MEN WHO OVERTURNED EMPIRES

By the same author

THE FOUNDATIONS OF LOCAL SELF-GOVERNMENT IN INDIA,
  PAKISTAN AND BURMA
THE UNION OF BURMA: A Study of the First Years of Independence
INDIA AND PAKISTAN: A Political Analysis
BALLOT BOX AND BAYONET: People and Government in Emergent Asian
  Countries
REORIENTATIONS: Studies of Asia in Transition
SOUTH ASIA: A Short History
EXPERIMENT WITH FREEDOM: India and Pakistan 1947
A NEW SYSTEM OF SLAVERY: The Export of Indian Labour Overseas,
  1830–1920
SEPARATE AND UNEQUAL: India and the Indians in the British
  Commonwealth, 1920–1950
THE BANYAN TREE: Overseas Emigrants from India, Pakistan and Bangladesh
RACE, CONFLICT AND THE INTERNATIONAL ORDER: From Empire to
  United Nations
THE ORDEAL OF LOVE: C.F. Andrews and India
A MESSAGE FROM THE FALKLANDS
BURMA: The Struggle for Independence, 1944–1948 (*two volumes*)

Men Who Overturned Empires

Fighters, Dreamers and Schemers

Hugh Tinker

The University of Wisconsin Press

Published in the United States of America by
The University of Wisconsin Press
114 North Murray Street
Madison, Wisconsin 53715

Published in Great Britain by
THE MACMILLAN PRESS LTD
Houndmills, Basingstoke, Hampshire RG21 2XS
and London

Printed in Great Britain

ISBN 0–299–11460–0

Library of Congress Cataloging-in-Publication Data
Tinker, Hugh
  Men who overturned empires.
  Bibliography: p.
  Includes index.
  1. Revolutionists—Asia—Biography.
2. Revolutionists—Africa—Biography. 3. Asia—
History—Autonomy and independence movements.
4. Africa—History—Autonomy and independence
movements.   I. Title.
DS35.T62   1987   960   87–6122
ISBN 0–299–11460–0

In affectionate memory of Stephen Koss

1940–1984

Master of the historian's craft
Greatly missed friend

Contents

List of Plates and Maps   ix

Introduction   x

1   The Edifice of Empire   1

2   The Nation Builders   23

3   The Winding Path of M.A. Jinnah   41

4   Jawaharlal Nehru: The Fading Dream   69

5   Country Boys Force the Pace: Aung San and Thakin Nu   97

6   Sukarno and the Vocabulary of Revolution   126

7   The Long March of Ho Chi Minh   158

8   Kwame Nkrumah: The Pursuit of Black Unity   181

9   White Over Black: Kenyatta's Kenya   208

Afterthoughts   238

Notes and References   241

Guide to Further Reading   250

Maps   260

Index   263

List of Plates and Maps

Plates

Between pages 96 and 97

1 Nehru and Jinnah assuming an affable appearance for the camera during their duel at Simla, May 1946
2 Jinnah and his sister Fatima at their New Delhi house a few days before he left the capital for Karachi, July 1947
3 Nehru addressing a press conference on becoming head of the Interim government, September 1946
4 Aung San marching through the streets of Rangoon to inaugurate the Constituent Assembly, June 1947, flanked by guards of the People's Volunteer Organisation, with Thakin Nu behind him.
5 Nu with Nehru on a visit to Delhi, March 1955
6 Sukarno returning from a foreign visit with his Japanese wife, Ratna Dewi
7 Sukarno and Nehru at the meeting of non-aligned states, Belgrade, September 1961
8 Ho Chi Minh greets his followers in Hanoi
9 Nehru visiting Ho Chi Minh soon after the Geneva Armistice, October 1954
10 Nkrumah with his Cabinet in formal chiefly robes after the 1954 election
11 A solitary Jomo Kenyatta, one week before his arrest, October 1952
12 Kenyatta and Nkrumah confer before the Commonwealth Prime Ministers' Conference, July 1964

Maps

Pages 260–62

India (with Pakistan, 1947) and Burma
South-East Asia
Africa in the era of independence, 1947–63

Introduction

The impetus to write this book came to fruition when my old friend of many years, Bob Frykenberg, suggested I might like to give some lectures at the University of Wisconsin, Madison. He spelled out what he had in mind: not a formal course for students working on a limited field, but a series in which we would hope to interest a wider audience. His sights were set on university faculty as well as students, and also the professional and political people who live around the state capitol. This meant ranging beyond a specialised subject, and he wanted me to attempt to illustrate the recent history of Asia and Africa – their re-emergence from colonial subjugation into full membership of the world family – as widely as I felt able.

This seemed a daunting assignment, but my particular tendency throughout my academic career has been to move tangentially from one interest to another, exploring a variety of widely separated topics. So another exercise in sticking my neck out was worth a try. How to make the approach wide-ranging without becoming so generalised that depth and definition would disappear? The solution I have attempted is that of comparative biography. The book I most enjoyed writing in more than 30 years of authorship was a biography of a remarkable Englishman who was an intimate friend of Tagore and Gandhi. When I left him to return to more formal historical writing – this time an immensely detailed documentary account of how Burma attained independence – it seemed much less satisfying.

That work on documents lasted four years and left me feeling that I had made a substantial contribution to the literature of the 'end of empire'. Yet had I not been compelled to remain at best an outside viewer – a voyeur perhaps – of the national leaders to whom eventually there was a 'transfer of power', in the accepted phrase? Yes, power was being transferred, prised from the Western overlord, but the contestants who became the successors were much less sharply delineated in my documents: and in the several other series of documents which have been compiled from the archives of Europe. It seemed well worth making the attempt to get behind the public postures of the new leaders as I felt I had been able to get inside the minds of those who were relinquishing control.

Can anyone who participated in empire as one of the White rulers – in however minor a role – do justice to the Asians and Africans who took over from empire? Someone like myself can never be wholly 'objective', and yet the experience did instil a certain sympathy with 'the other side': something like the empathy which the frontline soldiers felt for those they faced across No Man's Land on the Western Front in the Great War. Even across the divide of race and nation there was a recognition that this was an epic encounter. And now, 30 or 40 years have elapsed. It all seems like another life anyway. That world has gone forever.

When I was ten years old, my parents sent me to a rather odd little school at Sheringham in Norfolk. Most of the teaching was given by the headmaster, Hilderic Cousins. One day in a history lesson – or maybe it was a geography lesson, they tended to get mixed up – he was standing in front of the familiar map of the world where so many bits and pieces were coloured red for British and he observed, 'In your generation all this will disappear. You will see the British Empire come to an end.' In 1931, that was an astonishing statement. Few imagined any such dénouement. Now, in the 1980s, those who today are under 50 must think it all as distant and unreal as when in the middle ages half of France was ruled by England.

Although I did not belong to an imperial family, the chances of war found me arriving at the ports of Freetown, Durban and Mombasa when I was 19, before spending the next five years and more in India and Burma. The British Empire was under siege. I remember standing by the side of the exit route out of Burma in May 1942 and in the cinematic terms natural to my generation comparing the unending, bedraggled lines of refugees with the scene in *Gone with the Wind* when Atlanta is falling to the Union forces: 'It's just the same: the end of a whole way of life,' I thought. And yet the Japanese advance came to a halt and when the war was over the Empire was still intact. When we were on our honeymoon in Cornwall in the summer of 1947, into our idyll there came occasional nightmarish noises as the wireless told of terrible happenings in the Punjab. Places I remembered as sleepy, dusty and anonymous, were now in the centre of the storm. It all meant a good deal to me, for only 12 months earlier I had still been expecting to return to the subcontinent as a member of the Indian Civil Service.

Instead I became a lecturer at the School of Oriental and African Studies. Most of my students were young Asians and it seemed quite natural to treat them as belonging to my world and I to theirs. Elsewhere in the School, courses were being held for probationers going out to Africa in the Colonial Service. When we travelled out to Burma by sea in 1954, so many of the places we passed – Gibraltar, Malta, the Canal zone, Aden, Colombo – were still redolent of a past imperial age: we actually saw the last British Governor-General of Ceylon depart amid muted pomp as we lay at anchor in Colombo. Perhaps Suez was the moment when we all realised that the British Empire was not just fading away like a tropical sunset but was undergoing a convulsive spasm like a dying man in pain.

In my work I began to take a special interest in the end of empire. Having enjoyed access to many of the documents I published a short book, *Experiment With Freedom*, in 1967 which sought to explain how and why India and Pakistan had come about, 20 years before. In finding explanations it was much easier to grasp why the British went (the short answer is that they went when they had to, when the advantages of empire expired) than to understand why and how the national leaders arrived at their appointed goals. Why did Nehru, for almost all his political life a severe critic of British imperialism and committed countless numbers of times to wresting complete independence for the whole of India, accept a transfer of power which fell short of his objective on terms largely devised by the British? Why did Jinnah, a lifelong constitutionalist who subscribed to the concept of an Indian nation, carry through what was in effect a revolution by splitting the subcontinent into separate parts? To call Jinnah 'revolutionary' is to apply the same standard as one applies to George Washington who also carved out a new state, a new nation, where no nation had existed before (and this process is conventionally described as the American Revolution).

So one could go on, probing into causes and consequences. Too many British analysts have been content to apply the Transfer of Power model whereby, as in the White Dominions, independence is another step in a long journey towards severing the controls of the 'Mother Country'. Too many Asians and Africans have been content with the 'Freedom Struggle' model in which their countrymen all combined to topple over the colonial regime. It is now between 25 and 40 years since the countries considered here became independent. We have not yet succeeded in providing better explanations than those which like the Transfer of Power or Freedom Struggle models, are oversimplified, superficial. It is my hope to be able to claim, like those assembling to leave Baghdad at the end of Flecker's *Hassan*, who tell the Master of the Caravan:

> We are the pilgrims, master; we shall go
> Always a little further: it may be
> Beyond that last blue mountain . . .

Or maybe not; but anyway, 'a little further'.

Why were these eight leaders selected, and these eight only? Were there not others of whom it may equally be said that without them independence would not have been won, or won then? Others who come immediately to mind are Ben Bella of Algeria, Archbishop Makarios of Cyprus, Julius Nyerere, creator of Tanzania, Robert Mugabe, creator of Zimbabwe: while Nelson Mandela may – or will – join this company in the end. There are other towering figures in the Third World pantheon – Mao Tsetung, Nasser and Fidel Castro, while Frantz Fanon, ideologue of revolution, probably had a wider impact than any Third World statesman.

One might produce reasons why these other men were not included: concerning the last four, they did not lead their countries into independence, our main criterion. There seem to be good reasons for not widening the choice further. One is simply the limitations on the author's competence. Some among the chosen eight have been companions (in an intellectual sense) for 30 or 40 years, though others are only acquaintances. Inclusion of the two African leaders has stretched my scholarly credibility to the limit, as it is. A more fundamental reason is that to have added any more names to the list might have turned the book into a mere catalogue. Although the studies which follow may be called 'mini-biographies' I would claim that it has been possible to look at these men's lives and characters in some depth. In certain cases the evidence brought forward here has not been available in full-length biographies. By comparing their methods, their motives, and the resources they evoked in their followers and opponents it may be possible to view each of them in relation to their peers. The Asian leaders were very conscious of a camaraderie more important than any ideological differences, and though the two Africans were not so intimately involved they also shared many of their Asian counterparts' views and experiences. It is hoped that this book will not just provide accounts of eight important leaders but will also reveal them as actors in a drama wherein time and again they reacted upon each other. Sometimes we are able to view one of these actors through the eyes of another of them.

Readers interested in the source materials on which these studies are based will rapidly notice that whereas for Chapters 3–5 the sources are largely contemporary documents this is not so with the later chapters. For India, Pakistan and Burma it is possible to exploit the published series of documents which cover the last years of British rule (as listed in the individual bibliographies). These series were compiled by British historians from papers preserved in Britain to a large extent. The editors were sensitive to the importance of avoiding bias, but there is a built-in bias in the documents themselves whose writers became conscious of the importance of understanding the thoughts and actions of their adversaries only as these became of greater importance than those of their masters in Whitehall and Westminster. Nevertheless, the investigator who decides to exploit these series, not for what they tell us about the British but for what we can discover about the national leaders, finds much that is highly significant. In addition, there are collections of the letters of the national leaders, but these are far from comprehensive. So we fall back on published biographies: and we discover that Indian biographers of high academic standing have been at work, but that by comparison the yield from Pakistan and Burma is somewhat disappointing. The contemporary history of these countries has continued to be written, to a large extent, by Western scholars: or at any rate what is published in English.

For the remainder of the book, the narrative relies largely upon previous scholarly studies: of which, fortunately, there are a good number. For Sukarno and Indonesia, the great majority have been American, with Australian scholarship forming an increasingly important part of the work. One who takes a jaundiced view of this body of writing is an Australian-born journalist, Brian May, who spent four years in Indonesia and produced his own carefully researched account of the Sukarno years, *The Indonesian Tragedy* (1978). He castigated 'the guesswork which typifies much academic writing on Indonesia' (p. 84) and although this seems really too severe it is possible to understand why he became so disenchanted. A close reading of the literature uncovers large numbers of discrepancies between the different accounts; mostly of a trivial nature, like giving alternative dates for the various events. This poses problems for anyone who later tries to synthesise these differing accounts.

As a subject, Ho Chi Minh is even more baffling. The two Vietnam wars generated an enormous literature, mainly French and American, in which Ho constantly reappears. Yet the more carefully one compares the different accounts the more one discovers small yet significant differences between the various versions. One could, of course, deal with all this by explaining to the reader that A says this and B says that and C says something else again: but this is not intended as an exercise in pedantry. Where the various possibilities do not seem to make much difference the narrative adopts a policy of conflation. In other cases the most credible account is taken. This was the only chapter I felt obliged to refer to a specialist, Ralph Smith. I am grateful to him for rescuing me from a number of errors.

Because Ghana was the first independent state in Africa in modern times (if we exclude Liberia's phoney independence in 1847) this country received an amount of academic attention disproportionate to its size immediately before and after independence. It was also the first African situation where American scholarship made a significant contribution. Apter (1955), Fage (1959), Bourret (1960) and Austin (1964) charted the course of the new country's emergence. When Nkrumah was dispossessed early in 1966 this produced another crop of studies, such as Bretton (1967), Bing (1968) and Davidson (1973). All this is in addition to Nkrumah's own writings and those of Ghanaian chroniclers. The later productions vary widely in their interpretations of Nkrumah's downfall. The present writer, though lacking specialised knowledge, has tried to take up an independent intellectual position.

Historical writing on Kenya has focussed mainly upon White activities: see Huxley (1930), Oliver (1952) or Bennett (1963). A valiant effort to change the mould was made by Rosberg and Nottingham in *The Myth of 'Mau Mau'* (1966). A Dutch writer later declared that they 'developed and scientifically enshrined' a new myth, an African myth (Buijtenhuijs, 1973, p. 47). In this chapter the reader will find more attention given to the colonial overlords than elsewhere because they represented not Whitehall but the resident White settlers. The reality of repression and subdued resistance in Kenya was to preserve the White hegemony almost to the very last years before independence.

The writers mentioned above are listed in the 'Guide to Further Reading' which is intended to assist anyone interested in closer reading of the map on the road to independence which this book seeks to provide. There is no elaborate list of references in the 'Notes and References' section at the end of the volume. Those who are scholarly specialists can discover for themselves the validity of my sources. Others – whom I hope will form the majority – will not want to check up on where I get my information. They, I believe, will accept my 20 books and 40 years of reading and research as authority enough.

So, let us begin. Academic friends will, in different places, recognise signals showing them that I have listened to their ideas. One name only needs to be singled out: my dearest wife, Elisabeth, has as always read the rough draft, tidied it up, scrutinised the proofs, and in general kept me up to the mark.

HUGH TINKER

Biography is likely to remain one of the most effective means of promoting the true historical attitude on the part of a wider public.

David Thomson, The Aims of History (*1969*).

1

The Edifice of Empire

Empire! When did the name lose its dignity, its authority? For centuries empire represented an ideal, that of civilisation, universal order, peace.[1] In the ancient world the empires of Alexander, of the Indian emperor Asoka, and of Rome and China were accepted as exalted and sacred, conferring on their subjects law, order, tranquillity and a common sense of identity.

In Europe this traditional form of empire persisted in Austria (linked with Hungary) and Russia. The house of Habsburg occupied the Austrian throne from 1273 to 1918. They claimed the title of Holy Roman Emperor until this was abolished by Napoleon. Staunch supporters of conservatism and Catholicism, the Habsburgs received a wide measure of allegiance from their multi-ethnic subjects until their empire collapsed amid the ferment of revolution and nationalism in 1918. The Romanovs ruled Russia from 1613 to 1917. They too claimed to inherit the authority of Rome – or rather Byzantium – and combined religious and royal authority over the varied races under them.

The Rise of Maritime Empires

The overseas empires we are now to consider – those of England, France and the Netherlands – had little in common with the oriental and semi-oriental empires of middle Europe, the Middle East and Asia. They each began as trading ventures which then became instruments of their internecine military and naval struggles, mainly conducted in western Europe. Initially, their rivalry was with Portugal and Spain (who did establish their dominion in central and south America with some resemblance to the semi-oriental empires). Then, in the eighteenth century, the focus shifted from preying upon the wealth of the Lusitanian empires to a competition for primacy between the three northern maritime states. Each sought to secure the major share of the produce of the Western and Eastern seas: sugar and tobacco from the Caribbean, spices and fine textiles from the Indies. Each sought to gain hold of the ports or trading centres which dominated their spheres of activity. Initially, each intended to set up 'colonies' (in the Greek and Roman sense

1

of settlements of their own people in promising new lands). The Dutch established a colony in North America, centred on New Amsterdam, and another at the strategic tip of Africa, centred on Cape Town. However, their most successful venture was in Java where they built a port, Batavia, with canals and houses reminiscent of Amsterdam but where Dutchmen could not survive as settlers, and either made fortunes – and got out – or quickly died. The French created a colony on the St Lawrence River in Canada and peopled it with peasants from Normandy and Brittany – the *habitants* – whose descendants are there today. They tried to repeat the experiment elsewhere, in the Indian Ocean in the Île de France (Mauritius) and Bourbon (Réunion) where settlers, *habitants*, were also given land to cultivate. They failed, until sugar came to their rescue.

The British Model

The greatest success in transplanting colonies overseas was achieved by the British, whose people settled the North American coastline throughout its whole length. These adventures were undertaken to strengthen the trading power of the 'Mother Country' (a term employed by Bishop Berkeley who visited North America in 1728), but soon acquired a local or territorial importance as the settlers began to reproduce the social, political and religious institutions of the Old Country in a new and challenging environment. In England, the special significance of these colonies of settlement was only slowly perceived. In economic importance they could be equated with Barbados or Jamaica, where a White elite, the plantocracy, enjoyed wealth created by a Black slave workforce.

The difference between the mainland colonies and the sugar colonies was not total; when the protest against British taxation and arbitrary rule gathered momentum in the 1770s, emissaries were sent down to the Caribbean to urge the planters to join the mainland Americans. After all, there was little difference between the plantocracy of Virginia, cultivating tobacco with a Black slave labour force, and their counterparts in Jamaica or Barbados. However, the revolution did make all the difference. The Americans in rejecting George III found their legitimacy in the Republic of Rome which preceded the Empire of the Caesars. They adopted Roman political terms – the Senate, the Capitol – even though their system was actually based upon English Whig principles. Public buildings were all erected in the Roman manner. Their first citizen was named President, which now took on a distinctively republican connotation although its Latin origin, *presidens*, had denoted a governor.

Alternatives to the American Way

When in 1783 the British government recognised the independence of the United States few British colonies of settlement remained: only the maritime provinces bordering the Atlantic, and newly conquered Quebec. However, a new empire of conquest was rapidly expanding in India. Fifty years later there were new and important colonies of settlement, in Australia, New Zealand and South Africa (for this was how the Cape was regarded). What would be their future? Would they too demand independence when the time came: 'when the fruit was ripe to fall from the tree'? When colonial politicians agitated for representative institutions, with some blundering and hesitation their demands were met in London. The main concern was that they should not be a burden on the British taxpayer. Disraeli, who could enthuse about the oriental empire, had no time for the white colonies, demanding in 1867 to be told 'the use of these colonial dead-weights which we do not govern'. Gradually, the colonies of settlement achieved not just representative government but responsible government: as much independence as they wanted. Thus, by the 1880s, Australia, Canada, New Zealand and South Africa were excluding British subjects from India from their territories despite the disapproval of London, a policy celebrated by Kipling:

> Daughter am I in my mother's house,
> But mistress in my own.
> The Gates are mine to open,
> As the Gates are mine to close.

This growth of White colonial nationalism was not accompanied by any rejection of the Mother Country, because Mother was the guardian of the sealanes on which their trade depended: and the White colonies had the protection of the Royal Navy without payment. They showed their gratitude when war broke out in South Africa in 1899 with the Boer republics. Australians, New Zealanders and Canadians volunteered to pull the Mother Country out of the military mess it was in.

The White colonies – now termed Dominions – imperceptibly moved towards complete independence, but this did not seem to threaten the unity of the British Empire: indeed, Empire Day was celebrated with the greatest enthusiasm in these same Dominions. There was, now, a two-tier Empire: the lands of settlement, continually reinforced by migration from Britain, and the empire of conquest and absolute rule. The Indian Ocean was virtually a British lake. India was its centrepiece, with Burma, Malaya,

Ceylon and lesser territories like Aden as the periphery. What was to be their place in the Empire?

Earlier, among the British rulers of India, there were those who looked forward to a distant time when the Indians would re-emerge as the masters of their own house. Some, like Elphinstone and Munro, had thought this would come about by a renewal and rejuvenation of Indian institutions; others, like Macaulay and Trevelyan, his brother-in-law, had envisaged the gradual Anglicising of the Indian elite and their adoption of English political institutions. However, when the Indian National Congress was founded in 1885 and demands were made – politely, and with profuse declarations of loyalty – for instalments of self-government, the majority of Britons poohpoohed any such possibility.

The New Imperialism

By the 1880s the new imperialism was beginning to be popular not just among the ruling classes, but perhaps even more among the masses: the readers of the *Daily Mail*, the crowds who cheered Randolph Churchill with his Tory populist sentiments. Imperialism stirred in western Europe. France, smarting from defeat by Prussia, sought recompense in overseas annexations; the Dutch and the Germans also joined in the new expansionism overseas. It was important for trade but also important for prestige. And so began 'the scramble for Africa', and less conspicuously the 'Forward Movement' in South-East Asia and even the takeover of the islands of the Pacific: in which the United States, professedly anti-colonial in sentiment, played a major part in answer to the call of Manifest Destiny.

The modest demands of Indian progressives were greeted with reserve. From 1892 the Indian Legislative Council included a minority of Indian members, indirectly elected, and from 1909 this element was expanded. But Indian politicians were relegated to permanent – and ineffective – opposition. The previous generation of English Liberals such as Cobden and Bright had linked free trade with free political institutions, but now the Liberal voice was muted. One cause was the rise of Irish nationalism in a strident and anti-British form. Those who saw Ireland accommodated in some form of Home Rule, not unlike Dominion self-government, were outnumbered by those who insisted that Ireland must forever stay within the United Kingdom. Indians and other Asians studied the Irish question carefully: this, not the Canadian or Australian examples, seemed to have a message for them. Certain Liberal leaders, especially Lord Rosebery, ardently adopted the new Imperialist creed, and even those who had no stomach for further expansionism were cautious about relaxing hold over the existing territories, especially India. Gladstonian stalwarts like John Morley and James Bryce, exponents of trusting the people, felt uncomfortable about handing over to the Indians.

Bryce, publicist of American democracy, champion of the Boers in South Africa, found no parallel in India. Instead, he turned back (as so many Oxbridge intellectuals did) to a comparison with the Roman Empire. When Rome fell, western Europe was plunged into the Dark Ages: a British withdrawal from India would be the same: 'Everyone admits in his heart', he wrote, 'that it is impossible to ignore the differences which make one group of races unfit for the institutions which have given energy and contentment to another more favourably placed. . . . To India, severance from England would mean confusion, bloodshed, pillage.'[2] In 1912, the Liberal Secretary of State for India, Lord Crewe, told Parliament: 'There is a certain section in India which looks forward to a measure of self-government approaching that which has been granted in the Dominions. I see no future for India on these lines. The experiment of extending a measure of self-government . . . to a race which is not our own . . . is one which cannot be tried.'

Before 1914 the British aim in India was limited to giving selected Indians experience in the processes of administration and government, on the basis that Indians must prove their capability to conform to British standards. This may be described as political education; giving Indians the opportunity to demonstrate their familiarity with British constitutional methods with the promise that favourable performance could lead to greater opportunity. However, the ultimate control and management of the Indian political machine would be firmly retained in British hands. This, we must remember, was the climate of opinion in which two of our leaders entered adult life: in 1914, Jinnah was 38 years old and Nehru was 25.

The First World War: a Watershed

When war was declared, this brought spontaneous gestures of support for Britain from almost all the peoples of India, with the educated elite vying with traditional leaders to voice their loyalty. India was stripped of British troops for active service, while Indian soldiers held one-third of the British front line in France and Flanders during the terrible winter of 1914–15. Recruitment to the Indian Army went on; nearly a million men were enlisted; but the mood in India changed. The breakdown in Mesopotamia (Iraq) which condemned so many Indian soldiers to death in battle or grim years as prisoners revealed how India was being exploited. The war was not going well anywhere, and India's continuing support seemed important. In 1917, a new Secretary of State, Edwin Montagu, persuaded the Cabinet to make an important innovation. He was authorised to announce that the goal of British policy was 'the gradual development of self-governing institutions with a view to the progressive realisation of responsible government in India . . . Substantial steps in this direction should be taken as soon as possible . . . I would add that progress in this policy can only be achieved by successive stages.'

Despite its reservations, this statement indicated for the first time that India was embarking upon the same road as the White Dominions. The road might be long, but the end must be the same: the termination of British control over India, the end of the British Indian imperial system. India's new status was symbolised by separate representation at Versailles (like the Dominions) and separate membership of the new League of Nations (like the Dominions). However, the Dominions were represented by politicians of their own choosing; India was represented by 'safe' men chosen by the Secretary of State.

Self-Government by Instalments

As the first of the 'successive stages' in India's constitutional advance, certain of the functions of the provincial governments – the so-called 'nation building departments' – were placed under Indian Ministers who were elected members of the provincial legislatures. Montagu made it clear this reform devised by Lionel Curtis and called Dyarchy, was a temporary phase: within ten years – maybe much sooner – there would be a further major instalment of self-government.

Self-government on the instalment plan might have been acceptable to the pre-1914 Indian political leaders (among whom M.A. Jinnah may be numbered) but the scene was about to be transformed by the new politics of Gandhi. In 1914 he had been as loyal as other Indians, raising an ambulance unit for France among Indians resident in Britain. As late as 1918 he conducted a recruiting campaign for the British. However, he had learned in South Africa that political change was brought about by mass action, not by high-level consultation. Blunders in the immediate aftermath of the war, such as the introduction of arbitrary penal laws (the Rowlatt Acts) and the employment of repressive methods amounting almost to terror – as experienced at Amritsar – convinced him that Indians must demand and obtain immediate self-government, still not defined as independence.

The British replied by a mixture of carrot and stick (sometimes in reverse order). Gandhi was able to mobilise mass action: as one of his workers put it, he 'shifted politics from the drawing rooms of the educated . . . to the huts in the countryside, to the tillers of the soil'.[3] He evolved his unique approach of civil disobedience based upon self-sacrifice and non-violence.

The Nationalist Challenge in India

Gandhi's challenge was mounted in three major campaigns. The first against the Rowlatt Acts in 1919, took place in the aftermath of war when unrest in the north, particularly in Punjab, was fuelled by discontent among demobilised soldiers. Non-violence rapidly escalated into violence and Gandhi called off the campaign. However, his attitude to the British Empire had been permanently affected. A second campaign followed soon after, commencing in August 1920. Its goal was '*swaraj* within one year' (*swaraj*: full self-government). Its impact was much wider, but the attempt to set up an alternative administration and social services soon petered out. When a police station was set alight in February 1922 and the policemen were burned alive Gandhi again told his followers to stop, as they did not understand non-violence. Gandhi was arrested and jailed. The political movement passed from his hands. The third big campaign came in 1930–1 following the collapse of constitutional talks. Staging his salt march, his march to the sea, Gandhi aroused the whole country. Yet again the security forces contained the campaign. Gandhi returned to the conference table.

The civil disobedience campaign of 1930–1 had a counterpart in Burma on very different lines. There, a rural revolt broke out which paralysed 12 of Burma's 40 districts and almost a division of Indian troops were brought in before it was suppressed. Both in India and Burma unrest was fuelled by severe economic hardship. Yet although there was wide and simultaneous protest it did not succeed. The British were not easy to overthrow: the legitimacy of empire still held fast, though a little shaken. The British response was, as in 1917, to hasten slowly. First there was an inquiry into the working of Dyarchy; then there was another major instalment of self-government whereby almost all power at provincial level was given over to elected politicians, while an elaborate programme of reform at the all-India level envisaged the merger of British India and the Princely states in a new all-India legislature.

In these latter years the British much more deliberately cultivated those who remained their allies and supporters (as they supposed), the Princes, the Muslims, and other minorities. They sought to encourage the 'Moderates' while restraining the 'Extremists'. Self-government was now envisaged as a phenomenon which must come some time within the next half-century. However, Dyarchy – expected in 1919 to last five years, or ten at most – was still operative in the mid-1930s. Young Englishmen were still being appointed to the Indian Civil Service (ICS) and Indian Army and were assured that a lifetime career still awaited them. British business and industry still regarded India as one of their most important markets, and called on the politicians to keep it open.

It seemed as though the Indian National Congress was after all prepared to accept the 'self-government by instalments' approach when they took office in the provincial Ministries in 1937. But when war broke out in 1939 the response was entirely different from 1914. This time the Congress leaders adopted the former Irish political maxim: 'England's danger is Ireland's opportunity'. There was an immediate demand for a British declaration that India would be free: and the rejection of this led to stalemate, deadlock and confrontation. The old instalment plan technique was finished: though this was not immediately obvious to the British.

The British View of their Other Colonies

If there was recognition that India must, sooner or later, become one of the self-governing Dominions, there was scant consideration of this goal elsewhere in the empire. Burma, as a former province of British India (separated 1937), was set upon the same road; but for the rest – even for the 'model colony', Ceylon – the most that was envisaged was internal self-government, with Britain controlling defence and foreign relations. Unrest in the Caribbean in the 1930s served to arouse some awareness in London that the West Indies, neglected since the abolition of slavery a hundred years earlier, must be brought into the modern age. But how? Nationalism did not seem relevant: most West Indians still perceived Britain as the Mother Country and in Barbados they jokingly referred to their island as Bimshire, a kind of far-off English county. Africa was thought to be still awakening from savagery. In any case, there was the example of South Africa where, following full self-government, 'native rights' were steadily whittled away in favour of White hegemony. This seemed to provide the model wherever there were British settlers; Rhodesia, and even Kenya, possessed a vociferous White element who clamoured for political control and echoed the sentiments of 1776. If in

India independence was measured in decades, in Africa it was measured in centuries by Whitehall and Westminster.

An indication of how far British political leaders were prepared to go emerges from a colonial debate on 13 July 1943, initiated by Oliver Stanley, Colonial Secretary, 1942–5, and main architect of the new programme of colonial development. Stanley told Parliament that something more than a doctrine of trusteeship was now required: 'We are pledged to guide colonial people along the road to self-government within the framework of the British Empire.' However, he then went on: 'It is no part of our policy to confer political advances which are unjustified by circumstances, or to grant self-government to those who are not yet trained in its use.' A necessary preliminary was an advance in social and economic development. He singled out those territories which were well placed to advance down the constitutional road: Ceylon, where there was 'a promise of full internal self-government under the Crown'; Jamaica; and Malta. Not a long list.

In the debate, Sir Edward Grigg, one-time Governor of Kenya, sought to suggest that South Africa ought to be involved in British colonial policy in Africa: 'What authority have we to claim that responsibility, that power, that imperium, to use a Roman phrase, as our own?' His suggestion did not appeal to many MPs, though only one, Sir Richard Acland, spoke out in radical terms. He asked whether MPs imagined that the colonial empire was 'going to be ours' in 25 years' time? Five White nations controlled an 'enormous part' of the earth: would this 'extraordinary state of affairs . . . endure much longer?' He thought that Churchill especially was out of touch with reality.

Evidence of Churchill's view was given in January 1944 in a debate surprisingly initiated by Emmanuel Shinwell who sat with the opposition. He urged that the unity demonstrated by the British Empire in war should be consolidated in the peace. With that lead from the Left wing it was not surprising that the Prime Minister demonstrated his satisfaction with things as they were: the Empire, he pronounced, 'is not a sick boy'; on the contrary, it was 'more strongly united than ever before'. It was clear that he was thinking mainly of the White Dominions although he did indicate that he looked forward to a post-war 'Conference of the Prime Ministers of the Dominions, among whom we trust that India will be represented and with which the Colonies will be associated'. Well, it was something from the man who had so bitterly opposed the 1935 Government of India Act with its promise of a federation of all-India. But otherwise the colonial territories must wait until they had become politically mature.

The French Model

If the British vision of colonial independence was still vague it was a good deal more specific than in France or the Netherlands. France, the pioneer of Liberty, Equality and Fraternity, conceived of its empire entirely as an adjunct to the metropole. The British Empire in its heyday made some sense, providing the means of exporting goods and also people. The French Empire made no economic sense (despite attempts to fit it into the economic framework of *mise en valeur*). Its avowed aim was cultural, the *mission civilisatrice*, but its actual purpose was to prop up France's threatened great power status, particularly after the German victory in 1870. While some of its early pioneers were Catholic missionaries its most vigorous champions were naval and military officers. The French navy was particularly prominent in this field: until 1894, the colonies were controlled by the naval Ministry, and overseas possessions provided the main justification for a substantial navy.

The first major venture was the seizure of Algiers in 1830, ordered by King Charles X to prop up the Bourbon throne. This it failed to do: but his successor, the bourgeois King Louis Philippe, completed the occupation of the ports of Oran and Bone, beginning the process of European settlement of the coastal areas. However, French public opinion was lukewarm, and it was only after 1870 that an active colonial lobby developed. Its foremost activist was Jules Ferry, a socialist and opponent of Louis Napoleon and of the conservative republic which followed. Ferry was anti-clerical and a pioneer of secular public education, but he was also an imperialist; he wrote: 'An irresistible movement is bearing the great nations of Europe towards the conquest of fresh territories. It is like a huge steeplechase into the unknown.'[4] Under his lead, France acquired Tunisia (1881), French Congo (1884–5), Madagascar (1885) and Tonking (1885). When Léon Gambetta, the leader of the French resistance against Prussia, heard about Tunisia he congratulated Ferry with the assertion, 'France is becoming a great power again.'

However, Ferry's intervention in Tonking was to turn sour. The earliest French interest in Vietnam had been initiated through Jesuit missionary activity, bringing the Western cultural inheritance. Retaliation against them caused Louis Napoleon to seize Vietnamese territory in 1858, and further advances followed, bringing all Indo-China under French control. The reverse in Tonking in 1885 caused the downfall of Ferry and ended his dream of a new French empire in Upper Burma and south China. Further adventures in north-west Africa were still to come, justified by the first Minister for the Colonies, Theophile Delcassé: 'We wanted to make sure when the last parts of Africa were allotted that France received a share worthy of her power of expansion and of her importance as an instrument of civilisation.'

How was this 'civilising mission' exerted? A British historian of imperialism writes of the modern French empire: 'In theory it was liberal but in practice centralised and authoritarian.'[5]

In the 1790s the revolutionary armies had exported French revolutionary principles and practices throughout Europe as far as the Rhine. A decree of 1793 bestowed French citizenship upon the inhabitants of the French colonies (a measure which was quickly modified). Similarly, after 1870 the declared aim was *assimilation*, whereby those colonised would become citizens of a greater France. The process had begun in the old sugar colonies, Guadeloupe, Martinique and Réunion, and was extended to the three coastal departments of Algeria and to three departments in Senegal. All these sent deputies to Paris, elected by the citizen population. Elsewhere, citizenship was almost automatically acquired by the European settlers but the *indigènes* had to qualify for 'naturalisation', which could only be claimed by persons married to French citizens, those with a French secondary-school certificate and those who had served in the French army (not including the colonial levies). In practice, this status was difficult to acquire: thus, in Indo-China in 1938, out of a total population (estimated) of about 20 million, 2600 persons had been admitted to citizenship, most of them in the original colony of Cochin China.[6] At the same period, only 7817 inhabitants of Algeria had acquired citizenship out of a total of 8 million (the process involved renouncing Islam). For the remainder there was the status of *sujet* which bestowed obligations without privileges. They were liable to the *corvée*, they could not travel beyond their village area without a pass, and they were subject to detention or jail by administrative process instead of by judicial decision.

French rule required a much wider enforcement by French officials, police and military than in British colonies. Down to a level that can be equated with sergeant, all were (White) Frenchmen. However, the problem of persuading enough people to leave France to staff the empire led to devices to supplement the men from the metropole. In Annam (Vietnam) the corps of mandarins staffed the administration. Elsewhere in the empire the same political façade of 'protection' left the lower administration to chiefs and elders. The justification was that in time the whole empire would be as one with France.

Assimilation or Association for the Colonies

For the few who gained entry, *assimilation* represented admission into the civilisation of France in a way that British nationality never did for Indians or West Indians. For the few who had arrived, the *évolués*, there were no barriers. They could marry (White) French women, practise their profession in France, and receive full social recognition. Some Arabs and one or two Vietnamese rose to the rank of Colonel in the army. The highly educated Black or Brown Frenchman was welcomed, whereas to the British the 'educated' were under suspicion. What made this demonstration of the goal of equality meaningless was the slowness of the process. This was eventually recognised when the logical justification of the realities – the rationale of empire by the French which the British never attempted – replaced the concept of *assimilation* by that of *association* for the majority of the colonised. This may be defined as 'recognition that colonies should retain a separate identity and be governed pragmatically'.[7] This only took care of the short term.

The principal French exponent of colonial expansion described the situation in Algeria in respect of assimilation to the metropole as one of 'gross confusion'. He was able to suggest only the policy of *rattachement*, the linkage between ministerial policy and practice in France with that in the colonies.[8] A British specialist on Vietnam deduces that: 'The colonial power would be the ruler more or less in perpetuity and the subject people could aspire to self-determination only by identifying themselves individually with the French way of life – which of course meant assimilation again.'[9]

An aspect of the lack of a clear objective for the French colonies was a policy of fragmentation, or compartmentalisation. Nationalism might be neutralised by creating small and divided political and administrative units. Vietnam was divided into three: in the south, Cochin China, directly administered as a colony; in the north, Tonking, a protectorate with a strong infusion of military in the administration; and in the centre, Annam, with a titular 'emperor' still in place and parallel forms of administration, the French and the indigenous. Cambodia and Laos were separate Princely protectorates; the whole supervised by a Governor-General.

Similarly, Algeria was split between the coastal departments and the interior under military control, while the vast semi-desert territories of equatorial Africa were split up into an arbitrary assortment of colonies and protectorates, with Dakar, the seat of the Governor-General, as a special territory known as 'The Circumscription of Dakar and Dependencies'. This fragmentation policy gave no outlet for organised political demand, other than to the minuscule citizen elite.

The French possessions were riven by revolt right into the twentieth century. In Vietnam, from 1927 to 1931 there were rural outbreaks, mutinies among the troops, and assassinations of French officials. The regime replied with a policy of severe repression. In the interior of Algeria and in Morocco revolt was endemic. This was the general situation of outward stability and underlying instability until the fall of France in 1940.

The British Empire was under pressure during the Second World War, but apart from the colonies in the Far East and South-East Asia, conquered by Japan, control remained firm. India, and also Africa, provided important sources of military manpower: the Indian army was deployed in North Africa, East Africa, Italy and Burma. Three African infantry divisions also fought in Burma. India became a base for military supply and *materiel* second only to Britain in importance. The reconquest of Burma and Malaya in 1945 at first seemed to wipe out the defeat in 1942, though a sense of humiliation remained.

The French Grip Loosened

For the French empire, the war was a disaster. Throughout Indo-China the collaborationist Vichy regime was compelled to become the tool of the Japanese, who gave away some territory (part of Cambodia) to their Thai ally and who eventually destroyed the French administration and army. North Africa saw the collapse of the Vichy regime and a massive Anglo-American military presence. Syria, after the removal of the Vichy regime by British military action, had to be given independence by the Free French. Constitutional decisions about the empire's future could no longer simply be postponed. In 1946 a programme for a French Union was announced. There was some desire to emulate the British Commonwealth, but in actuality the new French Union reproduced the ambiguities of the past. Its constitution may be quoted at some length:

> France forms with the overseas peoples a union founded upon equality of rights and duties, without restriction of race and religion. The French Union is composed of nations and peoples who pool or co-ordinate their efforts and resources to develop their respective civilisations, increase their wellbeing, and assure their security. Faithful to its traditional mission, France intends to conduct the people under her charge to a state of free self-administration and the democratic conduct of their own affairs.

This might satisfy the inhabitants of Réunion or the French Caribbean: it was not enough for Vietnamese or Algerians.

The French Empire, like the British, was worldwide. The Dutch Empire was effectively concentrated in one zone, that of Indonesia (there were Dutch possessions in the Caribbean and Surinam − a slice of South America − but these were of minor importance). The archipelago of Indonesia covered a distance equivalent to one-eighth of the circumference of the Equator: wider, from east to west, than the United States. Its land area was 58 times greater than the Netherlands. However, the core of the archipelago was Java, with two-thirds of the total population.

The Dutch Model

Originally the Dutch came to purchase spices, but by the nineteenth century the main products were coffee and sugar. From 1830 to 1870 the Dutch operated the 'Culture System', a government monopoly which required the peasants to cultivate crops for export. From 1840 to 1874 a balance of 781 million Dutch Florins was remitted to the Netherlands as profit. This paid off the national debt, financed the construction of the Dutch railway network and restored Amsterdam to its financial importance. However, Liberal political paramountcy in the Netherlands after 1870 caused a gradual changeover to private trade and production, in which the sugar industry became the world leader. At the same time the Dutch expanded their activities into the 'outer islands' (partly to forestall Britain). This expansion was met by fierce resistance, especially in Sumatra, necessitating a much greater army in the East Indies.

With this greater involvement came a new consciousness of responsibility for the indigenous people and implementation of the 'Ethical Policy' followed. In 1901 Queen Wilhelmina spoke of the 'moral duty' which the Dutch owed to the Indonesians. It was more like Kipling's 'White Man's Burden' than any shift towards self-government. Policymaking was devolved from The Hague to Batavia, and indeed further along to the Dutch Residents. Dutch officials were given years of training before entering service and became the agents of a new programme of development concentrating upon the extension of irrigation and rural credit. Welfare was at the centre of Dutch policy: J.S. Furnivall made a comparison with British policy in Burma and declared: 'It was common to both policies, however, that they required a great expansion of official machinery. . . . In practice the new machinery [in the Netherlands Indies] was used in the interest of efficiency rather than of political education.'[10]

The resulting system was described as *Beamtenstaat*, the state as an efficient bureaucratic machine. In terms of material prosperity, the Netherlands Indies compared very favourably with India or Burma, but this was achieved by an even greater extension of the Dutch administrative apparatus. During its initial years, the Ethical Policy permitted a certain amount of indigenous participation in local government and tolerated organised religious and social activities. The first new organisation, called *Budi Utomo* (Glorious Endeavour), was founded in 1908 to foster education with an indigenous cultural basis: rather like Rabindranath Tagore's school, Santiniketan. This movement was confined to a Javanese elite of officials and intellectuals. Four years later a very different organisation was founded, *Sarekat Islam* (United Islam), originally composed of lower-middle-class members, such as traders, who had formed an association (*Sarekat Dagang Islam*) to combat the Chinese. Membership increased rapidly, and greatly alarmed the authorities.

The Dutch response mirrored that of the British – carrot and stick – although the carrot was late in arriving. In the Wilsonian euphoria of 1918 the Dutch held elections for a *Volksraad* or People's Council for the Indies. This resembled the limited legislature British India had acquired in 1892. It was a purely advisory body, with a majority of Dutch representatives. The other members were chosen on a racial basis (not so different from the 'communal' representation of Hindus and Muslims which the British had adopted). The minority of non-official members came from the Eurasian, Chinese and Indonesian (mainly Javanese) communities. This was in accordance with the judicial structure whereby the different communities were amenable to different legal systems ('like over like'), the great majority, the Indonesians, conforming to *adat* or customary law.

The *Volksraad* gave no outlet for popular political demand, though Eurasian Socialists linked up with their Dutch counterparts, strongly influenced by Marxism. *Sarekat Islam* was extensively penetrated by Marxist ideology. With Communists in key positions there were strikes and rural uprisings. The authorities replied with a campaign of repression. The right of assembly was suspended. Insurgent leaders were imprisoned and exiled. Attempts were made to provide a constitutional alternative. In 1925 and again in 1931 the *Volksraad* was broadened to provide an elected majority. The total (60) included 25 Dutch (15 elected), 30 from the indigenous peoples (20 elected), and five from the minorities (mainly Chinese). The consultative powers of the Council were strengthened, and if there was a conflict between the Council and the Governor-General the issue was referred to the Dutch parliament. This gave little satisfaction to Indonesian feelings. Though the members of the *Volksraad* were

conservative and unrepresentative they passed a motion in 1936 calling
for a conference to meet at The Hague and discuss the means whereby
self-government could be attained. This was rejected. The Governor-
General, de Jonge, declared, 'We have ruled here for 300 years . . . and we
shall still be ruling for another 300 years.'

Dutch Pluralist Philosophy

The plural system of political representation had its counterpart in Dutch
economic philosophy for there was held to be a Dual Economy.[11] The
peasant sector was seen as virtually static, because bound by the village
community, while the commercial and industrial sector was individualistic
and dynamic. This division fell along racial lines: the peasants were
Indonesians, the entrepreneurs were Dutch and Chinese. This separation
could be justified in theoretical or philosophical terms both from
Indonesian and Dutch concepts. In Javanese life there were supposed to
be *alirans* or streams to which different groups belonged: those who
followed the Islamic way, and those who belonged to the Hindu-Javanese
tradition. Within the Netherlands, politics and social welfare were
organised on confessional lines: Protestant, Catholic, and Socialist or
Secular. Dutch political parties and other institutions reflected these
different 'pillars', *verzuiling* as they were called. It followed that in
Indonesia the development of the Dutch and the Chinese elements were
envisaged as following different lines from those of Indonesians. The
Dutch among themselves distinguished between the *bliijvers* 'belongers'
and the *trekkers*: those who would retire to the Netherlands. Many of the
'belongers' were actually Eurasians, but were recognised as Dutch by law
(there were over 200 000 in 1930). This was in direct contrast to the
British view of the Eurasians in India who did not count as 'Domiciled
Europeans': though of course all (or most) of the inhabitants of the British
Empire could claim British nationality (some, like those from the Indian
Princely states, were classed as protected persons).

   The Dutch classification and subdivision of society, economic activity
and political development on lines supposedly rational excluded any
notion of Indonesian nationalism (indeed, the word 'Indonesia' was
prohibited by law). The emphasis was upon development and welfare.
Dutch colonialism was itself cocooned from external pressures, whether
those emanating from the Netherlands or from elsewhere in Asia. They
simply were not prepared for the disaster which swept it all away when
the Japanese invaded at the beginning of 1942.

Challenges to the European Imperial Network

In identifying the differences between three major European colonial powers have we sufficiently examined their similarities? Each of the three powers could take comfort in the conviction *not in our time*. After all, the European empires had withstood a number of shocks already in the twentieth century. The first major tremor was caused by Japan's spectacular victory over Russia in 1905. For a hundred years, the British in India had perceived Russia as a major threat, advancing through Afghanistan and Iran up to their border. Now, Russia was shown as unable to stand up to an Asian country which only 40 years before had emerged from medieval isolation. The Japanese victory thrilled young men throughout India and South-East Asia. Japan was just the first: they too could take their countries into the modern age and develop the same discipline and national spirit which had enabled the Japanese to challenge a major European power. However, it seemed that Japan was more interested in joining the European club than in encouraging Asian nationalism. Japan was an ally of Britain and France in the First World War. Some Asians were dismayed to see that by intervening in China, Japan too demonstrated an imperialist mentality. However, as a Buddhist country, Japan continued to send emissaries into South-East Asia and even into India, with long-term consequences.

As we have seen, the First World War had an impact in moving India forward towards greater self-government. The impact of the war was directly experienced by thousands of colonial peoples who were mobilised to assist the Allied war effort. Besides the troops from India there were Senegalese and Vietnamese soldiers fighting for France: some took part in the epic defence of Verdun. A French administrator wrote: 'The 175 000 soldiers enrolled during the years 1914–18 dug the grave of the old Africa in the trenches of France and Flanders.'[12] Besides the combatants there were labour corps from the British and French empires. Indians, Vietnamese, and Chinese (with an alert clerical assistant, Chou En-lai) toiled behind the allied lines. Thousands of young Asians and Africans saw the Europeans at close hand under intense pressure. All this was perhaps as important as the overtly political reaction to the war of Asian leaders who increasingly asked whether, if 'National Self-Determination' was an important allied war aim, they were part of this?

The Threat of Revolution

However, the impact of the war as seen from the allied side was less important than the Russian revolution, liberating this sprawling empire from despotism. Bolshevism, as it was labelled by its opponents, seemed to promise hope of liberation from Western oppression to Asians and Africans. The recognition of 'independent' republics in Central Asia, and abrogation of the 'unequal treaties' with China by the Soviet Union, seemed to herald a new relationship between Europe and Asia. The inauguration of the Third International in 1919 (usually termed the Comintern) promised world revolution setting the colonial peoples free. Its second meeting in 1920 was attended by delegates from 37 countries, including the Indian called M.N. Roy. (This name was his own invention, while his presence as a Mexican delegate was also ambivalent.) However, Roy's thesis on the national and colonial questions attracted as much attention as that by Lenin. Roy warned that the 'bourgeois democratic' politics of Gandhi was not promoting revolution, while Lenin did not believe that the Indian workers and peasants would bring about revolution. Roy remained important in the Comintern and attended the 1922 congress when the nine or ten Asian delegates also included Ho Chi Minh and Tan Malaka of Indonesia. However, as we have seen, the colonial governments with their obsessive fear of Bolshevism concentrated their intelligence resources against the Communists. In India 31 leading party members were arrested in 1929, tried, and in most cases sent to jail for lengthy periods (five, including S.A. Dange, received 12 years' imprisonment). Communism was suppressed in India, except as an ideology of intellectuals, and the same repression was effective in other colonial territories.

American Anti-Colonialism

The last external challenge to European colonialism was launched by President Roosevelt. As the first nation to shake off the colonial yoke, the United States had always adopted an anti-colonial stance, despite acquiring its own extensive empire in the Caribbean and the Pacific. Before his election in 1932, Roosevelt stated, 'The Presidency is pre-eminently a place of moral leadership', and this approach was applied especially to colonial questions. Americans felt strongly that the rapid overrunning of the Dutch East Indies, Hong Kong, Malaya and Burma by the Japanese early in 1942 demonstrated that the peoples of these territories had acquired no sense of 'belonging' with their colonial masters and therefore welcomed the Japanese as liberators. The fact that the Philippines, America's own dependency, was conquered with equal rapidity made no difference. Colonialism was exposed as morally iniquitous. The United States was committed to fighting Fascism and Japanese militarism; but was not associated with the European reoccupation of their colonies as part of the struggle.

Roosevelt became particularly incensed about the French record in Indo-China. En route to the Casablanca Conference in January 1943 he told his son Elliott: 'The native Indo-Chinese have been so flagrantly downtrodden that they thought to themselves: anything must be better than to live under French colonial rule! . . . Don't think for a moment . . . that Americans would have been dying tonight if it had not been for the shortsighted greed of the French, the British and the Dutch.'[13]

Even before the United States entered the war, Roosevelt had sought to invest the struggle with a moral purpose. In August 1941 he rendezvoused with Churchill aboard *Prince of Wales* off Newfoundland and with him agreed on an 'Atlantic Charter' to offer a better future for the world. The third article began, 'They respect the right of all peoples to choose the form of government under which they will live.' Churchill signed, accepting that this meant (in so far as it meant anything) that freedom would be restored to the peoples of occupied Europe. Roosevelt intended that the Charter should also apply to the colonial peoples. Yet the President's words were not supported by deeds, according to Wendell Wilkie, the American Republican leader. He proclaimed:

By silence on the part of the United States towards the problem of Indian independence we have already drawn heavily on the reservoir of goodwill in the East. . . . The people of the East . . . cannot ascertain from our government's wishy-washy attitude towards the problem of India what we are likely to feel at the end of the war about all the other hundreds of millions of Eastern people. They cannot tell from our vague and vacillating talk whether or not we really do stand for freedom.[14]

Churchill vigorously denied it was time to end empire, declaring at the banquet given by the Lord Mayor of London in November 1942, 'I have not become the King's First Minister in order to preside over the liquidation of the British Empire.' These were brave words (and true, inasmuch as this liquidation process was not launched during his premiership) but they were not meant to be policy.

Churchill's bravado did not please the American administration. A

British diplomat returning from Washington reported on, 'The existence of a feeling that the Netherlands East Indies, presumably also Malaya and Burma, might be established on a basis somewhat similar to that which the Americans had contemplated for the Philippines when once the latter had attained a nominal independence' (in 1933 the Congress had voted to give the Philippines independence after ten years, overruling President Hoover's veto).

These pressures produced a number of studies at Cabinet level in London. Churchill despatched a telegram to the Dominion Prime Ministers: 'There is a widespread and rooted feeling in the United States which regards the British Colonial Empire as the equivalent to the private estate of a landlord preserved for his own benefit.'[15] His conclusion was that 'we should do well not to resent but rather to welcome American interest'. He proposed a joint Anglo-American declaration that regional Commissions be established with representatives from both countries 'for consultation and collaboration'. The Colonial Secretary, then Lord Cranborne, objected strongly: 'We all know in our heart of hearts that most of the Colonies, especially in Africa, will probably not be fit for complete independence for centuries.'

The proposed British declaration did not go far enough to comply with American ideas: the document they produced started from the premise that colonial peoples had a right to independence. The British response was predictably cool: 'The emphasis through the document [delivered by Cordell Hull] on the conception of 'independence' is unfortunate.' As a counterblast, Oliver Stanley made his statement to parliament on 13 July 1943 warning there would be no self-government 'unjustified by circumstances'. However, in winding up the debate, Stanley let slip the news that there would be Commissions for certain regions 'mainly for consultation and collaboration'. MPs sat up; this appeared an important announcement, inserted at the end of the debate. The Colonial Secretary assured them that the Prime Minister was behind his decision.

Smuts weighed in with a speech insisting that those states which had assumed mandates over former German colonies should continue to exercise control unilaterally after the war: clearly this was intended to safeguard South Africa's position in South-West Africa. This was regarded as helpful by the British. Gradually, the Americans watered down their demands for international control and recognition of independence as an immediate goal. Even so, Roosevelt continued to take an inordinate interest in the status of Indo-China, challenging its future return to France at the Tehran conference. On his return to Washington late in January 1944 the President saw Lord Halifax and 'told him quite frankly that . . . I had for over a year expressed the opinion that Indo-China . . . should be administered by an international trusteeship'.

After April 1944 not much more was heard of an Anglo-American declaration on colonies. In part this was because the United States was now interested in annexing the Japanese colonies in the Pacific. However, the issue remained as an irritant and in May 1945, Lord Halifax reported from the San Francisco conference to establish a United Nations (UN) on the 'normal American tendency to represent Britain as the main obstacle towards progress in the direction of securing subject peoples from the Imperialist yoke'.

Thus the American threat to the European colonial overlords came to nothing, or almost nothing. The toppling of the Europeans came not from American pressure but from the forces of Asian nationalism pitted against powers no longer strong enough to enforce their rule upon their subjects. The Emperor had no clothes: but this had to be proved.

The End of Empire in Perspective

How significant was the formal termination of colonial rule? The first generation of the 'Freedom Movement' historians saw the attainment of independence as 'a new birth in freedom', and this view was encouraged by American scholars who deduced that because the birth of the United States released something like a political and social explosion in North America the same must have happened to these latter 'new nations'. Of recent years, revisionist historians, mainly but certainly not exclusively Marxist, have played down the notion of vital 'before' and 'after' differences. From another standpoint those who view the independence process in terms of a 'transfer of power' have also had a hand in lowering the temperature. They deny that the term 'revolution' has any relevance; things went on much the same with only the substitution of Asian (later African) leadership for the Western administration. Most Marxist historians see colonialism almost imperceptibly blending into neo-colonialism, while more conservative scholars have also emphasised continuities: was not the 1950 constitution of India modelled largely upon the British 1935 Government of India Act?

The emphasis upon continuity is justified with some of the new states; certainly for Ceylon (later Sri Lanka) and Malaya (later Malaysia) where nothing much changed at the formal moment of independence. In the case of the countries we shall consider the fact of independence did bring about tangible change, much of it dramatic. In Burma, Indonesia and Vietnam the contrast between the colonial system and the new fabric of independence was so striking that little argument is possible. For India and Pakistan it may be argued that much of the colonial structure survived 1947 and was only gradually modified by political pressures from groups and regions. However, the fact of partition – the fact that international frontiers appeared where previously there were no divisions of geography or culture – sent two 'nations' which previously had so much in common plunging off to discover new identities: a process which in the case of Pakistan led to the emergence of Bangladesh, because a common religious heritage proved less durable than a divided regional environment.

In Africa the application of revolutionary interpretations to the independence process often appears less justified than in Asia. In large areas of former French West Africa, France seems merely to have taken a back seat from which it continues to drive the political and administrative machine. Kenya, in structural terms, is not so different from the late colonial economy: yet the almost complete substitution of a Black elite for the former White bosses (with their Asian subordinates) has created something very like a race revolution. Of the Gold Coast – transformed into Ghana – one can only observe that the dreams of Nkrumah turned what might have been the smooth substitution of neo-colonialism for colonialism into a more dramatic, bolder venture.

This brings us back to the main thesis, that the re-emergence of Asia and Africa into the international arena was, fundamentally, the achievement of those men who ended empires. If now we view former Western dominance in Asia and Africa as a kind of freak, an aberration, almost an accident, it is because of the forces which these men personified.

So: what were those architects of independence like? Some were fighters; some were dreamers; some were schemers; and most were a mixture of all three.

2

The Nation Builders

These studies of men who led their countries into independence from Western colonial rule are designed to reveal how it was they emerged, how they attained the leadership of the national movements, what methods they employed in challenging the colonial power, how they conducted the final demand for independence, and what became of them when their countries shook off colonial rule. Every one of the 'new nations' has its great man, recognised as the architect of independence, and around most of these men legends have been formed to celebrate their achievement. Not in all cases: for some of them rapidly fell from power after independence and were cast into a limbo of neglect, such as befell Leon Trotsky in Soviet Russia. But in general their feats have been exalted as the legends assumed importance in assuring the new nation of its collective achievement in shaking off the bonds of alien subjugation. As these enhancements of the stature of the founders of the new nations of Asia and Africa received their place in these countries' historical records, these men became superhuman, demigods; their actual personalities became blurred in a cult, the cult of the Liberator, the selfless leader who sacrificed all for his country's freedom.

Assumptions about National Leadership Questioned

The purpose of this book is to show that in actuality these men were very different in their various methods of challenging the colonial power: and in most cases shrugging off the challenges of rivals who also cast themselves in the role of their nation's liberator. Some established their leadership by setting a noble example to their countrymen, by proclaiming a goal, by emphasising past national glories extinguished by Western conquest: in short by proclaiming an ideal which lesser men might emulate, if only in part. They taught their countrymen that if they wanted to shake off the colonial yoke then they must fight; they must cast off what Gandhi called the 'pathetic contentment' of colonial people in their servitude. They were told they had been free before: they could be free again. They must mobilise in order to gain that freedom. Such a direct challenge to what many regarded as the measureless might of the conqueror was by no means general. Most of the Afro-Asian leaders adopted a more realistic approach. They had studied in institutions of higher education on the Western pattern. Many spent time in Europe. On returning home, they took up professions which formed part of the superstructure imposed by the West: they were lawyers, professors, doctors, functioning in a Westernised context, within the colonial apparatus. When they came to plan for their country's freedom they sought to achieve this by assimilating Western institutions into a national political edifice, eventually negotiating a 'transfer of power' from their rulers.

Perhaps all this is labouring the obvious: but almost always the independence process has been viewed in one light only, that of a 'freedom struggle'. The leader is awarded the mantle of 'the Liberator'.

The Ideal: the Man of Valour

The Liberator! Portrayed in painting or sculpture in heroic pose, with sword drawn pointing towards the distant scene; or else in dignified stance with one hand resting upon a document which we believe to be the infant nation's constitution. Amongst these idealised figures we recognise the grave pose of George Washington: tall, erect, infinitely dignified, with a profile that any actor would envy.[1] We also recognise Vladimir Ilyich Lenin perpetually, it seems, arousing the people to action: orator, spellbinder, freedom fighter. So he appears on the banners at the parades in Moscow and in Peking. In Asia and Africa, similar larger-than-life statues have been erected of The Great Leader, the Saviour of His Country (to name only the titles awarded to Jinnah and Nkrumah). What were these men like in their actual lives? That is the purpose of this book: to reveal the man behind the myth; and to reveal that each one was cast in a different pattern.

The purpose of this book is not to cut these leaders down to size. In every case we are going to consider, these particular leaders *did* make unique contributions to their countries' independence. If they had not been in charge, their countries would not have become free when they did, and how they did. One man among these leaders was perhaps different from the others, inasmuch as he succeeded in giving a new shape to a new nation, giving it entirely new frontiers. Most of these leaders wrested imperial possessions from the Western overlords while endorsing the existing boundaries. M.A. Jinnah changed the old boundaries by his demand for a separate Muslim state, Pakistan.

The Reality: the Art of the Possible

Jinnah is actually the most surprising of these 'liberator' figures. The man hailed as Qaid-i-Azam, leader of the nation, was cast firmly in the constitutional mould. He seems, naturally, to belong to that type which the colonial powers identified as 'safe' leaders, men with whom they could do business more or less on their own terms. Such was Manual Quezon who opposed the American invasion of the Philippines in 1897 but thereafter threw in his lot with the occupying power and held a succession of offices under the Americans. Such as Bao Dai, the last Westernised Emperor of Vietnam, selected by the French to give a semblance of independence to the new Vietnam, who soon retired to end his days in the south of France. At one point, in the 1930s, when Jinnah was living in Hampstead, practising law in London, this must have seemed his role. Yet finally he thwarted not only British policy and purpose but also the superior bargaining power of Nehru and the Indian National Congress.

There were many cases in which the imperial authority selected their preferred candidate for a 'transfer of power' and arranged that the changeover take place while the favoured one was in the ascendant. This happened in Ceylon where D.S. Senanayake was identified as a trustworthy, pro-British figure. It was deemed better to hasten Ceylon's independence in order that he would inherit power and acquire the prestige of the architect of freedom rather than one of the several more extreme politicians waiting in the wings. The same was true in Malaya where, although the Communist jungle fighters were far from finished, power was handed over to Tungku Abdul Rahman, as a stalwart friend of Britain.

Among those selected for study in this book, few if any can be adequately understood as the embodiment of the freedom fighter, with no shade of qualification. Ho Chi Minh at once emerges as the seeming exception; yet even he would have been prepared to work with the French, if they had shown more imagination. Sukarno is another whom the Dutch very quickly identified as their enemy so that most of his life expressed defiance. Yet he, also, might have been mollified by policies less vindictive. All the others we are about to consider operated within the nexus of British imperialism, which was more pragmatic, less dogmatic than French and Dutch forms of empire. These men absorbed an education on the English model; all in their bid for national freedom entered into negotiations, more or less prolonged, with the British; all attained independence without an armed struggle against the imperial power. The term 'collaborator' has acquired an unpleasant association, yet these men were to a greater or lesser extent collaborators with British imperialism: even though their collaboration was directed towards the termination of colonial rule. In this there is a paradox: that these men whose efforts contributed substantially to the rapid extinction of 'the Empire on which the Sun never Sets' also (most of them) contributed to the emergence of the new Commonwealth which has played a major part in stemming the international decline of Britain into a third-rate power.

We need not be taken aback by this paradox. As we learn more about Europe under German wartime occupation we discover that the two categories of 'resistance' and 'collaboration' were by no means opposite and opposed. Many, perhaps most, in the occupied countries combined a measure of collaboration with some commitment to resistance. So it was with those who worked to end colonial domination. Among the men whose lives we are going to try to understand, all but one of those who were British imperial subjects spent periods in jail: some for a short time, but others for long terms of imprisonment. The exception is M.A. Jinnah, who eventually contemplated armed resistance, but did not actually have to put this into effect. Nehru, Aung San, Thakin Nu, Nkrumah and Kenyatta all suffered enforced detention by the British. They emerged to take a journey – in some cases long and roundabout, in others short – which led them to be welcomed at Government House and 10 Downing Street.

Freedom was attained by very different ways and means by men whose personalities and strategies were not fitted into a predetermined pattern but emerged from their very different backgrounds and evolved under very different circumstances.

The Liberator Image Re-examined

The model of 'the Liberator' is to be found in the story of two men who fought for independence in an earlier age and with a much less unequal balance between the imperial power and their opponents: we refer to George Washington and Simon Bolivar.

They raised armies of volunteers who took on the imperial forces and destroyed them. Washington went on to become a statesman, the Father of his Country; Bolivar won spectacular victories and failed to consolidate the political structure of the countries he had created. Both men illustrate the argument advanced earlier: that the Liberator draws heavily on the legacy of the imperial master. George Washington was a loyal servant of the Crown, holding the Royal Commission. As an army officer he served his king in the garrison of Barbados and on the colonial frontier in action against the French. In the colonial hierarchy he was an aristocrat, and maybe he would never have rebelled against British colonial rule if his plan to become a great landowner in the wilds beyond the settled frontier had not been frustrated by British policy towards the Indians. Having changed course, his changeover was complete.

Simon Bolivar was also from an aristocratic Venezuelan family of pure Spanish descent. He received his education in Spain and married the daughter of a Spanish nobleman. His conversion to the cause of colonial independence was more sudden than that of Washington. His vision of the future Latin America was oligarchic. He had no place for the peasant masses in the government. Although in his famous *Letter from Jamaica* he declared, 'We are a microcosm of the human race. . . . We are neither Indians nor Europeans, yet we are a part of each', in his campaigns the great Amerindian majority played no part. His troops were *mestizo* of predominant Spanish descent or else mercenaries from Europe – Irish and English mainly – and the descendants of the Incas looked on while the *blancos* fought it out among themselves.

The American revolution was even more a family affair. Indeed, it is better described as a civil war than as a war between two different peoples. The revolutionaries claimed that they were fulfilling English constitutional ideas ('No taxation without representation'). At least one-third of the population of the American colonies (more probably half) opposed the revolution. Called 'Loyalists' by the British and 'Tories' by the revolutionaries (who in turn claimed the label of 'Patriots' while the British called them rebels), the war eventually hinged upon the intervention of France and Spain as improbable allies of the revolutionaries. As the Loyalists lost (and departed to begin a hard life in Canada) the split between the collaborators and the freedom fighters was made to appear much clearer than it was in reality. The biggest losers were, of course, the North American Indians who now began the long enforced retreat into the deserts of the West.

The United States: an Irrelevant Case

Americans like to think that their experience provides the model for all other nations struggling to be free: and it must be granted that Thomas Paine's *Rights of Man* is one of the basic texts of anti-authoritarian resistance. Yet the American revolution seems in retrospect most like the European revolutions of 1848 in which middle-class liberals rose up against absolutism in order to secure representative institutions. The

difference was, of course, that the American revolution was successful –
and permanent. Later, non-Western opponents of colonial rule looked
much more for inspiration to France; and perhaps most of all to Italy and
Ireland. In those two instances they thought they saw a broad-based
popular revolt against alien rule, and they studied the ideas and
techniques evolved in Italy and Ireland. From Ireland they concluded that
a subject population could evolve its own reply to the agents and
collaborators of the imperial power by the weapon of the boycott, and
later by guerrilla revolt. From Italy they drew the lesson that freedom
could be won when the youth of the country renounced the social
controls accepted by their elders in the authority of Church and State.

The Mystique of the Italian Risorgimento

In the pantheon of those who fought imperial overlordship one name is
pre-eminent: that of Giuseppe Mazzini, whose 'Young Italy', the journal
Giovine Italia, had numerous imitators. In Europe his vision was taken up
by 'Young Ireland', and followed elsewhere. The 'Young Turk' movement
against the decadence of their country under the Sultans is best known,
but Gandhi also edited a journal, *Young India*, and movements named
Young Burma, Young Java, and Young China were founded. Equally
inspirational was the crusade led by Garibaldi to liberate Sicily from the
Bourbon yoke depending upon the enthusiasm of young volunteers from
north Italy: The Thousand. He became a hero in England and America as
well as in Europe.

The Element of Realpolitik

The hope that idealism and bravery could overcome empires encouraged
many an Asian and African intellectual. But was that the full explanation
of how Italy was unified and freed from systems of tyranny? Was there
not another actor in the drama equally important though lacking the
charisma of a Garibaldi and the vision of a Mazzini: Camillo Cavour, the
shrewd adviser of the Kings of Sardinia? It is suggested that in trying to
understand the ways in which Asian and African leaders wrested
independence for their peoples there were those whose contribution was
very like that of Cavour, though none may have taken him as their model.
In each of the leaders we are about to study there was one predominant
strain: the idealism of Mazzini, the courage of Garibaldi, or the statecraft
of Cavour. Probably in every one of them these elements were combined
reflecting the very different styles of the three Italian leaders.

Comparisons with Asia and Africa

Jinnah was almost wholly of the Cavour type: yet he was also able to call upon the idealism of the Muslim students of India at the critical moment and he certainly did not lack bravery in battling on while knowing that this would contribute to shortening his life, threatened by mortal illness. Nehru had all the idealism of a Mazzini and the personal courage of a Garibaldi. He lacked awareness of the limitations of his own and his party's capacity, to which Cavour owed his success, together with a willingness to accept allies and alliances – however distasteful – if these would bring his goal nearer. Of Sukarno we may say that he possessed an apocalyptic vision of a new order in Asia reminiscent of Mazzini and that he was prepared to gain his ends by methods as devious as any employed by Cavour. Nkrumah too combined a vision of a new Africa with an obsessive pursuit of total power which ended in his undoing. However, let us not anticipate the investigations we shall shortly begin on the lives of those chosen to illustrate the encounter between Afro-Asian nationalism and European colonialism. First we re-examine the three harbingers of Italian freedom.

In retrospect it seems amazing that within a period of just over ten years Italy was freed from foreign rule and unified after so many centuries in which the country had, in Metternich's celebrated phrase, just been 'a geographical expression' (*Italien ist ein geographischer Begriff,*). It is true that Italy was compelled to cede Garibaldi's birth-place, Nice, to France, while the upland Trentino had to wait another 50 years for its deliverance (owing to the betrayal of Garibaldi's great effort). That was a relatively minor price to pay for bringing together all the lands between the Alps and Sicily, divided and subjugated for centuries.

Austria, France and Spain dominated the whole country, either directly or through local autocrats under their influence. When the French revolutionary armies marched into Italy it seemed that the old order had been liquidated, as republics were established in the different regions. But Napoleon's dynastic pretensions created a new system of foreign control (albeit of a much more modern type). After Waterloo the old order was restored and the Austrian hegemony even more firmly imposed. The year 1848 seemed to bring liberation: it was then that the visionary Mazzini and the freedom fighter Garibaldi appeared to promise a new age. Yet once again the old order was re-established. Italy was still a geographical expression – in a foreign language.

Then, commencing in 1859, an Italian state began to arise through a series of military campaigns against the Austrian overlords and their

Bourbon clients. To those who cherished freedom, national self-determination as a high ideal, it was a miracle. But was it really a miracle or a combination of talents, each of which alone would have ended in the same bitter disappointments as in 1799 and 1848? That is the proposition which we now consider.

The Contribution of the Dreamer

Mazzini (1805 – 72) was, by the usual means of computing success, a total failure. His first political home was in the Carbonari ('Charcoal Burners'), a secret society with branches throughout Italy. They participated in a series of plots and insurrections and it was as a Carbonaro that he was denounced to the police and jailed for three months in 1830. Mazzini was compelled to live in exile, first in Marseilles, then in Switzerland, and from January 1837 in London. This became his home, which he quitted only for brief adventures in revolution. His main contribution was towards a religion, a faith of revolutionary nationalism. 'God . . . divided humanity into distinct groups upon the face of our globe and thus planted the seeds of nations'; 'The Country . . . is the sentiment of love, the sense of fellowship which binds together all the sons of that territory.' Young Italy became a network of secret societies with some 60 000 members, who planned and tried to execute revolts against the autocratic authorities. 'Weaving skein after skein of conspiracy, each more desparate than the last': all ended in bloody failure, but Mazzini was not dismayed.[2] 'Ideas ripen quickly when nourished by the blood of martyrs', he said. It looked as though his moment had arrived when, amid the revolutions of 1848, northern Italy threw off the foreign yoke. In February 1849, a republic was proclaimed in Rome; Mazzini, along with Garibaldi, headed the dictatorship of the triumvirate. They held out until July, when a French expeditionary corps recaptured the city for the Pope.

He dreamed of freeing Bourbon Sicily, and when Garibaldi landed with The Thousand Mazzini briefly joined him. He was then repeatedly elected Deputy for Messina in the new Italian parliament but refused to take his seat so long as the death sentence imposed in 1833 in his absence still stood: it was only rescinded in 1866. He still opposed the monarchy and in 1870 led an unsuccessful republican rising in Sicily. He was imprisoned, though released after the final liberation of Rome when the French forces withdrew. He felt no joy: 'I thought I was awakening the soul of Italy and I see only the corpse before me.' He died in 1872, a dreamer whose dream did not come true in the way he envisaged. He had written: 'The Countries of the People will rise, defined by the voice of the free, upon the ruins of the Countries of Kings and privileged castes. Between these Countries there will be harmony and brotherhood.' The reality was very different.

The Role of the Fighter

Garibaldi (1807–82) entered 'liberation politics' as a disciple of Mazzini. One of a seafaring family, he gained his master's certificate in 1832 and briefly served in the navy of the Kingdom of Sardinia. Then, in 1834, urged by Mazzini, he launched what was intended as an insurrection in Genoa. Like all Mazzini's plots, it failed, and Garibaldi had to flee to South America, where he became a naval captain with the rebel state of Rio Grande. He then took up the cause of Uruguay in its struggle against Argentinian hegemony and commanded an Italian legion, who became the first of the 'Redshirts', thereafter identified with all of Garibaldi's causes. He adopted a new style of fighting, derived from the gauchos of the pampas, and this guerrilla style was to give him his greatest victories.

When in 1848 Italy shook off absolutism, he returned with his legion to fight the Austrians. He headed for Milan, where Mazzini was leading the revolt and achieved some success. Then the defeat of the King of Sardinia ended hopes in north Italy. When the Pope fled from Rome, Garibaldi raised another force of volunteers and joined Mazzini in proclaiming the Roman Republic: 'Of political wisdom, Garibaldi was utterly devoid' proclaims a great Liberal historian, though he was 'a daring captain of irregular troops . . . [with] a certain Homeric grandeur'.[3] Threatened by a French army, Garibaldi repulsed their attack upon the Janiculum Hill. But he could not withstand French, Austrian and Neapolitan pressures: refusing to capitulate he led 4000 of his men through the enemy lines to safety. Once again, his was the life of an exile, in New York and Peru.

Meanwhile, Cavour was weaving his web of calculation to involve international support for Italian unification. The moment came in 1859 when, combined with the French, the army of Sardinia–Piedmont drove the Austrians from Lombardy. Cavour wanted to wean Garibaldi from Mazzini's influence and he was invited to command an army of volunteeers as a Piedmontese general. This force, called the Huntsmen of the Alps (*Cacciatori del Alpi*), made a brilliant advance up to Lake Como and beyond. When Louis Napoleon abruptly made peace, with much of north Italy still under the Austrian grip, Garibaldi was compelled to give up some of their highland gains. Then followed the spontaneous uprisings in north-central Italy which freed the country, down to the Papal States. Rebellion stirred in Sicily and Garibaldi quickly raised a thousand volunteer Redshirts to liberate the island.

The attitude of Cavour and his master, King Victor Emmanuele, was distinctly ambivalent. They feared that south Italy would become a republic on Mazzinian lines; but they could not oppose the swell of applause for Garibaldi (both internal and international) which accompanied his venture. Events took over. Within three months Sicily was freed from all Bourbon control. Garibaldi crossed to the mainland (with a British naval force benevolently on the horizon) and within one month he was in Naples, where he proclaimed himself 'Dictator of the Two Sicilies'. Anticipating the maxim 'If you can't beat them, join them', Victor Emmanuele led his regular forces into the Papal provinces, isolating Rome, and meeting up with Garibaldi to the north of Naples. Thenceforward, the initiative was with Cavour and his king. A hastily arranged plebiscite produced an overwhelming vote for a Kingdom of Italy with Victor Emmanuele at its head. Garibaldi retired to the home he had made on the little island of Caprera, and although elected by several constituencies to the all-Italian parliament he renounced the new regime. An abortive attempt to invade the territory of Rome in 1862 was foiled by the royal forces. Then in 1866 when Italy entered the war against Austria as Prussia's ally, he again took the field. The Italian forces performed somewhat dismally, but Garibaldi's Redshirts stormed up the sub-Alpine valleys to seize Trento, the most northern Italian-speaking city. Although Italy acquired Venezia at the peace treaty thanks to the Prussians, the Trentino was to be denied for another 50 years.

Garibaldi's last adventure came when, following Louis Napoleon's defeat at Sedan, a Republic was established in France and the old republican led forces which operated with considerable success against the Germans near the Swiss border. Retiring to Caprera, he refused all honours but remained the same simple, rugged, honest patriot and fighter for liberty he had always been, though enjoying the adulation of an international following.

The Statesman-Schemer

So far we have cast Cavour almost in the role of villain. That entirely minimises his stature as a man and as a statesman. Camillo Cavour (1810–61) belonged to an aristocratic family, yet in spirit he was in tune with the world of Peel and Cobden. As a young man he was an engineer officer in the army of Piedmont, which only bored him. Given charge of his father's estates, he made them a model property, run on a modern system of economics. As a youth, he had links with the Carbonari, but now his political ideas, following English and Swiss examples, looked towards constitutional nationalism. He founded his own newspaper, *Il Risorgimento*, in 1847 and the next year became a member of the Chamber of Deputies of Piedmont: he liked to repeat the aphorism, 'The worst of Chambers is better than the best of Antechambers' (where courtiers gather). He became a Minister in 1850, and Prime Minister in 1851. His chosen path was reform, not revolution. Like his two great contemporaries he was strongly anti-clerical and intended to eliminate the Church of Rome from the political sphere. He introduced legislation for civil marriage and encouraged religious tolerance in Sardinia–Piedmont.

His first venture into international politics was somewhat exploratory. Sardinia joined Britain and France in the war against Russia in the Crimea. This ensured that the Italian question was placed on the agenda at the Congress of Paris (1856) but brought no concession from Austria. However, Louis Napoleon was moved thereby to see himself as the champion of Italy. At a secret meeting at Plombières in the French Alps it was agreed that France would support the liberation of the whole of north Italy from Austria, in return for the adhesion of French-speaking Savoy and Nice (portions of the kingdom of Piedmont) to France. Napoleon proved a tricky ally; he backtracked on the Plombières agreement, and it was only the stiffness of the Austrians which (as in 1914) created a war situation. The campaign which followed was what Cavour had wanted; but Napoleon's unilateral ending of the war by the armistice of Villafranca upset all his plans. Enraged by this betrayal (for Victor Emmanuele endorsed the armistice) he resigned his office. Then the three grand duchies declared for Victor Emmanuele and Cavour came back. He had to pay the price Louis Napoleon had demanded at Plombières – the handover of Savoy and Nice – which in the contemporary atmosphere of western Europe did France no good, and encouraged Britain to consider the claims of Italy.

Cavour came back to power in January 1860. The plebiscites in the Duchies virtually doubled the territory of Sardinia–Piedmont. Then came the conquest of Sicily by the Redshirts, and Cavour was worried. With Mazzini there, the possibility of a republic of South Italy in rivalry with the northern kingdom was alarming. He determined to wean Garibaldi away from Mazzini, and sent Victor Emmanuele south to link up with the popular hero and win him over. King and conqueror met as equals; but with Cavour pulling the strings Garibaldi was outmatched. A parliament of Italy convened in Turin called for a plebiscite in the former Papal States and the Kingdom of the Two Sicilies. The verdict of 21 October 1860 for union 'announced the triumph of Cavour and the defeat of Mazzini. . . . The one man [Garibaldi] who could have fatally wrecked Italian harmony swallowed, when the moment came, his personal griefs, prejudices and vanities.'[4] This verdict by a British Liberal historian to whom Italian nationalism seemed an exhilarating contrast to the grimness of the *Realpolitik* which constructed a united Germany may play down the craftiness with which Cavour checkmated his adversaries. Yet Cavour had his ideals; he was working for constitutional monarchy and parliamentary government, whereas both Garibaldi and Mazzini believed in the simple yet dangerous solution of dictatorship. Cavour knew they must live with the Roman church, yet he intended to transform its place in the new Italy: 'A free church in a free nation' was his formula.

Cavour was a modern man: he would have found no difficulty in taking his place in the European Economic Community. He lacks the glamour of Mazzini and Garibaldi. Before his task was completed he died in June 1861. He did not see Rome become the capital of Italy: but also he did not have to confront the great social and economic problems which remained after the *Risorgimento*, the stark difference between north and south Italy.

By coincidence, each of this triumvirate was limited in his contribution to working for the freedom and unity of their country *before* the goal was achieved. They played no part in the testing times afterwards. The Asian and African leaders we are now to consider met their greatest challenge *after* independence (with the possible exception of Ho Chi Minh). We do not judge Mazzini or Garibaldi or Cavour by the Italian national experience during the remaining years of the nineteenth century. We do apply that test to the Afro-Asian independence-makers; though perhaps we exclude Jinnah, who in 1947 was already under sentence of death, and Aung San of Burma who was assassinated when he had already wrested freedom but before the formal handover by the British. In this book, although the main emphasis is upon the struggle for independence, the sequel has also to be placed in the balance.

The Italian Struggle as a Model for Asia and Africa?

Before we move on to the real subject of our inquiry, let us discover if we can draw any parallels between the Italian experience and that of Asian and African lands under Western colonial rule. Mid-nineteenth century Italy was controlled by Austria: the north, the most advanced part of the country, was mainly under direct Austrian rule. This was not oppressive for the mass of the population, while many of the upper class were associated with the administration. The Italian language was in official use, and Italian culture was respected. Nevertheless, Italian interests were subordinate to those of a central European empire. Italian army conscripts might serve in the Balkans or on some other frontier. The Austrian grip was extended by a system of subordinate states stretching down to Sicily. A few of them were well administered, but most were medieval systems of tyranny. When in 1851 Gladstone investigated conditions in the Neapolitan state he described it all as 'the negation of God erected into a system of government'. Pre-industrial societies were still locked into a feudal structure: but fear of revolution had brought into existence a network of spies and secret police which suppressed even the mildest forms of protest.

A certain parallel can be drawn with British India and also the Dutch East Indies. British India was well administered; the British officials were conscientious and fair, but it was an alien system of government. Indian interests were subordinated to those of Britain and a sizeable Indian army was maintained, always available to fight anywhere in the British Empire. Besides British India there were the Princely states, the largest, Hyderabad, with a population of 16½ million; the smallest, Lawa, 2808 persons. (There were 582 of these states altogether.) A few were run on modern lines, but most were of a medieval character. Although there was no secret police there were many spies and little room for free speech and criticism of princely rule.

The Dutch also recognised 282 Sultans in Indonesia, the Sultan of Jogjakarta being the most important. There was a well-trained corps of Dutch officials; many were enlightened men. Yet even more than British India, 'Netherlands India' was managed for the benefit of the metropole and successive policies contributed substantially to Dutch wealth. In Java, the traditional aristocracy, *priyayi*, formed the middle and lower echelons of the administration. They were known as Regents, or *kabupaten*, to the Javanese and watched over the rural peasantry.

Where the Austrian hegemony in Italy differed from Western colonialism in Asia and Africa was in its close identification with the religious apparatus. Austria was (and is) a devoutly Catholic country (so, of course, is France: but there the Revolution left a strong political tradition of anti-clericalism). In Austria the Church upheld the State, and the State the Church. The existence of a solid bloc of territory throughout central Italy directly ruled by the Church was an additional buttress to Imperial and Catholic control. The *Risorgimento* inevitably emerged as a challenge to clericalism: and the Church responded by asserting its place in the political system (a place which still remains strong in the 1980s).

There was no parallel to this situation in the British, French and Dutch colonies, though in minor ways all three sought to coopt the Christian population as their agents and supporters and in Kenya missionary support strengthened administration. However, the real power of religion was indigenous: in Islam, Hinduism, and Buddhism. Conscious that these religions could be mobilised as political forces hostile to Western colonialism, the Europeans sought to neutralise or placate these religions. True, the British in India inclined to favour Hindus more than Muslims at one period and Muslims more than Hindus later. But this favouritism in no way resembled the close alliance between Rome and Vienna, where both parties shared a common outlook and a common interest in maintaining the status quo, socially and intellectually.

Were there similarities between those who challenged the status quo in Italy and in Asia and Africa? There were indeed. The most active Italian patriots belonged to the urban bourgeoisie and were imbued with nationalist ideals in young manhood. For them, nationalism became a unifying force, more important than the regional and local associations which had identified Italians with a city (Milan, Florence, Siena) or a locality for hundreds of years. The Thousand who landed in Sicily came mainly from northern towns: but they hastened to support the Sicilian uprising because this was part of the all-Italian struggle. If the dynamic element was provided by the urban bourgeoisie, mass support was readily aroused among those previously regarded as supporters of the old order: the peasants and the city poor. If they did no more than hail Garibaldi as their liberator they convinced the agents of the *ancien régime* that they had to reckon with the people as active participants in the struggle.

There are close parallels in Asia and Africa. The initiative was taken by small numbers of educated, mainly urban leaders: but whereas the colonial rulers dismissed them as a small unrepresentative minority, when the struggle intensified those who had been unconsidered spectators showed they also had a part to play.

The 'Great Man' Thesis

Historians will remain divided for all time over the importance of personality – or a personality – in historical circumstances. At one extreme there is the view of Thomas Carlyle:

Universal history, the history of what man has accomplished in this world, is at bottom the History of the Great Men who have worked here. They were the leaders of men, these great ones; the modellers, patterns, and in a wide sense creators of whatsoever the general mass of men contrived to do or attain; all things that we see standing accomplished in the world are properly the outward material result, the practical realisation and embodiment, of Thoughts that dwelt in the Great Men sent into the world: the soul of the whole world's history, it may justly be considered, were the history of these.[5]

Marxist Emphasis upon 'The People'

An almost complete denial of the 'great man' basis of history runs through the entire literature of Marxism—Leninism. Out of a hundred illustrations we might produce, let us quote the following from Lenin:

Earlier historical theories ignored the activities of the *masses*, whereas historical materialism first made it possible to study with scientific accuracy the social conditions of the life of the masses and the changes in these conditions. . . . Marxism pointed the way to a comprehensive, an all-embracing study of the rise, development, and decay of socio-economic structures. People make their own history; but what determines their motives, that is the motives of people in the mass; what gives rise to the clash of conflicting ideas and endeavours . . . what are the objective conditions for the production of the material means of life that form the basis of all the historical activity of man . . . to all these matters Marx directed attention, pointing out the way to a scientific study of history as a unified and true-to-law process, despite its being extremely variegated and contradictory.[6]

Clearly, this study is concerned with the contribution made by great men to history: indeed, the role of Lenin himself amply demonstrates the difference that one individual can make to a movement. Frequently, there is a close connection between the man and the hour: Lenin and the Bolshevik group could do little in the 1905 revolution, yet seized the initiative in 1917. We think of Winston Churchill, widely considered a political mischief-maker for his part in the Gallipoli blunder of 1915 and his obstinate opposition to the India Bill in the early 1930s which largely wrecked any chance of a united India. His hour came in 1940. Although by 1945 he was no longer relevant, few would deny his claim to be a great man. Among those we now examine, some had to wait for years on the sidelines (like Ho and Sukarno), some leapt into prominence by exploiting new opportunities (as did Aung San and Nkrumah). Others ascended the political pathway steadily, and then assumed the position of overall leadership when they appeared right for the emerging situation (as Nehru and Jinnah did in 1946 – 7). Our study will not endorse Carlyle's absolute concept of Makers of History: rather of men who recognised that their hour had arrived, and bent the curve of history their way, instead of merely steering round the curve as most politicians do.

The Plan of the Book

The order in which these men and their countries are approached in this book is according to the order in which they secured independence from the colonial master. The only questionable case is that of Vietnam. The date of the French withdrawal from their former colony (1954) is taken as winning independence in the north, though a rival American client state functioned under siege in the south for another ten years.

The age at which these leaders achieved their goal is of some interest. Jinnah was 71 when Pakistan emerged in 1947; Nehru, his rival, was 58. In Burma, Aung San died a few months before independence at the early age of 31; his successor, Thakin Nu, was 41 when independence dawned in January 1948. Sukarno was 48 when the Dutch officially recognised the Republic of Indonesia in 1949. Ho Chi Minh was 64 when the French quit Indo-China. Nkrumah was 47 when the Gold Coast became Ghana in 1956, but Kenyatta was 69 or 70 when British rule in Kenya ended in 1963. Only Jinnah had become head of his country at a more advanced age: but whereas he survived little more than a year after Pakistan became independent, Kenyatta had another 15 years to preside over his country's affairs.

The different political pathways these men trod is also varied. Jinnah first attended the annual gathering of the Indian National Congress in 1904, aged 28, and became a member of the Viceroy's legislative council in 1910. Hence he had over 40 years of parliamentary politics before he became head of state. Nehru was urged by his father to stand for the provincial legislature in 1920, when he was 31 years old; but he refused to participate in the constitutional structure established by the British until finally he was elected to the Constituent Assembly in 1946. However, Nehru had acquired 30 years of experience of active Congress politics by then, outside the legislature.

In Burma Aung San and Nu also gained their first experience of parliamentary institutions when elected to the Constituent Assembly a few months before independence day. Sukarno's first constitutional role was as President of the Republic; Ho Chi Minh also stepped straight into the supreme position in his country's politics when he became President of the Democratic Republic of Vietnam in November 1946. Nkrumah was elected to the Gold Coast legislature in February 1951 while in prison and was released to become leader of government business: just five years before taking Ghana into independence. Kenyatta's transition from detainee to acknowledged leader was almost as abrupt. Set free, he entered the legislative council and negotiated independence terms before going on to contest a general election and become his country's first prime minister. What is surprising is the way in which these men, almost all inexperienced in government, assumed the supreme position and held it during the first critical years of independence.

Among these eight leaders, five remained at the helm until death removed them. Three, Thakin Nu, Sukarno and Nkrumah, were deposed by military coups. Nkrumah went after 10 years at the top, Nu after 14 and Sukarno after 20 years. This record seems impressive compared to the volatile politics of many new states, such as Nigeria with its continuous succession of leaders, civil and military, all of whom are deposed by death or sudden removal at brief intervals. However, to repeat the theme announced earlier, these names were carefully chosen because in the absence of these particular men it is probable that colonial rule would have persisted longer in their countries. They did not become leaders by chance: they were men of destiny. Apart from Nehru and Jinnah, for whom a dominant role could have been predicted 20 years before they finally reached the top, these men were outsiders, almost unknown, until their final attack upon the empires of western Europe.

The Impact of Independence?

They achieved a new kind of political system: the non-Western yet modern state. How far did they also change the social and economic systems inherited from colonial rule (and in many ways inherited from pre-colonial times)? Here the record seems faltering. In Vietnam, the revolutionary regime which Ho inaugurated has transformed an ancient civilisation into one almost totally unrecognisable. Some might say that Kenya has been transformed from a primitive, pastoral society into one where capitalism is dominant and a new African plutocracy has appeared: the 'Wa-Benzi' as they are called (from their ownership of a Mercedes Benz apiece). India has achieved lopsided economic growth and dubious social cohesion. Of some other countries it may be said that they have subsided, gently or violently, into economic anarchy and social and religious regression. However, this question is best left aside for another book.

Rudyard Kipling – not the most obvious choice to end this chapter – wrote:

> Cities and Thrones and Powers
> Stand in Time's eye,
> Almost as long as flowers
> Which daily die.

3

The Winding Path of
M.A. Jinnah

Indian Muslim Separatism

It was Jinnah's destiny to end up espousing a cause he had spent most of his life combating: that of Muslim separatism in India. Remembering the centuries of Muslim political dominance, many of their elite clung to past greatness and feared that because Western education was pioneered by upper-caste Hindus, especially the Bengalis, they would be deprived of their former position. When the Indian National Congress was started in 1885 Muslims were advised to keep aloof by their foremost spokesman, Sir Sayyid Ahmad Khan. Writing in 1881 he had observed, 'India is like a bride whose two eyes are the Hindu and the Mohammadan. Her beauty consists in this – that the two eyes be of equal lustre.' This might be interpreted as an acceptance of interdependence, but he then went on: 'Suppose that all the English were to leave India . . .? Is it possible that under these circumstances the two nations – the Mohammadans and the Hindus – could sit on the same throne and remain equal in power? Most certainly not. It is necessary that one of them should conquer the other and thrust it down.'

Despite this medieval imagery, Sir Sayyid was a moderniser, founding a college at Aligarh where Muslims could obtain higher education in an environment both Islamic and English. Under his influence, the Muslims largely kept out of the Congress: there were only two Muslim presidents of the organisation during its first 20 years. One of Sir Sayyid's followers convened a meeting at Dacca in 1906 which set up the Muslim League to safeguard the community's special interests. The honorary president was the Aga Khan, world leader of the Ismaili sect of Islam (which then numbered about 15 million). Jinnah was not present at this meeting and the Aga Khan later wrote that he 'came out in bitter hostility towards all that I and my friends had done. . . . He was the only well-known Muslim to take this attitude.'[1] This was all the more galling inasmuch as Jinnah was born an Ismaili.

41

An Outsider: Born in Karachi (1876)

Most of the leaders of the League were aristocrats, like the Nawab of Dacca, or members of the traditional official class, like Sir Sayyid. Jinnah belonged to a trading family (most of the Ismailis are business men) and was outside the mainstream of Muslim social and political consciousness. His family were Khojas, originally from Iran, but long domiciled in the coastal districts of western India. The family spoke Gujarati; also Gandhi's mother tongue. Jinnah's father had a Gujarati-sounding name – Jinnah-bhai Poonja. He took up trade in the port of Karachi as a hide merchant in a modest way: the family home consisted of two rooms. Here his son was born and named Mohammadali Jinnahbhai: his date of birth is officially recognised as 25 December 1876, though he may have been born the previous year.

His father prospered, diversified his business, and rose in the world, acquiring his own carriage. Trade in Karachi was booming, and he benefited. He was associated with a British managing agency whose Karachi manager persuaded him to send his son to their London office to acquire experience. The boy, not yet 17, departed in January 1893 with funds to support him for three years. Within three months he had abandoned the business and joined Lincolns Inn to become a barrister (May 1893). Legal training was then perfunctory, and M.A. Jinnah (for he had now anglicised his name) was called to the Bar in May 1896. This was an unusually early age to be admitted. He returned not to Karachi, but to the metropolis of Bombay where he was enrolled in the High Court in August 1896. Despite having no influence and no money he could not be denied. There were four difficult years, then he secured a temporary government appointment as Presidency Magistrate. The government would have made this permanent, but Jinnah was already certain he could do much better on his own as a barrister. His talent lay in a dramatic courtroom manner which convinced judges and juries. Assured of an income sufficient to meet his growing taste for fine clothes and stylish living, he took up politics.

Active in the Congress

At that time, active membership of the Congress entailed no more than participation in the annual gathering, held for the convenience of lawyers just after Christmas while the Courts were closed for the holidays. His introduction to Congress politics came in 1904. At that time the organisation was dominated by old men, most of whom had been prominent since its inception in 1885, like Dadabhai Naoroji (born 1825), Ferozeshah Mehta (born 1845) and S.N. Banerjee (born 1848). It was therefore quite remarkable that the Congress chose him to accompany a delegation to London in 1905, led by G.K. Gokhale (born 1866) and also including Banerjee. For obscure reasons the visit did not take place; but his selection was a tribute to his personality and persuasive powers.

In the next year the Congress was torn by divisions between the so-called Extremists (led by B.G. Tilak and Lajpat Rai) and the Moderates, composed of the old guard, and also the younger Gokhale, to whom Jinnah became a close associate. The Government of India would have preferred to have no politics at all, but obviously the Moderates were better than the Extremists. They also had the Muslim League to consider, for they were impeccable loyalists. Out of all this came the Morley—Minto reforms which expanded the provincial legislatures and the Viceroy's Legislative Council for all British India. Although the new councils were much larger there were still official majorities, even in those provinces most politically sophisticated. The system of election was largely indirect, with representatives chosen by local authorities as electoral colleges. However, to please the Muslims, a few of the legislators were chosen by electorates exclusively Muslim, while there were also representatives of the landlords.

In the first election, held in 1910, Jinnah was chosen to represent the Bombay Muslim constituency, becoming one of six Muslim members on the Viceroy's Council. At 34 he was by far the youngest member. Also elected for the 'General' (i.e. non-Muslim) Bombay seat was Gokhale, and the two men worked closely together in Council.

Reasons for Joining the Muslim League

Not until 1913 did Jinnah join the Muslim League when he entered as one of a group of 'progressive' younger men, almost all already in the Congress. They included the radicals Mohammad Ali and Abul Kalam Azad, and Fazl-i-Husain, a rising Punjabi liberal. They virtually took over from the older generation whose only purpose was the preservation of Muslim rights. They succeeded in persuading the League to adopt a programme aiming at 'the attainment . . . of a system of self government suitable to India by constitutional means by . . . preserving national unity, by fostering public spirit among the people of India, and by cooperating with other communities for the said purpose'.[2]

The annual gatherings of Congress and League were now, by agreement, held simultaneously in the same location. In December 1916 the Muslim League met at Lucknow with Jinnah in the chair, to be offered an agreement worked out by him with the Congress leaders whereby in any reforms scheme for greater self-government the principle of separate Muslim representation would be safeguarded. In the central or national legislature Muslims would be guaranteed one-third of the seats (they numbered somewhat more than one-fifth of the population of India). In all provinces where they were in a minority they were given weighted representation: thus, in the United Provinces (UP) where Muslims formed less than 15 per cent of total population they were to get 30 per cent of the seats. The price to be paid was that in the two major provinces where they formed a majority, Punjab and Bengal, they accepted fewer seats than their numbers warranted.

The Lucknow Pact was intended to take the sting out of communalism and to unite Congress and League to press the British government for reform. At this moment Jinnah was foremost in demanding full self-government. It was now that he was accorded the title of 'the Apostle of Hindu-Muslim Unity' by the poet Sarojini Naidu. It seemed as though he must become the recognised leader of India, and when the new Secretary of State, Edwin Montagu, visited India in 1917 he identified Jinnah as the outstanding politician: 'Jinnah is a very clever man and it is of course an outrage that such a man should have no chance of running the affairs of his own country.'

Gandhi Moves Centre-Stage

The Government of India was less impressed. Accustomed to regard Hindus, especially Bengalis, as troublemakers they had counted on the Muslims as loyalists. Yet now, some – notably Mohammad Ali and his brother Shaukat – were stridently anti-British and were interned. Jinnah might also cause trouble. Over the treatment of Indians in South Africa and the indenture system in the sugar colonies he openly rebuked the government. After the early enthusiasm for the war, by 1916 India was indifferent while the Muslims were uneasy about hostilities with Turkey. In April 1918 the Viceroy invited leaders to a conference to promote the war effort. Six leaders came from Bombay, including Jinnah (afterwards the Viceroy complained he had tried to raise 'extraneous political matters'). It was to Gandhi that the Viceroy turned to move a resolution on behalf of the non-officials calling for renewed support (Gandhi had led the stretcher bearers in the Boer war). He responded, and went off on a singularly ineffective recruiting campaign in Gujarat. This was Jinnah's first experience of being upstaged by the man who was soon to relegate him to the sidelines.

However, he now made a change in his personal life more revolutionary in its way than anything Gandhi ever attempted. In later life Jinnah always emerges as a public man, haughty, correct, remote, inflexible: a platform figure in contrast to the extraordinary genius now about to supplant him, whose engaging personality disarmed even his opponents and appealed to the millions. Yet now it was Jinnah who broke the rules and crossed the boundaries: he married outside his religion, almost unknown then, and in the 1980s still a rarity.

Jinnah's Romantic Marriage (1918)

When he went to England as a youth, Jinnah had been married in name at his mother's insistence to a child bride. She died while he was abroad. Now he intended to marry a charming girl who attracted him: this was the daughter of Sir Dinshaw Petit, a leading Bombay industrialist and a Parsi. He had one daughter, Ratanbai, known affectionately as Ruttie. Born in 1900 she was much younger than Jinnah. The most westernised and progressive group in India, the Parsis were still implacably opposed to any marriage outside the community. Sir Dinshaw absolutely forbade the match. Under Parsi law Ruttie could make her own choice when she became 18, and as soon as she could she gave herself in marriage to Jinnah. Her family cut her off. She went through the formality of conversion to Islam, but absorbed none of its teachings, happily taking ham sandwiches to her husband for an office lunch. Jinnah had never been devout and this marriage reinforced his secular outlook.

After political triumph he was now to suffer eclipse. He made a spirited gesture of defiance against the government by resigning from the Viceroy's Council in protest against the repressive Rowlatt legislation. But this personal gesture was obscured by Gandhi's new politics of mass action. After the Rowlatt *satyagraha* campaign of civil disobedience Gandhi took up the strange cause of the Caliph, the Turkish Sultan, deprived by the British of his leadership of the Islamic world. This cause was embraced by the Indian Muslims who joined Gandhi in *satyagraha*. Jinnah walked out of the Muslim League meeting which advocated direct action against the British government, to the scorn of his erstwhile ally, Mohammad Ali. The Ali brothers and Abul Kalam Azad called on all Muslims to depart from India, the *Dar-ul-Harb* or Land of Disorder, for Afghanistan. Many thousands sold up and quit. They had a stony reception.

Renounces Mass Action(1921)

A League minority joined Jinnah in his walkout. Fazl-i-Husain was one; he formed an inter-communal party in Punjab based on agricultural interests, called the Unionist Party. Similarly, Fazlul Huq formed a Bengali political group which bypassed the League. This provided no solution to Jinnah who was an all-India politician with no provincial stronghold. Re-elected to the central legislature in 1924 he worked with the 'Council Entry' portion of Congress led by Motilal Nehru in what they termed the National Party. That same year the League asked him to preside over their annual session. Jinnah would not commit himself to separatism. Speaking in the legislature in 1925 he declared: 'I am a nationalist first, a nationalist second, and a nationalist last. I once more appeal to this House, whether you are a Muslim or a Hindu, for God's sake do not import the discussion of communal matters into this House and degrade this Assembly which we desire should become a real national Parliament.'

When the Simon Commission came out to India to explore constitutional questions Jinnah persuaded a majority of the League to boycott the Commission, though the conservative Leaguers led by Sir Muhammad Shafi offered their cooperation. Jinnah joined with Motilal in drafting an alternative programme for self-government. He was prepared to scrap separate Muslim electorates and accept joint electorates – with safeguards – but the report issued by Motilal made no concessions (thanks largely to the influence of Jawaharlal) and Jinnah was driven to condemn the 'Nehru Report'. In this he was joined by the erstwhile radical, Mohammad Ali. Disillusioned with Gandhian methods, Mohammad Ali 'gradually drifted away from the Congress' (in Nehru's words). An attempt to stage a unity conference failed to secure any advance, though Jinnah was prepared to accept the Nehru Report subject to five amendments. These were rejected by Congress and the Muslims rallied under the Aga Khan to press separatist demands. Jinnah acquiesced in these demands: he had no real alternative.

At this moment his private life lay under the shadow of tragedy. His beautiful and vivacious Ruttie had gradually drifted out of his life, until he was formally separated from her. The daughter born to them in 1919, Dina, had not drawn them together although her father was devoted to her. Ruttie was neglected and simply pined away. She died in February 1929 before her twenty-ninth birthday.

Attempts to Regain Political Initiative

A last opportunity for Jinnah to take a leading part in the politics of inter-communal cooperation seemed to arise with the announcement by the Viceroy that a Round Table Conference would be convened to determine how, in due season, India could attain Dominion status. But when? Along with Gandhi, Motilal, Vithalbhai Patel (Speaker of the Assembly) and Tej Bahadur Sapru (the Liberal leader), Jinnah met the Viceroy in December 1929. Gandhi demanded immediate Dominion status: Lord Irwin explained that this was impossible, and Gandhi launched another massive non-cooperation campaign.

Although there was no immediate hope of bringing in the Congress leaders the Labour government in London went ahead with the Round Table Conference. Jinnah attended as one of the Muslim delegation of 16: he was the sole Muslim not committed to extreme separatist demands. Nevertheless, he spoke first, looking forward to 'the birth of a new Dominion of India'. Despite his long opposition to commualism he declared: 'There are four main parties sitting round the table now. They are the British party, the Indian princes, the Hindus and the Muslims.' That conference went surprisingly well, with agreement among these 'four parties' that the goal was an Indian federation. Nevertheless, Jinnah felt isolated and made the momentous decision to settle in London and practise before the Privy Council. He took an elegant house in Hampstead and brought over his daughter, Dina, and his sister, Fatima.

Exile in London (1930–35)

As a long-standing friend of Ramsay MacDonald he approached the Prime Minister for assistance in becoming a candidate for Parliament. This immaculate figure with his lofty speech was not to Labour's liking: he failed to win selection. Then he persuaded the Aga Khan to approach his Conservative friends to support his candidature as a Tory. This was equally unsuccessful. Was Jinnah totally cynical about British politics? Long before he had indicated that John Morley's book *On Compromise* was one of his favourites, but these actions seem to be taking the idea too far. This curious affair may only represent his own uncertain situation in 1931, or it may be an example of his later willingness to switch from one position to another quite opposite if this would advance his long-term strategy.

Deprived of a British political platform he retired into private life. He was always a loner; never more so than now. He earned enormous fees and could afford the trappings of wealth – a butler, a chauffeur, a Bentley, and dozens of Saville Row suits – yet there was little enjoyment in his life.

In his absence the Muslim League almost collapsed: in 1933 two rival sessions of the League were held. In 1934 Jinnah was unanimously invited to resume the presidency, but still he lingered, only returning to India in 1935. It is said that he re-entered Indian politics because an acquaintance reported a remark by Jawaharlal Nehru: 'Jinnah is finished.' The League's differences, between reactionary communalism and progressivism, were papered over. The Bengali maverick, Fazlul Huq, was brought back into the fold.

Due to the rearguard fight by Churchill and the Diehards a new constitution could not be implemented until 1936, and then only at the provincial level as the formation of the new federal parliament depended on adherence to the Federation by enough of the Princes to represent half the population of the Princely states, which was lacking.

Meanwhile elections for the provincial legislatures went ahead, on a much wider franchise. Separate Muslim electorates were preserved, so the task for the League was to appeal to 'their' audience. In Punjab and Bengal – key provinces – Muslims could expect to play the leading role: but only if they operated coalition politics, bringing in members of other communities. There was the Unionist Party formed by Fazl-i-Husain in Punjab, a rural coalition, designed to outflank sectional groups (like the Sikh Akali Dal) and to confront the predominantly urban Congress. An avowedly Muslim programme was unwelcome to the Unionists, and much the same situation prevailed in Bengal where the opportunistic Fazlul Huq needed Hindu allies to defeat Congress.

Returns to Lead Muslim League

Jinnah's call to the League to 'stand shoulder to shoulder with the Congress' did not impress the provincial leaders. In Punjab, Sikandar Hyat Khan, a powerful landlord and later Premier, told Fazl-i-Husain he had urged Jinnah's advisers 'to strongly pass on to him the advisability of keeping his fingers out of the Punjab pie. If he meddles he would only be encouraging fissiparous tendencies . . . and might burn his fingers.' Jinnah's response was to announce, 'I am going to smash Fazli', but the local power-brokers were too much for him and he departed saying, 'I shall never come to the Punjab again. It is such a hopeless place.'[3]

He did not have much better fortune elsewhere. The Aga Khan threw his weight against him. In consequence of all this confusion the Muslim League made a poor showing at the polls, winning only 108 of the 482 reserved seats. Their performance was worst in north-west India (already foreseen by the poet Iqbal as a separate Muslim state). In this vast area they won just four out of 153 Muslim seats. It was true that Congress did even worse in the Muslim constituencies, winning an overall total of 26: but in the General constituencies their performance exceeded all expectations: they had 716 victories. After much internal debate they decided to take office, and Congress ministries were formed in eight of the eleven provinces. A claim by the League to a share in a coalition in the UP (where both parties had fought the landlord politicians) was rejected. Nehru's estimate that Jinnah was finished seemed confirmed: he declared bluntly, 'There are only two forces in the country, the Congress and the Government.'

Fights Physical Disability

Jinnah's personal effectiveness was marred by a chronic chest infection (probably brought on by excessive smoking) which first appeared in 1936 and limited his ability to make public speeches. However, he threw himself into the task of transforming the League from a coterie of bigwigs into a mass organisation. At the 1938 annual session at Karachi the various provincial bosses who had shrugged him aside – notably Sir Sikandar Hyat and Fazlul Huq – were in attendance, as well as the former follower of Gandhi, Shaukat Ali. The first proposal for separate Muslim and Hindu federations within an all-India setting was advanced at Karachi, but not by Jinnah. He could see this was strengthening the provincial leaders, whereas his only power base was the national All-India Muslim League. In reply to Nehru, he declared: 'I refuse to line up with the Congress. . . . There is a third party in this country, and this is Muslim India.' It was but another step to insist that the League represented all Muslims while the Congress represented only the Hindus. In 1939 this idea seemed extravagant; but when in September the Viceroy announced, without prior consultation, that India was at war with Germany the Congress High Command ordered all their provincial governments to resign: which they did, though some with hesitation. By going out into the political wilderness the Congress wiped out its visible superiority over the League. The three provincial governments which still remained – in Punjab, Sind and Bengal – were largely in Muslim hands. Moreover, as Congress demonstrated its intransigence, the Viceroy and Governors increasingly made bids for Muslim support.

1940: the 'Pakistan' Resolution

It was in these circumstances that the League's annual gathering, held in Lahore in March 1940, came up with a new claim. The Lahore resolution emerged from a first draft by Sikandar Hyat (though he disavowed the final version which followed endless redrafting). As announced, the League claimed that 'the areas in which the Muslims are numerically in the majority . . . should be grouped to constitute independent states'. This resolution was moved by Fazlul Huq who was most interested in an autonomous Bengal. Jinnah in his presidential speech at last declared for separatism: the introduction of provincial self-government had shown that this would lead to 'permanent Hindu majority government'. He went on: 'The Musalmans are not a minority. The Musalmans are a nation by any definition. The problem in India is not of an inter-communal but manifestly of an international character and it must be treated as such.'[4] The press dubbed this the 'Pakistan Resolution'. Henceforward any discussion of India's future had first to dispose of the Pakistan issue. Gandhi professed himself unable to understand what it meant; Nehru brushed it impatiently aside.

What did the Lahore resolution mean? Jinnah refused to be tied down. The British were certain that it was intended as a bargaining ploy: the common change of Indian politics. Faced by a hostile Congress, the Viceroy cultivated Jinnah, who was ready to meet the head of the Government of India on equal terms, while steadily declining to be drawn into the war effort. Trying to mobilise political support, the Viceroy invited the Muslim premiers of Punjab, Bengal and Assam (where the League had formed a precarious ministry) to be members of a National Defence Council. All three – Sikandar Hyat, Fazlul Huq, and Sir Muhammad Saadullah – accepted. Jinnah summoned the Working Committee of the League and an ultimatum was issued: resign from the Defence Council or face expulsion from the League. Sikandar and Saadullah capitulated without fuss, though it must have been a bitter pill to the Punjab premier who had warned Jinnah to keep his fingers out of the Punjab pie. Fazlul Huq publicly protested that 'the principles of democracy and autonomy are being subordinated to the arbitrary wishes of a single individual'. Though he did eventually resign from the Defence Council he was made to pay: in December 1941 he was expelled from the League by Jinnah.

There was some uneasiness even among his closest associates at this display of intransigence. When Japan entered the conflict in December 1941 several considered that there should now be a national government:

but how to persuade Jinnah? As Sikandar wrote, 'The question is to bell the cat.' Some of the younger Leaguers felt that Jinnah should give way to the much respected Choudhury Khaliquzzaman as President of the League. Suhrawardy of Bengal was particularly vehement. Jinnah remained obdurate, emphasising that League participation in the war effort would mean accepting a junior role: 'The result will be that . . . we shall be once more reduced to a minority.'

The Political Meaning of Pakistan?

Next year the able leader of the Untouchables, Dr B.R. Ambedkar, published a study, *Pakistan, or the Partition of India*, in which he estimated the actual extent of the Muslim-majority areas which would go into the new polity. Because he calculated the population figures carefully, his map anticipated the Pakistan which was to emerge with uncanny accuracy. This Pakistan would incorporate substantial areas in eastern and north-west India. But it also showed that the two key provinces of Punjab and Bengal would be split, while out of the province of Assam claimed for Pakistan only Sylhet District would be included. Ambedkar's analysis should have had a sobering effect on both Congress and the League. 'The ghost of Pakistan will be there,' he wrote, 'casting its ominous shadow'. Both chose to ignore the dangers. Jinnah's critics had demanded what benefit Pakistan would bestow on the traditional Muslim centres of Delhi, Lucknow and Hyderabad? Only the somewhat lame 'hostage' argument had been forthcoming: Congress must treat their Muslims decently so that Pakistan would be good to its Hindus and Sikhs. Now it was made clear that key areas in the main bastions of the hypothetical state, Punjab and Bengal, must be sundered. Jinnah ignored all this: for him Pakistan must be . . . because it must be. Congress also brushed aside the stark fact that unless Muslim claims were satisfied, the outer parts of the subcontinent would justly demand separation. In the Congress camp only the south Indian leader C. Rajagopalachari responded positively.

The year 1942 was a year of challenge. The Japanese were fast approaching. Cripps flew to India to try to mobilise Indian nationalism against the threat. His main effort was directed to persuading Congress. He invoked his personal friendship with Nehru. He advanced a dual plan: national association with the war effort now, and machinery for devising an independent Indian Union when the war ended. As a gesture to the League, Cripps proposed including a provision that provinces who wished to defer entering the proposed Union could remain apart (Smuts told Churchill this could create another Northern Ireland). As Congress rejected the plan, Jinnah's reaction was not tested.[5]

In August 1942 Gandhi issued his 'Do or Die' call, and the Congress leaders were arrested. There were strenuous efforts to topple the Raj, especially in the districts around Banaras, before the revolt was suppressed. These 'August Disturbances' ended any possibility of dialogue between Congress and the Raj and left Jinnah as the sole important figure on the scene. He continued to resist British approaches, while not discouraging Leaguers from participating in activities like the Air Raid Precautions organisation in the big cities, which helped the League to build up the local infrastructure it had lacked. While the Congress was suspended the League was able to cobble together ministries in four of the 'Pakistan' provinces, giving their claim some semblance of legitimacy.

When the war was over Wavell as Viceroy convened an all-party conference at Simla despite all Churchill's opposition to a new initiative. His intention was to obtain agreement on a new, national Executive Council: in effect a national government. As regards the Congress and the League, there would be parity between Hindus and Muslims: 50:50, an immense concession to the Muslims forming at most one-quarter of the population. Additionally, four members would represent the minorities.

1945: Jinnah Asserts Leadership of All Muslims

The Congress, through its president, now Abul Kalam Azad, accepted the 50:50 formula, though it went far beyond the historic Congress claim to represent all the peoples of India. Wavell explained to Jinnah that he could nominate four out of the five Muslim members, but the fifth would be a Unionist. When the Viceroy stuck to this position, Jinnah declined to allow the League to join the new government.

Wavell never learned that Indian politics was all about bargaining, so he accepted this refusal and announced that the formation of the new Council must be postponed. If he had gone ahead, it seems certain that Jinnah would soon have been compelled to acquiesce. Twelve months later Wavell did go ahead and form a new Council without League participation, leaving Jinnah to give way three months later. As it was, Simla represented victory for Jinnah over Viceroy and Congress: a successful assertion of the claim that only the League could speak for the Muslims.

The Simla conference took place just as a new Labour government entered office. After fresh consultations, the Viceroy announced that elections would be held, both for the provincial legislatures and for the central Assembly (still set up on the old model). The League organisation was still rudimentary at the local level, but the campaign was boosted by hundreds of volunteer workers: idealistic Muslim students, especially from Aligarh. They carried a simple message: that the League was their champion and Congress their enemy. Behind these crowds of volunteers were the Muslim political bosses; calculating, opportunistic, self-serving. Only six months earlier (6 May 1945), Jinnah had written: 'Corruption is a curse in India and amongst Muslims, especially the so-called educated. . . . No doubt this disease is common, but amongst this particular class it is rampant.'[6] He now had to appeal to the people through these intermediaries. In Punjab, the landlord supporters of the Unionists deserted their old party in droves. In Bengal, the straightforward but ineffective Nazimuddin (former Premier) was pushed aside by the more politically sophisticated – and more ambivalent – Suhrawardy. He sought to broaden his support by pressing Jinnah to declare an 'amnesty', mainly directed towards getting Fazlul Huq into his camp, but this was too much for the Qaid-i-Azam (as Jinnah was now universally known) to swallow. The most hopeless situation was on the North-West Frontier where a League ministry led by Aurangzeb Khan had collapsed in March, rather to the relief of the Governor, Sir George Cunningham, who had told Aurangzeb: 'If Ministers went on as they were doing, either I must give up the Governorship or I must get new Ministers.'[7] Khan Sahib, pro-Congress leader of the Red Shirts, formed a new Ministry.

Elections: the League Triumph

This was the background to the elections. First, in December 1945, came elections for the Central Assembly on the limited franchise. The League won every Muslim seat, except for the man from the Frontier, who subsequently joined them. They polled 87 per cent of the vote. Then came the provincial elections in February 1946, a better test as the electorate was so much larger, and actual political power was at stake in new Ministries. Once again, the League performed impressively, receiving 75 per cent of the popular vote and gaining 439 of the 494 Muslim seats. However, the score according to provinces was less satisfactory. Bengal was the one unqualified success, with Suhrawardy's followers winning 113 of the 119 seats. Outside the League, Fazlul Huq was the only prominent Muslim to survive. Suhrawardy was able to form a Ministry with independent support. In Punjab, Unionist domination was broken, and the League won 75 of the 86 Muslim constituencies, with four other Muslims hastily jumping on the bandwagon. This left them just short of the 88 needed for a majority in a legislature of 175. Negotiations with other groups broke down: the price demanded by the 22 Akali Sikhs was a separate Sikh state in any future Pakistan. Jinnah ignored advice from his local supporters that a deal must be struck with the others. Eventually a 'Unionist' coalition was patched up, led by the former Premier Khizr Khan Tiwana, now leader of a tiny rump.

In Sind it was much the same story: the League did well, winning 28 seats while the breakaway League group under G.M. Syed gained only four seats. The total number being 60, the League were just short of a majority but, unlike the Punjab, the Government eventually acceded to the claims of the League as the largest party to form the government. Assam was never a Muslim-majority province, and despite winning 31 seats in a House of 108 the League was condemned to opposition. On the North-West Frontier, there was a campaign marked by skulduggery and bribery. Cunningham recorded, 'The election campaign is fiery, and all the Muslim members are killing sheep in order to get votes. Apparently, ten votes per sheep.' Despite all this, the League only secured 17 of the 36 Muslim seats (the total was 50). Congress won a clear majority and formed another Ministry. Despite the shift in the balance of political forces, the position after the 1946 provincial elections was much as in 1937, with Congress in control of eight out of the eleven provinces: though the League eventually secured two Ministries, whereas in 1937 it had none.

The Viceroy Questions the Appeal of Pakistan

As soon as Labour had come into power, Lord Wavell tried to impress on the New Secretary of State, Lord Pethick-Lawrence (21 August 1945) the urgency of confronting Jinnah. He wrote, 'I am sure the Pakistan idea is stronger in the Muslim minority Provinces than in the Pakistan Provinces.' However, he insisted, 'We cannot evade the issue', and 'The crudity of Jinnah's ideas should be exposed.' Pethick-Lawrence informed the Cabinet that there was 'no clear scheme of partition', hence there should be no statement.

Early in 1946 the Cabinet decided to send a mission to India to negotiate about the end of Empire, and inquired from Wavell how 'Pakistan' would look. Wavell replied (7 February 1946) with a district-by-district listing of 'genuinely Moslem areas'. He enclosed a map showing how Pakistan would be delineated according to the 1941 Census. This anticipated the shape of the future Pakistan even more precisely than Ambedkar's study. Even this delimitation did not solve the problem of the Sikhs: 'The problem is one which no version of Pakistan can solve.' While Nehru and other Congress leaders were in regular correspondence with Labour friends like Cripps, Jinnah had no firm British connections, though some Tories encouraged the League. When the Cabinet Mission arrived in March (its members being Pethick-Lawrence, Cripps and A.V. Alexander) the favoured status of Congress was made clear: speaking in Parliament on 15 March Attlee affirmed, 'we cannot allow a minority to place a veto on the advance of the majority'.

On 24 March Wavell recorded in his diary: 'The Three Magi have arrived. They are pleasant and friendly but I am still doubtful whether they have got any definite plan in their heads.'[8] Quite the opposite: the Mission saw their job as reconciling the claims of Congress and League, paying most attention to the former. It was soon clear that the two sides were impossibly far apart, and the Congress leaders gave no indication that they considered it necessary to accommodate the League in their future government. Wavell had all along urged the need for a fall-back plan, and on 11 April the Mission acquainted Attlee with their thoughts. They favoured an Indian Federation with a centre mainly confined to Defence and Foreign affairs: the alternative appeared to be a divided India with the 'Pakistan' portions limited to the minimum extent outlined previously by Wavell. They *must* get some agreed scheme, otherwise 'we risk chaos'. If 'Pakistan' offered 'the only chance', would the Cabinet agree? With virtually no discussion, the Cabinet agreed on the same day that although Pakistan would be 'weak' they would accept this alternative 'if that seemed to afford the only chance'.

Instead Cripps evolved his 'Three Tier Formula' which would create a sort of Austria–Hungary, allowing the two new states to remain one country by forming groups of provinces as the League wanted while retaining a slimmed-down central government. This seemed to also meet the Congress demand, and Cripps was optimistic they would accept. He rightly observed that for the plan to succeed it *must* 'have the support of one side. If Jinnah would not play, he inevitably drove us into the arms of Congress.'

Jinnah Confronts the Cabinet Mission (1946)

Jinnah continued the game he had successfully followed throughout the war: he would, and he wouldn't, play. When confronted with the minimum Pakistan offer he found this 'definitely unacceptable'. A.V. Alexander wrote in his diary: 'I have never seen such a man with such a mind twisting and turning to avoid as far as possible direct answers. I came to the conclusion that he is playing this game, which is one of life and death for millions very largely from the point of view of . . . a legal negotiation.'[9] Each member of the Mission had a try, and Jinnah seemed inclined to the Three Tier solution, if assured Congress would also accept. Unfortunately the main spokesman for Congress as its current President was Abul Kalam Azad, and as a Muslim he desperately wanted to find a formula which would appease his former League friends. He therefore went further than the High Command was prepared to go.

Reality burst in when the Mission adjourned with the Congress and League leadership to Simla to work out details. Nehru was especially cold towards the proposal: he insisted upon a strong centre, while he shrugged aside the idea of an intermediate authority formed by groups of provinces. To obtain Congress acceptance the Three Tier formula was diluted. Nevertheless, the conference broke up without agreement. The Viceroy noted after his last interview with Jinnah that he 'looked tired and ill . . . badly in need of a rest'.[10]

The Mission was driven to a course it had shrunk from at the beginning. On 13 May they issued a Statement embodying *their* plan, accepted by nobody. This began with a massive demolition of the practicality of the Pakistan demand. Their verdict was that: 'Neither a larger nor a smaller sovereign state of Pakistan would provide an acceptable solution. . . . We are therefore unable to advise the British Government that the power . . . should be handed over to two entirely separate sovereign states.'

Woodrow Wyatt, newly elected Labour MP, was hovering on the fringe of the Mission (described by Wavell as a 'minion' of Cripps). He met Jinnah on 25 May and reported that he was 'very nervous'; he was 'bitterly hurt' by the 'onslaught' on the idea of Pakistan. What the subcontinent really needed was a 'surgical operation': this simile was to become familiar upon his lips. It implied that if blood must be shed, so be it. They 'had never expected the British to give them Pakistan. . . . They knew they had to get it by their own strong right arm.' Was this just hyperbole, or was he thinking of resorting to force? At this time, he summoned Colonel Iskander Mirza, a Political Officer familiar with the Frontier. He told him they had failed to influence the Mission and asked Mirza to leave his Delhi desk and 'disappear' into the tribal territory. He received a large sum to encourage the tribesmen to launch a rising with the cry of 'Islam in Danger'. However, before he could set off, Jinnah advised him that he would try another strategy. The armed rising would be held in reserve.

Having failed to secure agreement on the constitutional future,

Viceroy and Mission tried to persuade Congress and League to participate in an interim government. On 3 June, Jinnah inquired from Wavell whether if one party accepted the plan, and agreed to enter an interim government, while the other held out, the Viceroy would go ahead with the interim arrangements? Wavell replied that the Mission agreed that they would go ahead, though 'we hope that both will accept'. Accordingly, on 6 June the Council of the League signified its acceptance of the plan based on 'compulsory grouping' of provinces as 'the basis and the foundation of Pakistan are inherent in the Mission's Plan'. Accordingly, they would negotiate the League's entry into the interim government. Next day Jinnah gave Wavell his terms for entry: 'The only portfolio he would consider was that of Defence.' So participation was by no means unconditional, but the twisting and turning were over.

The Collapse of His Strategy

It seemed certain that the Congress would reject the proposals of the Cabinet Mission, leaving Jinnah to extract victory from near disaster. On 13 June Azad, as retiring Congress President, informed the Mission that they could not join an interim government on the lines suggested. Then, quite unexpectedly, on 25 June Azad sent a long letter about the constitutional position. This rehearsed the usual reservations but the final paragraph read: 'While adhering to our views [that grouping was only an option] we accept your proposals and are prepared to work them.' Meeting to consider the letter the Ministers 'agreed that although cleverly worded the last paragraph . . . must be regarded as an acceptance of the long-term proposals'. Wavell disagreed: 'an acceptance by Congress which they meant to break was worse than a refusal'. However, the Cabinet Ministers had been over three months in India and now they could return with some sort of agreement: they grabbed it. Because Congress had accepted the long-term plan but still (at Gandhi's insistence) held out for more in the Interim Government its formation had to be postponed.

When Jinnah was informed, his first reaction was muted, though he declared that 'every move the Delegation had made had been at his cost'. Two days later he issued a statement which was more vitriolic: it included a warning to the British Government that any further modification of the position 'will be regarded by Muslim India as going back on the part of the Cabinet Delegation and the Viceroy on their pledged word in writing and as a breach of faith'. The Governor of Punjab commented to Wavell: 'Jinnah is in a very bad temper . . . and although the charge of bad faith is without foundation nearly all Muslims and many intelligent Hindus think he has been outwitted.' Soon after Jinnah wrote an angry letter to Attlee stating 'the Mission had shattered their hopes for an honourable and peaceful settlement'. Was it possible that 'the British Government will still avoid compelling the Muslims to shed their blood?' All this cannot have reassured the Prime Minister.

Nehru's Equivocation

As if to rub in their differences, Nehru – newly installed as Congress president – made a statement (10 July) underlining their rejection of grouping: 'We have agreed to go into the Constituent Assembly and we have agreed to nothing else.' Patel called this speech 'emotional insanity' and it confirmed the League in abandoning negotiation. A few days later, Wavell made another effort to form his interim government, issuing identical invitations to Jinnah and Nehru based on the previous formula (six Congress, five League, three minority members). The Viceroy ruled that neither Congress nor League could object to any name submitted by the other party. Nehru promptly declined: Wavell told Pethick-Lawrence, 'Congress are convinced that they have got us on the run and we ought to correct that impression at once.'

The League response was even more negative. In resolutions passed at Bombay on 29 July, the Supreme Council withdrew their acceptance of the Mission's proposals, while also putting aside constitutional methods, announcing that 'the time has come for the Muslim nation to resort to Direct Action'. This was undefined, except as a 'coming struggle', but it seemed that Gandhi's erstwhile critic was now prepared to resort to Gandhian mass civil disobedience. Not surprisingly, Jinnah turned down Wavell's terms for joining an interim government (31 July).

From London, the Secretary of State urged the Viceroy to press Jinnah further. The League had precipitated 'a most dangerous situation' but they could not let both the main parties drift into opposition. To this suggestion Wavell replied with, for him, uncharacteristic political subtlety; he would put the onus of approaching Jinnah upon Nehru by commissioning him to form a government: 'We can have some chance of using the present situation to good effect if we can put responsibility for satisfying the League on Congress' (1 August).

This move did not produce the results intended. Nehru accepted the invitation to form a government, and clearly assumed that henceforth he was *de facto* Prime Minister of the Provisional Government of India. He formed what was, in effect, a Congress ministry with amenable adherents, so Wavell had lost his principal asset – control over the machinery of central government – and Jinnah was left out in the cold.

Nehru Forms a Government: Without Jinnah

Nehru approached Jinnah and gave him certain assurances, but a meeting resolved nothing. Jinnah observed, 'There will be no more meetings.' Without warning, the political climate was tragically darkened by communal violence in Calcutta. Direct Action Day, August 16, passed off with processions and speeches throughout most of India. In Calcutta it marked the start of four days of bloodshed at the end of which about 4000 were dead, besides thousands wounded and houses destroyed. Suhrawardy as Chief Minister was awarded most blame for provocative speeches and failure to take timely action. But the evidence suggests that most victims were Muslims: Jinnah in his current negative mentality declared that 'it was an organised plot to discredit the Muslim League on the part of Hindus'. The Killing had its biggest effect on Wavell who concluded that Britain had lost control and must leave India before everything collapsed in chaos. But did the League orchestrate violence? And was Jinnah interested in demonstrating that without their participation no administration could function properly? At this time all his speeches carried echoes of bloodshed. Himself aware of his impending end, was he prepared to visualise the end of India if Pakistan was denied? Such conjectures do not seem fanciful. When his Calcutta lieutenant M.A.H. Ispahani bewailed, 'I sincerely hope that such a tragedy will not be repeated. . . . We want to remain peaceful if the Hindus allow us' (20 August), Jinnah made no reply.[11]

Meanwhile, Nehru and the interim government had their hands on the levers of power. How could Jinnah stage a comeback, which was not also a climb-down? He issued elliptic statements: 'The wound is too deep and the negotiations have led to too much bitterness and rancour for us to prolong the present arguments' (9 September). What could that mean? Wavell gave an interview to him on 16 September. The Viceroy recorded: 'Jinnah was quite friendly throughout, was polite, and much less discursive than he often is. In fact he was at his best.' At a further interview on 2 October, Wavell urged him to 'come into the Government at once and unconditionally'. Again he recorded 'Mr Jinnah was friendly and reasonable throughout.'

The Qaid-i-Azam was seeking to gain some concessions he could take to the League Council as evidence of change, but none was forthcoming. Jinnah extracted the meaningless undertaking that he could nominate someone who was not a Muslim: he wanted to appear as the friend of the Untouchables. After yet another meeting (12 October) Wavell noted: 'It is obvious that the League wish to come in, that Nehru . . . has done nothing to smooth the path for them, and that the Coalition Government if formed will not be all pulling in the same direction.' This proved an accurate prophecy.

The League Belatedly Enter the Government

Next day Jinnah signified his readiness to enter the interim government for 'very weighty grounds and reasons which are obvious and need not be mentioned'. The Qaid did not put himself forward: he had no intention of accepting Nehru as his leader. Liaqat Ali Khan was the principal nominee, and Jogendra Nath Mandal, an Untouchable, was among the other four. There was a final wrangle over the posts that the League would receive: Nehru wished to deny them anything important, and the best they could obtain was Finance: which doubtless was regarded as beyond any Leaguer's competence. However, Liaqat, who took the post, had the advice of an exceptional civil servant, Muhammad Ali, CIE, OBE, who knew all about finance. This uneasy new partnership between Congress and League began on 26 October 1946.

With the new combination installed, two main questions remained to vex the Viceroy. The League had not repealed its resolution renouncing the Cabinet Mission Plan: technically, its participation in government depended on accepting the plan, but Jinnah continued to be vague about renewed acceptance. Also, the League having taken part in elections to the Constituent Assembly had not signified its readiness to join an Assembly while the question of grouping remained unresolved. Both these issues were connected to the overall question: was Jinnah prepared for any solution other than the oft-declared formula of a full five provinces Pakistan? London, the Viceroy, and the Congress were united in refusing to entertain this. One of the few British politicians Jinnah was still prepared to speak to frankly was Woodrow Wyatt. When the Attlee government invited Nehru, the Sikh, Baldev Singh, Liaqat and Jinnah to London early in December to make another effort to resolve the grouping issue before the Constituent Asembly got down to work, Jinnah talked to Wyatt. He insisted that Congress had never accepted the Mission's plan and vowed he would 'do all he can' to stop them seizing power. 'Only the creation of Pakistan can deal with the situation', he averred; he no longer accepted any plan for a minimum government at the centre. When Wyatt asked if the Congress adopted the grouping plan 'in its entirety' would he reconsider, the answer was an unequivocal 'No'. It emerged that his real policy was for British rule to continue to ensure 'a period of tranquillity'. This illusion that the British Raj might still be upheld for a further period was his only solution to the imbroglio.

When Jinnah talked to Ministers – still the Cabinet Mission trio – he was calmer than of late. When Alexander tried to reassure him that there was still the authority of Parliament as a safeguard against *force majeure*, he retorted that 'he now understood the function of Parliament . . . was simply that of registering the decisions of the Constituent Assembly'. It was a fair assessment. In another chat with Wyatt, the latter observed that the British were unlikely to stay on in India 'for any appreciable period. At this he [Jinnah] was shocked and startled and for a moment could think of nothing to say.' Eventually, he announced that there was no objection if the British went straight away: but this was not the case if they delayed departure until giving Congress time to get hold of 'so many official positions'. Although the London visit slightly encouraged the League, it only provided a pause before the Congress-controlled Constituent Assembly got down to its work.

Disharmony at the Centre

Meanwhile, the Interim Government was a house divided. Liaqat introduced a budget which bore heavily on big business. As an avowed Socialist, Nehru at first gave his approval: but he was speedily made aware that the Marwari millionaires who supported Congress were asserting that this was an anti-Congress move. The League further exacerbated the situation by passing a resolution on 31 January 1946 calling on the British Government to accept that the Cabinet Mission plan had been nullified by Congress and that the Constituent Assembly should be dissolved. Predictably this was condemned as 'defiance' by all the non-League ministers (not merely the Congress quota) and they called for the dismissal of the League ministers.

Wavell was aware that mainly as a result of his nagging Attlee was about to announce the termination of British rule by mid-1948. He was not aware that Attlee was also about to sack him in favour of Louis Mountbatten. Wavell therefore temporised until on 20 February Attlee fired off his double bombshell in parliament. There was then a pause upon the all-India scene, though not in Punjab where inter-communal conflict, originating in the strongly Muslim west of the province, caused Khizr, leader of the rag-bag coalition ministry, to resign. The Muslim League boss declared that he had the strength to confront the legislature, but the

Governor was unconvinced; moreover he anticipated that to form a government from one community only was to precipitate civil war in the province. He suspended ministerial government under Section 93.

One of the mysteries of the day is why Jinnah did not make more effort to woo the Sikhs, whose capacity to disrupt the life of the central Punjab was clear to anyone. Early in the London visit (3 December) he did urge Baldev Singh to support Pakistan: 'provided they did so the Muslims would see they got a proper share of power'. This was an isolated approach, overtaken by bloody events in Punjab during the following months which totally alienated the Sikh community from their Muslim neighbours.

A New Viceroy: Mountbatten

When the new Viceroy landed at Delhi airport on 22 March, there to greet him was Nehru – and Liaqat Ali. Jinnah was absent. Mountbatten arrived with somewhat meaningless instructions from Attlee to work for a unified India. It was a cruel paradox that Wavell, who never accepted the solution of Pakistan, was treated with contumely by the Congress leaders while Mountbatten – who rapidly perceived it offered the only way out – is adored as their friend. Mountbatten disguised a ruthless pursuit of power behind a façade of charm. He had captivated Churchill and Roosevelt, and also Nehru whom he had befriended in Malaya.

He embarked upon a whirlwind programme of interviews with the Indian leaders, starting with Nehru (24 March). The viceroy asked Nehru to tell him about Jinnah, and was told he was 'one of the most extraordinary men in history. A financially successful though mediocre lawyer, Jinnah had found success late in life. He had not been politically successful until after the age of 60.'[12] It is difficult to think of a more disparaging and disingenuous description of his opponent. The Viceroy posed the question: what if Jinnah were granted his Pakistan? Nehru answered, 'It might be possible to frighten Jinnah into cooperation on the basis of the short time available.' Mountbatten next met Liaqat, for an inconclusive discussion. Meetings with Patel, Rajendra Prasad, Azad, Gandhi and again Nehru, Gandhi and Patel followed. On 3 April, he met Liaqat a second time and asked him for his suggestion for the future constitution. Liaqat replied that his Congress colleagues were 'utterly impossible people to work with, since there is no spirit of compromise or fair play in them'. He added in what may have seemed rhetorical language: 'I consider the position now so intolerable that if Your Excellency was only prepared to let the Muslim League have the Sind

Desert I would still prefer to accept that . . . than to continue in bondage to the Congress.'[13] This was the man Wavell had commended to George VI for his 'imperturbable common-sense'.

Mountbatten Rebuffed by Jinnah

Not until 11 days after his first meeting with Nehru did the Viceroy invite Jinnah to see him, having first extracted a 'List of Awkward Questions' from his staff. Mountbatten noted, 'He was in a most frigid, haughty and disdainful frame of mind.' Jinnah made the now familiar observation that the only solution was 'a surgical operation', implying clearly that if communities had to be sawn asunder, this was a price that must be paid. Mountbatten made the somewhat lame retort that first they must administer an anaesthetic. Clearly Jinnah's determination had impressed him, for at his next staff meeting he said that to bring in Jinnah they would have to accept Pakistan – 'a truncated version if necessary' – but that would be the end result; 'Things would take much longer than was anticipated.' Clearly Jinnah had made a dent in Mountbatten's calculations. Having confronted his adversary, the Viceroy decided it was no use keeping him at a distance: they met again two days later. Now, Mountbatten was on the defensive; when he underlined the British Government's intention to depart before June 1948, Jinnah asked him: 'How then do you propose to leave . . . is it then your intention to turn this country over to chaos and bloodshed and civil war?'

Then followed daily meetings. Mountbatten played his ace: partition might be granted, but only if Punjab and Bengal were partitioned. Jinnah was taken aback, and Mountbatten pressed home his advantage: 'I am afraid I drove the old gentleman quite mad.' Next day (10 April) he had recovered his composure and reiterated the demand for 'a surgical operation'. His argument was that time did not permit changes in the boundaries; the five 'Pakistan' provinces should be handed over intact. The Viceroy countered with insistence that only the 'moth-eaten' Pakistan was on offer; which would be 'almost unworkable'. However, Mountbatten realised that he was not getting through: 'He gave the impression that he was not listening. He was impossible to argue with.' The meetings ended in deadlock. The Viceroy later recorded 'On 10 April I warned Mr Jinnah categorically that if I finally decided to recommend to HMG that there should be a partition of India then . . . the partition would follow the boundaries of the communal majorities. Mr Jinnah replied "I do not care how little you give me so long as you give it to me completely. I do not wish to make any improper suggestion to you but you must realise that the new Pakistan is almost certain to ask for Dominion Status within the British Empire.'[14]

This should have been music to Mountbatten's ears, for he ardently desired that India should not leave the Commonwealth, but he testily replied, 'I could not possibly recommend to HMG that they should take on as a member of the Commonwealth so severe a liability as Pakistan was likely to be.'

Jinnah Accepts a 'Truncated' Pakistan

If for Jinnah the moment of truth had finally dawned, this did not prevent him continuing to campaign for the 'full' Pakistan. However, he was no longer interested in any compromise formula with Congress which he was convinced they would renege upon. Mountbatten turned his persuasive powers upon the 'moderate' Liaqat who was equally distrustful of Congress but who imagined that an alternative would be for the British 'to stay for five years and gradually transfer as liquidator the Central subjects to the successor authorities' (21 April). The League had no conception of the urgency of the Cabinet's commitment to pulling out of India. The Viceroy continued to believe that some *via media* between the Cabinet Mission Plan and 'this mad Pakistan' was possible; yet even he was not hopeful. Lord Ismay, his principal adviser, put him right on his rejection of Pakistan's application to stay in the Commonwealth: 'If forced into a position whereby only part of India wanted to remain in the Commonwealth he felt that HMG might consider accepting such an application.' In his resilient style, Mountbatten decided to use this shrewd advice to influence the Congress decision: when he spoke to Nehru's confidant Krishna Menon he 'absolutely shuddered' at the prospect of a Pakistan in, and an India out of the Commonwealth.

These moves had little effect upon Jinnah. His mood was now fatalistic. Yet the provincial leaders of the Muslim League had no inkling that Pakistan could only be won by accepting the partition of Punjab and Bengal. Jinnah had been too successful in preaching the inevitability of the 'full' Pakistan. A way out seemed to open when Suhrawardy informed Mountbatten that he believed he could preserve Bengal 'as a complete entity' (26 April). He received encouragement, though Ismay could not believe this. Surely, Ismay inquired, 'he must have misunderstood you?' But it did become an option: the same day Mountbatten asked Jinnah for his reaction and was informed 'I should be delighted. What is the use of Bengal without Calcutta. . . . I am sure they would be on friendly terms with us.' Indeed, this had been envisaged in the Lahore resolution.

Mountbatten once more reverted to the advantages of the grouping formula. Jinnah's rejection was total: 'The leaders of the Congress are so dishonest, so crooked, and so obsessed with the idea of smashing the Muslim League that there are no lengths to which they will not go. . . . He begged me not to ask him to reconsider the Cabinet Mission plan again.'

For a month, the united Bengal plan was promoted. Sarat Chandra Bose, leader of the Congress in Bengal, was in favour and wrote asking for Gandhi's blessing. For several days, the Mahatma did not reply: eventually he delivered a categorical negative.

As Mountbatten evolved his plan, Jinnah remained a bystander. The Viceroy's senior adviser, Sir Eric Mieville, showed the draft plan to Nehru and Jinnah: he reported that the former 'only made two comparatively small points' but the latter 'did not react favourably. . . . Whilst he did not definitely reject it, he said [it] would lead to terrible complications . . . and bloodshed.' The apprehension that Jinnah would reject the plan provides the most charitable explanation for Mountbatten's extraordinary conduct in discussing the plan with Nehru at Simla with no reference to Jinnah. This backfired, and Nehru's reaction almost torpedoed the plan. However, Mountbatten was able to reassure him eventually (after a hasty visit to London) and on 3 June Congress and League alike accepted the plan, which provided the 'motheaten' Pakistan Jinnah had all along resisted.

The League's Impotent Fury

He still had to face the Council of the League and obtain their formal assent. This was forthcoming; but the meeting was invaded by a motley crowd of objectors who were forcibly ejected by Muslim League National Guards (the *Ansars*). Jinnah remained in control. Later, when someone tried to ingratiate the Qaid by praising the League's support for Pakistan he replied roughly: 'Don't talk to me about the Muslim League. I and my stenographer created Pakistan.'

While the Congress leaders tried to tempt Mountbatten into handing over power prematurely, Jinnah sat it out. The last storm in a tea-cup occurred over the selection of a Governor-General for the new Pakistan. Nehru invited Mountbatten to become their first Governor-General, and it seemed a good idea to suggest he should do the same for Pakistan, thus preserving a tenuous unity. Jinnah was prepared to accept the Viceroy as Supremo, presiding as a coordinator over separate Heads of State for the two new Dominions. This was said to be constitutionally impossible, and

Jinnah concealed his intentions for about six weeks until on 4 July Mountbatten's insistent questioning produced the answer: Jinnah would be Governor-General of Pakistan. The response was vitriolic: Mountbatten indicted Jinnah for 'megalomania'. Suggesting that his power as Prime Minister would be stronger than as Governor-General, Jinnah replied, 'In my position it is I who will give the advice and others will act on it.' After unavailing attempts to bring about a change of mind, Mountbatten slammed out of the room. It was not his finest hour: for as his Press Secretary recorded, 'He has misled them [the Cabinet] and put them in a false position by overselling the likelihood of a joint Governor-General-ship.'[15]

Not much remained to be accomplished. Jinnah sold his opulent houses in Bombay and Delhi and prepared to move to Government House in Karachi (adequate accommodation for a minor governor but hardly for a Head of State). The upheaval seems to have bothered him not at all: far more upsetting was his daughter Dina's news that she was staying in Bombay as the wife of a Christian Parsi. Jinnah remonstrated, but she pointed out that she was merely doing what he had done.

Back to his Birthplace as Governor-General

Jinnah and his new Cabinet flew to Karachi on 7 August. On 11 August Jinnah was elected President of the Constituent Assembly, in addition to being President of the League and Head of State. His position was impregnable, fortified by the absence of potential rivals. In Bengal, Suhrawardy remained in Calcutta to assist Gandhi in the task of peacekeeping: Fazlul Huq, though back in the League, had no backing. The Punjabi politicians had played no significant part in creating Pakistan; the most powerful, Fazl-i-Husain, Sikandar Hyat and Khizr, were either dead or out of politics. On the Frontier the only real leaders were Khan Sahib and his brother, whose pro-Congress stand disqualified them from power. In Sind, Ghulam Hidayatullah, previously Premier, was rewarded by becoming Governor (all the other governors were British officials). The only other important leaders were Liaqat and Nazimuddin, both impeccably loyal to the Qaid. Jinnah's previous vulnerability to provincial political bosses was at an end.

At the inaugural meeting of the Constituent Assembly, Jinnah made a long speech which included some remarkable passages:

> Work together in a spirit that every one of you, no matter to what community he belongs . . . no matter what is his caste, colour or creed

is first, second and last a citizen of this State with equal rights, privileges and obligations. . . . In course of time all these angularities of the majority and minority communities . . . will vanish. . . . You may belong to any religion or caste or creed – that has nothing to do with the State. . . . We are all citizens, and equal citizens of one State. . . . You will find that in course of time Hindus would cease to be Hindus and Muslims would cease to be Muslims; not in the religious sense . . . but in the political sense as citizens of the State.[16]

There are echoes here of his 1925 speech in the central assembly. It seems to have little relevance to the new Muslim homeland, but we must remember that in August 1947 about 20 per cent of the people of the West wing – even in the 'motheaten' form – were non-Muslims while in the East wing the proportion was more than one-third. Jinnah hoped to reassure them: but as communal conflict escalated even further, Hindus and Sikhs clamoured to be moved to the new India. About 6 million trekked out, and probably 8 million Muslims from East Punjab and the minority provinces moved in. Apart from a few Parsis and communities of Christians, mainly Untouchables, the West became solidly Muslim. In East Pakistan, even after some Hindus had left they accounted for one-quarter of the total, together with small numbers of Buddhists and Animists.

Unresolved Questions: Kashmir

Soon after the British departure the great majority of the Princely states acceded to their 'host' countries. Two of the biggest states held back: Hyderabad, with a Hindu majority and a Muslim ruler, the Nizam; and Kashmir, with a Muslim majority and a Hindu maharaja. Both signed standstill agreements while they tried to avoid final commitment. Sirdar Patel rang up Colonel Iskander Mirza who was handling Pakistan's border affairs and said, 'I will give you Kashmir if you leave Hyderabad to me.' Unfortunately Jinnah thought he could exploit the Hyderabad situation, while he regarded Kashmir as already in the bag. A freelance British airline operator began flying in arms to Hyderabad, using Karachi as his base. Negotiations were strung out for a year; at last the Indian Army was ordered to invade the state, and the Nizam's regime came to an abrupt end.

In Kashmir, there was no clean ending. Impatient with the impasse, Jinnah was attracted to his earlier plan of mobilising the Pathan tribesmen. They began to enter Kashmir in mid-September, and at first Liaqat Ali denied government involvement. However, on 25 October Iskander Mirza revealed to Cunningham, back as Governor on the Frontier, that Liaqat was in the know. Jinnah had become aware of what was happening but insisted, 'Don't tell me anything about it. My conscience must be clear.' The decision to let loose the tribesmen proved disastrous. The Maharaja escaped to Delhi and offered Mountbatten his accession to India, which was reluctantly accepted. The tribes delayed, looting and killing, and had not reached the state capital, Srinagar, when a Sikh battalion was flown in and held them at bay. They were steadily driven back. Jinnah wanted to order in the Pakistan forces, but it was explained that if the two new Dominions went to war all the remaining British officers and NCOs would be withdrawn on both sides. This harmed Pakistan much more than India. Jinnah instructed Cunningham to give all assistance to the tribesmen: he accepted this, 'provided I didn't have to do one thing and say another'.[17] The conflict dragged on until a ceasefire was agreed in January 1949, after Jinnah was dead.

Jinnah's Decline and Death (1948)

By carefully taking rest between the taxing sessions with the Cabinet Mission, Wavell, and then Mountbatten, Jinnah succeeded in concealing his physical decline, though his hollow countenance and staring eyes could not be disguised. However, in only one of the documents (Wavell's note after Simla) is there any hint that others realised he was a sick man. For six months after the move to Karachi he kept up the illusion of normality. He even managed a visit to Dacca in March 1948; his only glimpse of the East Pakistan he had created. From June he ceased to perform public duties and went up to the hill station Quetta, from where he was taken to a remote mountain top, Ziarat. The doctors knew that there was no hope: to the tuberculosis of the lungs was added lung cancer, and finally pneumonia. It was decided to take him back to Government House, Karachi, where he died on 11 September 1948. He had survived long enough to see his country through its first year, past the worst crises of national survival.

'He goes furthest who knows not whither he goes,' declared Oliver Cromwell. Jinnah was an outstanding example of a traveller who pressed on as an act of will even when he could not see journey's end.

4

Jawaharlal Nehru: The Fading Dream

Although Jinnah was able to inspire awe, and respect from many who did not actually like him, and finally cult status as the maker of Pakistan, he had few friends, if any. His greatest admirers, like Hassan Ispahani and the Raja of Mahmudabad, were not intimate with him. Only to his sister Fatima was he completely himself: for he could not even keep the love of his wife, Ruttie, and his daughter, Dina, who meant so much to him.

By contrast, Nehru was adored by thousands. To a whole generation of young Indians he was a comrade and a hero. He seemed disarmingly open and appealing. The rugged old soldier, Wavell, who received more abuse than sympathy from Nehru, recorded after he had taken tea with his wife, son, and personal staff: 'They all like him.' This empathy is reproduced in all the biographies of Nehru in which an element of hero-worship overcomes the detachment which the biographer ought always to adopt to the subject.

One felt this empathy between the great man and the multitude whenever Nehru appeared in public. Most had no idea what he was talking about; nevertheless, they felt he understood them and their needs. That overworked term *charisma* truly applied to this man. And yet he was apart from the crowd. Often, as they pressed to receive the benison of personal contact, he would strike out angrily, repelling those who wanted to worship. There is a paradox of a man much loved and sought after, who often found himself alone. He wrote of himself: 'I have become a queer mixture of the East and West, out of place everywhere, at home nowhere.' He had more in common with his adversary, Jinnah, than he would have cared to admit. Haughty, aloof, he too found no real marriage of mind and body with his wife, who also died young, leaving him with a blank in his personal life. However, the comparison should not be carried too far. Unlike Jinnah, born almost on the borders of the subcontinent, in a family of no importance, outside the mainstream of his religion, Jawaharlal Nehru was born in the heart of India, a Brahman of the highest, in conditions of wealth and privilege.

Born to Privilege (1889)

'An only son of prosperous parents is apt to be spoilt. . . . When that son happens to have been an only child for the first eleven years . . . there is little hope for him to escape this spoiling'; so Nehru began his revealing *Autobiography*. He was born on 14 November 1889, the son of a highly successful, wealthy lawyer, Motilal Nehru. They were Saraswat Brahmans, from the Kashmiri Pandit community, long domiciled in the Delhi – Agra area. Motilal had settled in Allahabad, capital of the UP and seat of its High Court. Much of his legal practice was concerned with the litigation beloved by wealthy landlords, the *taluqdars* of UP. His earnings enabled Motilal to adopt an opulent lifestyle. He built a mansion in the Civil Lines, the 'White' appendage to the city. His household was compartmentalised into European and Indian sections. Motilal had discarded all the Brahmanic conventions. In a public speech which anticipated Jinnah's similar statement by many decades he declared he was an Indian first and a Brahman afterwards. On returning from a visit to Europe, he refused to undergo the penalties which caste authority dictated must be observed by anyone who crossed the Black Waters. Wearing English dress outside his private apartments he had as many British friends as Indians. Prominent among them was a high-flying administrator, Harcourt Butler, about whom was repeated the rhyme he 'tickled the tail of a Taluqdar' ('I tickled his tail so successfully/That now I am Sir Harcourt and the next LG'). He was a kindred spirit: also a *bon viveur*.

Motilal was devoted to his only son (for other male offspring were still-born) and smothered him with affection. Jawaharlal ('Jewel') was unlike his outgoing, ambitious, arrogant father. He was shy, unsociable, and like his mother who was another Brahman of Kashmiri origin, married to Motilal at 14. She preserved an orthodox Hindu outlook despite acquiescing in the demands of her dominating husband. She tried to instil orthodox religion in her son, but early on Motilal placed him under an Irish tutor who was also a Theosophist and Jawaharlal's outlook reflected this vaguely ethical, vaguely oriental, vaguely mystical influence. When he was 15 the boy was taken to England to be placed in school at Harrow: this choice – and the later choice of Trinity College, Cambridge, for university – must have owed a good deal to the family friend the children called 'Uncle Harcourt', for the Butlers had a close connection with Harrow and Trinity.

Education in England

The family installed him at Harrow in 1905, and although he underwent the usual horrors of public school existence in those days, he was not unhappy but he was restless. In 1907 against the advice of father and headmaster he sat the not very formidable Trinity College entrance examination and went up in October of that year. Cambridge, and Trinity especially, were then at the peak of intellectual brilliance and influence, but none of this rubbed off on the young Nehru. He read Natural Sciences, and although (as he later admitted) he did not do much work, he obtained a respectable Second Class degree. Both father and son rejected the idea of working for the examination for the ICS (which some of his close relatives were to enter) and instead he read for the Bar in the Inner Temple. The next two years (1910–12) were passed pleasantly and expensively in London, and he returned to Allahabad to join his father's legal practice. His sister found him 'reticent and not disposed to express his feelings': the opposite of his ebullient father. Jawaharlal went to the annual Congress meeting at Bankipur in December 1912: not out of political conviction, but almost as an expected occurrence for his father's son. The onset of the Great War made little impact on Allahabad. The next important event in his life was his marriage in 1916.

An Arranged Marriage

Despite his seven years in England he made no attempt to escape an arranged match. The bride, chosen by his father after much searching, was also a Brahman of Kashmiri descent belonging to the Kaul family of Delhi. When his wife Kamala lay dying, Nehru reflected: 'I was 26 at the time and she was about 17, a slip of a girl, utterly unsophisticated. . . . I was far more grown-up than she was. And yet with all my appearance of worldly wisdom I was very boyish and I hardly realised that . . . [she] required gentle and careful tending.'[1] His sister recalled that the wedding was 'lavish to the point of ostentation. . . . Evening after evening there were feasting and gaiety in which it seemed as if no one in the whole province had been left out.'[2] Their only child, a girl, named Indira, was born on 19 November 1917: her grandfather concealed his disappointment behind a joke.

The year 1917 saw his first serious venture in politics. The Theosophist leader, Mrs Besant, launched the Home Rule League for constitutional advance, and Jawaharlal became Secretary of the Allahabad branch. This was still drawing-room politics. The new Gandhian politics was first seen in 1919 with a call for *satyagraha* or civil disobedience to protest against the Rowlatt Acts. Events became violent in Punjab where at Amritsar the military launched a campaign of repression. Only gradually did the truth emerge because the province was sealed off from the rest of India. It was in October 1919 that Jawaharlal managed to get to Lahore to investigate what had been done. His father still hesitated to commit himself to the politics of *satyagraha* but from thenceforward Jawaharlal was Gandhi's follower. When the first provincial elections were announced, implementing Montagu's reforms, Motilal urged his son to stand for a UP constituency, but Jawaharlal declined. In the non-cooperation campaign of 1920–1 he found fulfilment: it was 'a wholehearted expression of the self'.

His new situation brought about a strange contrast between the old world and the new. He escorted his wife, mother and sister to the fashionable hill station Mussoorie in May 1920: Kamala was already suffering from ill-health. The government required him to give an undertaking not to contact the Afghan delegation also staying in Mussoorie. Nehru refused, and was ordered to leave. His father appealed to Sir Harcourt Butler, now Lieutenant-Governor. At first Butler supported his officials, but when Motilal emphasised that he must join his 'sick mother or wife as the case may be' Sir Harcourt issued orders to withdraw the ban.[3]

Although implacably opposed to the Raj, the Nehrus were never really outsiders. Jawaharlal now became involved with peasant protest against landlord exploitation. This persuaded him that the root cause of unrest in India was economic, not social or religious. This conviction of the paramount importance of radical economic change was to remain the basis of his political thought throughout his life. The campaign continued throughout 1921: which Jawaharlal recalled as 'full of excitement and optimism and buoyant achievement'. In May his beloved sister, Nan, was married to another young lawyer, Ranjit Pandit. This ceremony, in total contrast to her brother's wedding, was austere in its simplicity: 'The list of guests read like a political convention', she recorded. Chief among them was Gandhi. Although brother and sister were now physically separated, the bond of affection was unbroken: probably his sister was closer to Nehru than wife or daughter.

Introduction to Jail (1921)

Late in the year, the government decided to crack down on the movement. Many were arrested, and on 5 December the Nehrus, father and son, were taken in. Jawaharlal was sentenced to six months in jail. As a Class A prisoner he had certain privileges; he could receive unlimited books and periodicals and had writing materials. He was allowed limited freedom of movement. One of his biographers shrewdly observes that Jawaharlal was much better prepared for jail than most middle-class Indian lads because he had been at an English public school: the poor food, spartan conditions, total absence of privacy, and meaningless rituals and routines were very similar.[4] Because there was an error in his indictment he was released after three months.

However, he was not at liberty for long. In February 1922 there occurred a massacre of some police constables by a Congress mob and Gandhi called off civil disobedience, declaring that the people were not yet ready for *satyagraha*: for Gandhi this was a basic question of morality and spiritual enlightenment. For Nehru it was just a technique which embarrassed the British, and he deplored the move, though even he recognised that things had got out of hand: 'any unknown man who wanted to do so could take charge of a Congress Committee. . . . There was no way of checking them.' Sensing they had the Gandhians on the run, the government arrested the Mahatma and others not in jail, including Nehru. This time he was given 21 months. Conditions were crowded – so many Congress workers were now inside – but Nehru accepted it all as a monk accepts a monastery. He was glad to be freed from the endless distractions of political campaigning.

Once again he was discharged prematurely, after ten months, in January 1923. His father was already at liberty and Motilal believed that civil disobedience had reached a dead end. He decided that the government could best be opposed from within the system so he tried to convert the Congress to 'Council Entry'. Only a minority agreed with him, not including his son. Motilal was elected to the central legislature in 1923. He rapidly emerged as the outstanding figure on the opposition benches. His son also ventured inside the system by standing for the Allahabad municipal council and was made chairman. His two years in this post, 1923–5, were taken very seriously and he worked much harder than most of the councillors.

Yet this did nothing to resolve the main question: where were they going? Gandhi's solution was to immerse himself in the 'constructive programme' of social uplift; he observed a 'year of silence' throughout 1926. This was no solution to Nehru who began to realise the limitations of the movement he had identified with: 'The average Congressman is notoriously not a revolutionary, and after a period of semi-revolutionary action he resumes his humdrum life. . . . Larger issues seem to fade off in his mind and revolutionary ardour, such as it was subsides.'

Encounters Socialism in Europe

All the while Kamala's health was deteriorating and in March 1926 the Nehrus went to Switzerland, without finding any cure. The trip enabled Jawaharlal to meet European intellectuals, especially Socialists. He attended the Congress of Oppressed Nationalities in Brussels in February 1927. This was organised by Willi Muenzenberg, a Communist (later expelled), and was largely funded by the Party. Nehru was prominent, though emphasising nationalist rather than Communist aspects (as when he praised the 'noble example' of Kuo Min Tang China). A League Against Imperialism was founded, and he later served on its nine-man executive committee. In November 1927, accompanied by Motilal, he was a guest of the Soviet Government at the tenth anniversary celebration of the revolution. This visit – a mere three or four days – made a great impression. It was the subject of his first book, _Soviet Russia: Some random sketches and impressions_, an uncritical panegyric,

Next month, at the annual Congress held in Madras, Nehru moved a series of resolutions which reflected his newly-articulated leftward stance. He demanded complete independence (no association with Britain), identification of Congress with the League Against Imperialism, and denunciation of British militarism. These were all carried. Gandhi was not present, and he told Jawaharlal 'you are going too fast'. He added that his speeches were 'encouraging mischief-makers and hooligans, I do not know if you still believe in unadulterated non-violence'. Elsewhere he wrote, 'We have almost sunk to the level of a schoolboy's debating society.'

Nehru Repudiates 'Gradualist' Reform

Next year, in reply to the Simon inquiry, Motilal Nehru's committee produced their own programme for constitutional advance. Jawaharlal formed a pressure group to oppose any 'moderate' formula being adopted by the All Parties Conference. This Independence for India League brought together Jawaharlal and Subhas Chandra Bose, the impetuous Bengali radical, as joint secretaries. When the Simon Commission visited India they were met by increasingly hostile demonstrations. At Lucknow in November 1928 Nehru was out at the forefront and received the full force of the violence meted out by mounted police. Gandhi praised his disciple; 'It was all done bravely.' Nobody could have done more to demonstrate that non-violence meant discipline and courage.

Meanwhile there was pressure to accept Motilal's report, a compromise to satisfy the Liberals. Eventually Jawaharlal and the League acquiesced, though he privately thought the report was 'futile'. When presented to the Congress at Calcutta in December 1928 it was adopted. As he was to do so often, Jawaharlal accepted a position he did not believe in for the sake of unity.

The year 1929 was a time of waiting. The election of a Labour government in Britain seemed hopeful, but the sole outcome was an announcement by the Viceroy, Lord Irwin, reaffirming the goal in India as Dominion status. When the Viceroy's talks with political leaders broke down, the Congress prepared to resume the struggle with their annual gathering at Lahore in January 1930. There was a general feeling that Gandhi should take over the presidency but he insisted that what he called 'the Crown' should be assumed by Jawaharlal: who, feeling he had attained that high office only by default, felt 'annoyed and humiliated'. Nevertheless he used the office vigorously, almost ruthlessly.

Congress President (1930)

At Lahore Gandhi moved a resolution affirming the goal as complete independence: Dominion status was thrown aside. Bose moved an amendment whereby Congress would set up a parallel government implementing 'complete severance of the British connection'. Nehru repudiated this course in his presidential speech as a move 'to paralyse government and compel government to abdicate': which, of course, it was. But was not this his policy also? The amendment was defeated. When the new working Committee (the so-called High Command) came up for election, ten names were proposed which had to be accepted or rejected en bloc. Those Congressmen who had entered the legislatures were ordered to resign, and Motilal gave an example which he appealed to all the others to follow. One Indian historian writes that 'the Congress under Nehru's presidentship had to act as a steamroller'.

As always, Gandhi remained the super-president of Congress. He decided to launch a new civil disobedience movement against the government monopoly of salt manufacture. Irwin held back, but inevitably there was a clampdown. Gandhi was arrested, and also Jawaharlal and Motilal. This may be an appropriate place to list all the periods Jawaharlal spent in jail:

> 5 December 1921–3 March 1922
> 12 May 1922–31 January 1923
> 14 April 1930–11 October

19 October 1930–26 January 1931
26 December 1931–30 August 1933
12 February 1934–4 September 1935
30 October 1940–4 December 1941
9 August 1942–15 June 1945

From jail, Nehru wrote to Gandhi: 'For myself I delight in warfare.' But as his principal biographer observe 'Few even among the Congress leaders shared Jawaharlal Nehru's zest for battle.'[5] Gandhi was doubtful, and the Liberal leaders Jayakar and Sapru induced him to ask the Nehrus, father and son, to consider negotiation. They were conveyed from their jail in the UP to his jail near Bombay. It was evident that Motilal was seriously ill. He was released, and died on 6 February 1931. Soon after, Gandhi had discussions with the Viceroy and the Gandhi–Irwin pact was agreed on 4 March. Thereby the Congress prisoners were released.

Launches Peasant Struggle

Jawaharlal went his own way, launching a campaign with Communist support to arouse the rural poor of the UP against the landlords. Rent was not paid and the landlords were attacked, even murdered. In June 1931 he made a speech declaring that his objective was 'the total expropriation of all landlords'. It was piquant that at this moment when his position was virtually indistinguishable from that of the Communists he was expelled from the League Against Imperialism as an Asian Kerensky.

After much hesitation, awaiting the call of 'the Inner Voice', Gandhi decided to participate in the second Round Table Conference. He was bitterly disappointed, and on return to India resumed civil disobedience. The new Viceroy, Lord Willingdon, had little interest in dialogue with Congress. Gandhi was arrested, while Nehru was sentenced to his longest period of imprisonment yet. However, just as Gandhi withdrew from the crowd into his ashram, so Nehru found peace when 'inside': his condition could be called jail-happy. It was not that he wrote to his sister Nan (7 April 1932): 'Prison is the best of universities if only one knows how to take its courses. Physically, of course, one has the chance of regular and simple living, mentally its effect is still more noteworthy. . . . The enjoyment of life becomes keener. So three cheers for jail.'[6]

Writes *Autobiography* in Jail (1934–5)

Gandhi and Nehru were both released late in August 1933. Soon after, the two men met, and it was clear that they differed widely on future policy. Gandhi decided to devote a year to his constructive programme, working for the Untouchables. Although the evidence is not clear it would seem that Nehru announced that he would launch a programme of rural mass struggle, but was dissuaded, against all his convictions. He was now sadly adrift. British officialdom entirely misread the situation and saw Nehru as supplanting the Mahatma. He was arrested again. The next prison term was remarkable in yielding the *Autobiography* which he wrote entirely between June 1934 and February 1935. It shows an amazing detachment from his physical conditions, his political difficulties, and his emotional problems revolving round the deteriorating health of Kamala.

During this time in jail, there was an important development in the Congress which reflected his influence among younger members. The first move came from outside, under the influence of the Communist intellectual known as M.N. Roy. His group published proposals for the formation of a Congress Socialist Party: these appeared while Nehru was still at liberty, but he did not respond. In March 1934, with Gandhi's blessing, a group of Congress moderates revived the All-India Swaraj Party to contest the elections which would be held under the 1935 Government of India Act. As a reply, an All-India Socialist Conference was held at Patna in May; this city was already associated with the emerging radical leader, Jayaprakash Narayan (known as JP). He became Organising Secretary of the new Socialist Party within the Congress, with other young Marxists like M.R. Masani as activists. They looked to Nehru as their natural leader, yet on his emergence from jail he refused them all encouragement.

His release was sanctioned after many, including Rabindranath Tagore (to whom Nehru had entrusted his daughter's education), had pleaded that he be allowed to join his dying wife who had gone to a clinic in Germany in a last desperate hope of cure. His time with her was interrupted by visits to England where he met Labour leaders and also the Liberal imperialist, Lord Lothian (with whom he engaged in a massive correspondence). Nehru was aroused by the growth of fascism in Europe; he was virtually the only Indian leader to feel any connection with world affairs. He got to know V.K. Krishna Menon, originally from Kerala, but brought to England in 1924 to become the Theosophist hope by Mrs Besant. The two men had this background in common, as well as being intellectuals, socialists and loners. His new friend had sufficient influence on Nehru to decide about the United Kingdom publication of his *Autobiography* (the first publication was in India). He also met Subhas Bose, whom the Government of India had virtually exiled to Europe.

In his absence he was re-elected President of Congress, after Gandhi had inquired 'Whether you will allow your name to be proposed for the Crown of Thorns'. The Government of India noted, shrewdly, 'He is afraid of Nehru drifting to the Left more and more and thinks . . . thereby . . . he will have him as his chief henchman for his next campaign.'

Nehru Loses his Wife (1936)

Nehru did not know whether to stay with his wife or return: she gave him his answer by dying on 28 February 1936. All he could do was to dedicate the *Autobiography* 'To Kamala, who is no more'. Although his British publisher went bankrupt, the book was an instant success and was reprinted 14 times by 1941, when with an additional chapter it continued reprinting.

Taking up the Presidency, Nehru found that the party was moving rapidly away from his own policies. Bose urged him to fight to lead Congress 'in a progressive direction': 'your position is unique' (4 March 1936). Rafi Ahmad Kidwai, one of his UP friends, rebuked him for not strengthening the High Command with radicals; instead, he said, strictly constitutional newcomer like Rajagopalachari and Bhulabhai Desai would make the High Command 'more reactionary than the one it has replaced' (20 April 1936). These Right-wingers, headed by Rajendra Prasad, nevertheless felt aggrieved by 'the preaching and emphasising of socialism' and tendered their resignations en bloc (29 June 1936). Nehru tentatively offered to Gandhi to resign the presidency, evoking a flood of letters from the Mahatma of which the import was: 'How I wish you would put down your foot on "insane" programmes and save your energy for the common good' (30 July 1936). Nehru acquiesced in Gandhi's renewed insistence on loyalty and unity. He acquiesced in Congress contesting the elections, and when they unexpectedly won success in most of the provinces he acquiesced in a policy of office acceptance. Even Nan (Mrs Pandit) stood for election and in due course took office in the ministry.

In UP Nehru played a role, though it may not have been decisive, in rejecting any notion of a Congress–League coalition. He told Pandit Pant, the incoming Congress Premier, 'I am personally convinced that any kind of pact or coalition between us and the Muslim League will be highly injurious. It will mean many other things also which are equally undesirable.' With this rupture between the two major parties came severance of personal relations with many former Muslim members of Congress who had been close friends, notably Choudhury Khaliquz-zaman. To Nehru, a product of the Mughal cultural inheritance, quite without religious conviction, any political position based on religion seemed medieval. To him class not caste was the basic factor in politics and ideology.

Travels Abroad: Europe Again

With no part to play in the new Congress politics of ministerial government Nehru once again embarked on foreign travel. In May 1937 he attended the second All-Burma Students' Conference at Mandalay at the invitation of the President of the Students' Union, Aung San, himself the future Prime Minister of Burma, who declared 'That a leader of millions . . . should be standing amidst us and instructing us makes us feel depressed for Burma that is denuded of leaders.' His words were resented by Dr Ba Maw, then Premier, who deliberately insulted Nehru, telling him to keep out of Burma. In June 1938 he went to Europe, where he first spent five days in Barcelona to talk to the Republicans about the progress of the civil War, then went on to England where he was feted by the Left and by leading Liberals but also by international celebrities like Paul Robeson. He visited Paris, Geneva and Czechoslovakia: he would have liked to go to the Soviet Union but could not obtain a visa.

Nehru had been Congress President for two years. His term had been extended to avoid a change while the elections took place. As Gandhi thought over the next choice he looked with favour on Subhas Bose. The choice was surprising, for if Nehru was content to preach revolution Bose intended to practise it. However, Gandhi was not altogether happy with the way in which Congress ministries were fulfilling British plans under the 1935 Act which the Mahatma had denounced as satanic. So he planned for Bose to succeed Nehru at the end of 1937.

Falls out with Subhas Bose (1939)

As President, Bose revitalised the Congress machine and endeavoured to induce the new ministries to take practical steps to implement state planning (at this time Bose was labelled Socialist, though already the correct term might be totalitarian). He continued to fight the policy of implementing the 1935 Act, as Rajagopalachari and others seemed content to do. Increasingly, Gandhi regretted his elevation, while Patel was openly hostile. To all appearances the two young leaders remained close comrades. On 19 October 1938 Bose thanked Nehru for 'all your letters' adding, 'You cannot imagine how I have missed you all these months.'

In January 1939, the Working Committee met at Bardoli, north of Bombay, and after Bose had departed Gandhi talked about choosing a successor. There was no great enthusiasm to stand, and the choice fell on Pattabhi Sitaramayya, a lacklustre Gandhian. Nehru was present, though he disclaimed any part in the choice. Despite Gandhi's personal support, Sitaramayya failed to defeat Bose: he received 1377 votes to 1580 for Bose. JP and the Socialists mobilised the younger element behind him. Apparently recognising his failure, Gandhi told Nehru he would be absent from the forthcoming session (3 February 1939). However, the Mahatma was rallying his forces for renewed attack.

Nehru's part in the next few weeks showed him at his most hesitant and equivocal. He professed not to understand what the intentions of Bose were: 'I am entirely at sea' (4 February). Bose's first reply was brief and friendly (10 February). Then came the bombshell: obeying Gandhi, all the members of the Working Committee resigned en bloc, except for Nehru, who issued a statement on 22 February and then resigned. It was not surprising that Bose told him: 'I find . . . you have developed a tremendous dislike for me.' Remorselessly, he exposed Nehru's inconsistencies and his 'nebulous' ideas: 'You call yourself a Socialist. . . . How a Socialist can be an individualist as you regard yourself beats me'; 'If the Working Committee had another member as talkative as yourself I do not think we would ever have come to the end of our business' (28 March). And so it went on, for what in its printed form covers 21 pages. Nehru replied at almost equal length, more in sorrow than in anger (3 April). The correspondence dragged on, but Bose had discovered the bitter truth: that no-one could out-manoeuvre Gandhi when challenged. He resigned, and the safe Gandhian, Rajendra Prasad, took over the presidency.

It was typical of Nehru's capacity to recognise – somewhat selectively – his shortcomings, that when he put together a collection of his correspondence for publication nearly 20 years later (*A Bunch of Old Letters*, 1957) he included the entire series of exchanges of February–April 1939.[7] He also seems to have confessed to Taya Zinkin about the same time: 'I subordinated myself to Gandhi although I was in agreement with what Subhas was trying to do.'[8] In a moment of crisis he had failed to come out decisively.

The outbreak of war in September 1939 also found Nehru in two minds. He had strongly condemned Fascism and rebuked the Chamberlain government for appeasement. He had visited China and witnessed Japanese aggression. The pact between Germany and the Soviet Union revealed the common intentions of the two totalitarian empires, and now Germany had invaded Poland. At first it appeared that Gandhi would roundly denounce Nazi aggression, as Rajagopalachari and Patel actually did: surely, then Nehru's voice would be raised against totalitarianism? But when the Congress High Command spoke, although they condemned fascism and offered their assistance, this was on condition that India was recognised as 'an independent nation'. Bose would have launched an all-out struggle against Britain, as would JP who declared an armed struggle was justified: 'If this does not accord with Gandhiji's principles that is not my fault.'

Dilemma: Fascism or Imperialism the Main Enemy?

Nehru felt quite otherwise, and unusually he wrote to Lord Linlithgow, the Viceroy, to tell him, 'How much I desire that the long conflict of India and England should be ended and that they should cooperate together. I have felt that this war with all its horrors has brought this opportunity to our respective countries and it would be sad and tragic if we are unable to take advantage of it' (6 October 1939). Nevertheless, he observed, it was like a Greek tragedy and they seemed to be moving to a predestined end.[9] The Viceroy's reply showed no recognition that a generous gesture was required. The Government stalled; and the Congress ministries resigned.

The political stalemate was not broken when Hitler overran France and threatened to invade England. In August 1940 Nehru wrote of the Government of India: 'They sleep, even though waking on Simla hills. . . . The sands of time run out here in India as in Europe and the world. So many of my colleagues have gone back to prison and I envy them'[10]

On 13 October 1940 the High Command decided to launch a symbolic *satyagraha*, offered by selected individuals. Vinoba Bhave was chosen by Gandhi to go first. He was arrested for speaking against the war and jailed. Nehru was nominated the second *satyagrahi*, and whereas the unknown Vinoba was given three months, Nehru was sentenced to four years in jail. Once again, he was to be released prematurely. On the eve of Pearl Harbor he was set free, and the Viceroy appealed for united support against Japan. Nehru gave his answer on 20 December 1941: the essential precondition was recognition of Indian independence.

A visit to India by Marshal Chiang Kai-shek and his wife in February 1942 had 'Nehru sticking to him like a burr' according to one of the Governors.[11] Nothing occurred to resolve the political deadlock though Chiang publicly expressed support for 'India's aspirations'. At this time Nehru was involved in a personal dilemma: his daughter, Indira, indicated that she intended to marry a Parsi of Allahabad, Feroze Gandhy. Her father was reluctant to agree, but Indira persisted. Eventually the wedding was fixed for 26 March. This important event was overshadowed by another of international importance: the arrival in India on 22 March of Sir Stafford Cripps with a mission to bring the nationalists into the government in order to arouse India to resist the Japanese advance. As ambassador in Moscow, 1940–1, he was credited with creating comradeship between Russia and Britain. On return to England he became a member of the War Cabinet (19 February 1942). Churchill's stock had slumped with the disastrous defeats in South-East Asia and some saw Cripps taking over. He leapt at the idea of going to India: if he succeeded, he believed nothing could stop his advance. The plan he brought (approved by the Cabinet) conceded India's right, straight after the war, to work out a constitution for immediate independence. This went a long way to meet the previous demands of Congress. In the meantime, portfolios on the Viceroy's Council would all be held by politicians, except for defence.

Did the plan really have any hope of success? As soon as Cripps released the details Gandhi described them as 'A postdated cheque on a crashing bank'. It was not an unfair description. Cripps pinned his hopes on Nehru, whom he had met before and regarded as his friend. Nehru did not arrive from Allahabad until 29 March when Cripps noted he 'was tired and not well'. He said little, and Cripps deduced that Congress had already decided to reject his scheme. At their next meeting Nehru complained about British shortcomings: they had no intention of resisting the invader. On 2 April Nehru and Azad brought a long letter of rejection from the Working Committee. Yet on 7 April Nehru made a speech in which, while condemning British imperialism, he expressed solidarity with China, Russia and the United States. He urged his countrymen to 'fight any invading army. It was more dignified and honourable for India to go down fighting with soul intact.'[12]

Dialogue with Cripps Fails (1942)

This came just when Cripps turned to the newly-arrived special envoy from Roosevelt, 'Colonel' Louis Johnson, for assistance. Johnson met Nehru and Azad and, ignorant of India as he was, thought he had persuaded them. Cripps decided to make a last personal appeal to Nehru: 'Leadership – the sort of leadership you have – can alone accomplish the result. It is the moment for the supreme courage of a great leader' (7 April). All this to the Hamlet of Indian politics! On 8 April United Press reported Nehru and Johnson in agreement. To the latest Cripps offer, Nehru made counter-proposals which Cripps attempted to meet. He was

being drawn increasingly beyond his Cabinet brief. Despite all this, on 9
April Nehru wrote gloomily to Johnson. Azad and he had just had two-
and-a-half hours with Cripps (significantly, this meeting is the only one of
which no record was kept). He went on: 'The whole picture that emerged
from our talks took me aback and I suddenly discovered that the very
premises on which we had been discussing this subject during the last four
days were unjustified. The whole structure that we had tried to build so
laboriously in our minds was without any real foundation.'[13]

Next day came the confirmation from Azad that Congress had pulled
out. He claimed that Cripps had led them to expect 'a National
Government and a Cabinet consisting of Ministers', with the Viceroy's
role reduced to that of 'constitutional head'. Instead, this 'new'
government would be like the old 'in all essential features . . . we cannot
fit into it'. Two days later Cripps departed, leaving an atmosphere of
increased mistrust and suspicion. He had oversold himself, and never
again regained the commanding position in government he had held
early in 1942.

For Nehru also the breakdown was another misadventure. According
to a former Congress Premier of Madras, Dr P. Subbarayan, Gandhi and
his supporters 'Made a fool of Jawaharlal who never knows his own mind
and is not prepared to oppose the wishes of the majority of the Working
Committee for fear of losing popularity'.[14]

The war continued to go badly. Yet by June the Burma front had
settled into a stalemate which was to persist for another two years:
neither the British nor Congress could know this. Gandhi was again
making the running. He called on the British to withdraw: India would
await the Japanese and if necessary respond with passive resistance. The
Working Committee met at the end of April to issue a resolution. Nehru
opposed the demand for the withdrawal of British troops, but only
Rajagopalachari among the top leaders stood up to Gandhi: the
resolution issued on 1 May rejected cooperation with the British and
adopted a policy of non-violent resistance though the population were
advised 'not to put any obstacle in the way of British forces'.

Yet Gandhi wanted more: on 14 July the Working Committee's call for
Britain's withdrawal was interpreted by Gandhi as 'open rebellion'. Nehru
believed 'It is Gandhiji's feeling that Japan and Germany will win.'[15] His
private correspondence showed Gandhi moving nearer to the use of
physical force than ever before. On 8 August the High Command
demanded the immediate transfer of power to Congress and called for a
mass struggle 'on the widest scale'.

Congress Rising Fails: Jail Again, 1942–5

In London and New Delhi preparations had been agreed to forestall a Congress revolt. Early on 9 August Nehru and all the other leaders were arrested. Gandhi was taken to luxurious confinement in the Aga Khan's palace at Poona and the Working Committee were incarcerated in the Mughal fort at Ahmadnagar, far from any city. For nearly three years there was silence in Congress politics. Spontaneous risings occurred, especially in the Bhojpuri areas of eastern UP and west Bihar. Though leaderless they were difficult to suppress and stretched military resources to the limit. The only front-rank leader to organise the revolt was JP who escaped from jail. Before he was arrested in March 1941, JP had protested against 'the farce of *satyagraha*' and began organising underground resistance. After his escape he issued 'Letters to All Fighters of Freedom'. He was contemptuous of Gandhi's protestations that he had not expected violence: what did he expect after all his brave words about rebellion? And yet when he was recaptured in November 1942 his condemnation of Congress leaders totally excluded Nehru: 'He is an out and out anti-capitalist', declared JP: he hoped that Nehru would be able, while interned, to 'devise something new on socialist lines and overcome Sardar Patel's pro-capitalist policy'.[16]

However, the evidence is that Nehru and his fellow internees merely bickered with each other. This, his longest time in jail, was largely passed in cultivating flowers. He did write one book, *The Discovery of India*, between April and September 1944. Rambling, repetitive, yet with shafts of insight, Nehru himself called it 'this jumble of ideas' near the book's end. Regarded as among the more intransigent leaders, he was not released until 15 June 1945. JP and some other socialists still remained in jail.

When Wavell met Nehru at Simla on 2 July for a long talk, the Viceroy said, 'There was much on all sides to forgive and forget. And I meant it.'[17] Nehru played no part in the Simla Conference and only began to resume public work in September.

Militant Rhetoric Confronts Realities

Wavell had returned to London for consultations with the new Labour government. He perceived clearly enough, 'They are obviously bent on handing over India to their Congress friends as soon as possible.' When elections were announced, the work of central organisation fell to Patel, but Nehru took the lead in arousing the people from the platform. His language was increasingly violent: 'A revolution is inevitable. It is only a question of time when it comes' (27 October 1945); 'India must . . . prepare herself for a mass battle for freedom, which may come sooner than people expect' (12 November); 'If a country was unprepared for revolution to free herself, the nation was dead. Congress had never allowed the flag of revolution to be lowered' (same day).

Alarmed by these inflammatory words, Wavell — a plain man who meant what he said — asked Nehru to meet him. Nehru seemed uncompromising. He said that 'Congress could make no terms whatever with the Muslim League under its present leadership', which he described as 'Hitlerian'. He insisted that relations between ordinary Hindus and Muslims were improving all the time, and was unmoved when Wavell reminded him 40 had been killed in recent communal riots in Bombay. The Viceroy warned that 'the preaching of violence must eventually lead to violence'. After these exchanges Wavell concluded that Nehru 'Is quite incapable of considering any views which do not coincide with his own'. Nevertheless the Viceroy confided in his diary, 'I cannot help liking him.'

Early in 1946 Nehru replied to a friendly letter from Stafford Cripps. After denouncing British policy in the past he went on to castigate the Muslim League and its 'Nazi technique'. He insisted that there was 'A definite revolt against it among Muslims, and I believe this is growing'. He did not think the League would be effective: their leaders had 'spent their lives in soft jobs. . . . They will subside.' The letter rambled on in typical fashion and at one point Nehru observed disarmingly, 'I sometimes feel that I am rather out of date.' Near the end he added 'If conflict comes, obviously I shall be in the middle of it' (27 January 1946). Cripps sent a copy to Pethick-Lawrence remarking, 'This will interest you.' Obviously he believed this was the real thing.[18]

Intimacy with Mountbatten starts in Malaya

The stage was set for the Cabinet Mission. When the Three Magi first arrived Nehru was on a trip to Malaya which was, in its way, to be a more important experience for him than the negotiations. The visit was to offer sympathy to the Indian community, who had suffered severe privations during the Japanese occupation, and — to an undisclosed extent — also to bolster the collapsed morale of Bose's Japanese-sponsored Indian National Army or INA (some of whose officers had been symbolically represented by Nehru in their trial in the Red Fort, Delhi).

The military authorities intended to cold shoulder Nehru but were overruled by Mountbatten as Supreme Commander. He directed that

Nehru must be treated as if he were Prime Minister of independent India: he was attended by the Commissioner of Labour who was reminded that Nehru had not long left jail and was in a strange world: this was 'a magnificent opportunity to begin the cure'. Nehru was driven straight-away to meet the Mountbattens. He fell victim to their fascination and agreed to adjust his programme to avoid giving prominence to the INA. Nehru's speeches were mainly about the future in Asia where India and China would be brothers. Altogether he made 20 speeches in eight days and met 60 000 people. At the end he was 'extremely weary'. The Mountbattens – Dicky and Edwina – exercised their charm in special ways: 'He had met an English couple he could trust.'[19]

Nehru came into the discussions with the Cabinet trio during the Simla adjournment. He stated the position from which he was not to budge during the following months. He declined to consider 'a vague and airy Centre'. As regards the proposed Groups, 'this was a matter for the Constitution-making body. . . . The Centre must be capable of function-ing.' The Groups would form 'an unnecessary intermediate body': 'Industrialisation and progress [planning?] were only possible on an all-India basis.' 'The Congress contemplated that the all-India Constitution-making Body would decide the Union constitution and would also decide the main lines of Provincial constitutions.' When British officials drew up a list of Points for Agreement, Nehru observed that both sides agreed with much of this: maybe any disputed points could be decided by an impartial arbitrator? He had private meetings with Jinnah over this proposal, but they could not agree. The last two meetings between all the parties on 11 and 12 May degenerated into a wrangle between Nehru and Jinnah. The conference ended in failure.

Before they all left Simla Wavell had an interview with Nehru. This found him in a frame of mind very different from the talk of revolution six months earlier. Nehru stressed that the Viceroy 'should realise that it [the Congress High Command] was a body with many different tendencies and stresses, including a very strong element of extremists which had lately been gaining ground. . . . It was by no means certain that the present Working Committee would retain their influence over the more extreme elements.' There was some double-talk in all this. JP had at last been set free on 12 April 1946. Nehru may have been apprehensive, but he also wanted to keep his regard. JP continued to be militant. He stirred up groups in the Bihar police to mutiny and he made a tour through Punjab in which he urged the formation of district cadres 'That could overrun the police, murder British officials and take over charge' (or so the Governor alleged). Yet one of Nehru's first acts on resuming the

Congress presidency in July 1946 was to bring JP on to the Working Committee. When Wavell asked Nehru whether JP 'was going to become constitutional or that the Working Committee was going to be revolutionary?' Nehru laughed and said "Both I hope". He . . . was a very fine fellow and really not at all inclined to violence.'

Jawaharlal was still intent on riding two horses at once. In urging a return to mass action, JP was only wanting to follow the same course that Congress had taken in 1921, 1931 and 1942. However, with Patel in the driving seat this would not happen again. The situation was too explosive: mass action could so easily follow a communal pattern, Hindus versus Muslims. And so Nehru once again abandoned the way of struggle to which he was emotionally committed.

The Cabinet Mission plan, watered down and adulterated, was still not acceptable to Congress. On 24 June Gandhi told Cripps he was advising against acceptance. For a second time he had thwarted that supple negotiator. Nehru dashed off to Kashmir on behalf of Sheikh Abdullah late in June. He was arrested on the orders of the Maharaja. This was the old Nehru, the knight errant, not the new careful constitutionalist.

Dismisses Cabinet Mission Plan

As Congress President Nehru hastened to acquaint the press with his own view (and, it was assumed, that of Congress) on the grouping plan. He demolished it brick by brick, concluding, 'You see this grouping business approached from any point of view does not get on at all' (7 July). Doubtless this was the view of other Congress leaders, but it was folly to say it openly at this delicate stage. Patel certainly thought so, blaming his psychology: 'He feels lonely and he acts emotionally.' Azad wrote: 'I must place on record that Jawaharlal's statement was wrong.' His first major biographer called it 'a serious tactical error'.[20] If Jinnah was looking for a reason to withdraw from the commitment he had made – which had proved so unprofitable – this was not presented to him. Desperately seeking to break the deadlock, Wavell invited Congress and League to form a government. Nehru declined, but when the Viceroy renewed the invitation to *him* to form what was in effect a Congress ministry, after the usual bargaining Nehru agreed (10 August). A large measure of power had fallen into his hands. The new Interim Government was sworn in on 2 September. Although Wavell continued to preside over the Executive Council, Nehru held preliminary meetings of his 'Cabinet', where decisions were agreed, thus making the main meeting much of a formality.

Elections to the Constituent Assembly had taken place (10 – 22 July): the Congress filled 201 of the 210 general seats and the League obtained all but five of the 78 seats reserved for Muslims. JP and the Left wing refused to take part, and the four Sikh seats remained unfilled as they could not agree on policy. Nehru and Patel pressed for the Assembly to be summoned; Wavell stalled, insisting that first an accommodation must be made with Jinnah. Nehru made certain concessions, notably that the Leader of the Assembly should be drawn from the League (8 October). An argument with Wavell over the position of a senior police officer led to a veiled threat that 'other consequences will inevitably follow' (11 October). When Jinnah decided to join the government, Nehru refused to give the League any of the three major portfolios. Wavell concluded, 'Congress are determined to keep the League out of the Government' (24 October). Both Viceroy and League had to give way to Nehru's obduracy; this must have confirmed him in the belief that before long Congress would have its way in everything. The strain of this confrontation produced in Nehru a temporary physical and nervous breakdown.

The Interim Government Divided

In September, Nehru's London friend, Krishna Menon, had again come into the picture. Nehru sent him to the UN General Assembly as an alternate delegate. Mrs Pandit headed the delegation, and Krishna Menon gave her trouble; he 'constantly flouted the united decision of his delegation by saying he was responsible only to the Prime Minister' (as Nehru already liked to be called).[21] Notwithstanding, Nehru gave his friend a commission as an unofficial roving ambassador. Wavell suggested he should first consult Liaqat Ali as principal League Minister. Nehru was furious: 'I am unable to accept this', he told the Viceroy. He accused the League of functioning as a separate block because they demurred at accepting his decisions (21 November). The same day in a speech at Meerut he accused the Viceroy of being in collusion with Jinnah, or what he called 'a mental alliance'. He warned Wavell that they might resort to struggle: 'Our patience is fast reaching the limit.'[22] To this kind of verbal violence Jinnah retorted by announcing that the League would boycott the Constituent Assembly, whose postponed meeting was fixed for 9 December.

When the Secretary of State invited a small Congress – League mission to come to London, after the usual initial refusal Nehru agreed to go. In their meetings, Nehru evaded all attempts to induce him to recognise the Three Tier constitution. In answer to a direct question from Cripps, he emphasised the need to go ahead with the Constituent Assembly: 'The Muslims would come in anyway sooner or later.' He restated the Congress view that the Sections were optional: 'He could not see why the Muslim League should not come in [to the Assembly] and put any questions of interpretation to the Federal Court. The only other test was the test of battle.' Jinnah and Nehru eventually confronted each other at a final meeting, when Attlee presided. Here, Nehru showed that he realised that the unity he desired might not prove attainable: 'They could not conceive of any constitution imposed over one part of the country by another. . . . To some extent it was true that this was a conflict between Indian points of view but he was convinced that unless Indians had a free hand other difficulties would arise.'

On return to India, everyone resumed where they had left off. The League continued to boycott the Assembly and the Interim Government continued to quarrel. In his first private talk with Wavell Nehru 'worked himself up into a denunciation of His Majesty's Government . . . [their] stock in India was down to zero so far as Congress was concerned'. Wavell observed that the Cabinet were doing all they could to preserve Indian unity: 'Nehru burst out that he would sooner India was divided into a hundred parts than that they should in any way abandon their principles and give in to the Muslim League.'

Congress Leaders Face Reality of Inter-Communal Conflict

At their next meeting, the atmosphere was very different; 'Nehru was subdued', and accepted 'that obviously they could not force a constitution on a reluctant province'. Attlee's statement of 20 February had induced a certain new realism in Congress thinking. On 9 March Nehru told Wavell that Congress had at last accepted the British interpretation of the Grouping formula, except that they called for the partition of Punjab and Bengal. If Congress had made this clear nine months earlier, much might have been different.

Mountbatten's task had been greatly simplified by Wavell's long duel with Congress, League and Cabinet. All three were now in a more realistic frame of mind. Among the Congress leaders he met in the first days, Mountbatten found Gandhi delightful but quite impractical, Patel bigoted and difficult to know, and only Nehru a man he could understand: 'most sincere', 'convincing', with 'fairness of mind'. As early as 31 March, Mountbatten was trying to produce a plan: 'a form of Partition with a central authority for reserved subjects; this to be an experimental arrangement'.

Among Congress leaders, Patel was the most realistic about what was happening and would happen. Responsible for the Home portfolio, he knew how far the security situation had degenerated. The mutiny among Indian Navy ratings in Bombay harbour had indicated that even the armed forces were no longer completely reliable, thanks largely to the Congress campaign of sustained denigration. Looking ahead to the relationship of the Princely states to the provinces he could foresee many attempting to 'go it alone'. An early handover by the British was essential if there was to be a functioning administration to take over a country that could still be governed. Patel was not bothered about the term Dominion status which so offended Nehru: his confidant, V.P. Menon, the constitutional adviser, convinced him that this would speed up the process of transferring power as they need not wait for a new constitution and a treaty with Britain before taking over. He tried to rush the British government into conceding Dominion status to the Interim Government, which would have delivered the League into his hands. As it became clear that this was not on, he accepted the creation of Pakistan, though he intended to ensure that the Muslims did not receive more than the bare minimum of territory. As he told the Constituent Assembly later: 'I agreed to Partition as a last resort when we had reached a stage where we could have lost all.'[23]

Patel could deliver the Congress – or its solid centre. He could not deliver Gandhi: but since the Cabinet Mission, Gandhi had been in the wilderness. Nehru was the key to pushing through a realistic takeover. His acquiescence in the partition of Punjab and Bengal seemed to indicate agreement with Patel. Mountbatten wanted to make sure: and so he invited Nehru – with the now ubiquitous Krishna Menon in attendance – for a House Party at Viceregal Lodge, Simla (the original intention was to ask Gandhi, Jinnah, Nehru, Liaqat Ali et al. to Simla, but the others were omitted).

Moment of Truth at Simla

Nehru had been shown the plan Mountbatten was sending to London. As we have seen, the Viceroy feared objections by Jinnah but not by Nehru, and – as with the Cabinet Mission plan – the calculation was that if Congress was in favour the League would be compelled to go along. Instead, when they reached Simla, Nehru reverted to what he called 'The Cabinet Mission's Plan with Modifications', which ruled out Pakistan. The Viceroy decided to give Nehru the opportunity to study the Partition plan at leisure: he kept the draft overnight, and next morning addressed a long epistle to Mountbatten:

The relatively simple proposals that we had previously discussed now appeared . . . in an entirely new context which gave them an ominous meaning. . . . The picture of India that emerged frightened me. In fact much that we have done so far was undermined and the Cabinet Mission's scheme and subsequent developments were set aside and an entirely new picture presented.[24]

The similarity of the language employed with the language of his letter to Cripps of 9 April 1942 is striking. Once again, the dreamer had awakened, and was unprepared for what lay ahead. But Mountbatten did not suffer from the limitations which had restricted Cripps. Modifications were introduced to satisfy Nehru, and after a hasty visit to London for Cabinet approval Mountbatten presented his plan to the Indian leaders on 2 June with Nehru, Patel and J.B. Kripalani representing Congress. When the moment arrived, Nehru indicated 'that there could never be complete approval of the plan from Congress but on the balance they accepted it'.

Mountbatten also saw Gandhi, who was observing a day of silence. His written notes showed he would not oppose the plan. When the letter of acceptance from the Congress Working Committee arrived later, signed by Kripalani, it contained the sentence, 'We earnestly trust that when present passions have subsided . . . a willing union of all parts of India will result therefrom.' This disguised what was undoubtedly the expectation of many in Congress, including Nehru and Patel, that Pakistan would be a hopeless mess and the League would come back – on terms dictated by Congress. A second meeting of leaders took place next day, and Nehru was untypically silent; perhaps reserving himself for a radio statement that evening. This was restrained and statesmanlike. He still could not fully accept the reality, observing that the plan 'envisages the *possibility* of these areas [the future Pakistan] seceding from India; on the other hand it promises a big advance towards complete independence'. He continued, 'It is with no joy in my heart that I commend these proposals to you, though I have no doubt in my mind that this is the right course.'

A few days later Mountbatten asked JP to a meeting, hoping to neutralise his opposition as he had that of Gandhi. JP declined, and continued to campaign for a people's revolution. But he received no support except from a few likeminded Socialists. When the full All-India Congress Committee (AICC) met to ratify the agreement on 14–15 June, Patel was centre-stage; this was his affair. The AICC voted to endorse the Mountbatten Plan by 153 to 29, with 36 abstentions. The tiny minority was composed of Socialists, some Gandhians, and some Nationalist Muslims. The great majority had their eyes firmly fixed on the accession of power.[25]

Tryst with Destiny

British rule ended on 14 August and the Constituent Assembly met at midnight to perform the formalities of assuming power. Nehru made a speech – probably largely spontaneous like most – which captured the mood of the hour in felicitous phrases: 'Long years ago we made a tryst with destiny, and now the time comes when we shall redeem our pledge, not wholly or in full measure, but very substantially . . . A moment comes, which comes but rarely in history, when an age ends and when the soul of a nation long suppressed finds utterance.'

A new age: but the old legacy of caste and communal division flared into an orgy of killing. Nehru, together with Mountbatten (for another ten months still Governor-General of India), worked tirelessly to restrain the frenzy. Campbell-Johnson remained Mountbatten's press officer, and on 13 September 1947 he recorded:

He [Nehru] vindicates one's faith in the humanist and the civilised intellect. Almost alone in the turmoil of communalism . . . he speaks with the voice of reason and charity. The negotiations for the transfer of power between March and August did not seem to me to evoke his full powers. A certain moodiness and outbursts of exasperation were the visible signs of overstrain; but now, somehow, he has renewed himself and in this deeper crisis he is shown at his full stature – passionate and courageous, yet objective and serene.[26]

Surely Campbell-Johnson was right? From the time of the Cabinet Mission to 15 August 1947, Nehru's judgement was continually at fault. He reached his full stature as the leader of independent India, and if this were a complete biographical sketch instead of a study of his part in the end of empire the years that were now to come would have been given the main focus. As it is, only the briefest account follows.

Amidst all the killings, the assassination of Gandhi on 30 January 1948 came as the greatest shock. Once again, Nehru found the right words: 'Even in his death there was a magnificence and complete artistry. It was from every point of view a fitting climax to the man and to the life he had lived.' The same was not true of Nehru's departure from this world. After years of achievement it came as an anti-climax.

The Good Years

The first decade after independence produced the great years, when India provided an example to all Afro-Asian countries looking for freedom.

India's foreign policy was virtually Nehru's own creation. The first major success was the acceptance by the tradition-bound White leaders of the British Empire that in the new Commonwealth an Indian republic could be a full member. This development made possible the future Commonwealth membership of the new Afro-Asian states. More central to Nehru's vision was the concept of an Asia united in brotherhood and free of Western domination. In a dark moment in 1940 he had written, 'My own picture of the future is a federation which includes China and India, Burma and Ceylon, Afghanistan and possible other countries.' He endeavoured to realise this vision in relations with neighbouring countries in the 1950s. Burma, led by U Nu, was linked in a special relationship of friendship. But more important was the cultivation of friendship with Communist China, despite their divergent ideologies. When China accepted what was known as Peaceful Co-Existence through *Pancha Sila*, the five principles, in an agreement of June 1954, including 'mutual respect for each other's territorial integrity', it seemed that this was guaranteed. However, China persisted in raising questions relating to the frontier imposed by the British in 1914, and Nehru persisted, equally, in adhering to the British McMahon Line, though Foreign Department records showed how sketchy was the claim. As with the Grouping question, Nehru was not prepared to consider any other than his (or his department's) interpretation.

However, the exact boundaries of remote mountain tops seemed of little importance compared to India's other foreign policy successes. It was India who, as honest broker, was able to break the deadlock over the negotiations for ending the war in Korea, and India again whose mediation secured a formula at Geneva in 1954 which ended the first Vietnam war.

At home, the successful mounting of general elections at regular five-year intervals demonstrated that a largely illiterate electorate – by far the largest in the world – could play a meaningful part in the choice of a government. The apparatus of centralised planning seemed to be stimulating rapid industrialisation, especially in the sphere of heavy industry. The virus of communalism appeared dormant, though a new phenomenon – the demand for drawing new state boundaries on linguistic lines – was perceived by Nehru as reversing the spirit of Indian unity which was so dear to him.

About ten years after independence, India's shining example as the world's greatest democracy began imperceptibly to fade. In the sphere of planning the emphasis on heavy industry, particularly steel production, was obviously draining India's foreign exchange, while steel exports proved disappointing. The public was becoming disillusioned with planning which seemed to create a web of controls, termed Permit Raj. The demands of linguistic groups created political instability in south and central India. Nehru was compelled to give way and accept new states on linguistic lines, though standing out against the claims of the Sikhs for a Punjabi-speaking state which they would dominate. However, the greatest crisis came in worsening relations with China. Increasingly, Nehru had become the central figure in a coterie of his personal admirers, among whom Krishna Menon exercised a special influence.

Nehru had little in common with most of his political colleagues. The avowed Gandhians seemed to point to the past. The machine politicians, weighing up calculations about caste and community, filled him with contempt. He sought the company of intellectuals, in particular, three Fellows of the Royal Society: S.S. Bhatnagar; Professor P.C. Mahalanobis, his planning guru; and Homi Bhabha, top atomic scientist.[27] Most important was Krishna Menon. He was brought into the Cabinet as Minister without Portfolio in 1956 and in 1957 became Minister of Defence. He shared Nehru's obsession with Pakistan's aggressive intentions and also his nonchalance about the problems of India's north-eastern border. He switched around the generals, preferring those who were politically sympathetic. In 1962 Portugal's obdurate refusal to discuss the future of Goa was broken by launching an invasion into that territory. The operation was not well managed, but Portuguese resistance was nominal. This success encouraged the idea of emphasising India's claims in the Himalayas. The front was extended in the area of Tawang, a Buddhist monastery situated right on the border.

Conflict with China: Disillusion

The Chinese retaliated by advancing rapidly, brushing aside Indian army resistance. In his reaction to the invasion, Nehru lamented he had been 'out of touch with reality', in an 'artificial atmosphere of our own creation'. Did it occur to him that this was a re-enactment of his attitude to the Cripps proposals in 1942 and to the Mountbatten plan at Simla? Almost certainly not.

Even before the war with China, Nehru was visibly ageing. U Nu, the Burmese Prime Minister, recalled: 'With advancing age he began to wilt and to tire, and he sometimes went to sleep on the sofa when U Nu was around.'[28] His view of what was important in Government became ever more hard to understand. One day he urgently called his principal research officer to his office: 'I am very worried about Thermidor', was his opening observation. Being an historian, the research chief knew that the Prime Minister was not bothered about the performance of some nuclear reactor but was referring to the phase in the French revolution when, in reaction against the Terror, Robespierre was overthrown. 'Do you think they should have executed Robespierre?' asked Nehru. They discussed this problem for some time until the research officer observed, 'Prime Minister, you have a Cabinet meeting and they have already been waiting some time.' Signing to the research officer to come with him, Nehru entered the Cabinet room where he continued to dilate on the question of Thermidor. Krishna Menon whispered 'Should the Cabinet be spending their time on this matter?', but the monologue continued until Nehru had exhausted the subject, when they turned to the mundane items on the agenda.

The Dream Dies (1964)

Nehru never recovered from the shock of China's 'invasion', as it was portrayed in India. He felt betrayed by the country he had seen as the great partner in Asia in the days of *Hindi-Chini-Bhai-Bhai* ('Indians and Chinese are brothers'). He still made an impression on his foreign visitors of internationalism and humanism and he still made speeches to respectful crowds, though these were increasingly incoherent. Let his sister Nan tell of the last days:

> Bhai had been slowly going down in health since the Chinese attack. In January 1964 at the annual session of the Congress . . . he had a mild stroke from which he recovered enough to resume his daily tasks. He had been pained and disillusioned over the China incident, he had been deeply hurt by the knowledge that advisers who he had trusted had misled him. . . . He seemed to have no will left to live.[29]

Pained he no doubt was: but like many great men he had wanted only to hear from those who would tell him what was agreeable to know. He died on 27 May 1964. His will was read over the radio by Mrs Pandit. He rejected 'the shackles [of religion and tradition] that bind and constrain her [India] and divide her people and suppress vast numbers of them . . . I wish to declare with all earnestness that I do not want any religious ceremonies performed for me after my death. I do not believe in any such ceremonies and to submit to them . . . would be hypocrisy.'[30]

Nevertheless, the full Brahmanical ceremonial was performed at his cremation and his grandson lit the funeral pyre to the chanting of the Brahman priests. Even at his passing his ideals, his dreams, were thwarted by the traditionalists.

1. Nehru and Jinnah assuming an affable appearance for the camera during their duel at Simla, May 1946. *Popperfoto*

2. Jinnah with his sister Fatima at their New Delhi house, a few days
before he left the capital for Karachi, July 1947. *Popperfoto*

3. Nehru addressing a press conference on becoming head of the
Interim government, September 1946. On the left sits Sardar Patel;
the second right is Rajendra Prasad. *Popperfoto*

4. Aung San marching through the streets of Rangoon to
   inaugurate the Constituent Assembly, June 1947. He is flanked
   by guards of the People's Volunteer Organisation. Immediately
   behind, left, is Thakin Nu (both in Burmese head-dress).
   Popperfoto

5. Nu with Nehru on a visit to Delhi, March 1955. *Popperfoto*

6. Sukarno returning from a foreign visit. Behind is his Japanese wife, Ratna Dewi. *Popperfoto*

7. Sukarno and Nehru at the meeting of non-aligned states, Belgrade, September 1961. *Camera Press*

8. Ho Chi Minh emerges from his cottage in the former French Governor-General's residence in Hanoi to greet his followers. *Camera Press*

9. Nehru visiting Ho Chi Minh soon after the Geneva armistice, October 1954. *Popperfoto*

10. Nkrumah with his Cabinet in formal chiefly robes after the 1954 election. On the right of Nkrumah sits his old ally, K. A. Gbedemah; second from left, standing, is Nathaniel Welbeck. *Popperfoto*

11. A solitary Jomo Kenyatta near his home, one week before his arrest and trial, October 1952. *Popperfoto*

12. Kenyatta and Nkrumah confer before the Commonwealth Prime Ministers' Conference begins, July 1964. *Popperfoto*

5

Country Boys Force the Pace:
Aung San and Thakin Nu

In negotiating with Jinnah and Nehru the British were dealing with leaders they had to recognise as their political and also social equals. As an outstanding barrister, Jinnah enjoyed a distinction equal to – for example – Stafford Cripps. Nehru, educated at Harrow and Cambridge, could be at home in any English country house, as when he stayed at Blickling Hall with the Marquess of Lothian. Moreover, both these leaders served immensely long political apprenticeships before finally winning independence; Jinnah was at the forefront of Indian politics for nearly 40 years before he got his Pakistan; Nehru was hailed as the Crown Prince of Indian nationalism over 20 years before he was able to keep his tryst with destiny. By contrast, Aung San and Thakin Nu were unknown less than ten years before they compelled the British to concede their demands.

When they first had to negotiate with the Burmese leaders, Attlee, Pethick-Lawrence and their colleagues thought they were dealing with a bunch of rustics, uncouth, and ignorant of the ways of high politics. On 5 November 1946 Pethick-Lawrence commented on their 'political immaturity', and again on 9 December he told the Cabinet that: 'We are dealing with a body politically immature, singularly lacking in experience of the outside world, and with no appreciation of the weakness of Burma or of the difficulties . . . she is likely to face.'[1] They were to discover that these country lads were the equals – perhaps the superiors – of their Indian counterparts in political sagacity. Aung San may not have known which knife and fork to use when he dined at Government House but he had a sure grasp of the realities of power. Neither Nehru nor Jinnah gained all that they wanted (or what they had announced as their objectives) but Aung San and Thakin Nu did obtain all their demands, despite British objections.

Traditional Forces in Burmese Politics

These young men represented a different kind of leader from those we have so far considered; the Burma from which they sprang had been

97

influenced by the West far less than India, and only a tiny middle class had
assimilated Western education. The British conquest had been achieved
by forces predominantly Indian. Indians formed the mainstay of the urban
workforce and (along with Chinese) provided the infrastructure of trade
and manufacturing. The economic superstructure was entirely controlled
by a handful of big British firms. The Burmese remained peasant farmers;
paddy cultivation was their customary way of life.

Traditional Burmese culture centred upon the monasteries, found in
every village and town, so that in the 1920s more than half the males in
Burma were literate in their mother tongue (compared to a literacy rate of
13. 9 per cent in India). This old world survived largely intact, particularly
in Upper Burma, annexed only in 1886: when years of guerrilla resistance
followed. Hence, by the 1920s and 1930s, only a tiny minority of
Burmese politicians had come up via the ladder of education and training
in Britain, by which Gandhi, Jinnah and Nehru had risen. Such were U
Chit Hlaing, a member of the English Bar, who led the *Wunthanu*, the
original political movement for 'the preservation of the nation', and Dr Ba
Maw, graduate of Cambridge and Bordeaux, first Premier after separation
from India in 1937.

Most of the leaders in Burma in the 1920s and 1930s appealed to an
older tradition. There were the political monks, U Ottama and U Wisara,
and there was the supposed king, Thupannaka Galuna Raja, known to the
British as Saya San, whose revolt in 1930 affected one-quarter of Burma.
Neither of these styles provided the basis for the emergence of Aung San
and Nu. A few years earlier Aung San might possibly have taken to the
jungle, bandit or resistance fighter according to one's viewpoint, known
only within a few miles of his own home. Nu might have been a village
schoolmaster, or a teller of tales, respected for his piety. Because they
were able to participate in two kinds of experience which were new and
unexpected – radical university politics in the 1930s, and Japanese stage-
managed 'independence' in 1943 – 5 – they became successively prime
ministers of Burma and the architects of independence. Leadership by
rural, lower-middle-class folk remains rare in Asia. These two pioneered
their own forms of politics; and this was indeed creating a revolution in a
way that Nehru and Jinnah, despite their involvement in mass politics, did
not attain.

Leaders From the Countryside

The man who was known first as Ko ('Elder Brother') Nu, then *Thakin* Nu,
and finally U Nu was born in 1907 at Wakema, a small market town (9000

people) in the lush Delta of Lower Burma. His parents ran a cloth store. Aung San (successively called *Bo*, or 'Captain', and *Bogyoke*, 'General') was born in 1916 at an even smaller place, Natmauk, in Magwe District in the dry plain of Upper Burma. He claimed his family were 'rural gentry', meaning they were hereditary headmen. His grandfather, Bo Min Yaung, had fought as a guerrilla against the British when they occupied Upper Burma. For men like these a university education would have been unthinkable a few years earlier, but in 1920 Burma obtained its own university on a campus outside Rangoon. Under intense political pressure the strict academic standards which first prevailed were relaxed, and entry was broadened. Nu entered in 1926 and was awarded his BA in 1929. He left for a few years to manage a national school, independent of the British system, but returned to read law.

Student Politics

The early 1930s were a bad time; the world depression particularly hit Burma as agricultural prices dropped. In the 1920s it had been relatively easy for the students to obtain good jobs: but not now. Their frustration created a climate in which nationalist politics could flourish. Ko Nu was elected President of the University Students' Union; the students looked up to him as their mentor. Aung San became editor of the student magazine *Oway*. Between them they transformed the Union from a social centre into a political cockpit. Nu specialised in inflammatory speeches in earthy, often vulgar, Burmese. As a youth he had been a rip. The tolerance of the university authorities was strained too far. Nu was expelled for his extravagant language, and so was Aung San who published an article about the Burmese university bursar entitled 'Hell-Hound at Large'. The student body thereupon came out on strike. At the end of four months the Principal readmitted the two offenders under pressure from Dr Ba Maw as Premier. Nu promptly left, but Aung San remained as President of the Union.

They and other student leaders joined a fringe political group, *Do-Bama Asi-Ayone*, 'We Burmans', modelled on Sinn Fein in Ireland. They adopted the prefix of *Thakin*, previously employed exclusively by the British and equivalent to Sahib. Nu found himself the 'treasurer without treasure' in his own words. The party was too poor to pay the electric light bill and their parliamentary wing, *Komin Kochin*, only won three of the 132 seats in the legislature. However, they were not interested in parliamentary politics but in arousing the workers. Their first major venture was to organise a strike amongst the workforce of the Burmah

Oil Company in 1938. Though the strike was broken, the strategy of urban industrial action had been demonstrated.

Leftist Causes

Alongside these activities, Thakin Nu – whose literary leanings were already emerging – set up the *Naga-Ni* or Red Dragon Bookshop just off the university campus to sell the publications of the Left Book Club and also Marxist literature. His associates were Thakin Than Tun and Thakin Soe. Than Tun's background was much the same as that of Aung San and Nu. He was born in 1913 in Toungoo District in central Burma. He went to a village school and to the Teachers' Training College. He worked as a vernacular teacher. Soe was an employee of the Burmah Oil Company. Nu's literary friends included Ko Thant (later Secretary-General of the UN) and Thakin Thein Pe, who achieved early notoriety as author of *Tet Pongyi*, 'The Modern Monk', a satire on decadence in the monastery. He spent some time in Calcutta where he came into contact with the Indian Communist Party. They linked up with the Thakins and in 1939 the embryo of a Burmese Communist Party was formed with Aung San as Secretary-General, Thakin Soe as leader, and H.N. Goshal, a Burma Indian (also known as Thakin Ba Tin), as another early member. Early in 1939, Aung San was arrested for conspiring to overthrow the government. He was soon released. As Communists they followed the Party line only loosely. As we have seen, Aung San had a great admiration for Nehru and in 1940 he attended the annual Congress at Ramgarh, regarded by Communists as bourgeois.

Nu's Solidarity With China

The war in the Far East produced cross-currents among these young radicals. Nu was drawn strongly to the Chinese struggle against Japan and paid a visit to China under KMT auspices. Aung San saw in the Japanese a strength which could overthrow the British Empire. Rangoon was sprinkled with Japanese: ostensibly doctors, dentists and business men, they were actually secret agents. In May 1940 a reporter from a newspaper, *Yomiuri Shimbu*, arrived. He was actually Colonel Suzuki Keiji, known as Minami Matsuo.

Aung San Joins the Japanese (1940)

The CID were not unaware of these activities. They responded by arresting politicians under wartime emergency rules. First they caught the small fish: in July, several Thakins – Than Tun, Soe, and Nu. Then in August a big fish was taken into the net: Dr Ba Maw, the late Premier. A warrant was out for Aung San, but Suzuki helped him and another young Thakin, Hla Myaing, to escape by ship. This was a Chinese vessel which made port in Amoy. There are different versions of how they got to Japan, but eventually they were accepted as useful allies and were sent back to recruit more potential fighters in Rangoon. It is not even clear whether they travelled in a Japanese or a Chinese ship: but either way they made secret contacts with Thakin friends who agreed to accompany them back to Japan. They were given intensive military training on Hainan island prior to going to Thailand in preparation for the invasion of Burma which was at an advanced planning stage.

In Bangkok the little band had a final celebration in December 1941. According to custom, they each contributed blood from their veins to a silver bowl and all drank therefrom. This *thwe-thauk*, or blood drinking, sealed eternal comradeship and they all assumed titles signifying their compact: Aung San became Bo Teza (Fire General), Thakin Shu Maung, a former postal employee, became Bo Ne Win (Sun of Glory General), Hla Pe, who had assisted the first escape, was Bo Let Ya (Right Hand General), while Aung San's first fellow-traveller, Hla Myaing, was Bo Yan Aung. The band became known as the Thirty Comrades, their heroic status reflecting the company gathered round the great king Alaungpaya, although they were 68 in number. Colonel Suzuki also took a Burmese pseudonym as Bo Mogyo (Thunderbolt). The group were accompanied by a slightly older Thakin, Tun Ok (born 1907) who was expected to head the civil government.

Launch of the Burma Independence Army (1942)

The Thirty Comrades entered the southernmost districts of Burma alongside the rapidly advancing Japanese. They recruited their soldiers from the more adventurous or the more unruly on their route. The Japanese tried to control them; Bo Mogyo was in overall command, and 'battalions' were commanded by Japanese. However, the BIA or Burma Independence Army (as it was called) acquired an unenviable reputation for indiscipline. Their worst excesses were committed when they reached the Delta districts where amid the Burmese there were villages of the Karen minority. Treated with contempt by the old Burmese kings, the Karens had welcomed British rule and, probably more important, their best people had become Christians under the influence of the American Baptist missionaries. When the Japanese invaded, most of the population showed indifference, or actively welcomed the invader. The Karens in the army fought them stoutly and the civil population passively resisted. They now felt the retribution of the BIA, whose conduct was aggressive, often violent. Aung San had given them an example in the early stages of the advance when he accorded summary trial to an Indo-Burmese or Muslim-Burmese headman who had assisted the British: Bo Aung San ran him through with a bayonet.

The Japanese High Command pulled out the BIA, sent Colonel Suzuki back to Japan, and finally disbanded his private army in July 1942.

One cause of friction was the discontent of BIA officers over the failure to implement promises of independence made publicly by General Iida of the Japanese army when the BIA first entered Tavoy in the south. Aung San had planned to set up a government at Moulmein, but was put off. Thakin Tun Ok was appointed head of a *baho asoya* or central administration for a brief while until the Japanese turned to Ba Maw, released from Mogok jail, who headed an 'Independence Preparatory Committee'. He called in the veteran politician Ba Pe (his former rival) and also approached some Thakins. In March 1943 Ba Maw paid an official visit to Tokyo accompanied by Aung San. They were invested with Japanese decorations and Aung San was given the rank of Major-General. To the Burmese he was *Bogyoke*, the historic term for general.

Burma's 'Independence' (1943)

All this was in preparation for a proclamation by General Kawabe on 1 August 1943 declaring that Burma was independent, and was at war with Britain and the United States. Ba Maw was named as *Adipadi*, Head of State, with a government which was a mixture of old and young politicians. Aung San became Minister of Defence, Thakin Nu was Foreign Minister and Than Tun was Minister for Agriculture, while Thakin Mya (an older man) was named Deputy Prime Minister. The new government established relations with some countries under Axis control and actually sent an Ambassador to Japan.

In place of the BIA the Japanese now created a Burma National Army (BNA), much smaller in number and under strict Japanese control. Bo Ne Win was named as its commander. Six infantry battalions were organised and a so-called Pom Pom battalion. Discipline was much stricter than in the BIA and face-slapping by Japanese instructors was an everyday occurrence. The best officer material was sent to Japan. The BNA was dressed in Japanese uniform; they were required to salute the Japanese, but not vice versa.

The propaganda value of Japan's 'gift of independence' in the Greater

East Asia Co-Prosperity Sphere was emphasised by a gathering of heads of puppet states in Tokyo in November 1943: besides Ba Maw there were the heads of Manchukuo, Thailand and the Philippines, with Subhas Bose as head of the Free India Government and the unknown 'Prime Minister of China' recognised by Japan.

The politics of collaboration was not accepted without dissent. Nu only joined the government belatedly and reluctantly; he confessed to 'suddenly wake up to find "Made in Japan" printed on his forehead'.[2] Thakin Soe never accepted the occupation and organised a resistance movement with virtually no support from the British. Thakin Thein Pe made his way out to India where he received scant encouragement until he was taken up by the cloak-and-dagger organisation, Force 136, which was desperately trying to justify its mysterious and expensive existence. Burmese agents were infiltrated into Rangoon and returned, reporting early in 1944 the emergence of an anti-Japanese or anti-Fascist movement. Later that year Thein Pe told Force 136 that there were many 'sympathisers' and even some activists; he added 'Thakin Nu is what I may call an active sympathiser. He gave shelter to our party workers.' He concluded, 'Aung San is now brought back to party line. He understands his past mistakes and means to amend them. . . . After all, he is a true patriot. . . . Yes, he is anxiously waiting for the word from us.'[3] The Japanese were increasingly suspicious of their Burmese supporters; they even organised the assassination of Ba Maw which however, misfired. This year of 1944 saw the supreme Japanese effort to break the deadlock which had bogged down the Burma front. A series of attacks were launched in March, with the main thrust into the Manipur plain. Bose committed his INA to the attack with the slogan *Chalo Delhi* ('Delhi here we come'). The attack was broken; 50 000 Japanese troops died in the operation while the fighting spirit of the INA was destroyed. The BNA was assigned duties in the rear areas. Aung San observed the disaster with an appraising eye. This was the turn-around in the fortunes of the war.

The Japanese Retreat (1945)

The forces under Mountbatten as Supreme Allied Commander were launched into Upper Burma and into Arakan. After fierce fighting, Mandalay was captured (20 March 1945). Aung San got through a message that he was ready to come over to the Allies while the Japanese understood that he would be fighting for them. The rising was timed for 10 April, but because of the speed of the British advance was put forward to 27 March. Instead of moving against the British they disappeared into

the jungle and their *Bogyoke* announced, 'We are now at war' – at war with
Japan. Simultaneously, Than Tun – touring central Burma – went
underground in his native Toungoo. He was contacted by a mission from
Force 136 who did not find him cooperative. The most effective
operations against the Japanese were launched by the Karens of the
border hills who had never given up, awaiting the British return. They
virtually wiped out a Japanese division.

Before he departed, Aung San wrote a farewell letter to Ba Maw, 'My
dear Adipadigyi'. Cryptically he said, 'I shall be coming back to Rangoon
and if conditions do not worsen so unexpectedly I hope to meet you
again.' He went on:

> These are dark days for us. The Japanese troops are withdrawing . . .
> and I shall not be surprised if, before monsoon, the war in Burma is
> over. . . . I have every confidence that our cause will win ultimately,
> war or no war, peace or no peace, the struggle for our national
> independence must go on till it ends in victory. . . . Meantime I wish
> you to be prepared for the worst.[4]

The worst happened when British-Indian forces took over Rangoon on 3
May. The Japanese army had pulled out on 23 April, taking Ba Maw
along with them; Thakin Nu and his wife also went along. Thakin Nu's
journey ended near Moulmein, but Ba Maw pressed on and finally
reached Tokyo where he went into hiding, eventually surrendering to the
Allied occupation authorities.

Aung San Confronts the British

Meanwhile, the senior British military commanders were at cross-
purposes over the treatment to be accorded to the BNA and the resistance
identified as the AFO (Anti-Fascist Organisation). Force 136 asked
permission to arm the AFO. The military advice given to Mountbatten
was that they should not be armed, but he overruled this and gave his
recognition to the AFO. He had to tell London what he was doing, and
this was not easy. In the prevailing atmosphere, those who had
collaborated with Japan were traitors. Mountbatten thought otherwise:
he was strongly under the influence of his Cambridge friend Peter
Murphy, a Communist, whom he had added to his staff. He justified his
policy to the Chiefs of Staff by arguing, 'We shall be doing no more than
what has been done in Italy . . . in turning people who were
satellites . . . into co-belligerents.'

The Cabinet were much less happy about this, as were Mountbatten's own staff: however, General Slim, in command of 14th Army, showed more understanding, declaring (19 April): 'Help already given by BNA has gone long way towards expiation of political crimes.' The Civil Affairs Service, formed to provide a military administration and recruited mainly from British civil servants ejected from Burma, objected strongly to this policy. So did the Governor, the ex-Cabinet Minister, Sir Reginald Dorman-Smith, when he heard what was happening. Slim continued to support Mountbatten. With the campaign against the Japanese army still raging he observed, 'We have in Burma a potentially dangerous situation . . . not dissimilar to that which developed in Southern Ireland after the [last] war.'

Eventually, when Rangoon was won, Aung San crossed over to meet General Slim. He claimed to represent a Provisional Government of Burma whose President was Thakin Soe. Slim informed him that 'he and his army have no legal status'. This meeting took place just when the AFO was passing a series of resolutions which demanded the 'right of self-determination . . . forthwith' and the organisation of a national army. Dorman-Smith cabled in alarm protesting against 'even semblance of recognition' for Aung San's claims. Mountbatten tried to reassure him, but added, 'I foresee having to fight a civil war against 10 000 armed Burmese soldiers at a time when it is vital that my forces should be better employed.' He inquired whether Dorman-Smith had 'alternative sugges-tions'?[5]

Just one day after the Slim–Aung San meeting, a Statement of Policy was given to the House of Commons (issued as a White Paper). This emphasised that after military government was terminated the civil Governor would return to function as sole authority until December 1948. Thereafter, a general election would take place and the legislators would be invited to draw up a new constitution on Dominion lines. Even then, the hill areas occupied by the frontier tribes would remain under 'a special regime under the Governor'.[6] This uninviting prospect was offered to a people who, in name at any rate, had tasted independence.

Communist Leadership in National Movement

The AFO now called itself the Anti-Fascist People's Freedom League (AFPFL) and its general secretary and political spokesman was Thakin Than Tun. He issued statements cast in tones of reason, doubtless to reassure the British. If Mountbatten was worried about a possible rising, the AFPFL had cause to be worried about British repression. Trained members of the BNA numbered 7000 at most, and the forces under Mountbatten (not all in Burma, of course) numbered one million. A rising could be put down; even though the BNA might dissolve into guerrilla bands it could not hope to take over the country. Than Tun continued to call for a national government but made it clear that armed struggle was, for the present, not envisaged. The message was 'cooperation'.

Aung San Protects his Burma National Army

During these months the main concern of Aung San was the future of his BNA: Mountbatten announced that all the men considered suitable would be enlisted in a newly-raised army on British lines. The intention was to distribute the men of the BNA (now called Patriot Burmese Forces: PBF) as individuals among the new battalions. Those unfit would be demobilised. Those against whom criminal offences were proved would be tried. This programme held no appeal to Aung San who saw his army as his main weapon in the demand for independence. Meeting after meeting was held at which he found reasons for further delay.

Meanwhile, the campaign in Burma was coming to an end with the virtual extermination of the Japanese forces trying to escape over the Sittang river. Mountbatten now faced the precarious venture of a seaborne invasion of Malaya and Singapore, but just as this was launched came the news of the atomic bomb and the Japanese surrender. Mountbatten's task was not simplified when General MacArthur saddled him with the additional responsibility of taking over Indonesia and Indo-China, previously within the American sphere. Moreover, the new Labour government was anxious to speed up the demobilisation of British servicemen. Mountbatten was heavily dependent on the formations of the Indian Army under his command; he had no wish for a trial of strength with Aung San.

With the Japanese surrender, Dorman-Smith pressed the new Labour Government for the return of civil administration to Burma. He issued an ultimatum: unless there was an early return, he would resign. The Burmese also were quick to realise that a new situation had emerged. Than Tun stepped up the propaganda campaign to end military government. A mass conference was convened to formulate demands and some 5000 or 6000 attended. Shops in Rangoon were closed. It was a symbol of the new mood in the country that ordinary people wanted to participate in politics whereas in the past protest had been expressed through local guerrilla risings and religious demonstrations. The mass rally now became a powerful expression of national feeling. What became known as the Naythuyein Mass Meeting heard Aung San speak about the Burmese contribution to the Allied cause; he saw Labour's victory as a sign that imperialism was on the way out and he affirmed that '99 per cent of the PBF would be unwilling to serve in the fighting forces of a country that was not free'. Hesitant when speaking in English, Aung San was eloquent, even verbose, in Burmese. Than Tun followed, presenting a manifesto, 'World Peace and Free Burma', in which he proposed the immediate establishment of a Provisional Government. The contribution of these two speakers was significant: Aung San supplied the inspiration, Than Tun produced a programme. Which was to prove more important?

Trying to sort out the problems posed by Dorman-Smith and the BNA, Mountbatten arranged a high-level meeting at Kandy, attended by the British military top brass and Aung San, Than Tun and other representatives of the former BNA and the AFPFL. At a preliminary meeting of the British commanders Slim bluntly observed that 'the root of the trouble lay in the fact that the Burmese distrusted us'. However, it seemed as though agreement had been reached when Aung San and Than Tun signed the so-called Kandy Agreement on 7 September, whereby the BNA/PBF would be embodied in the regular army as separate units under their own officers. The new Burma Army would have a British Inspector-General and two Deputies, one from the PBF and one from the ethnic minorities who had made such an important contribution to harassing the Japanese. Mountbatten tried to tempt *Bogyoke* with the post of Deputy Inspector-General and the British rank of Brigadier: he was too shrewd to be side-tracked in that way. He was not ambitious for British rank.

Dorman-Smith also came to Kandy (though he refused to meet the BNA and AFPFL leaders). Somewhat reluctantly Mountbatten agreed to hand over the administration in Burma the following month. When Attlee was consulted he wrote, 'There is an obvious risk in moving so fast', but he acquiesced.

The Civil Governor Resists the New Nationalists

On his return to Rangoon in mid-October, Dorman-Smith announced that he would go further than the 17 May statement: he would appoint an advisory council. He invited the AFPFL to submit names, but when they demanded the right to nominate a bloc of their own people to the council he rejected their terms and chose his own council from among superannuated pre-war politicians. Later he was able to bring in the malcontent Thakin, Tun Ok. The Governor conducted negotiations with AFPFL through intermediaries. This was typical of his aloof, olympian style. The main go-between was U Tin Tut, the senior Burmese member of the ICS. He was trusted by Dorman-Smith and increasingly he won the confidence of Aung San. However, he could not bring the two sides together. Dorman-Smith was advised by his Private Secretary and others that AFPFL was going to split into factions. This was not totally without justification: there were signs of tension between Aung San and Than Tun supported by the Communists.

A decision which was to affect future events in Burma was now concluded in New Delhi. British Indian forces had been despatched to Java as part of Mountbatten's directive to disarm the Japanese and rescue allied prisoners of war. As we shall find, they became embroiled in the nationalist struggle. Mountbatten, Wavell, and Auchinleck as the Commander-in-Chief India were deeply concerned about the effect this would have on Indian national feeling. At an Inter-Command conference it was decided that if a similar situation emerged in Burma the Governor should be warned that Indian troops would not be available to quell a national rising. Mountbatten hoped this would stimulate a sense of urgency from Dorman-Smith, but he was not stirred. Even a danger that spelled immediate trouble was allowed to simmer. Aung San's action in bayoneting a headman in 1942 now became known. The Governor referred the question to the Cabinet, who advised that if there were 'a strong *prima facie* case . . . proceedings would have to be instituted'.[7] Having obtained this ruling the Governor did nothing. He seems to have supposed things were quietening down: 'Aung San is a tired and deflated little man', he told London.

Mass Mobilisation

However, the AFPFL was far from inactive. In mid-November another mass meeting reaffirmed the Naythuyein resolutions and called for the dissolution of the recently formed Governor's Council. An All-Burma Congress of the AFPFL was held in the precincts of the great Shwe Dagon pagoda, 17−23 January. According to Than Tun there were 100 000 present at the open sessions, while even the Governor's Secretary admitted that numbers were 'some 20−30 000'. This was quite an achievement for an organisation only a few months old. The keynote speech was delivered by Aung San, who accused the Governor of economic Fascism: 'the Governor is the dictator of Burma.'

Besides mobilising thousands in mass rallies, thus involving the common people as Gandhi had done in India in 1921 and 1931 and somewhat chaotically in 1942 (but not in the final tussle for power) Aung

San also constructed a power base in the People's Volunteer Organisation or PVO (in Burmese, *Pyithu Yebaw Tat*). Some 5000 former members of the BNA were now enlisted in the regular army, but this left thousands more outside, restless and discontented. They were given uniforms; there was a rudimentary organisation; they practised drilling and, in secrecy, weapons training. Early in 1946 there were over 150 units or *Tats* with nearly 6500 members. The Code, or Rules of Conduct, commanded that 'Duties . . . shall be faithfully and strictly carried out with an iron will, ready to meet death.'[8]

During these months, Thakin Nu withdrew from active politics and retired to a little town (or large village) in the Delta, Moulmeingyun, where he was writing a book called *What is Marxism?* He did make a visit to Rangoon, either in December 1945 or January 1946, when he called on the Governor who noted on a draft 'Nu snubbed'. He also brought together Aung San and Than Tun, for he was worried about the obvious rift between them.[9] Although married to sisters (the daughters of a Christian), the two men were temperamentally quite different. Than Tun – often called the 'brains' of the League – was methodical, well-organised, even-tempered and versed in international Marxism. Aung San was moody, given to long silences and sudden outbursts, eloquent in rhetoric, impetuous, erratic: and a hero to the people. The two were actually complementary in what they had to offer, but increasingly differences emerged. Nu's efforts to bring the two men together were only partially successful.

The position of Thakin Soe, who had the longest record of underground resistance, was even more unclear. Supposedly he was in disgrace for an affair with a female student (the AFPFL, and particularly the Communists, were strictly puritanical) but he was preaching a stiffer line against the British than any of the others. Finally, in March 1946, Soe's group broke away to form the 'Red Flags' (as they were called), while Than Tun's following were known as the 'White Flags'.

Aung San Accused of Murder

A potentially explosive element was introduced when Thakin Tun Ok publicly accused Aung San of the headman's murder, and his widow petitioned the Governor for justice. Belatedly, Dorman-Smith sought London's permission to prosecute, and at first Attlee – in charge of the affairs of Burma while Pethick-Lawrence was in India with the Cabinet Mission – agreed that the law must take its course. However, when Pethick-Lawrence was informed he objected: a prosecution might prejudice their discussions with Indian leaders. Dorman-Smith was ordered to hold back. There followed a frantic exchange of telegrams between Rangoon and Whitehall in which the Governor offered various solutions to the prevailing deadlock, finally coming up with the unexpected suggestion that a new coalition ministry was possible with Paw Tun, the last premier of Burma before the invasion; U Saw, his predecessor as premier, an unscrupulous schemer who had been interned for dealing with the Japanese; and Aung San, previously portrayed by Dorman-Smith as a murderer and an enemy.

Confusion Over the Murder Charge

Now he wanted to promote this triple alliance: he told Attlee, 'The iron appears to me to be hot. With what force do you think I should strike?'[10] This was the last straw for Attlee. Dorman-Smith's erratic behaviour had exasperated him already. On 7 May 1946 he cabled Pethick-Lawrence: 'It is obvious he has lost [his] grip. He changes his position from day to day. I am convinced he must be replaced.' The Governor was instructed to return.

The AFPFL renewed their demand at a meeting of the Supreme Council of the League, 16–23 May. They condemned the Governor's 'unrepresentative, powerless Executive Council'; they demanded a real national government; and in case of the demand not being met, they signalled a 'freedom struggle' and empowered the Supreme Council to take all necessary actions. As before, Dorman-Smith belittled the demands of Aung San; a 'definitely puzzled man' he was called. However, the next move indicated that the political temperature was rising fast.

The Governor Defied, and Replaced

The PVO increased its show of strength, choosing as a special focus the little town of Tantabin, 40 miles from Rangoon, where the first BNA action against the Japanese had been staged in 1945. There were parades on 13, 14 and 15 May 1946. Dummy rifles were carried. On 18 May a procession of 1000 to 1500 persons marched in defiance, beating drums and carrying flags. The police and the Burmese magistrate in charge ordered them to disperse, and then fired, killing three and wounding others. Afterwards 81 were arrested. Dorman-Smith, yielding to Aung San's personal intervention on 23 May, ordered release of the detainees: this was against the advice of his Chief Secretary. Subsequently Dorman-Smith agreed that the ring-leaders, 50 in number, *should* be prosecuted.

All this reinforced Attlee's determination to get a new governor installed as soon as possible.

The arrival of Sir Henry Knight, a senior member of the ICS, not a political appointment, created an interval for reassessment. It was known that his was a temporary posting. At first it was conjectured that Dorman-Smith had gone to London to obtain a new policy, but on 5 August it was announced that he had resigned 'for health reasons' and was to be succeeded by Major-General Sir Hubert Rance, whom Mountbatten had appointed in May 1945 to head his military administration after he fell out with the Civil Affairs officers who wanted to get rid of Aung San.

During his brief period as Governor, Knight did his best to boost the sagging morale of the civil service, and also to improve the flow of imports. He found an ingenious legal device to eliminate the possibility of Aung San facing prosecution, thus clearing the way for his being invited to join the Executive Council. More controversially he outlawed Thakin Soe's Communist Party because of its armed threat to government as well as to rice production in the Delta districts. Thakin Thein Pe exerted himself to bring the two Communist parties together again, on the grounds that both 'Had a common object . . . in contesting British imperialism'. Knight asked Aung San to meet him on 9 August; he looked 'very thin'. He told the Governor that 'Rance *must* come out with a new policy, with proposals that go beyond the White Paper [of May 1945]. . . . If not, it is no use his coming.' Knight passed this on to London, but in actuality when the Cabinet approved a 'Line of Policy for Sir H. Rance' this began by stating the objective as: 'To secure within the scope of the White Paper of 1945 and the Act of 1935 an Executive Council more representative and broader based'. He was told not to promise any date for attainment of Dominion status: 'There is no advantage in fixing paper dates', and he was even told not to use the term Dominion status and on no account to make any reference to independence. Armed with these unpromising instructions he arrived and assumed his post on 31 August 1946.

Aung San Outfaces the Communists

During the last days of Knight's governorship there was a significant change within the central management of the AFPFL. As General Secretary, Than Tun had held an important policy-making role. Now the Supreme Council of the League elected a new General Secretary, the moderate Socialist Kyaw Nyein. He received 52 votes while the Communist candidate, Thein Pe, got only 33 votes. Aung San was consolidating his overall position.

The New Governor Walks into a Crisis

In his first speech Rance acknowledged, 'I have not returned to Burma prepared to announce epoch-making changes.' Changes were on the way; but not because the British government or the Governor initiated them. Dorman-Smith and Knight had managed to stone-wall for almost a year; largely because *Bogyoke* was occupied in building up his power base. Now that he was secure he could begin to take action. However, crisis was precipitated by an event outside the AFPFL. On 5 September the Rangoon police went on strike, demanding better pay. Their grievances were genuine: Knight had negotiated a temporary settlement but now their union called them out. Rance quickly decided that the Executive Council he had inherited from Dorman-Smith was useless while most of the senior British officials seemed to lack any ideas. As regards the political solution, Rance told Pethick-Lawrence, 'I'm playing a lone hand here.' Rance sought an early meeting with Aung San, but he replied that he was sick with dysentery. Seeking to interpret the political aspect of the strike, Rance concluded that the veteran Ba Pe was manipulating the policy: 'I suspect he is Aung San's evil genius.' Was this illness real, or assumed in order to gain time? When Rance gave an interview to U Saw, the former premier, on 12 September he told the Governor that he did not consider Aung San 'a strong character, as initially he was controlled by Than Tun and now he was in the pocket of U Ba Pe'. Regarding his illness, Saw commented 'that this conformed to his idea of Aung San's character . . . [he will] always be sick when anything big is on hand'. Future events were to disprove U Saw's analysis.

Rance was convinced that a change of policy was necessary: he told Pethick-Lawrence, 'we are in one big morass here which has to be cleared'. London agreed that he should offer AFPFL improved terms of entry into the Council. This was against the threat of the strike spreading throughout the public services.

Perhaps this prospect also worried Aung San. At any rate he wrote to Rance (17 September): 'I am worried about the whole situation deteriorating throughout the country. . . . Here I am, helpless in bed, and I must remain quiet, God alone knows how long. I feel I must meet you instantly.' Rather quaintly, the Governor observed that it was 'strange' for a Buddhist, 'although not perhaps a practising one', to invoke the name of God; he concluded that Aung San's wife, Khin Kyi, with her Christian upbringing inspired this: Rance went to their house at nightfall under conditions of secrecy. Rance tried to convince Aung San of British goodwill but he replied that when Dorman-Smith had first returned 'there was more goodwill being shown by Burmese to the British than ever before'. He alleged that Dorman-Smith had repelled them: 'down came the iron curtain'. Concerning the current strike he declared 'AFPFL originally had nothing to do with it but now they were backing it and he was finding difficulty in restraining some of his party from adding fuel to the fire.' Thakin Soe was 'very active and the country might well swing in that direction'.

Rance departed feeling 'more hopeful'. Aung San's combination of terms for possible cooperation with hints of possible insurrection was shrewdly devised. While the Governor felt his way towards a political solution, military intelligence feared 'open rebellion'. In view of the embargo on the employment of Indian troops to suppress Burmese nationalism, the Acting Supreme Commander South-East Asia informed the Chiefs of Staff that substantial British reinforcements must be despatched from Malaya, weakening the position in that territory whose rubber was much more important to Britain than Burma's rice: and incidentally delaying the troops' repatriation and demobilisation, a politically sensitive issue.

As an unwanted distraction, an attempt was made to assassinate U Saw on 21 September: he was not killed, but his sight was badly impaired. Ba Pe blamed 'Those damned Communists', but Saw firmly believed that Aung San was responsible and stored up a grudge against him.

Aung San Assumes Lead in New Council

Rance reached agreement with *Bogyoke* on the composition of a new Executive Council. The AFPFL did not get things all their way: they had to accept six seats on the new Council (no better than Dorman-Smith had offered the previous year). However, Aung San obtained the Defence portfolio (previously supervised by the Governor) and was Deputy Chairman of the Council: exactly as Nehru had just become in Wavell's Council. This was vitally important to the Burmese who attached the utmost importance to keeping up with India in constitutional advances. Like Congress in India the AFPFL secured the key Home ministry. Besides the six AFPFL members, U Saw was given a minor post. Thakin Ba Sein, the first leader of *Do-Bama Asi-Ayone*, who had fallen out with the younger Thakins and formed a rival party, came in. Most important was the inclusion of U Tin Tut, no longer in the ICS, who was given the vital Finance ministry. He was regarded as an independent, but increasingly he became Aung San's adviser, supplying the inside knowledge of British forms of government and administration which *Bogyoke* lacked.

Among the AFPFL nominees was just one Communist: Thakin Thein Pe. This reflected the changed balance of power. The first task was to deal with the strikers, and Aung San achieved this at considerable cost. When the settlement was negotiated the Communists attempted to prolong the strike, but with limited success. Rance noted, 'There is no doubt Communists are out to embarrass AFPFL as much as possible' (21 October). The AFPFL members of the Council therefore came up with an announcement intended for public consumption as much as for adoption by the Council. This laid down a future programme in which, among the many proposals, they called for Burma's recognition within the family of nations and admission to the UN, and finally 'the establishment of a sovereign state in the very near future'. Should these objectives not be realised 'we shall not hesitate to resign'.

Break With the Communists

At a conference of the Supreme Council of AFPFL commencing on 1 November, Aung San made the inaugural speech. His main target was again British imperialism, and he compared Burma with India where a 'Divide and Rule' policy had 'estranged' Hindus and Muslims. Burma was 'in a politically stronger position' though 'in bad shape, economically and financially'. At this meeting the differences between the Council-entry portion of AFPFL and the Communists at last reached breaking-point. The Communist attack was led by Thakin Chit, formerly of *Do-Bama*, who taunted Aung San's following as the 'Dominion Status AFPFL'. Trades union leaders supported the Communists and Thein Pe made what was called 'a humorous speech': he commended Aung San 'to the care of worthy guardian angels like Thakin Nu, Thakin Kyaw Nyein and U Ba Pe'. It would appear that this advice was sarcastic.

Than Tun wound up; 'He solemnly stated that the time for parting of the ways had verily come.' When he had finished the Communists walked out, and were then expelled by unanimous decision. In the enormously long statement which followed the Communists were branded as 'Vipers in the bosom'. The AFPFL were left to prove that they had not sold out.

Demand for Independence within One Year

In a memorandum drafted by Tin Tut detailed demands were advanced: in effect that Burma's political advance would be in step with that in India. Rance urged the Cabinet to accept the need for a new policy but the unhelpful response was 'do your best to put the brakes on'. The AFPFL raised their demands in a statement made public on 13 November: the British Government must announce before 31 January 1947 that Burma would be free within one year. Because the Cabinet still hesitated, the AFPFL insisted on further concessions: the next election must choose a Constituent Assembly 'for the whole of Burma'. Under the 1935 Act the hill areas were excluded from the political process. Rance told London that the 'Time for equivocation is past. In my opinion HMG must now be prepared to be definite or accept the consequences.' These consequences were spelled out by Field Marshal Montgomery to the Cabinet: 'The situation might require up to two [British] Divisions. These did not now exist.'[11] Reluctantly the Cabinet acquiesced. They had just experienced the utterly fruitless meeting with Nehru and Jinnah: it was not a good moment to turn down the Burmese. Rance's proposal to ask an AFPFL delegation to come to London for discussions was accepted, and Attlee informed parliament that they would 'hasten forward the time when Burma shall realise her independence'. The policy enunciated as recently as August 1946 was now scrapped in December.

Nu's Political Comeback

While these momentous changes were happening, Thakin Nu was installed as Vice-President and Treasurer of the AFPFL. Aung San overcame his plea that he just wanted to go on writing and brought him to Rangoon. Nu regretted the break with the Communists, but accepted that it was inevitable. He later claimed that he initiated the demand for independence within one year: he asserted that he saw the Governor who promised to pass on his message to London. But Rance sent no such report. What does seem clear is that Nu was one of the hardliners: he was suspicious of the British Government's intentions, particularly with regard to keeping the Frontier Areas apart on 'Divide and Rule' lines.

When the delegation for London was selected, Aung San was automatically leader. Tin Tut went along as his adviser and draftsman. Besides the AFPFL delegates (who also included old Ba Pe and Thakin Mya, Home Member) there were two from other parties: U Saw and Ba Sein. Presumably Rance wanted to emphasise the 'All-Party' nature of the group. Kyaw Nyein went along as an Adviser, and Rance also wanted Thakin Nu to go: he was, he told London, 'The most important member of AFPFL Working Committee excluding Aung San' (29 December), but he remained behind to give direction to the League while the others were in London. If the discussions did not go well it would be his responsibility to organise 'mass struggles and freedom fights'.

Aung San travelled separately from the others, stopping over in Delhi to confer with Nehru who warned him to examine the British proposal 'with particular care . . . and not to be caught by it as I was'.[12] The *Bogyoke* had lunch with Lord Wavell who recognised him as 'a strong character' but also warned Pethick-Lawrence that their negotiations would be difficult: 'He struck me as a suspicious, ignorant but determined little tough.'[13] While in India Aung San gave a press conference where he snapped out that he was 'Hoping for the best but prepared for the worst'.

Negotiations in London (January 1947)

Among those Cabinet Ministers entrusted with the discussions the view was expressed that in talking to the Burmese they would not encounter 'the purely "Bazaar approach". The more frankly we could discuss with them the better.' They were still bruised from the Nehru–Jinnah encounter! The talks lasted from 13–27 January 1947, with ten formal meetings and a lavish exchange of memoranda. A mood of trust began to emerge, and an agreed formula began to evolve, although the concessions were mainly from the British. A sticking-point seemed to be the Burmese demand for the Frontier areas to be brought into the constitutional process. Attlee and his colleagues clung to the established view that the Frontier peoples were a special British responsibility which could not be abandoned.

Eventually agreement was reached that a Committee of Enquiry composed equally of AFPFL members and representatives of the hill peoples would ascertain their true wishes. Cripps drafted the agreement with his customary dexterity in skating round tricky corners, and they all met to finalise the agreement on Sunday evening, 26 January. At the beginning, Aung San sprang a surprise: they wanted the British to sign, while they waited until they returned to Burma to signify their agreement. However, this was too much for Attlee and Cripps: they flatly declared, 'Unless agreed conclusions were reached there was no point in negotiating.' The startled Burmese team withdrew, and returned saying they would endeavour to join in agreed conclusions. A last-minute hiccup remained; U Saw and Ba Sein announced that they could not sign, but Aung San brushed this aside: 'Let them resign and say they do not agree with the final statement and do not accept any responsibility for it.'[14]

Next day the agreement was signed by Attlee and Aung San and the delegation departed: apart from the two dissidents they were well satisfied.

Meanwhile, Burma waited uneasily. Nu had told Kyaw Nyein to send him a one-word message when the end was reached: 'Orange' would mean success, 'Lemon' would indicate the failure of the talks; but there were neither oranges nor lemons. In Rangoon Nu announced: 'AFPFL is not calling for a general strike among workers at the present time. But should the fight start there will be country-wide strikes involving all classes of workers.'

The Red Flag Communists did not threaten: they acted. On 13 January a mob stormed the Secretariat, the headquarters of the administration. The police responded with their *lathis*, iron-bound staves, and the Communists were arrested and expelled. Nu commented, 'The public got fed up with Communists' rowdyism. . . . Press and public do not take the incident seriously'; however, five days later all public services in Rangoon came to a standstill at AFPFL behest and most shops and bazaars were closed. Clearly, Nu was barely in control. On 21 January the Communists numbering up to 3000 made another assault on the Secretariat and were again repulsed. The reply by the AFPFL members of Council was to demand that the Red Flags should be banned. Rance remained uneasy. Despite their differences it seemed likely that if no result was reported by 31 January the AFPFL and Communists would both revolt. Before news of the agreement could be circulated a rebellion did start in three districts: Myaungmya, Magwe and Tavoy. AFPFL envoys were hastily flown to these places to persuade them to stop. Chaos had been averted, though strikes in the public services sputtered on.

Leaders of the Hill Peoples Accommodated

Aung San's return did much to calm the situation. He claimed that AFPFL demands had been conceded in full. The tide was flowing strongly his way. His next triumph was to secure agreement from important Frontier leaders to an agreed constitutional solution. The hill peoples were sending their representatives to a gathering at Panglong in the Shan States. Aung San suspected that this meeting would be 'fixed' by the British to prolong the status quo. Nu said openly that, 'although the London agreement looked very well on paper he strongly suspected that HMG had first of all made sure that the frontier peoples would not agree to any form of union with Burma'. However, *Bogyoke* went up to Panglong and discovered that the more shrewd and realistic Frontier leaders had grasped that a new political situation was emerging. The Shans and Kachins claimed their own states within a Union of Burma: this was accepted. The Chins were content to receive a 'Special Division'. Only the Karens remained outside this atmosphere of unity. Along with the Frontier leaders, Aung San signed a special Panglong Agreement on 14 February. The hill peoples would be associated with the constitutional process.

Resounding Election Victory

The time for the general election was approaching. With Aung San riding high the AFPFL had almost no opposition. The White Flag Communists contested 13 of the 91 general constituencies (each returning two MPs) and won in three of them. No other party risked ignominious defeat. The 176 AFPFL MPs included every important figure, save one. Thirty MPs prefixed their names with *Bo*, indicating that they had been in the BNA and were now active in the PVO. With support from the MPs chosen from the Frontier areas AFPFL was unassailable.

Thakin Nu was the one prominent leader to stay out of the Assembly. He flatly rejected the pleas of Aung San to stand for election. One who did put up was Ba Pe, but Aung San was nauseated by his persisting with the corrupt practices which had disfigured pre-war parliamentary politics: and anyway his usefulness was exhausted. Ba Pe was sacked from the Cabinet early in May: Aung San told the public that his Ministers 'enjoyed an untarnished reputation for incorruptibility and honesty of purpose [and] should not be made to suffer on account of anyone who strayed from the path'. Soon after, Ba Pe resigned from the Assembly.

Aung San's Lifestyle

The *Bogyoke* certainly lived up to his words. A Reuter correspondent wrote of meeting him:

> Squatting on a chair in the barely furnished living room of his modest residence. . . . A few hard wood and cane chairs around an ordinary round table and a small flower pot with withered wild flowers were the only furniture in the room. The walls were bare, the floor uncarpeted. . . . Aung San . . . wore only a plain white singlet and a multi-coloured *lungyi*. . . . Now talking fast and excitedly, now seeming absorbed in thought, Aung San discussed Burmese politics for nearly two hours. The cares of office and the strain of political campaigning seemed to have left their mark on him.[15]

There was much to do. He informed Attlee (13 May) that independence must be attained 'early in 1948' (Attlee had already announced that

Britain was leaving India before June 1948). The next move was to bring forward the draft of the new constitution: the first that the Secretary of State knew of this was when he read a report in *The Times* (20 May) headed 'A Republic of Burma'. The draft was unveiled to a Convention of the AFPFL members of the new Assembly in Jubilee Hall, 20–23 May. The first clause proclaimed that Burma would be 'an independent sovereign republic'. This put paid to British hopes that Burma would stay in the Commonwealth as a Dominion owing allegiance to the Crown. Winding up the Convention, *Bogyoke* claimed that they were framing 'a new type of democratic government that best suited the Burmese'; it was largely drawn from Yugoslavia. He admitted 'time alone would prove whether or not the form chosen was the best'. He was working for unity among all the peoples of their country and he hoped this would lead to 'the complete unity of all South East Asia countries'.

All this was news to Rance, for although Burma was not formally independent he had been excluded from decision making since the Attlee–Aung San Agreement had transferred virtually all power to the Council, functioning as a Cabinet. The British had never envisaged such a rapid build-up to this situation: India's constitution was not finalised until 1950, while Pakistan had to wait until 1956 for its soon-overthrown constitution!

Nu becomes President of Constituent Assembly

At this juncture, the MP for Mergui was travelling to his distant constituency when he was drowned at sea. Aung San renewed his appeal to Nu to come in. He asked for time to consider, but this was brushed aside and Nu, willynilly, became MP for Mergui, a place he had never previously visited. It was natural that he should be President of the Constituent Assembly when it met. First, however, he was chosen to lead another mission to London.

The Burmese had appeared content with the constitutional timetable until Mountbatten's announcement that India and Pakistan would become independent – as Dominions – in mid-August. They had always attached importance to keeping level with India, and now they renewed the pressure. It was explained that the Dominion status option was open to them, with the same timetable as India; but if they became a republic this would require more contentious legislation and the negotiation of an Anglo-Burmese Treaty. Nu's task in London was somehow to keep the republic, while securing constitutional concessions. He found Attlee and his colleagues friendly, but unyielding. Nu advanced the ingenious suggestion that instead of the existing Commonwealth structure there should be a federation of Socialist states. Attlee dismissed the suggestion as neither 'desirable or feasible'. All Nu could secure was agreement that the 'Interim Government' of Burma would be called the 'Provisional Government' and the Members of the Executive Council would be Ministers, and their chief recognised as Prime Minister. With these cosmetic concessions he returned. Almost immediately he confronted the biggest crisis of his political life.

Aung San Assassinated: Nu becomes Premier

On 19 July, gunmen burst into the Council chamber where Aung San was holding a cabinet meeting. Aung San, his deputy Prime Minister, Thakin Mya, and five other Ministers were murdered. One of the gunmen had been instructed to kill Thakin Nu, who was elsewhere, but he could not bring himself to slay this man known for his religious piety. The Cabinet already suspected that U Saw was planning some act of retaliation (he resigned on returning from London and did not attempt to contest the election). Arrested the same day, Saw was found to have concealed large stocks of arms and ammunition in sealed containers in the lake near his house.

It emerged that these had been supplied from British army depots on indents supposedly from the police. Certain British officers had been friendly with Saw, while Military Intelligence had been indicating since May that Saw was planning to seize power. All this encouraged many Burmese to believe that British interests were behind the assassinations. Fortunately the Governor seized the initiative and the same day called on Nu to take over as Prime Minister. Nu built his team around the nucleus of surviving Ministers. Bo Let Ya became his Deputy, responsible for Defence, Kyaw Nyein became Home Minister and Tin Tut took on Finance; this appointment, Rance commented, 'is certainly speeding things up'.

Nu made his first priority his public insistence of confidence in the Governor and the British Government. He pressed on with measures to stiffen national security by recruiting ten battalions of auxiliary armed police (many from the PVO). An early decision was a Defence Agreement with the United Kingdom (29 August) whereby a British military mission would help to train and equip the armed forces: no other foreign power would provide military assistance. Nu returned to his old idea that a reconciliation with Than Tun and the White Flags could be arranged: it did not work. Another major concern was the continuing estrangement of the leaders of the Karens. Early in September the Secretary of State (now Lord Listowel) paid a brief visit with the dual object of tidying up loose threads in Britain's future relationship with Burma while also endeavouring to mediate between the AFPFL government and the Karens, who still attached great importance to the British connection. Despite conciliatory moves by Thakin Nu, and earnest pleas from Listowel, the Karens could not even be brought to agree among themselves.

The Constituent Assembly now finalised the provisions of the Constitution, enacted on 24 September. In his speech proposing its adoption, Nu declared that the regime would be leftist, but he warned against the people expecting that a new millennium would dawn on the morrow. Though he claimed all the peoples of Burma were now united he admitted that this unity 'is only in the initial stages . . . tender and fragile'.[16]

Nu Signs Independence Treaty

Accompanied by a delegation of his Cabinet colleagues, Nu arrived in London on 15 October for a treaty ceremony to ratify the end of British rule. Much still remained to be settled, but the treaty was signed at 10 Downing Street on 17 October by Attlee and Nu for the two countries. Article 1 read: 'The Government of the United Kingdom recognises the Republic of the Union of Burma as a fully independent State.' The necessary legislation went through Parliament in November, despite Churchill summoning the Conservatives to oppose the Bill. Independence Day was fixed for 4 January 1948.

Thakin Nu made yet another attempt to bring the White Flag Communists back into the AFPFL. This was repulsed, though Than Tun claimed that they desired unity which was the wish of the masses: 'The Rightists of the AFPFL submitted to the Imperialists in the Nu–Attlee Treaty, now also they are doing the same in discarding the Communist Party.' He concluded by claiming that the Communists 'have adhered to our principles of AFPFL'.

Post-Independence Dangers

A further danger threatened. A large part of the PVO inclined towards the Communists. An attempt was made to accommodate them by founding a Marxist League, of Socialists and PVO. It was against this uneasy background that independence was celebrated in a brief euphoria which all too soon evaporated. Nu had indicated his intention to retire from office six months after independence, but events made that impossible. At the end of March, Than Tun made a defiant speech in Rangoon's Bandoola Square and then vanished, setting up an underground resistance based on Toungoo. Soe was already in revolt in the Delta. Nu replied by promoting yet another Leftist unity programme. There was no response; instead a major part of the PVO went underground while all the former BNA battalions of the army except that commanded by Ne Win mutinied and joined the rebels. Nu was still supported by the minorities, including the efficient units of the Karen, Kachin and Chin Rifles. Amid all this turmoil, Nu followed Gandhi in announcing to his wife that henceforth he would live in celibacy (like the Mahatma, he waited until after they had five children). From now on he slept in a hut behind their house. He tells us in his autobiography that this decision produced a breakdown in his wife's health, but it was all part of his efforts to become a pure Buddhist leader and hence bring benefit to Burma. Among the disasters of 1948, Tin Tut was assassinated in September. Inevitably the Communists were blamed, but it was whispered that the order was given by a prominent member of the government.

The PVO rebels went back to their old game of harassing the Karens who had been restless ever since their claims to a separate state on ambitious lines had failed. They now had a Karen National Defence Organisation (KNDO) which was armed. At Christmas 1948 the situation exploded with the KNDO fighting the PVO, and then units of the Karen Rifles fighting the ex-BNA units of the Burma Rifles. The Delta towns, and even Rangoon, came under threat. The civil service unions chose this moment to strike for better pay. In March 1949, Nu toured Upper Burma to try to calm the panicky officials. In his absence, the Socialists gave him an ultimatum: he should hand over to the Communists. Nu refused; and the Socialists, led by Kyaw Nyein, resigned. Nu reconstituted his Cabinet, bringing in General Ne Win as Minister of Defence.

Slowly, the situation improved. Mandalay, the rebels' biggest prize, was recaptured in April. By November the initiative had passed to Nu's government, and the next two years saw the rebellion reduced to the scale of jungle resistance. Those who had deserted Nu (who in 1950 discarded the prefix Thakin and was called U Nu) now thought again: as Nu wrote later: 'Only when the tide turned did the opportunists return to the government's side.'[17]

Nu Wins Through

There followed a few years when the situation looked bright. Nu launched his *Pyidawtha*, or Welfare State; he also sought to inspire his people through Buddhism. In 1951 the World Peace Pagoda was built, and in 1954 the Sixth Great International Council of Buddhist monks and learned laity was opened (the fifth had been at Mandalay in 1871 under the patronage of King Mindon). The Council closed in May 1956, the 2500th anniversary of the Buddha's decease. All seemed set fair. Then in 1958 a split opened in the ruling AFPFL. The background was another move by Nu to withdraw from politics. This set the various factions manoeuvring, while Ne Win also came in. There were two AFPFLs: the group led by Nu was labelled the 'Clean AFPFL'; that led by Kyaw Nyein was called the 'Stable AFPFL' (presumably emphasising continuity). Rumours of a military coup were rife (1958 was the year of General De Gaulle, General Ayub Khan in Pakistan, and other military takeovers). Nu decided to pre-empt any coup by offering to propose to parliament that Ne Win should take over as Prime Minister.

Ne Win governed for two years, and then staged another election. He calculated that the 'Stable AFPFL' would win, with support from the army. Instead, Nu scored a landslide victory, winning 159 seats to the 41 the Stable group secured. He renamed his party *Pyidaungsu*, emphasising its attachment to the soil. His campaign was marked by an insistence that the people, *Ludu*, formed the nation (he wrote a play called *The People Win Through*). He categorised the politicians who would deceive the people under the label 'Mr Zero'. Nu had given some delicate promises in his campaign. He undertook to make Buddhism the state religion (Aung San had thrown out any reference to Buddhism in the 1947 constitution), and he promised to create two new ethnic states, one for Arakan, and one for the Mons of Tenasserim. It was this which led to his downfall.

Nu Ousted

A conference on constitutional reform opened on 1 March 1962. At 2 a.m. next morning he was awakened by noise in the compound. A squad of soldiers had arrived to arrest him. Along with all the other leading politicians (including Kyaw Nyein and the Socialists) and the leaders of the ethnic minorities he was interned. This time General Ne Win was getting rid of the 1947 constitution and with it the AFPFL and both groups of leaders. He formed his own party, *Lanzin*, to promote 'The Burmese Way to Socialism'.

Nu was incarcerated for more than four years. He was then released, on condition he went into exile. At first he was associated with a motley collection of opposition leaders who tried from Thailand to organise a new resistance movement (the Communists and the Karens were still in the field: Than Tun was gunned down in 1968). Then Nu went to India to the Buddhist centre, Bodh-Gaya, near Patna. His Buddhist piety led representatives of the thousands of Untouchables who had embraced Buddhism to invite him to be their leader. He declined. He was still writing. He published an autobiography in 1975: he chose to portray himself as a rapscallion (internal evidence suggests that it had been written in jail). Some passages in *Saturday's Son* verge on the gross, as when he speaks of his own denunciation of Soviet Communism: 'Mother-fornicating Russians. . . . Stalin comes nowhere near General Aung San, even when the latter is baring his penis and pulling the foreskin back.'[18]

Nu's Buddhist Apotheosis

This was one U Nu, but not the deeper man, who had searched for so many years for enlightenment. In 1980, Ne Win released all political prisoners and invited those like Nu who had been in exile to return. Nu was no longer concerned with politics; he devoted himself entirely to Buddhism. He did not retire into a monastery but lived in Rangoon as a layman, under constant police surveillance. He appealed for funds to begin a translation of the *Ti Pitaka*: within one week the public subscribed more money than he needed. The 'Three Baskets' comprise the teachings of the Lord Buddha, 40 volumes in all: the *Vinaya* (Rules of Conduct), *Sutta* (Discourses) and *Abhidhamma* (Exposition of the Four Ultimate Realities). Nu proposed to write an outline or, as he called it, 'a glimpse of the *Ti Pitaka*'. During 1981–2, three instalments were issued amounting to more than 2000 pages. As editor, or commentator, Nu sometimes introduced his own experiences to illustrate the Buddha's teachings. He tells us that as Prime Minister:

He was more often than not obsessed with the heated debate in the Parliament or the thoughts of a corrupt minister in his Cabinet or the undue influence of his party men or some such matters. . . . Sometimes while he was chanting sermons, his mind flitted about in all directions. . . . The words came out of his mouth automatically, without himself being conscious of what he was chanting.

Despite all his endeavours, Nu felt he had not fully acquired *jhana*, which he defines as 'extraordinary mental concentrations' which exclude fleshly attachments. There are four *jhanas*, the fourth, both 'ordinary' and 'extraordinary', on a much higher plane than others. Nu relates:

> The author is, honestly speaking, a person without indomitable will. He does not have the unflagging diligence. Therefore, his attempt to acquire the fourth *jhana* (ordinary) in about the middle of 1962 failed. He could not go beyond the second *jhana*. He deceived himself that writing of religious books . . . is far more important. . . . Though he never got the *abhinna* [achievement of freedom from sensuality, rebirth, speculation, ignorance] he got the intellectual satisfaction that even the lowest *jhanas* could accomplish such mini-miracles.[19]

So we leave U Nu, once freedom lover and statesman; now contemplative mystic. Some Burmese regard him as a future Buddha. Almost all Burmese regard Aung San as a national hero and martyr. With his death on the brink of independence, he receives all the acclaim for this achievement and none of the obloquy attached to subsequent conflicts: even though his former BNA and his PVO became heavily involved in the insurgency. He is a figure in Burmese mythology, like the kings Alaungpaya and Anawratha who united the Golden Land in centuries past. His enigmatic features gaze down in every public place of assembly. Few stop to ponder what he was actually like as a mere man.

6

Sukarno and the Vocabulary of Revolution

Viewing each leader in turn as one of his particular generation, Sukarno comes after Jinnah and Nehru and before the Burmese leaders. Jinnah and Nehru were fully adult before 1914: Jinnah was already an experienced politician. Throughout the 1920s they were acknowledged as leaders of national status and by 1939 each was at the head of his political movement: though in the case of Jinnah some thought he was past his prime. Nu and Aung San only grew to early manhood in the 1920s and 1930s. In 1939 they were still politically unknown outside their own little circle.

Born at the start of the twentieth Century, to Sukarno the Russo-Japanese war which signalled the reawakening of Asia can have meant nothing: neither did other political events before 1914. Though the Netherlands and the Dutch East Indies were largely insulated from the full impact of the Great War, the 1920s saw the first stirrings of contemporary nationalism in Indonesia and the young Sukarno responded. His rise to prominence in political leadership was punctuated by long periods of withdrawal enforced by the colonial government: in this respect he was like Nehru during these same years, also held incommunicado by the colonial power.

Sukarno's moment came in 1942 when Japan overran South-East Asia: the same moment as for Aung San and thereafter for Nu. During the next three years, when Nehru was totally isolated from political involvement, Sukarno became spokesman almost overnight for Indonesian nationalism. When the war ended, the political journeys of Jinnah, Nehru – and very soon also Aung San and Nu – were obviously getting near to their hoped-for destination. It soon became evident that their overlords, the British, intended to hand over power at an early date. In India and Burma the fundamental question was no longer *if* or *when* would the British give up, but who would inherit their legacy? In India, who could bargain most successfully, Congress or League? In Burma, who would win the final struggle, Communists or Nationalists?

Indonesia in the years immediately after the Japanese surrender was in tumult. The British, when they arrived, had only the most limited objective: to disarm the enemy and release their captives. Their softly-softly approach to Indonesian nationalist claims was quickly overwhelmed. The Dutch returned, determined to reintroduce their former system of control with only watered-down self-government. For a further four years, Sukarno found himself at the centre of a political maelstrom of which the outcome seemed obscure. At times, his grip on the nationalist forces appeared to be failing. If, now, we place him in the pantheon of Afro-Asian leaders who decisively influenced the course of events it is because he was a survivor, to whom the drama of revolutionary struggle was an end in itself. To him, independence was not something achieved: it was a *leitmotiv*, a mode of existence. He was no hero: his final exit was ignominious. Yet during his day he featured as a significant Afro-Asian leader, a 'charismatic' personality like Nehru who made a far greater impact on the international scene than Nu with his disarming frankness and humility.

Yet Sukarno's background corresponded much more to that of the Burmese. He too was a country boy, and like Aung San he claimed descent from gentry, though his family circumstances were equally modest. He too received his higher education not in the metropole but in a newly-founded colonial college, thus opening up horizons which previously would have been closed to Indonesians like him.

Sukarno: Name of Magic Power

The man who became Sukarno was born on 6 June 1901.* His father was descended from the Javanese nobility, *priyayi*. Though his own circumstances were modest, he was entitled to be called *Raden* (chief) Sukemi Sosrodihardjo. As *priyayi* he obtained an education in a Teachers' Training School and was sent off to the little island of Bali. This island alone in Indonesia has clung to the old Hindu religion and culture. There he met his future wife, Idayu Njoman Rai, said to belong to a Brahman

---

* Readers may have noticed the name spelled Soekarno elsewhere – the form he always used. In 1972 the government switched from an orthography based on Dutch pronunciation to one conforming to Anglo-American norms. This will be employed: hence *priyayi* not *prijaji*, Surabaya not Surabaja, *wayang* not *wajang*. The new practice is not altogether consistent. *Pancha* (five) is still written *Pantja*; Sjahrir (a prominent politician) has not become Shahrir. Jogjakarta, although pronounced Yogyakarta, is seldom spelled like that.

family. They married and had a daughter. Sukemi applied for a transfer back to Java and was sent to Surabaya, a major port. There a son was born and named Kusno Sosro. His sister died, and to avert evil influences the boy was given a new name: Sukarno, or Karno. This was highly auspicious, being a modern rendering of Kerna, King of Awangga, in east-central Java. This mythical prince was one of the Pandavas, the heroes of the Javanese epic, *Bharata Yudha*, taken from the Hindu classic, the *Mahabharata*. The *Bharata Yudha* — in Raffles' translation, the 'War of Woe' — was between the 'good' Pandavas and the 'evil' Kauravas who had usurped their realm by stealth (the parallel with the Dutch in Java was obvious to anybody). Kerna is represented as valorous:

> His wish was that nothing should avert the war
> For he feared the loss of his character for courage[1]

This was no ordinary name, and it was familiar to almost all Javanese for the *Bharata Yuda* was famous as performed in the *wayang kulit*, the so-called shadow play, though that description does not do justice to the whirling world beyond the lighted screen; a world of magic. And magic was always close to Sukarno's imagination as he acquired Western knowledge.

Only in 1914 were Indonesians admitted to schools where the medium was Dutch (these were intended for Dutch and Eurasian students). As his father was a teacher and *priyayi*, Sukarno was among the favoured few. His father coached him in Dutch, and also introduced him to theosophy. By now they were living in a small town, Modyokerto. Sukarno was sent to Surabaya, where he experienced loneliness and sought shelter in the Theosophical Society library where he became acquainted with the great Europeans from Rousseau to Marx. His heroes included Mazzini and Garibaldi. He lodged with the scholarly Tjokroaminoto whose household was a kind of ashram, and who introduced the latest arrival to the new nationalism of Sarekat Islam. Sukarno joined an off-shoot which in 1918 began to be called *Jong Java*, Young Java.

College Years and Marriage (1922)

In 1921 he went on to the Technical College at Bandung, founded only the previous year. It was about now that he was married to his *guru* Tjokroaminoto's daughter, a girl of 15. It was more like a betrothal than a marriage and they did not live together. Most of the College students were Dutch; in the year of Sukarno's enrolment there were 29 Dutch, six Indonesian and two Chinese students. The atmosphere was not conducive to nationalism, yet he found ways of joining in discussion groups outside. Another important development was his growing attraction to his landlady; in 1922 he divorced his teenage bride and married Inggit Garnasih. She shared none of his growing absorption in politics but was attuned to him in the world of magic.

The major radical political force was the *Partai Kommunis Indonesia* (PKI). Founded in May 1920, this was the first Communist party organised in Asia. They became active in the trades unions and increasingly militant. Sukarno came under the influence of their man Musso. There was an ill-organised series of revolts; first in west Java in November 1926 and subsequently in Sumatra in January 1927. The government easily quelled these revolts; 4500 supporters were jailed and 1300 exiled in Dutch New Guinea. The PKI was banned and did not re-emerge until 1946. Sarekat Islam was damaged by its association with the PKI: hence, as Sukarno began to appear on the political stage, there was something of a vacuum. His first notable work in print appeared in *Indonesia Muda* ('Young Indonesia') and was a series of articles on 'Nationalism, Islam, Marxism'. Already he was arguing that these three different ideologies were facets of the same truth. Despite his limited education he was widely read, absorbing the ideas of the European Marxists in the medium of French, German and English as well as Dutch. One who knew him in the Bandung period, Takdir Alisjahbana, recalls: 'A fascinating personality . . . few [were] able to resist his charm. . . . To all this must be added his famous talent for oratory, and his resonant carrying voice. . . . He possesses a skill of dramatisation that fascinates and moves his audience.'[2]

Founds National Party (1927)

On what may have been chosen as an auspicious day, 4 July 1927, Sukarno founded his own party, known as *Partai Nasional Indonesia* (PNI) or *Persatuan Nasional Indonesia* (Indonesian National Unity). He aimed to break the mould of the multi-party system which the Dutch had initiated.

This was almost the only time during the twentieth century when Dutch rule assumed a relatively progressive face. A.C.D. de Graaff arrived as Governor-General late in 1926 and appealed to the nationalists for cooperation while some Dutch officials endeavoured to counteract their countrymen's reactionary spirit by forming *De Stuuw* (Forward

Movement). Among them was Dr Hubertus Van Mook, destined to be the head of the post-war administration. Sukarno began to tour Java, addressing massive crowds on the theme of the awakening of national consciousness. He urged the formation of a 'Brown Front' to overcome the White Front of Dutch dominance. He cited the example of India, where Gandhi was creating an 'indissoluble union' to include the objectives of Indian Muslims. At other times he was scornful of *anhimsa*, non-violence, and he criticised Gandhi and Nehru as 'philosophemes' inclined to philosophical concepts which weakened the Indian nationalist movement. His speeches ignored most social issues which had so concerned Sarekat Islam. He concentrated on attacking Dutch interests, claiming that 'Our opponent indeed already feels the earth tremble under his feet.'[3]

Despite his magnetic personality and his enormous popularity the PNI was slow to win members: one calculation is that by September 1929 there were less than 6000. Sukarno's speeches became ever more extravagant. He revived the legend of the Prophecy of Jayabhaya (reigned 1135−57) who foretold that the *Pringi* (*Feringhi*, Europeans) would conquer Java but that 'the Prince of Kling' would send armies to drive them out and then, after five years, 'return to his own country'.[4] A 'Prince of Kling' would come from south India, but Sukarno interpreted the prophecy as applying to Japan. His prediction excited the people in their thousands and the Dutch authorities found it necessary to explain away the Jayabhaya legend. Sukarno's defiance could not be ignored indefinitely by de Graaff, and on 29 December 1929 he was arrested.

Jailed for Bold Rhetoric (1930)

His trial was a long-drawn-out affair. To the Dutch judge the case was a miasma of fact and fantasy. The prosecution attempted to show that the PNI was connected with the League Against Imperialism with which Nehru was then linked. Mohammad Hatta was involved with the League: Hatta resided in the Netherlands from 1921 to 1932 and became an MP in the Dutch parliament: but his association with the PNI started only on his return. The evidence against Sukarno was flimsy and when he was eventually sentenced to four years' imprisonment in December 1930 one eminent Dutch professor, J.M.J. Schepper, condemned the verdict as violating the great Dutch legal tradition. De Graaff commuted the sentence to two years, and in actuality Sukarno was released on 15 December 1931.

During his absence his PNI disintegrated. Former members were drawn into Hatta's 'new PNI' or *PNI Bahru*. Opponents formed Partai Indonesia (Partindo). Hatta was assisted by another Holland-returned politician, Sutan Sjahrir, who had also spent several years in the Netherlands and become an admirer of the Dutch Socialist movement. However, they had to accept the enthusiasm with which Sukarno was welcomed back. He had not adjusted to prison life as Nehru was able to do; he had found it 'a shattering experience'. Now, he had the adulation of the masses again. He became known as 'Bung Karno'. *Abang* means elder brother, and *bangsa* the nation, the people. Sukarno was hailed as the Elder Brother of the Indonesian people.

'Marhaen': Symbol of Exploitation

During the next 20 months while he was at liberty Sukarno launched a campaign on quasi-Marxist lines. This centred upon the philosophy of Marhaenism, drawn from the name of a poor peasant he once talked to. He declared that 90 per cent of Indonesians belonged to this class of small farmers, labourers, urban workers: and he did not direct his attack upon the other 10 per cent but upon the Dutch who had exploited them and the Chinese entrepreneurs who lived off their labour. Instead of the class struggle enunciated by Marx he externalised the struggle and insisted that all Indonesians could live in harmony in a *gotong-royong* 'mutual help' society. In this philosophy he was in accord with Gandhi who believed that in India employers and employees shared a common interest. Sukarno went beyond Gandhi to declare war on the foreign exploiters. Independence would provide a 'golden bridge' whereby the Marhaens could attain a just social order.

These ideas were expounded to mass audiences. They yielded ample results. Out of the former PNI, Sukarno had taken up Partindo, and within one year its membership soared to 20 000. The authorities could not allow this to develop further. The relatively liberal de Graaff had been replaced as Governor-General by de Jonge, a hardliner (it was he who pronounced that Dutch rule would continue for another 300 years), and the Colonial Minister was H. Colijn, whose notorious book, *Colonial Problems of Today and Tomorrow* (1928), had declared that the Indonesians could not expect self-government 'in the humanly foreseeable future': indeed, he dismissed the notion that there was any Indonesia: 'The islands . . . are a unity for the reason that they compose the Netherlands Indies and for that reason alone.'

Sukarno should have anticipated what happened: his arrest in August 1933. But already he was taken with 'monumentalism', in Professor

Alisjahbana's words, 'fond of everything spectacular and imposing', a manifestation of *der Machtmensch* described by Nietzsche, 'the will to power'.[5] After three months of being examined in prison, awaiting sentence, he announced his renunciation of non-cooperation. The news shocked his thousands of admirers. One who was no extremist, Dr Sutomo, wrote: 'It was he who had demolished the crumbling walls that had divided the various groups of the people from one another. . . . For them he was Bung Karno. . . . They saw in him only the prophet of freedom.'

Sukarno then announced his withdrawal from Partindo because he no longer accepted its policies. His foremost biographer attributes this withdrawal to his inability to endure the prison existence. Needing the adulation of the masses he abhorred solitude – the complete opposite to the introspective Nehru.[6]

Banishment (1934)

His apparent apostasy did not secure his release. The Dutch colonial *exorbitante rechten* gave the Governor-General power to send anyone considered a threat to peace and order into exile. In February 1934 he was transported to Flores, the remote island in the Lesser Sundas, far from Java. His political rivals, Hatta and Sjahrir, were also transported to the Dutch equivalent of Devil's Island, Boven Digual in New Guinea. Probably Sukarno's renunciation of non-cooperation did ensure a less severe fate for him. He was permitted to take his family with him, but the only intellectual companionship he found was among the Catholic missionaries: the local inhabitants remained strangers to him.

Although banned from any political correspondence he was allowed to explain his position on non-cooperation: 'While it could be a source of strength for our movement [it] could never really furnish an ideal. . . . I have always been able to accept non-cooperation only as an effective instrument of nationalist propaganda. . . . I have never been able to base a philosophy upon it.' It was now that he became 'converted' to Islam. Of course all Javanese are formally Muslims, but most incorporate Hindu and animist elements in their religion. Those who are strict are called *santri* and for them Islam is all-embracing. Sukarno did not follow that path; rather he examined the modernist position adopted by the Aligarh school in India. He criticised the backwardness of Islamic orthodoxy; neverthe-less he wrote on 17 October 1936, 'a soul that was only superficially Islamic has become a soul convinced of Islam . . . a soul that daily rendered homage to HIM'.

Sukarno suffered from malaria; in 1938 he was moved to Benkulen in Sumatra, perhaps for humanitarian reasons (in 1936 Hatta and Sjahrir were moved from their vile jungle camp), or perhaps because the Dutch hoped that a more Islamic environment would complete his 'conversion' from politics to religion, for Islam in Sumatra was more powerful than the syncretic faith of Java. He was closely associated with the Muhammadiyah, inspired by an Egyptian reformist movement. The Muhammadiyah accepted government aid for its schools and was therefore abhorrent to radical nationalists. They now provided Sukarno with a vehicle for polemic and controversy which enabled him to regain a place in the public eye. He explained his position in an article, 'Sukarno by Himself', which appeared in June 1941: 'There are men who say Sukarno is a nationalist; others say he is no longer a nationalist but a Muslim; and others again say he is neither nationalist nor Muslim but a Marxist. . . . What is this Sukarno? Is he a nationalist? A Muslim? A Marxist? Readers, Sukarno is – *a mixture of all these isms.*'

War: Sukarno's Fascist Leanings

He grew ever bolder in what he wrote. The occupation of the Netherlands by Nazi Germany in 1940 left the Indies isolated, out on a limb. However, the Dutch authorities made no move to conciliate national feelings. A question in the *Volksraad* about the Atlantic Charter was answered evasively. Some of their opponents, like Hatta and Sjahrir, expressed sympathy for the sufferings of the Dutch, but Sukarno offered no word of sympathy. Alisjahbana declares that even before the war he 'showed a leaning towards . . . German Fascism with its mythbuilder Alfred Rosenberg, its agitators Hitler and Goebbels'.[7] What is certain is that he quoted approvingly words he attributed to Nehru: 'Even if the Indian people do not agree with Nazism and Fascism, even if the Indian people recognise the evil of Nazism and Fascism . . . they will surely part company with the British. They have no wish to help the British in the present war.'[8] As was his custom, Sukarno adapted Nehru's actual words to reflect his own hostility to the Dutch and his growing admiration for Japan. Increasingly, he envisaged a great war in the Pacific and many others shared his expectations: the prophecy of Jayabhaya was again on everyone's lips. Surely, this was the promised time?

Following their occupation of Malaya and Singapore the Japanese invaded Indonesia. The disastrous naval battle of the Coral Sea on 27 February left Java exposed; on 9 March the Dutch commander-in-chief surrendered. The Governor-General was taken prisoner, though the

Lieutenant-Governor, Dr Van Mook, escaped to Australia. Almost everywhere the Japanese soldiers were received with shouts of *Banzai*: the Japanese made much of the Jayabhaya prophecy and most Indonesians believed that now they would be free. However, it was quickly made plain that independence was not on the Japanese agenda. Two weeks after their arrival the Japanese banned the Indonesians' flag. They even partitioned the archipelago into three quite separate military commands; Sumatra, Java, and the Great East. Their role was to provide oil, tin, rubber, sugar and other essential materials for the Japanese war economy. Thousands of Indonesians were conscripted into labour corps, and these *romushas* were treated with that callous indifference verging on brutality which characterised Japanese practices throughout South-East Asia.

Adopted by the Japanese (1942)

Sukarno awaited events in his Sumatran exile. He was contacted, and one week after the Dutch surrender agreed to cooperate with the Japanese. They were in no great hurry to make use of him; not till 9 July was he returned to Java without ceremony in a small motor launch. Hatta and Sjahrir were already back home. The three men met, and it soon became clear that their intentions were different. Sjahrir was not prepared to cooperate; the others decided to go along with the Japanese in order to extract concessions from them.

There was a new corporate directorate, the *Empat Serangkai* or 'Four Leaf Clover', representing important elements in the national life. Sukarno was included as the populist leader of the masses (his seven years in exile notwithstanding); Hatta was chosen as a cosmopolitan intellectual; Jaji Mas Mansur was former chairman of Muhammadiyah; and Dewantoro was an educationist, sponsor of national schools on similar lines to Tagore. They headed an organisation called *Pusat Tenaga Raiyat*, 'Centre of Power for the Countrymen', or *Putera* in common usage. What had they gained? They applied to the Japanese for permission to fly the national flag and sing the national song, *Indonesia Raya*. After six months the answer came back: 'No'. Early in 1943, Tojo Hideki announced that Japan would bestow independence on Burma and the Philippines. There was no reference to Indonesia which was allotted the status of a colony.

Increasingly a public figure, Sukarno experienced another change in his private life. A girl he had come to admire in Sumatra was brought to Java to be his third wife after he divorced Inggit. Alisjahbana has identified a leading aspect of his personality as 'idealised sensualism'. He was drawn irresistibly to 'beautiful women with full breasts'. His new wife Fatmawati gave him his first son, Guntur, whose name means 'thunder'.

The Indonesian nationalists acquired a friend in Rear Admiral Maeda Minoru, head of military intelligence. Like Colonel Suzuki he developed a romantic sense of identification with these people so very different from his own, rather like Lawrence of Arabia. They needed any friend they could find, for Japan had no intention of making any real concessions. Sukarno was accorded the title of *Pemimpin Besar*, Great Leader, but his role was largely confined to that of speechmaker, which he performed very effectively. Yamamoto Moichiro, Colonel – later General – who became *Gunseikan*, head of the military government, looked down on Indonesians as 'natives'. He made it clear that they must carry out orders 'exactly'. This was the job of the Central Advisory Committee, *Tjuo Sangi In*, for which Sukarno was chief Adviser.

Experience was being acquired in other ways which would serve to advance independence. The machinery of government, previously firmly under Dutch control, was now staffed by Indonesians almost to the top level. Many were *priyayis*, formerly the lower echelons of the administration. They were formed into *Djawa Hokokai* (Javanese Service Movement) and instructed to organise neighbourhood associations for communal purposes. Islam was mobilised through a Consultative Council, *Majlis Sjuro Muslimin Indonesia*, or *Masjumi*. Both these developments were based on traditional leadership but new prospects were opened up by the formation of auxiliary military forces known in Indonesian as *Pembela Tanah Air*, Fatherland Defence Force, *Peta* for short.

Japanese – Indonesian Military Forces

Beginning in October 1943 this force was formed into battalions (*Daidan*) about 500 strong. Their junior commanders were mainly young urban middle-class men, the sort who had formed the audience for Sukarno. Trained by Japanese instructors they became tough and disciplined. Their numbers expanded rapidly until there were 66 *daidan* in Java and another three in Bali: a total not far short of 35 000 (five times larger than the BNA). The *Peta* was intended only for local defence but there was also the *Hei-Ho* whose strength in Java was close on 25 000. The officers of the *Hei-Ho* were all Japanese; their role was mainly to operate as labour battalions.

Role of the *Pemuda*, 'The Young Braves'

These young soldiers were potentially political activists. Even before the war the *sumpah pemuda* or 'Youth Oath' had been a pledge of Indonesian unity, and now the *pemuda* were poised to become the standard bearers of national revolution.

There was virtually no resistance movement, except on distant Ambon whose Protestant inhabitants had formed the backbone of the Dutch Indies Army (very like the Karens in Burma). Sjahrir later acquired the reputation of a resistance leader, but although he refused to collaborate with the Japanese all he really did was to monitor the declining fortunes of Japan on his illegal radio. A more important development was the re-emergence of an illegal PKI. Paradoxically this was encouraged by Admiral Maeda. Wikana, arrested by the Dutch in 1940 for PKI activities, was recruited. Also involved was the veteran Communist, Tan Malaka, who returned from abroad only in 1942 and was employed to speak on 'Radio Tokyo' (actually at Bantam). Then there was Subardjo, who was a former journalist on the daily *Matahari* (Sun) as was also Iwi, an outlawed Communist. These and other radicals were introduced by Maeda into his political training school, *Asrama Indonesia Merdeka*, and encouraged to indoctrinate *pemuda* students among whom was Aidit, the future Communist leader.

Japanese Encourage Hope of Independence (1944)

During 1944 the tide of war in the East turned against Japan, although the Allies were still far from her shores. Tojo resigned, succeeded as premier by Koiso Kuniaki, another general, pledged to intensify the fight, but more aware of the need to conciliate Japan's underlings. On 7 September 1944 it was announced that Japan would grant independence to Java – perhaps along with Sumatra – after the war. Permission was given to fly the national red and white flag and to sing *Indonesia Raya*. The standing of Sukarno and the other collaborators revived. He had been denounced (rather unfairly) for assisting the recruitment of the *romusha* forced labour to a total of perhaps 500 000. Liable to serve wherever they were sent, only 70 000 returned. Resentment at press-gang methods had caused sporadic revolts in rural Java, though the full extent of this horror was not yet known. Meanwhile, Sukarno was again the idol.

The Japanese had calculated cleverly. Sukarno and his associates could expect little sympathy from the returning Allies; surely then the Dutch would be restored? An appeal to nationalism was the best method of anchoring the Indonesians to the victory of Japan. Even so, political progress was slow. The *pemuda* showed their discontent; on 14 February 1945 a *Peta* battalion stationed at Blitar in east Java, far from the capital Jakarta (as Batavia was known after 1942) marched out of barracks in protest. The rising was suppressed, but it was an ominous sign.

A Preparatory and Organisational Committee was belatedly convened. The 62 members met on 28 May 1945. It represented all shades of opinion, but it was dominated by Sukarno. His ideas were those adopted. He rejected parliamentary democracy, the 'Ins' versus the 'Outs'. He pleaded for *mufakat*, an Islamic term for the *gotong-royong* he had long advocated: consensus, harmony, unity. He called for a *Führerstaat* in which the President would personify the general will. He enunciated a philosophy for the future Indonesia, entitled *Pantja Sila*, the Five Principles, on 1 June. He asked the Committee 'Upon what *Weltanschaung* do we intend to establish the state of Free Indonesia?' These principles were Nationalism: extending from Sumatra to Irian [New Guinea], Internationalism (meaning links between nations), Consultation (*mufakat* again), Social Justice, and finally Belief in God.

Sukarno's Dream of Greater Indonesia

On 11 July Sukarno told the Committee: 'At no time . . . have I declared that my struggle was confined to the claim to the former Dutch held territory. . . . In fact I have on one occasion in my life dreamt of a Pan-Indonesia which will include not only Malaya and Papua [ie. Australian New Guinea] but also the Philippines.'

Sukarno was rebuffed when he asked that there should be a Greater Indonesia including the British territories, Malaya, Singapore and North Borneo. Marshal Terauchi, Commander-in-Chief of the Southern Region, dismissed this claim (17 July) though he agreed that the former Netherlands Indies would be given Japanese-style independence. On 7 August Sukarno announced the formation of a Committee for the Preparation of Indonesian Independence (*Panitia Perisiapan Kemerdekaan Indonesia*: PPKI). Together with Hatta and the new President of the PPKI, Sukarno flew to Dalat in Vietnam. There Terauchi informed them that independence would be proclaimed. According to a Japanese source, Masaaki Tanaka, the appointed day would be 7 September. All this occurred after the two atomic bombs had been dropped on Hiroshima and Nagasaki. When they returned, thousands awaited them at the airport with Yamamoto to the fore.

Sukarno: Bringer of Independence

When they reached Sukarno's residence, Sjahrir burst in upon them to say that Japan was sueing for peace. The two leaders went to military headquarters for confirmation and were told that the staff were otherwise engaged. They managed to see Maeda who dropped hints and told them to be circumspect. It was decided to convene the PPKI next day, 16 August. When the members arrived they found Sukarno and Hatta missing. It transpired that the previous evening students from the *Asrama Merdeka* led by Wikana along with student followers of Sjahrir presented an ultimatum to Sukarno: you must proclaim independence immediately. Sukarno procrastinated; tempers flared up, the students withdrew. Later (most accounts say early in the morning) the students returned and compelled Sukarno and his family, and also Hatta, to come away with them; their destination was the *Peta* barracks at Rengasdenglok, about 70 miles away. There they argued inconclusively, and the students prepared to stage a coup in Jakarta.

Pemuda Force Sukarno to Declare Independence

Maeda came to hear of all this: his advice was to go ahead with independence. They all went to Maeda's residence in Jakarta; he sent messages to the high command, but nobody turned up. This was not surprising as by now instructions had been received from the Allies prohibiting any further Japanese initiative. However, Maeda insisted that the proclamation be given, pledging his own word on behalf of Japan. A short statement was drafted and signed by Sukarno and Hatta. Next morning it was publicly read out by Sukarno: 'We, the people of Indonesia hereby declare Indonesia's independence.' It was signed 'In the name of the Indonesian people, Sukarno--Hatta, 17 August'. Next day, the PPKI adopted the constitution agreed the previous month. As President, Sukarno appointed and dismissed all the Ministers, who were responsible to him. He also had the right to make laws with the agreement of the elected assemblies. Until these were chosen (and this never happened) all State powers were exercised by the President assisted by an advisory committee (KNIP) which he appointed. On 31 August Sukarno named his Cabinet.

A major setback was the disappearance of all military force: the Japanese disarmed and dissolved the *Peta* and *Hei-Ho*. It was about their last overall assertion of authority, and was carried out smoothly and simultaneously so that the Indonesians were unable to reply. However, as in Burma, the demobilised soldiers did not just return to civilian life: they formed a quasi-military organisation similar to the PVO, though on an ever larger scale, the People's Security Organisation, *Badan Keamanan Raykat* (BKR). Many Japanese officers were sympathetic: they pictured themselves as bringers of independence to fellow-Asians against the

West. Arms began to be transferred to the BKR under local arrangements; they even acquired some tanks.

Struggle or Negotiation?

Sukarno's role, as so often, was to articulate and dramatise the attainment of the national will. One course forward was that symbolised by the young activists – *perjuangan*, or mass action – and at the same time as BKR was being created *badan perjuangan*, 'struggle groups', were formed. One such was the *Barisan Banteng*, Wild Buffalo Corps (whom the British called the Black Buffaloes). The course which Sukarno sought to follow included *perjuangan* but also hoped to extract dividends from diplomacy (*diplomasi*). In a major speech on 2 September he brought this out: 'The policy now adopted by the Indonesian republic must be oriented to the international world. For this the prime condition is *diplomasi*. . . . Behind that *diplomasi* . . . must be a power force. . . . We are now organising the aggregate will of the people . . . a will to feel themselves independent.'

Sukarno's pretensions were criticised by Sjahrir in a manifesto called *Perjuangan Kita*, 'Our Struggle', which exposed the rhetoric of revolutionary nationalism. No-one could label him 'collaborator', and a wide spectrum of the population began to look to him in the chaotic aftermath of the Japanese defeat. Supported by 50 members of the KNIP advisory committee, Sjahrir denounced the 'Japanese Fascist mentality' of the presidential regime and demanded that legislative authority be shared with the KNIP. Sukarno gave way.

Indonesia Made British Responsibility

Perhaps the disorganised regime might have been overwhelmed by the arrival of the occupation forces if as much, or worse, confusion had not also halted them. When South-East Asia Command (SEAC) was formed in 1943, Mountbatten was assigned responsibility for retaking Malaya and Sumatra. Java and the Great East were to be regained by General Douglas MacArthur and his South-West Pacific Command. MacArthur's headquarters were in Australia and a Dutch military and civil planning and propaganda unit worked alongside him in Brisbane. The general was drawn directly into the invasion of the Philippines and plans to invade Japan. He decided to shift responsibility for the Dutch Indies onto other shoulders, judging that anyway it was, in language he was accustomed to, a 'can of worms'. Mountbatten resisted this enormous additional responsibility, and it was actually only on 15 August, the day after Japan's surrender, that Indonesia and also Indo-China south of the 16th parallel were assigned to SEAC (though there was an American joke that this stood for 'Saving England's Asiatic Colonies').

Plans for the reoccupation of Malaya were well advanced and some ships had already put to sea. Then, with characteristic egotism, on 19 August MacArthur used his position as Supreme Commander of all forces in the Far East to issue an order that no surrender might be taken from any Japanese commander and no landing attempted before the formal signing of the surrender in Tokyo Bay. All operations had to be halted. The signing ceremony, fixed for 28 August, had to be postponed until 2 September because of a typhoon. Meanwhile the British warships had to ride out the monsoon. This postponement of the SEAC invasion timetable by two weeks meant that British forces did not land in Singapore until 9 September. The surrender ceremony applying to Southern Region on behalf of Marshal Terauchi was held on 12 September.

British Military Occupation Delayed

Since Java had been outside his area, Mountbatten had no intelligence about conditions there. British forces arriving in Malaya and Singapore had received a warm welcome; the same might be expected in Indonesia (in Sumatra the British arrival proceeded without serious incident). These illusions were encouraged by the assurances given by Van Mook and other Dutch administrators that the Indonesians would welcome their return also. Reality soon dawned. Some of the Dutch civilian internees walked out of the camps which had been their prisons for three-and-a-half years, despite instructions to stay inside. Many were roughly handled; some were killed. One of the few to grasp what was happening was Lieutenant-Colonel Laurens Van der Post, the South African writer who had been a POW and who spoke Dutch. Until he was contacted the arriving forces had no idea of what to expect.

The cruiser _Cumberland_ was the first ship to arrive at Tanjong Priok, the port for Jakarta, on 15 September, five weeks after the republic had been proclaimed. Dr Van der Plas, the senior Dutch official aboard, went on shore and then hastily re-embarked. It was not what he expected. The British assignment was to disarm the 60 000 Japanese troops and liberate the 100 000 allied prisoners, many being women and children. They were instructed not to interfere in the internal politics of Indonesia but to hand over, in due time, to the legitimate authority: that is, the Netherlands. It proved quite impossible to carry out the task assigned without involvement in the still fluid political situation.

The task of recovering POWs and disarming the enemy was given to 23 Indian Division whose advanced elements landed on 2 October at Jakarta. Already relations between the British and the Dutch were those of mutual incomprehension. On 30 September Mountbatten had listened to an exposition of the situation by Captain J.P.H. Perks of the Dutch navy who informed Supremo that: 'The Indonesian forces were not organised, that . . . all resistance would collapse as soon as the Allied forces appeared. . . . Negotiations implied weakness: the use of force which the Dutch had employed for three centuries was the most suitable course to pursue.'[9] These sentiments were held equally by the Dutch government, newly returned to The Hague. Pieter Gerbrandy, the leader of the wartime government, was an authority on the Indies, proud of the historical record like most of his countrymen. Mountbatten attempted to persuade the Dutch to adopt the same liberal policy he had followed in Burma. He had some success with Van Mook but none with Admiral Helfrich, commander of their forces in the East. Van Mook was rebuked: the Dutch ambassador in London advised that any Dutchman who negotiated with Sukarno would be tried for treason.

The British forces were instructed to move only into key areas from where they could carry out their task of rescuing POWs. Besides Jakarta, these were Bandung (one brigade), Semarang (an improvised brigade) and Surabaya (one brigade). They were in position by the end of October. Their deployment was accompanied by bizarre, often bloody encounters between Indonesians and Japanese garrisons. The most curious incident was at Surabaya where there was a major pre-war Dutch naval base. Admiral Helfrich smuggled in a Dutch naval officer, Captain Huijer, who ordered the Japanese commander to deliver all arms into his custody. Having no-one to guard them he entrusted them to Sudirman, formerly of *Peta*, who undertook to guard the arms pending the Allied arrival. Sudirman promptly handed over a vast cache to the city *pemuda*.

Occupation Escalates into Warfare

This was the situation when the British-Indian brigade began to disembark on 26 October. Initially all went well, but fighting flared up; whether started by Indonesian or British provocation depends on your witness. The senior British officer in Java, Major-General D.C. Hawthorne, prevailed on Sukarno to fly to Surabaya. He patched up an agreement, but later the same day (29 October) the local British commander, Brigadier Mallaby, was shot dead. Bitter fighting followed. Three days later a new formation arrived, 5 Indian Division. After a week of negotiations, fighting was resumed: Mountbatten's report goes on,

'Our casualties were very heavy . . . concentrations of naval and artillery fire were put down and bombing attacks were made by Thunderbolts and Mosquitos' (bombing planes). Fighting continued for three weeks; British casualties numbered 1000, the Indonesians lost many more and the city became a desert.

Sukarno also mediated at Semarang where *pemuda* extremists attacked the Japanese garrison and were in turn attacked, losing an estimated 2000 in six days. British troops guarding 11 000 ex-prisoners were under siege. On 1 November Sukarno was called in and a ceasefire arranged. His interventions were resented by many, and when he declared: 'Don't let us be forced to face alone the whole military power of England and the Allies. . . . If there are problems we must and shall follow the path of peace', although this was sound advice, it was not to the liking of his audience.

Sukarno Loses Control

Power was slipping from his hands. Hatta, as Vice-President, announced the KNIP would provide a Working Committee to 'share responsibility for the fate of the Indonesian people'. Sjahrir and his colleague Amir Sjarifuddin were designated *formateurs*; in Dutch constitutional terms, those who put together a new government. This development occurred before the disastrous events at Surabaya and Semarang. Then on 12 November Sjahrir became Prime Minister; Sukarno was now in effect merely ceremonial head of state. The government was in Sjahrir's hands.

The government of India told Mountbatten that no more Indian troops would be sent to Java. Out of the 30 battalions there, only four were from the United Kingdom. General Christison in overall command insisted that no more Dutch troops should come in, while the Dutch civil affairs units (NICA) were demilitarised, placed under British control, and renamed Allied Military Administration. It was all very tense. Sjahrir seemed more likely to be acceptable to the Dutch government and late in November he indicated his willingness to begin 'tripartite' negotiations. The response of Dr Logermann, Dutch colonial minister, was to reject negotiation as 'impossible'. Mountbatten saw this as 'a virtual declaration of war'.

The country was sliding into chaos, or as the British official historian puts it, there was a vacuum 'into which the British military authorities were quickly sucked'. Typical of this situation was an incident on 13 December 1945 when the greater part of the village of Bekasi was burned in retaliation for the murder of the British and Indian crew and passengers of a crashed Dakota by the Wild (or Black) Buffaloes. There was 'bitter and adverse comment in India': and of course even more in Java. Mountbatten offered the British government two courses; either there should be negotiations between Dutch and Indonesians with a view to bringing in a general ceasefire (Plan X) or else punitive action against 'Known or suspected terrorists' (Plan Y). The second course was advised by Ernest Bevin.[10] Fearing some such development, Sukarno and Hatta slipped away from Jakarta to the inland city of Jogjakarta whose Sultan commanded the allegiance of his subjects and who was also loyal to the Republic. Sjahrir remained in Jakarta to negotiate. This weakened his position as a symbol of the national struggle.

New Indonesian Army Formed

The British had to reckon now with an Indonesian army. The *Tentara Keamann Raykat* (TKR) was formed out of the BKR. Although some senior staff officers were from the old Dutch colonial army the leaders of the fighting formations were almost all ex-*Peta* and ex-BKR. They were armed exclusively with Japanese weapons: Colonel Sudirman, the most successful in obtaining arms, became army commander. Amir Sjarifuddin was Minister of Defence and there was some friction between him and Sjahrir on one side with their 'resistance' reputation, and officers who were 'collaborators'. Sukarno regained importance as consensus figure: 'If it should ever turn out that Sjahrir is not maintaining the demand for 100 per cent Merdeka . . . then I have the right to dismiss him', he told a wildly cheering crowd on 17 February 1946. On 28 February Sjahrir resigned from the premiership: but Sukarno and he needed each other, even if they suspected each other: on 2 March he was back as Premier.

Meanwhile Plan Y was being put into effect. Despite his knowledge of the trigger-happy propensities of the Dutch soldiery Mountbatten agreed to the introduction of Netherlands forces, previously held back in Malaya, early in March 1946 because 'the quality of these Netherlands troops was far superior to that of the forces which had originally landed in Java'. Their numbers soon equalled two divisions in strength. The senior Dutch officer ordered them to extend the territory they occupied to double the previous area. Control – such as it had been – was passing out of British hands. On 4 April, Lord Inverchapel (sent as diplomatic intermediary) accompanied Van Mook and Indonesian negotiators to The Hague. Agreement was confined to arrangements for evacuating Dutch internees to the ports. There was a new Lieutenant-Governor, Dr Blum, and a new Dutch commander, Lieutenant-General Spoor, replacing Helfrich. Sjahrir continued to negotiate with them. This inevitably made him suspect to the more militant. Sukarno was not loath to encourage his detractors.

Communist Bid for Power

On 29 April the PKI emerged as an open party. Its leader, Tan Malaka, had made an abortive bid for power and was in jail, but Wikana and others were active, having the Wild Buffaloes as their allies. Ex-*Peta* elements in the army distrusted Sjahrir who created the elite Siliwangsi division as a highly professional force to counterbalance the largely out-of-control TKR. Sudirman decided to act. On 27 June Tan Malaka and other leading Communists were set free and Sjahrir was kidnapped just as Sukarno had been the previous August. An ultimatum was presented to the President to appoint Tan Malaka head of the government with Sudirman in total control of the armed forces. When this was followed by the demand that Sukarno resign, the President resisted. Sudirman realised his error. Sjahrir was liberated by loyal troops and Tan Malaka rearrested. On 31 October Sjahrir announced his third Cabinet. Its 31 members included four Communists. Consensus was again in fashion. Sukarno had demonstrated once again in a crisis that he represented unity.

The first post-war Dutch government, a centrist coalition reflecting the myriad interests represented under the List System, was led by the Labour Premier, Professor W. Schmerhorn. The election of 1946 reflected a small swing to the right and the new Premier, Dr Louis Beel, belonged to the Catholic People's Party. It was Schmerhorn, however, who was despatched to lead a negotiating team to meet the Republican leaders. Their discussions produced the Linggajati Agreement, as it is called from the hill station where they met (12 November).

Abortive Netherlands – Indonesian Agreement (1946)

The Dutch recognised the Republic as the *de facto* authority in Java and Sumatra. A federal state would be created, the constituent units including the authorities which the Dutch had inspired in the 'outer islands'. The whole conglomerate would be part of a Netherlands – Indonesia Union with Queen Wilhelmina as head (the model of the British Commonwealth is obvious). This compromise was hard to swallow and the final signature was not appended till March 1947. Linggajati enabled the British to leave with a good grace, and the last units were withdrawn by 30 November 1946. They had pleased nobody. Sjahrir complained to President Truman that they had reimposed Dutch rule. The Dutch complained that they had strengthened the hands of the Indonesians: they were presented with a bill by the Dutch for the use of barracks, railroads, and other facilities during their occupation (which was not paid).

Endorsement for Linggajati had to be obtained from KNIP. A bloc in this assembly known as *Benteng Republik* (Republican Fortress) utterly opposed the deal. Sukarno decreed that the total would be increased from 200 to 514. Resistance was prolonged from December to February 1947 when at length Sukarno secured approval for the change by putting his position to the test: if they refused, they must find a new president. He declared (25 February): 'I am neither a president *à la française* nor *à l'americaine*. I am a president of the Indonesian revolution . . . guiding and leading the people.' The new body included 80 representatives of Workers and Peasants, the numbers of *Masjumi* were almost doubled and there were greatly increased numbers from Sumatra. Although Sjahrir was responsible for Linggajati, his Socialist group dwindled. He paid a visit to India to attend the Inter-Asian Conference. He was entertained by the Viceroy whose press officer reported the lunch with Sjahrir and 'his buxom, blonde Dutch wife': 'Sjahrir must be the smallest statesman since Dolfuss, the Austrian pocket premier.' It was good public relations: but the Dutch were planning their counter-attack.

On 27 May they presented an ultimatum. Sjahrir made concessions, but they wanted more; three Left-wing members of his Cabinet withdrew support and he resigned on 26 June. No alternative was practicable, and on 20 July the Dutch launched their euphemistically named 'police action'. They thrust deep into Republican territory. The UN called for a ceasefire but before this was agreed the Dutch secured all major ports and the authority of the republic was confined to a mere one-third of Java, centred on Jogjakarta.

UN Intervention

Australia brought the issue to the UN: with a Labour government in office, and militant solidarity with Indonesia among the dockworkers, normally conservative White Australia was supporting Asian nationalism. On 30 July 1947 the UN Security Council ordered a ceasefire. The Dutch continued to probe into Republican territory until they had established a satisfactory perimeter, the 'Van Mook Line'. The new Indonesian army, under yet another name, *Tentara Nasional Indonesia* (TNI), although huge in number proved deficient against the hard-hitting Dutch.

A UN 'Good Offices' Committee was formed: Australia was nominated by the republic, Belgium was the Dutch choice, and the United States provided a 'neutral' chairman. The American position was equivocal: Roosevelt's anti-colonial sentiments had been offset by a growing awareness of the need to support Western Europe against Communism. For Dean Acheson this was the major consideration. The Good Offices Committee convened on board the US naval transport *Renville* anchored off Jakarta. They had to bring together bitterly opposed forces.

When Sjahrir resigned, his successor was Amir Sjarifuddin, a Christian and supposedly a moderate. Sukarno's role throughout the long crisis was to reassure his bewildered countrymen, especially all those outside Java apparently abandoned to the Dutch. His belief in *diplomasi* rather than struggle, *perjuangan*, was severely tested, but he continued to maintain a balancing act.

Negotiations in *Renville* arrived at a precarious agreement, signed on 17 January 1948, by which the Van Mook Line was accepted, in return for virtually nothing. A plebiscite was promised in the areas surrendered to the Dutch. Dr Frank Graham, the American chairman, persuaded the Indonesians to accept these humiliating terms by telling them that this would internationalise the dispute: *diplomasi* again. Sukarno urged acceptance over the radio, arguing, 'If ideals can be achieved peacefully why should we fight?' His appeal fell on deaf ears. Amir had to resign, and Hatta was asked to be *formateur*. He now became Premier of a broad-based Cabinet responsible to the President: virtually a return to 1945.

The attempt to legitimise Renville met widespread opposition. Talks with the Dutch went on, but although the Republicans withdrew their forces behind the new agreed boundaries there was no move to begin the plebiscite in Dutch-occupied areas: to the contrary, on 9 March an interim federal government was installed for their projected United States of Indonesia. Of the 16 ministers, nine were Dutch.

An unexpected diversion was the announcement by USSR on 26 May that they would exchange consuls with the Republic. This contravened the Dutch understanding that Renville banned foreign representation. To please the USA the Republic stalled. The Communists responded with hostility. Amir now announced that he had all along been a Communist! From Moscow the sinister Musso returned after 20 years in the Soviet Union. He arrived in Jogjakarta on 11 August and was immediately elected Secretary-General of *Gerakan Revolusi Rakyat* (People's Democratic Front) dominated by Communists. Their line was that the Dutch Communists had been wrong to advise cooperating with the Netherlands: a national revolution was the only path to freedom.

Almost simultaneously, a general election in the Netherlands had produced a Labour-led coalition. If this seemed propitious, the fact that the Catholic People's Party assumed control over Indonesia proved calamitous. The new colonial minister, E.M.J.A. Sassen, was committed to a tough line. Van Mook was recalled home and the outgoing Catholic premier, Beel, was sent out as High Commissioner.

Attempted Communist Takeover

Trouble was brewing in the 4th (Senapati) Division stationed around Surakarta in east Java. The situation was complicated by the presence at Madiun of the Tan Malaka battalion. Tan Malaka was released from jail. Fighting broke out between army units. The Red Flag was hoisted over Madiun town hall.

Sukarno proclaimed a state of emergency and called on the people to choose between himself and Musso: 'My beloved people, in the name of the struggle for Indonesian independence I appeal to you.' Musso replied by abusing Sukarno, reviving the accusation that he had recruited *romusha* slave labour, accusing him of a sell-out to America. Musso was backed by 30 000 rebel troops, but the crack Siliwangsi Division launched an attack. Musso was killed; Amir was executed. The revolt was over.

The Dutch Kidnap Sukarno

However, the Madiun revolt gave the Dutch a big opportunity. Their federation was in being: 15 states, with only the Republic lacking. On 19 December Jogjakarta was seized by Dutch paratroops. Sukarno, Hatta, their ministers and Sjahrir (retained as an adviser) were all arrested and flown off to places of exile. In the confusion Tan Malaka made another bid for power. There was an element of choice in Sukarno's arrest; he could have escaped into the surrounding countryside, but he awaited capture, perhaps calculating that in arresting him the Dutch were outraging international opinion. If so, he was right.

India Mobilises International Pressure

First to respond was Nehru, who convened a conference of Pacific and Indian Ocean states, including Egypt, Ethiopia, the Philippines, Australia and New Zealand, but not Britain or the USA. They agreed to ban the Dutch from their ports and airfields and demanded that the UN Security Council take action.

On 28 January a UN resolution called for the cessation of hostilities, the release of the Indonesian leaders and the restoration of their authority within the Van Mook Line. The resolution called for the resumption of negotiations and transfer of sovereignty to a United States of Indonesia before 1 July 1950. The Dutch had ignored previous resolutions, but this time the United States exerted pressure by suspending part of the aid programme. Sassen resigned from the colonial ministry but his successor, Beel, also belonged to his party. The agreement made by Dr H.J. Van Roijen with Muhammad Rum, a second-rank leader, under the auspices of the American H. Merle Cochran, left much of the recaptured territory in Dutch hands, but accepted the principle of a Round Table Conference and the release of the captured leaders. Before they returned, Tan Malaka (called by some Father of the Republic) was executed by order of Colonel Nasution.

Dutch forces did not leave Jogjakarta until 30 June and Sukarno and the others returned there one week later. They returned as heroes. Hatta re-formed a Cabinet, and a month later departed for The Hague to lead the Republican delegation. The Sultan of Pontianak in Sumatra led the rival delegation from the 15 Dutch-sponsored states. The conference lasted from 23 August to 2 November. It was eventually agreed that sovereignty would be transferred to a United States of Indonesia (USI) before 30 December 1949.

Dutch Recognise Federal Indonesia (December 1949)

There would be a Union with the Netherlands under the Dutch Crown. The considerable Dutch business interests were safeguarded against nationalisation or expropriation. The Dutch colonial army would be disbanded by July 1950 and all units withdrawn from Republican territory. The agreement left the Indonesians dissatisfied in two important respects. They had to assume a national debt of 4300 million guilders (US $1130 million) of which 1.291 million guilders ($339 million) must be paid in foreign currency. The main charge was for military operations waged against the Republic! The status of West New Guinea (West Irian) was left to be determined within one year: meanwhile, Dutch rule continued there.

Sovereignty was formally transferred on 27 December; but the occasion was unlike the independence celebrated in India and Pakistan on 15 August 1947 and in Burma on 4 January 1948. This was more like a pause in the struggle. Sukarno was elected President of the USI. He directed four *formateurs* to submit names for the federal Cabinet and chose Hatta as Prime Minister and Foreign Minister. The Cabinet included two Sultans from Sumatra and South Celebes (Sulawesi) though most of its members were Republican politicians. Sjahrir was not among them. Only later did Sukarno reveal the full venom of his animosity ('While I was taking hammer blows on the head his entire underground effort can be summed up by saying he sat quietly and safely away somewhere listening to a clandestine radio'). Sjahrir never again held Cabinet office.

The uneasy beginning to the federal republic was shattered by the eruption of 'Turk' Westerling into Java. Westerling, a Dutch officer, had pacified (or terrorised) Sulawesi in 1946. Part of the Dutch legacy was a separate state in west Java, Pasundan. From there he issued demands to the Republic and failing any reply captured Bandung (22 January 1950) and planned a coup to depose the USI government in Jakarta. He was disavowed by the Dutch government and compelled to leave hastily, but his buccaneering had done no good for the federal idea or for the Netherlands.

Also in January 1950, Sukarno paid a state visit to India which was returned by Nehru in June: in a typically ruminative speech (so different from Sukarno's declamatory style) Nehru told his audience,

> Our mind tries to skip over this colonial period to some extent as we pick up old threads again – the old threads that have to be picked up in a new way because new conditions have arisen. . . . So, we become more and more intimately connected . . . by bonds of mutual understanding and interest and, if I may say so, even of mutual affection.

Politicians are accustomed to making this kind of speech on a foreign tour, but we may believe that Nehru, with his almost mystical sense of Asian-ness, meant every word.

Dutch Retain New Guinea

The new state was beset by many problems but over-shadowing all was the Dutch refusal to hand over New Guinea. This issue was exploited by Sukarno until the Duth finally gave way, in 1962. He then found another foreign territorial issue in the inclusion of the British North Borneo territories in the newly-formed Malaysia. In a sense, his whole presidency was dedicated to his own vision of an Indonesia stretching 'from Sabang to Merauke', next to what was then Australian New Guinea.

The first move was to liquidate the federal structure and instal a centralised system. Westerling's rash adventure provided a starting point. All the outer states capitulated to the Republic except for the most easterly islands which proclaimed a Republic of the South Moluccas. The TNI arrived to take over but were opposed, mainly by Ambonese ex-soldiers of the Dutch colonial army. By November 1950 resistance was virtually over. Many of the rebels were evacuated to Holland where a South Moluccan government in exile addressed pathetic appeals to the UN, which were ignored. On 14 August 1950 the new set-up was endorsed by the legislature established by the USI who thus ended their own existence. As Vice-President, Hatta affirmed that the revolution had been completed. Sukarno insisted that it had to go on 'with united forces and tireless energy'.

As if to signal their displeasure the Dutch parliament passed a constitutional amendment in 1952 incorporating West New Guinea into the Netherlands and closing off further discussion of the issue.

Trials of Indonesian Democracy

Already the Indonesian multi-party system was demonstrating its inherent weakness. There were over 20 parties. In the parliament the strongest were *Masjumi*, the Islamic party founded under Japanese auspices with 49 members; the PNI, Sukarno's old party refounded in 1946, with 36 members; the Socialists (PSI), Sjahrir's party with 17 members, and *Indonesia Raya*, with 17 also. The PKI came next with 13: in total there were 232 MPs. In 1952 *Masjumi* split into two, one group calling itself *Nahdatul Ulama*. The fragility of the parliamentary system was already apparent.

A major legacy of the revolution was a swollen undisciplined army. Parliament attempted to reduce its numbers and in so doing upset regional and sectional forces. On 17 October 1952 tanks were lined up in front of the presidential palace and a group of officers led by Nasution called on Sukarno to dissolve parliament. The President handled the officers coolly; the plot was a half-baked affair, and it fizzled out. Nasution was allowed to retire. All was far from well in parliamentary politics. There were five prime ministers between September 1950 and March 1956. All headed coalitions on the Dutch model, for despite their hatred for the Dutch they accepted their constitutional forms as their own. When at last a general election was held on 29 September 1955 it was with proportional representation on the Dutch list system. The new parliament of 257 MPs included 57 PNI, 57 *Masjumi*, 45 *Nahdatul Ulama* and 39 PKI. The once prestigious PSI returned 5 members only; indeed, none of the other 23 parties represented were in double figures: most had one or two members. These phantom parties increasingly became the butt of Sukarno's scorn.

Asian–African Conference (1955)

The year 1955 was most memorable for what was probably the high point of Sukarno's presidency, the Bandung Conference, which assembled in April. Invitations went out to 25 countries. The majority were in Asia and the Middle East. The only African states invited were Ethiopia, the Gold Coast, Liberia and the Central African Federation: this White-dominated state came up with the sole refusal. Both North and South Vietnam came, but not North or South Korea.

Nehru saw himself as the central figure; the veteran of the fight against colonialism and the apostle of non-alignment. He expected to act as sponsor to Chou En-lai in the unfamiliar field of international diplomacy, but it was actually Chou who took over centre stage (as *The Times* pronounced, 25 April 1955, 'It has been Mr Chou En-lai's week'). Nehru had to acknowledge that he demonstrated 'reasonableness, restraint and good breeding', but also he was seen to possess authority and a firm grasp of Afro–Asian realities. The final communiqué was notable for its extraordinary length and a good deal of self-congratulation (as when it referred to 'the age-old tradition of tolerance and universality' which the assembled countries personified), yet no-one could deny its significance as a symbol of the Third World renascence.

Sukarno was about to become the storm-centre of his country's affairs after several years of standing above the battle. Indonesia attempted to reactivate the New Guinea (or West Irian) question through the UN. The Bandung communiqué had stressed the urgency of an early solution, and strong Afro–Asian support was expressed for the Indonesian case at the UN though eventually the familiar device of a Good Offices Commission was accepted. Impatient at the delay, Indonesia abrogated the Netherlands–Indonesia Union on 13 February 1956. There was no Dutch response, and it was shown that a nice observance of legality was not essential.

Sukarno Preaches Politics of Consensus

During 1956 dissatisfaction with the existing system simmered and eventually boiled. On November 28 Hatta resigned from the office of Vice-President, deploring the drift towards chaos: 'All our rebellions and our splits, our political anarchy and adventurism, and all the steps taken in the economic field which have created chaos, are the result of the fact that our national Revolution was not dammed up at the appropriate time.' The revolts he mentioned were being led by dissident army officers in Sumatra and elsewhere. Sukarno denied Hatta's indictment. For him the problem was 'free fight liberalism'. He declared (24 December 1956): 'For 37 years I have worked for unity. . . . How can I, who have worked for unity . . . say "Hey, Indonesian people, unite, unite, but . . . the Communists are not included?" . . . Can we create unity while bunging . . . the Communists down a mouse-hole?' This was a prelude to his speech on 21 February 1957 when he proclaimed his *konsepsi* (conception) of what was to be Guided Democracy. He called for a *gotong-royong* Cabinet composed of all political groups, including the PKI. He invented a new slogan, *Nasakom*, meaning Nationalism, Religion (*agama*) and Communism.

Army commanders in the outer islands proclaimed a state of emergency and replaced civilian governors by military men. In this crisis the last parliamentary Cabinet resigned and was replaced by a 'business cabinet' (*Kabinet karja*) headed by Djuanda, not identified with a party. Attempts were made on Sukarno's life. On 14 March 1957 Sukarno declared a nationwide state of war and siege and assumed full powers. In July 1959 he dissolved the Constitutional Assembly and reinstated the 1945 constitution by decree.

Against this background the escalation of the dispute over West Irian was a welcome diversion. Acts of violence were committed against Dutch people and firms; 45 000 Dutch citizens were expelled. This was to continue until by 1962 300 000 Dutch citizens had been sent back to the Netherlands, 280 000 of them being 'Brown Dutchmen', Eurasians, strangers to Europe. These measures caused economic chaos; in particular, 80 per cent of inter-island traffic had been carried in Dutch ships which now moved hastily out of the archipelago.

1962: Dutch Quit New Guinea

At last, in 1962 the Dutch abandoned their costly and useless possession. An agreed formula provided for a brief period of UN control before Indonesia moved in, early in 1963. The final ceremony was witnessed by U Thant as UN Secretary General. The Papuans were supposed to be consulted but the method – reference to tribal councils – provided only nominal assent.

1963: Sukarno President for Life

In the aftermath of this triumph, in May 1963, Sukarno was elected President For Life by the People's Consultative Congress which had replaced parliament. At the same time Britain devolved its last colony in

South-East Asia to the new Malaysia. Sukarno denied that this would be truly independent: 'There was a world revolution of new emerging forces against the old established order . . . a revolution against the exploitation of man against man. That is why we support the struggle of the people of North Kalimantan' [Borneo].

Confrontation with Malaysia

This speech signalled another of those magic slogans or *mantras* in which Sukarno delighted, *Nefo* (New Emerging Forces). The struggle produced one of his most memorable images, *Konfrontasi*, confrontation. In July 1963 Sukarno's intentions were clearly expressed: 'We will destroy Malaysia. Malaysia is against our ideal, against our evolution, and against our State – our revolution is a confrontation to destroy the old order and build a new order in Indonesia and elsewhere.' Sukarno hoped to employ the same techniques as had broken Dutch resistance in New Guinea. The British replied by building up their forces in the jungles and coastal waters of Borneo: for there was still a defence agreement with Malaysia. A 'Crush Malaysia' propaganda campaign was mounted. However, the international support which had been so important over West Irian was generally lacking. *Konfrontasi* brought further economic decline. Inflation –rampant since independence – now went mad. The Indonesian rupiah, worth ten to the dollar in the 1950s, was 300 per \$1 in 1961, by late 1963 it was 1200 per \$1: by 1965 12 000 rupiah bought only one dollar. Sukarno's reply to this economic stagnation and disruption was again monumentalism: the national monument 110 metres high in Merdeka Square; the Istiqlal Mosque, largest in South-East Asia; the stadium for the Asian games or *Ganefo* (Games of Newly Emerging Forces) built by the Soviet Union.[11]

'New Emerging Forces' as Alternative to UN

The USSR was one friend, China was another. When Malaysia was admitted to the Security Council of the UN in December 1964, Sukarno played his last card: he took Indonesia out of the UN, declaring (in words made familiar by Hitler) 'our patience has come to an end'. He attempted to launch a rival international body *Conefo* (Conference of New Emerging Forces) to bring about a world 'without imperialism or exploitation'. This envisaged association with the revolutionary states: China, North Korea and Communist Vietnam. His internal policy was the same.

Communist Party Given New Strength

The alliance between Sukarno and the PKI grew ever stronger. By 1963 there were over 2 million members in the PKI while 12.5 million were in Communist mass organisations. Sukarno made it clear where his *Nasakom* doctrine was leading (17 August 1964): 'I am a friend of the nationalists, but only the *revolutionary* nationalists! I am a friend of the religious groups, but only of the *revolutionary* religious groups! I am a friend of the Communists, because the Communists are *revolutionary* people!' The PKI formed the spearhead. Sukarno planned to employ these forces to counterbalance the growing political threat posed by the army. Certain military commanders were, however, PKI sympathisers, including the air force chief, Air Vice-Marshal Omar Dhani, who visited Peking and negotiated the delivery of 100 000 small arms to equip a people's militia or Fifth Force. This was the situation in 1965 which triggered off the '30th September Movement': (invariably called in Indonesia by another acronym *Gestapu*, for *Gerkang* (movement) September, and *Tigapolu* (thirtieth).

Sukarno's Waning Sexual Potency

The prelude to the crisis was occasioned by Sukarno's apprehension that his physical powers were failing. He had always been proud of his virility. Like any Eastern potentate he was celebrated for his wives. In 1955 he had followed the example of King David of Israel who coveted Bathsheba, wife of Uriah the Hittite. Sukarno became fascinated by Hartini, wife of an oil magnate. Despite the scandal, he married her in 1955. Later, he married Ratna Sari Dewi, a Japanese bar-girl of ethereal beauty, and Hariati, thus completing the quartet allowed under Islamic law. Hence, his fifth wife, Yurike Sanger, did not have their status in the eyes of the Muslim community. Like an old-time Mormon, Sukarno kept each of his wives in a separate establishment in a different part of town. Perhaps it was not surprising that he complained of physical debility. In June 1961 just before his sixtieth birthday he told Hartini that he was old by Indonesian standards. He did have a kidney weakness, but although he was no longer as trim and fit as before he was still an impressive man. Yet it began to be whispered secretly that he was dying.[12]

Probably the *putsch* of 30 September 1965 was intended to pre-empt the power struggle which must ensue when the President died. What happened is not in dispute; *why* it happened has never been properly explained.

The Plot Against the Generals (1965)

Just before dawn on 1 October, six generals and brigadiers were murdered and their bodies thrown down a well at a nearby military base, Halim. Their most important intended victim escaped: General Haris Nasution, chief of staff (retired in 1952, then recalled) managed to escape from his house and jump over the garden wall amid a hail of shots. His five-year-old daughter was killed. Unaccountably, Lieutenant-General Suharto was not on the death list, and it was he who brought the Siliwangsi division into action, and occupied Jakarta. The murders were executed by troops under Lieutenant-Colonel Untung, commander of the palace guard, but other more senior officers were involved, notably Brigadier-General Supardjo. They were supported by two battalions of paratroops and other crack forces. At 7.20 a.m. the radio announced that the *putsch* was 'an internal affair of the army'. Those purged were said to be in the pay of the CIA, and described as 'counter-revolutionary'. It was announced that a Revolutionary Council had taken over.

While all this was happening, Sukarno was at the house of his Japanese wife, Dewi. He set out for the presidential palace about 6 a.m. but heard the place was surrounded. He went to Hariati's house and decided to make for Halim, where he met Air Vice-Marshal Dhani and General Supardjo. Without declaring for or against the coup, Sukarno issued an ordinance stating he had taken over command of the armed forces.

General Suharto Takes Over

This was an empty gesture as Suharto had already assumed that position. Hearing of his movements, Suharto ordered the president to leave Halim as an attack would shortly go in. He travelled to Bogor where his wife Hartini was waiting in the palace there. Suharto visited Sukarno at Bogor and told him firmly who was in control. Sukarno made a radio broadcast of sublime meaninglessness:

> Brothers, because there is a misunderstanding which can lead to a contradiction . . . to remove the doubts among the people and to build a more powerful unity. . . . We must remain alert and not permit any fighting to develop between the Air Force and the Navy because this

will only benefit the neo-colonialists, imperialists and others. I order the Armed Forces to be united to save the nation and the revolution.[13]

Such rhetoric had gone down well in the past, but now made little impact. Already the army was moving against the PKI, and soon there were mass arrests and executions. By 13 October the CIA in Washington was claiming that there was 'incontrovertible evidence' of Sukarno's involvement in the *putsch* in conjunction with the PKI in order to eliminate the military. The State Department was said to be 'unconvinced' by the 'rather meagre' evidence.

Although Sukarno fought to retain his authority he was steadily out-manoevred by General Suharto, hitherto little known, so that *The Times* (2 March 1966) had to announce: 'Remarkably little is spoken of him. . . . He is reckoned of average intelligence . . . and is said to have a moderate faith in Islam.'

This shadowy figure organised the extermination of thousands labelled as Communists: 150 000 is given as 'a conservative figure'. Thousands more were exiled in labour camps on distant islands with no hope of release.

Were the Communists responsible for *Gestapu*? This is flatly denied in the influential though anonymous 'Cornell Paper' issued from the university in January 1966 which accepts that Sukarno and the PKI became involved but claims they did not initiate the plot.[14] The paper blames dissident army officers such as Untung and Supardjo who wanted to get rid of Masution and the general staff. Whatever the truth, the Communists were ruthlessly eliminated and Sukarno humbled. The chosen instrument for his humiliation was the student body – those same *pemuda* who had forced Sukarno his hand in August 1945.

Sukarno Stripped of Office

Endless demonstrations in Merdeka Square called for his removal. 'Hang him, hang him', they cried, and demanded that he go on trial. The students were encouraged by highly respectable people like Mrs Mang Sudewo, wife of a Brigadier-General, who ran a kitchen to feed them. The Speaker of the People's Consultative Congress assured the students, 'The end of the modern Pharaoh of Indonesia is imminent.' On 5 July 1966 that Congress, which had made him President For Life, revoked this decision and also handed over the authority to appoint Cabinets to General Suharto.

In January 1967, Sukarno offered to go into exile providing he could retain his office. This was refused, and next month he handed over what powers still remained to Suharto. In March Suharto was sworn in as acting President and in December 1967 Sukarno was placed under house arrest in Bogor. Not until March 1968 did the general adopt the full Presidential title and role, stripping Sukarno of everything.

Last Humiliations

His personal life followed the same pattern; of his wives only Hartini did not secure a divorce from him. On 16 June 1970 he became seriously ill and died five days later. He was buried in an obscure grave at Blitar in East Java: not so far away from the kingdom of the legendary Kerna. But nobody remembered that any more.

7

The Long March of Ho Chi Minh

Among these creators of new states none is quite like Ho Chi Minh who, despite having the spotlight of publicity turned upon him by the world's press, remains in many ways a mystery man. The first problem is his name. Was he first Nguyen Tat Thanh? Known for more than 20 years as Nguyen Ai Quoc, 'Nguyen the Patriot', under this name he was reported as attending international conferences and became the author of numerous articles. However, as an undercover man for the Comintern he also used innumerable pseudonyms. Some of these will be mentioned, but the reader need not try to remember them. He assumed the name Ho Chi Minh, 'the Enlightened', at some time between 1942 and 1943 and soon thereafter he began to acquire fame. In this account he will be called 'Nguyen Ai Quoc' until 1941/2 and 'Ho Chi Minh' or 'Ho' thereafter.

A Mystery Inside an Enigma

Yet that is not the end of the mystery. There are puzzles about many of his movements, recorded differently by different writers; and when he emerged as a national and international leader, almost immediately a myth-making process began. This may also be true of Aung San, Sukarno, and others; but the careful investigator can disentangle myth from reality for most of their important moves and decisions. One reason for Ho's elusive quality is that he became used to operating unobtrusively; so far as possible, invisibly. He seems to have maintained this style to the end. Nobody could have been more opposite to the flamboyant Sukarno, or even the haughty Jinnah or the mercurial Nehru.

The American major, Archimedes Patti, who headed the cloak-and-dagger Office of Strategic Services (OSS) mission which was in part responsible for assisting Ho into power in 1945, was asked, 'What impression did he make on you?' He replied: 'Really he didn't impress me very much, to be honest about it. To me he was just another old Vietnamese' (Ho was then 55). However, this unassuming manner concealed an iron will. The image of 'Uncle Ho' fostered in national propaganda was almost as illusory as that of Uncle Joe for Stalin. Ho possessed a nerve which never cracked; he pursued his chosen ends with complete ruthlessness. And yet, to those who came to know him well, like Jean Sainteny, his adversary and friend, he was warm, relaxed, affectionate. In endeavouring to give an account of his life one cannot really be satisfied that the truth is emerging: not the whole truth.

The subject of this study was born in the village of Kim-Lien in the Nghe-An province, about half way between Hue and Hanoi. His birthday is officially given as 19 May 1890. Like other Vietnamese of his day he was given two names; his first, 'sacred' name bestowed at birth was Nguyen Van Coong (modification of *Cung* and meaning 'respectful'). His second, literary name assumed when he went to school was Nguyen Tat Thanh ('Nguyen destined for success'). He belonged to a family of literati. His father, Nguyen Sinh Huy, a notable Chinese scholar, was awarded a doctoral degree. He gave up his minor post in the administration because he refused to conform to French practices. He joined the Scholars' Movement in 1907, was arrested, and some say imprisoned on the notorious island of Pulo Condor, where political prisoners were exiled. On release he became a practitioner in Chinese medicine.

Travels to the West

Nguyen Ai Quoc was the youngest child. Unlike his older brothers he went to a Franco-Annamite school and obtained a certificate in 1907. He seems to have taught for a while, but already politics called him, and with his father's support he took ship for France. He signed on as a steward, having acquired some skill in cooking. He remained at sea for a few years and probably visited the United States. Then he came ashore in London and obtained a position as a cook in the Carlton Hotel. Here he acquired some proficiency in English. He spent most of his free time working for the Overseas Workers' Union, a clandestine anti-colonial organisation chiefly recruited from Indians and Chinese. His new friends urged him to go to France, where he could do effective political work among the thousands of Vietnamese the war had brought to Europe to fight as soldiers, in the labour corps, and as civilian employees replacing the French who were fighting. He made his living as a photographer (or one who retouched photographs). In 1919, like many from countries under Western domination, he tried to interest the Versailles Conference in self-determination for his country. He was ignored.[1]

At first he was associated with various Left-wing groups – anarchists, syndicalists – but eventually he joined the Socialist Party. His hero was Jean Jaurès (1859–1914), who in 1904 founded the newspaper *l'Humanité*. Jaurès worked for reconciliation – especially at the international level – and discouraged conflict. He contributed to *l'Humanité*, *'Souvenirs d'un exile'*. These articles were signed by his newly assumed name, Nguyen Ai Quoc. It was perhaps in the spirit of reconciliation that he became friendly with a policeman responsible for supervising the Vietnamese in France, Louis Arnoux. They met at a café near the opera, and Arnoux urged his political chief Albert Sarraut to meet this remarkable young man (Sarraut had previously been Governor-General of Indo-China). That is one version: another is that Arnoux was using Nguyen as a police spy, a charge that was to be made again and again. However, we need not assume a sinister motive for these meetings. Arnoux was intelligent, and Nguyen Ai Quoc enjoyed their conversations. Unlike most of the Vietnamese revolutionaries he was never anti-French and he welcomed the company of French writers, politicians, and even of one general, Leclerc.

Helps Found French Communist Party (1920)

He made his first important political appearance at the Socialist Congress in Tours in December 1920. A contemporary photograph shows the young Vietnamese addressing elderly bearded French Socialists: paying no attention at all. He had been reading Lenin's *Imperialism: The highest stage of capitalism*, and his ideological position had hardened. Hence, when a large majority of the delegates at the Tours Congress voted to join the Third International, against the advice of their leader, Léon Blum, the political heir of Jaurès, Nguyen Ai Quoc was among them. He stated a little later, 'At the start it was patriotism not communism which moved me to believe in Lenin and in the Third International.' However, he was now a founder-member of the French Communist Party, taking part in the Communist Congress at Marseilles in December 1921. *L'Humanité* was now a communist paper, and we find him writing in its columns condemning 'The indifference of the proletariat in the metropole with regard to the colonies. . . . To the French worker a 'native' is an inferior.'

In 1922 he published his first book, *Le Dragon de bambou*, ridiculing the reforms in Annam. He also published a study of colonialism in general which his biographer describes as *'si malhabile, si médiocre'* that he doubts if Nguyen Ai Quoc was the real author.[2]

He paid his first visit to Russia later that year, participating in the Fourth Comintern Congress of November–December 1922. The Comintern was the Third International, established in 1919, and at an early stage the

Indian M.N. Roy emerged as its colonial theoretician, almost equal to
Lenin. At the Fourth Congress Roy emphasised the counter-revolutionary character of bourgeois nationalist movements, such as Congress
under Gandhi; Tan Malaka of Indonesia urged that international
Communism should support pan-Islamic movements, the opposite
argument. Zinoviev, presiding over the Congress, blurred these differences and declared that just as the Russian Communist Party was assisting
the Chinese communists, so the French and Dutch parties should take care
of Indonesia and Indo-China; a curiously neo-colonialist policy which was
to persist for several years. Nguyen Ai Quoc does not seem to have been
prominent in these discussions although he was included in a group
photograph with Roy, Tan Malaka, and other Asian delegates including
three from Japan.[3]

He returned to Paris and edited *Le Paria* (The Untouchable). Now the
picture becomes confused, for Nguyen Ai Quoc returned to Moscow in
1923 for training at the *agitprop* school called the University for the
Toilers of the East. He took part in the Fifth Comintern (June–July 1924)
where he did make a mark. He called for a more energetic anti-colonial
policy by the French and British Parties and demanded that the
Comintern take 'some concrete steps immediately' in South-East Asia. He
emphasised the role of the peasants as a revolutionary force: 'The rising of
the colonial peasantry is imminent.' He declared that risings had already
begun 'but each revolt is drowned in blood'.

International Communist Agent (1925)

Doubtless because he impressed the Congress he was asked to join
Mikhail Borodin as Comintern agent in Canton. He arrived (probably) in
January 1925. His assignment included organising a pan-Asian
propaganda, 'League of Oppressed Peoples of Asia'. This achieved little
success. His main work was among his own countrymen. By mid-1925 he
had organised the *Viet-Nam Coach-Mang Thanh-Nien Hoi*, Vietnam
Revolutionary Youth Association, usually called *Thanh-Nien*. He was
much influenced by Sun Yat Sen at this period. A network of conspirators
was created in Vietnam, but probably more important was the training of
potential leaders, many of whom were enrolled in the Whampoa Military
Academy, staffed largely by members of the Soviet Military Mission led
by General Galen. This academy was to produce the leaders of the KMT
armies and many KMT administrators: and, paradoxically, many Chinese
Communist generals. Alongside them were young Vietnamese; the best
known later was Pham Van Dong who in 1955 became Prime Minister of
North Vietnam.

The deplorable side of this training programme was that candidates who were deemed 'unreliable' were betrayed to the French Sûreté on their return to Vietnam. Even more despicable was the betrayal of Phan Boi Chau, a nationalist leader who had been fighting the French since 1908. This venerable leader was lured to Canton by Nguyen in 1925 and persuaded to go on to Shanghai to an address just within the French concession. There, he was arrested. It has been alleged that Nguyen Ai Quoc received 100 000 piastres (a fortune) for this act. On being returned to Vietnam, Phan Boi Chau was sentenced to a term of hard labour, later commuted to house arrest (he remained in Hue till his death in 1940).[4]

All these activities suddenly came to an end when Chiang Kai-shek broke with the Communists after the USSR had tried to take over the KMT. Nguyen Ai Quoc had a Soviet passport (thus escaping the fate of the Chinese Communists) but had to leave with Borodin and Roy, making an epic journey across the Gobi desert. Back in Europe he once again faded into the shadows, though it seems probable he attended the Congress of Oppressed Nationalities in Brussels, along with Nehru and Hatta. He was sent to Thailand, where he toured Vietnamese villages on the eastern border. He seems to have adopted the saffron robe of a Buddhist monk.

Enters Hong Kong (1930)

By January 1930 he had arrived in Hong Kong where he established the Vietnamese Communist Party which soon merged into the Indo-China Communist Party or *Dong Duong Cong-San Dang*. The meeting to implement this merger of separate groups is said to have been held during a football match on 3 February 1930 (presumably the match distracted attention from the little group). The party formulated a ten-point programme: complete independence for Indo-China, a government of workers, peasants and soldiers, an eight-hour day and equality for men and women.

While this idealistic programme was being assembled a massive revolt broke out in Vietnam: bigger than any outbreak since 1908 or 1916. A Vietnamese battalion mutinied at Yen Bay near Tonking, killing the officers and NCOs. This was suppressed, and the leaders guillotined. The mutiny was not Communist-inspired, but the spirit of rebellion was exploited to incite peasant risings. One was centred in Nghe-An, Nguyen's birth-place, while in Cochin China (known to the Vietnamese as *Nam Bo*) several revolts broke out in the Mekong delta. The French employed troops and also aircraft to crush the rebels, yet they were unable to impose their control completely for several months. Among the rebel leaders was Truong Chinh, born 1909, whose real name was Dang Xuan Khu (he also assumed a literary name). He was on the Sûreté list and was arrested in November 1930 and sentenced to 12 years penal servitude in September 1931. He went to the infamous Son-La forced-labour camp in the jungle on the Thai border where hard-core Communists were able to indoctrinate their fellow convicts.

Arrested: then Freed

The Sûreté had not overlooked Nguyen Ai Quoc who was living in Hong Kong, posing as a Chinese, Sung Mancho. Acting on a French tip-off, the British police arrested him on 6 June 1931, along with a young woman, Li Sam, described as his niece but more probably his mistress. The arrest was irregular in many ways and he was freed from the threat of deportation on 20 August 1931. His case was handled by a British lawyer, F.H. Loseby, apparently instructed by the League Against Imperialism. Another deportation order was served, and the case was taken before the Privy Council in London. D.N. Pritt, KC, later Chairman of the Society for Cultural Relations with the USSR, appeared for Nguyen Ai Quoc, and Stafford Cripps for the Hong Kong government; he quickly decided that he had a weak case and deportation to French territory was dropped. Nguyen Ai Quoc now applied to visit Britain, but this was refused. He secretly visited Singapore and on return to Hong Kong was again arrested. But for the authorities this was enough, and he was shipped off to Shanghai on 6 January 1933.[5]

Next he was at the Lenin School in Moscow, 1933–6. These were the years of Stalin's purges, and it was fortunate that he had spent so long away at a great distance. One who then worked at Moscow University, Nguyen Khanh Toan, suggests that during his Moscow years he was provided with a Russian wife.

With the emergence of Léon Blum's Popular Front government in France, repression in Vietnam was relaxed. Truong Chinh and most of his fellow prisoners were released. The better atmosphere did not last long. With the outbreak of war in Europe the Communist Party was banned in France, and hundreds of Vietnamese communists were rounded up, including Truong Chinh. He was able to persuade his judge to free him and he quickly disappeared. An order for the arrest of Vo Nguyen Giap also went out. He was a licentiate in law of Hanoi University working as a history teacher. Giap went underground, but his wife and her sister – also revolutionaries – were caught. Giap's wife was sentenced to life imprisonment, and died in jail; her sister went to the guillotine. Giap escaped, and went underground, as did Truong Chinh.

Meets Underground Vietnamese Communists (1941)

Nguyen Ai Quoc reappeared in the borderland of Yunnan. A key meeting took place between 10 and 19 May in 1941: the 8th plenum of the Indo-China Communist Party (ICP), where the veteran agent from the Comintern probably had his first encounter with Truong Ching and Vo Nguyen Giap. The young leaders who had founded the underground movement and endured the hardships of physical struggle were reluctant to accept this stranger as their mentor. However, they were shrewd enough to recognise that his international contacts could contribute an essential element to their hitherto isolated effort. His overall leadership was acknowledged, but the younger group retained actual control over their organisation and this dichotomy persisted throughout all the years that followed.

Those who participated in the 8th plenum became members of the *Tong-Bo*, the central committee of the ICP. Truong Chinh was appointed Secretary-General. As a front to the core organisation a League for the Independence of Vietnam was formed: *Viet-Nam Doc-Lap Dong-Minh*, usually known as the *Viet Minh*.

Assumes Name 'Ho Chi Minh': Harsh Captivity

Nguyen Ai Quoc went into Yunnan early in 1942 to link up with the many other Vietnamese exiles who were known collectively as *Dong Minh Hoi*. They were under the patronage of Marshal Chang Fa-kwei, the commander of the units of the KMT army throughout the area. He was not in control of security and Ho Chi Minh (as we may now begin to call him) was suspected by them as a Japanese spy.[6] He probably tried to get himself cleared by borrowing someone else's papers after his arrest. It did not work out like that. Ho was made a prisoner, a convict, 'loaded with chains, covered in sores, put amongst the worst bandits, associated with the condemned, like one dead'. His way of staying sane was to compose poems in classical Chinese which he somehow kept with him.

> The clouds embrace the mountains,
> The mountains clasp the clouds,
> Alone I go, heart trembling,
> Looking towards the southern sky
> I think of my friends.[7]

How long was he held in captivity? Bernard Fall says very precisely that he was held from 28 August 1942 to 16 September 1943. Other writers give different dates, none so precise, but all are agreed that he was a prisoner. Marshal Chang (who later ran a restaurant in Hong Kong) insists that Ho was never imprisoned by him.[8] The next question is why was he eventually released? The most probably explanation is that Chang discovered that the man he had previously selected to head the *Dong Minh Hoi*, Nguyen Hai Thanh, was ineffective: and argued that a now chastened Ho Chi Minh would be more inspiring while still following the Chinese line. A few writers suggest that the Allies (that is, the American OSS) demanded his release so that they could get better reporting on the situation inside Vietnam than the aged Nguyen Hai Thanh, long absent from his own country, was able to provide.

While Ho was incarcerated, Vo Nguyen Giap was training guerrillas for action against the French. Although Japanese forces entered French Indo-China in 1940 they left the administration and armed forces intact. Their own forces there were not large, for Vietnam was merely a staging-post. Hence when Giap began operations there was no contact with the Japanese. His first action was on 22 December 1944 when he led a band of 34 against a French outpost (one is reminded of Aung San and his Thirty Comrades). They captured several outposts and with the arms they gathered were able to equip larger forces. Giap behaved ruthlessly towards the French-led levies and even village chiefs who were condemned as French collaborators. Giap, remembering his wife's sufferings, felt a hatred towards France which Ho with all his old associations never experienced.

Ho made contact with the OSS and their chief, Colonel Helliwell, who agreed to give supplies, arms and equipment in return for information. Although the OSS remit was vague, it was shaped by Roosevelt's general anti-colonialism and his special venom concerning the French record. FDR made it clear there must be no assistance to the French; indeed he was ready to transfer Indo-China to Chiang Kai-shek, who was too realistic to rise to the bait. While the Viet Minh forces were deployed in the liberation of the northern border provinces they were also able to create a reserve (one writer estimates 10 000 troops) who were trained for the 'big push'. Ho seems to have remained in Kunming until 1945 where he cultivated the OSS, portraying himself as a Communist who was above all a nationalist. To Major Patti he stated (in excellent English), 'I put in fifteen years of service to the Party and I believe I paid my debt. From now on I am independent and I can do as I find best for my country.'[9] Just what an American would like to hear!

French Collapse: Underground Forces Advance (1945)

The situation altered abruptly on 9 March 1945 when a Japanese *putsch* liquidated the whole French administration and military power overnight. By then, the British were in Mandalay and the Americans had landed in Luzon. The Japanese interned those who surrendered without a struggle and killed all those French elements who put up a resistance. General Alessandri fought his way out into Yunnan with a force of 6000. They received a stony welcome. A Free French representative was there, Jean Sainteny, who had a heroic resistance record. He opened negotiations with the Viet Minh and was given a statement amounting to a demand for a substantial handover of French authority.

Ho moved steadily nearer the plains as his guerrillas consolidated their hold. By mid-1945 they controlled about one-third of northern Vietnam. As they advanced they conscripted able-bodied males into their army. Sainteny tried to persuade them to accept French fighters in their advance, but he was given a brush-off. Finally, six representatives of France and the United States were parachuted into Viet Minh headquarters on 16 July 1945. They achieved very little.

Like everyone else, the Viet Minh were unprepared for the A-bomb and the Japanese surrender. In the north, Ho was able to move fast. He sensed what he called '*le moment favorable*' (a slogan from Lenin) and on 13 August proclaimed the Committee for the Liberation of Vietnam, which he claimed was 'equivalent to a provisional government'. On 21 August he arrived in Hanoi. A spectator records seeing 'a strange person in shorts, walking stick in hand, crowned by a peculiar sun-helmet, coloured brown'. This was actually the garb worn by most of Hanoi's pedicab drivers. He took a packet of American cigarettes from his shirt pocket; the spectator when told his name was surprised, and asked 'Are you the famous revolutionary?' Ho replied 'I am a revolutionary. When I was born my country was a land of slaves. Since adolescence I have longed for its liberation. That is my sole virtue.'[10]

Vietnamese Independence Proclaimed, Hanoi

Next day, Major Patti arrived by plane, bringing Jean Sainteny who claimed to resume the authority of France. He moved into the palace of the Governor-General. He found the French officials and soldiers had all been interned and he was virtually a prisoner. There was nobody to oust the Viet Minh, and this was accepted by the Emperor of Annam, Bao Dai, whom the Japanese had acknowledged as ruler. On 26 August he abdicated and recognised the Democratic Republic of Vietnam. This was officially proclaimed on 2 September when Ho read a declaration to a vast assembled crowd:

> All men are created equal. They are endowed by their Creator with certain unalienable rights, among these are life, liberty, and the pursuit of happiness. . . . Nevertheless for more than eighty years the French imperialists abusing the standard of Liberty, Equality and Fraternity have violated our Fatherland. . . . They deprived us of all liberties. They have enforced inhuman laws. . . . They have built more prisons than schools. . . . We are convinced that the Allies who recognised the principle of equality of all peoples at the conferences of Teheran and San Francisco cannot but recognise the independence of Vietnam. . . . Vietnam has the right to be a free and independent country; and in fact is so already.

The new red flag with its yellow star was hoisted and among those saluting and standing to attention were the American officers. They had come a long way very fast.

British Occupy Saigon and South

In the south, it was all different. At Potsdam Mountbatten had been given responsibility for accepting the Japanese surrender south of the 16th parallel. As in Indonesia, he had to implement this decision with virtually no guidelines. Major-General Gracey had to take over. The Saigon river was closed to shipping, so on 13 September his division began to fly in via Bangkok.

Douglas Gracey was a typical Indian Army officer. Commissioned in 1914, he had fought at Gallipoli with his Sikhs. Since 1943 he had been in action with the 20th Indian Infantry Division. He took good care of his men and he believed that soldiers should stay out of politics. His instructions were to recover the allied prisoners of war, to disarm the Japanese, and to hand over to the lawful authority as soon as possible.

However, although General Leclerc, whose armoured division had liberated Paris, was waiting at Kandy, the only French force within thousands of miles (other than the Vichy forces now interned) was the 5th Colonial Infantry Regiment in Ceylon. Gracey was on his own.

While independence was being proclaimed in Hanoi on 2 September there was a rising against the French in Saigon. British and Australian POWs who had freed themselves tried to quell the disorder. On 21

September, Gracey (whose division was not yet all in Saigon) issued a general order stating that the transition from war to peace conditions would be carried out all over southern Indo-China under his command. No demonstrations were permitted; looters and saboteurs would be shot. Two days later he released and armed the interned Vichy troops. They attempted to take over the city; for three days they fought the Viet Minh, and in the cross-fire Lieutenant-Colonel Dewey of OSS was shot dead. Gracey was compelled to make use of Japanese troops against the rebels. The conflict was abated. A strong protest against Gracey's action was sent by the Democratic Republic of Vietnam to the British Prime Minister on 26 September. This was said to constitute 'a great violation of our national rights . . . and non-observation of attitude of neutrality by the British disarmament forces'.[11]

Mountbatten was worried by these developments. He urged Leclerc to compromise: 'You cannot put back the past: there is a new situation.' Leclerc replied, 'What you say makes sense but it is not French policy.' Leclerc arrived in Saigon in October with the first French reinforcements. He was in military command, but supreme political authority was given to Admiral Thierry d'Argenlieu, a strange, remote figure previously a Carmelite monk. His principal qualification was total loyalty to de Gaulle. He did not actually arrive until early in 1946; meanwhile, Leclerc consolidated his hold over the south and Gracey's role was phased out. By the end of January 1946 only two British-Indian battalions remained. Although the French now controlled Saigon and the other towns the rural areas were largely in Viet Minh hands. Their leader, Tran Van Giau, used extreme methods to enforce compliance from the people which probably went beyond the policy of Ho.

KMT China Occupies North

The KMT Chinese entered Tonking in massive numbers. General Lu Han had 180 000 troops with him and they lived off the country in the traditional Chinese manner, looting and exporting industrial plant to China. Having experienced a Chinese jail, Ho was cautious in his dealings with them. He was compelled to accept the 'nationalist' Vietnamese who now came in from China in a United Front government. Under these circumstances, Sainteny and his colleagues seemed to offer the possibility of an insurance policy.

Ho first met Sainteny on 28 September 1945. The latter wrote: 'This ascetic man . . . was a person of high calibre. . . . His wide ranging culture, his intelligence, his unbelievable activity and his absolute impartiality won for him his unique prestige and popularity with the population.' (It should be recalled that when he first appeared in Hanoi in August, everyone asked 'Who is Ho Chi Minh?') Sainteny realised that a military reconquest demanded too high a price. He told his superiors in Paris that 300 000 troops would be required to achieve anything (an accurate estimate of what the French eventually had to commit in Indo-China). 'We should negotiate', he concluded.

Ho separately reached the same conclusion. He restrained his more intransigent lieutenants; he fostered the image of Uncle Ho. On 11 November he publicly dissolved the ICP. The Viet Minh made a deal with the Vietnamese 'Nationalists' whereby they were guaranteed a proportion of seats in the new national assembly elected early in 1946.

Ho Forms Coalition Government (1946)

France signed an agreement with China whereby in return for giving up the territorial concessions in the treaty ports, handing over the Yunnan railway, and meeting sundry other Chinese demands, they agreed to withdraw their troops from Indo-China by 15 March. Negotiations went on in Hanoi between Sainteny and Ho. Meanwhile, on 2 March Ho formed a coalition government. The Foreign Minister was Nguyen Tuong Tam who had been in south China but not as an associate of Ho Chi Minh (he fled from Hanoi in June 1946). The Minister of the Interior, Huynh Thuc Khang, was non-party. He was placed in overall charge when Ho went to negotiate in France. Leclerc supported the move to negotiate; d'Argenlieu was hostile, but the new Colonial Minister, Marius Moutet, was (for the time being) persuaded. It was a near thing.

French warships approached Haiphong on 6 March, and despite the agreement were fired on by Chinese batteries. They replied in kind, and proceeded to land. The Viet Minh viewed this development with alarm and a declaration for all-out war was issued. This was overtaken by the convention also concluded on 6 March between Ho and Sainteny. The convention was avowedly made on behalf of the Government of the Republic of Vietnam and for Admiral d'Argenlieu. Accordingly, France recognised the Republic 'as a free State, having its government, its parliament, its army and its finances and as part of the Federation of Indo-China and of the French Union'. Reunion of *Nam Bo* with the north would be accepted by France if ratified by popular referendum. In return, the introduction of the French army was agreed, though under careful conditions: only 'French of metropolitan origin' were to come – no colonial troops. These were to be phased out completely within five years. Further negotiations would determine the diplomatic relations of Vietnam with foreign countries and the future status of Indo-China (that is, Vietnam, Cambodia and Laos).

Ho put all his authority into the acceptance of the convention by his wilder supporters. To receive Sainteny he asked the former emperor Bao Dai to stand with him and endorse the agreement.[12] To his supporters he said 'Keep calm and maintain discipline. I will not let you down.' The French became increasingly equivocal. A conference was held at the hill station, Dalat, between Giap and Pierre Messmer. The demand that *Nam Bo* come in with Vietnam was resisted; the referendum must wait until conditions were more stable. On 30 May Ho left by plane for France to work out a settlement. Two days later d'Argenlieu proclaimed a separate republic for Cochin China with its own army and separate budget: he had yielded to the *colons*. Unknown to Ho, his seeming friend General Leclerc was also working against him: on 6 June he warned Georges Bidault that Ho was *'un grand ennemi de la France '*.[13]

Ho Heads Negotiations in France

In the French general election of 21 October 1945, 75 per cent of electors had voted for Communist, Socialist or Popular Republican Movement (MRP) candidates. The resistance record of the Left, compared with collaboration on the Right, was a major factor. However, when the Assembly presented a new constitution to be decided by referendum, the MRP joined the Right in telling the electors that there were inadequate guarantees against Communist subversion and against disintegration of the French empire. By a narrow margin the draft was rejected on 5 May. A second Assembly was elected on 2 June and produced a modified constitution which was endorsed on 13 October. The head of the government, the MRP resistance leader Bidault, was a believer in the continuing *mission civilisatrice*. He cold-shouldered Ho, who insisted that at the national parade on Bastille Day he be placed next to Bidault. The Communists were scarcely more sympathetic. Their leader, Thorez, had deserted from the army and been stripped of his citizenship in 1939. He made his way to the Soviet Union. He returned to France in November 1944 and was rehabilitated, but was under some pressure to demonstrate his patriotism, including support for the empire.

Ho was kept hanging about at Biarritz. A conference was convened at Fontainebleau, but France was represented mainly by officials, not politicians. There was nobody from the Communist Party. In desperation, on 5 August, Ho declared: 'I have come here to make peace. Do not send me back to Hanoi empty handed.' When eventually a *modus vivendi* was reached on 14 September this purported to 'bring provisional solutions to the most important questions of immediate interest arising between France and Vietnam'. This covered secondary problems and made no concessions concerning independence within the French Union which Ho had expected. On 19 September Ho embarked on a packet boat which took four weeks to reach Hanoi. He was said to be in good spirits, but this was assumed: he feared he would be denounced as a traitor on his return. When he landed on 20 October it seemed that the magic of Uncle Ho had not faded. He still hoped for a settlement, but each time he sent a communication to Bidault it was unaccountably held up by d'Argenlieu. General Valluy, the military commander, demanded that all Viet Minh forces be withdrawn from the Haiphong area, following a brush with the French navy. At this moment d'Argenlieu was in Paris, and he persuaded Bidault to teach the Vietnamese a lesson. This took the form of an artillery bombardment in which 6000 were killed. By 28 November the French had total control of Haiphong and its airport and harbour.

End of Negotiation: Hostilities Begin

A last chance of compromise seemed possible when the veteran Léon Blum became the head of government in December: his pre-war record towards Vietnam had been good. Yet the message which Ho despatched on 15 December did not reach Paris until 26 December, and then yielded no response.[14] Ho could no longer restrain the hardliners. On 19 December hostilities began. The Viet Minh attacked in Hanoi; many French people were killed and wounded, among them Sainteny who had always pressed for compromise. The French forces won back the city, but when they reached the residence of Ho Chi Minh they found he had gone. Next day he issued a proclamation: 'Save the country. We will win. Long live the independent, indivisible Vietnam.'

Thus began the French phase of the Vietnam conflict which was to last eight years. It would cost France over 77 000 of her sons, including 2000 officers (among them the sons of two Marshals of France and of 20 Generals) and even heavier casualties among the Foreign Legion, the colonial troops from Algeria, Morocco and Senegal: and of course the Vietnamese soldiers conscripted by France to fight the Viet Minh.

French policy sought to create a substitute for independence by designating the protectorates of former French Indo-China, and subsequently Cochin China, as associated states within the French Union. Bao Dai was persuaded to become head of state. At first French military activity seemed to succeed. The Red River delta was cleared of the Viet Minh, who retired to the hills.

Aid from Communist China Received: 1949

The situation altered radically when in 1949 Mao Tse-tung's forces reached the border of Yunnan. Thereafter, the Viet Minh could rely on a supply of weapons (mainly American, taken from the defeated KMT). From 1951 a Chinese advisory unit was stationed in Tonking under Wei Kuo-ch'ing. Ho himself had especially good relations with the Chinese leaders in Kwangsi down to the 1960s. France appointed one of her finest generals, de Lattre de Tassigny, to take command in 1950.

De Lattre was a commander in the Napoleonic style but he was also a desert general who relied on an arc of Beau Geste-type forts. Gradually, taking heavy losses in men, the Viet Minh infiltrated into the Delta. The French expeditionary forces numbered 250 000 men. General Giap had about the same number of soldiers, but these were reinforced by para-military elements. His strategy was later described in his own book, *People's War, People's Army*.[15] This emphasises the importance of support from the civilian population, while 'disintegrating the enemy' by propaganda. Gradually, the French people turned against the *sale guerre*.

France Disillusioned: the United States Intervenes

In 1952 a secret meeting took place in Rangoon between the Deputy, Jacques Raphaël-Leygues and Viet Minh representatives. This was abruptly called off when the United States promised a sizeable increase in military aid to the French in Vietnam.[16] Laniel became Premier in 1953, announcing that his government 'was ready to seize all occasions to make peace, whether in Indo-China or at the international level'.

Ho seemed ready to respond when he gave an interview to a Swedish journalist, Löfgren. This reflected his former affections:

> I have always felt great sympathy and admiration for the people of France and the partisans of peace in France. It is not only the independence of Vietnam which is today exposed to severe attacks. The independence of France is also seriously threatened. . . . American imperialism drives the French colonialists to continue and extend the war of reconquest in Vietnam with the object of making France weaker and weaker and overtaking her place in Vietnam. . . . The struggle of the French people for independence, democracy and peace and an end

to the war in Vietnam forms one of the important factors in the endeavour to solve the Vietnam problem.[17]

Ho Chi Minh's outburst was a reflection of the growing American involvement in the suppression of the movement they had previously supported. American military supplies first arrived in June 1950. By 1952 they were contributing $400 000 000 a year and John Foster Dulles gave enthusiastic support as part of his anti-Communist crusade.

Ho was correct in identifying America as early as 1953 as the principal enemy. His message got through: Laniel approved a proposal to send a Socialist Deputy, Alain Savary, to open up preliminary talks, but Bidault, now Foreign Minister and still a hawk, refused: 'Ho Chi Minh is giving in; do not support him by this contact.' A few months earlier, in July 1953, a new French commander took over in Vietnam: General Henri Navarre. He is supposed to have reported back that the war could not be won; but the United States exerted strong pressure to continue. General Giap realised that his best course was to knock out the French before American aid increased decisively.[18] In a series of lunges he cut off a sector of north Vietnam and isolated much of Laos. Navarre's reply was to establish a massive fortified camp near the Lao border at Dien Bien Phu. It was here that the French finally threw in their hand.

France's Last Stand: Dien Bien Phu (1954)

Navarre committed 12 infantry battalions, artillery and some tanks to a place that could only be supplied by air. He calculated that the Viet Minh would be destroyed in any attempt to capture his position. Giap launched his assault on 13 March; for nearly two months the fighting raged. What was a total surprise to the French was the appearance of heavy enemy artillery, hauled up the steep mountainsides. Soon after midnight on 7 May the Viet Minh overran the last French positions held by the Foreign Legion and Algerian colonial infantry. Those who were not dead marched away into captivity. With prescience Ho proclaimed: 'Great as was the victory it was no more than a beginning.'

On 8 May the international conference at Geneva to resolve the Vietnam imbroglio was opened. Bidault spoke intransigently. Pham Van Dong represented the Democratic Republic, and put forward eight conditions which still included the possibility of 'free association within the French Union'. There was no response from the United States or from Bao Dai's henchman. On 25 May, Dong suggested demarcation of zones of control, representing a single holding', on which a ceasefire might be based: or in plain language, partition. There was still no French response, until at 2 a.m. on 18 June the Radical Socialist Pierre Mendès-France assumed the premiership, promising to find a solution within 30 days.

Vietnam Formally Divided, North and South

Mendès-France succeeded: on 21 July the conference issued a final declaration. This followed an armistice agreement signed by representatives of France and the Democratic Republic the previous day accepting the division of the country along the 17th parallel with a demilitarised zone between. Military regrouping was to be completed within 300 days, and the introduction of new forces into either part of Vietnam was prohibited. The final declaration had no signatures appended (the United States and the Bao Dai regime remained aloof). Nevertheless, according to Article 7, 'The Conference declares . . . the Viet-Namese people [shall] enjoy the fundamental freedoms . . . established as a result of free general elections by secret ballot. . . . General elections shall be held in July 1956 under the supervision of an international commission. . . . Consultations will be held on this subject between the competent representative authorities of the two zones from 20 July 1955 onwards.'[19]

The USSR and the People's Republic of China had recognised what we may now call North Vietnam since 1950. India and Burma, while sympathetic to the struggle, had awaited results. Now both Nehru and Nu visited Ho Chi Minh soon after his return to Hanoi.

Friendship of Nehru and Nu With Ho

Nehru noted in his diary for 17 October 1954: 'He came forward – almost leapt forward – and embraced and kissed me. Obvious that this was not a showpiece. He felt it and meant it. Fine, frank face, gentle and benign – not at all one's idea of a leader of a rebellion.' Nu did not set down his impressions till many years later, but they are very similar:

> As the Burmese delegation was entering the guest house, President Ho Chi Minh, who had playfully concealed himself behind a door, sprang out and without saying a word embraced U Nu and kissed him on the cheek. . . . That day Ho Chi Minh was wearing a khaki shirt and khaki trousers. The shirt was not new and the trousers lacked a crease. His clothes were not merely unpressed but looked as though he had been wearing them for two or three days. . . . Ho Chi Minh was so free of cant and pretence that it was as though he was totally oblivious of the

fact that he was president. Seeming him so patently honest, so wanting in pride, and so unpretentious, U Nu was filled with reverence. . . . U Nu did not know that Ho Chi Minh was a bachelor. Therefore, when he inquired after the president's family, asking how many sons and daughters he had, Ho replied with a smile that he had many. . . . U Nu asked 'But how many?' A laughing Ho Chi Minh had to tell him that all the people of Vietnam were his children.

This was Uncle Ho, as two representative Asians saw him.[20] Soon, some of his 'children' were to endure harsh treatment. First, there was an exodus of thousands of Catholics to the south, where they became the most implacable opponents of the Communist north. This exodus was mainly caused by the anti-Communist attitude of their priests: and most of all by the new premier of what we may now call South Vietnam, Ngo Dinh Diem. Diem, an ardent Catholic, a former mandarin, was plucked out of a Maryland seminary to become premier by the Americans in 1954.

However, the brutal application of the new land collectivisation programme in the north must be ascribed in part to Ho Chi Minh, even though he ceased to be Prime Minister in August 1955. Active leadership of this programme was taken by Truong Chinh, Secretary-General of the *Lao Dong*, the cover name for Workers' Party, which the Communists now used. The land reform which Truong initiated followed the prevailing Maoist line. Almost all, except the poor peasant occupiers, were indicted as reactionary landlords. They were brought before tribunals formed of peasants and deprived of their land. They were executed or sentenced to long periods of forced labour. Within a short while it became clear that this policy was damaging the rice crop. The north had always relied upon importing from the Mekong delta; this source was now cut off. Truong Chinh and others of his group were removed from office, confessing to 'major errors'.

Ho Calms Discontent in North

Ho resumed charge of the Party Secretariat. When the 10th Plenum of the Central Committee met in September 1956, Vo Nguyen Giap read out a long list of errors, some quite devastating: 'We have failed to realise the necessity of uniting with the middle-level peasants. . . . Executed too many honest people. . . . Failed to respect the principles of freedom of faith. . . . We resorted to . . . disciplinary punishments . . . executions. . . . Worse still, torture came to be regarded as a normal practice.' A rehabilitation programme restored most 'middle peasants' to their homes and wives, leaving those who had benefited from their expropriation resentful. This reversal of policy came too late to prevent an outbreak in a Catholic area, the Quynh Luu revolt in part of Nghe-An province, in mid-November 1956.

Anticipating Mao's 'Hundred Flowers' experiment in liberalisation, the intellectuals who had been cowed into silence were now encouraged to speak out. There was some indirect criticism of Ho. One poem taken as applying to him runs:

> People who live too long,
> Are like lime pots,
> The longer they live,
> The worse they grow.[21]

By 1957 it was judged that the crisis of confidence was over. Ho's biographer insists that he was never blamed for the excesses; the people distinguished between their revered leader and his 'entourage'. Emphasis was given to the simplicity of his life-style. Although he occupied the palace of the former French Governor-General he actually lived in the gardener's lodging and grew flowers and tomatoes. He dressed the same as all other Vietnamese: a drab tunic suit and sandals made out of old lorry tyres.[22] It does appear that from the late 1950s he took a back seat, leaving the direction of affairs to a collective leadership: Giap as military chief, Pham Van Dong as Premier, Truong Chinh as formulator of ideology, Nguyen Duy Trinh as planner and programmer and Le Duan, brought back from the south, taking over as party chief from Ho late in 1957.

Moves for Reunification Resisted by South

In foreign policy first priority was given to implementing that part of the Geneva accords which provided for elections throughout Vietnam, originally scheduled for July 1956. Innumerable communications passed between Pham Van Dong and the Co-Chairmen of the Geneva Conference, representing Britain and the Soviet Union. The British Government professed to 'have always regarded it as desirable that these elections should be held and have advised the Government of the Republic of [South] Vietnam to enter into consultation with the Viet Minh authorities [sic] in order to ensure that all the necessary conditions obtain for a free expression of the national will'. In the next sentence the British Government added that they 'do not agree' that South Vietnam 'were legally obliged to follow this course'.[23] It was stalemate, and as neither Ngo Dinh Diem nor his American masters intended to allow nationwide elections what had seemed the main advantage of the Geneva agreement was denied to the Democratic Republic.

As in divided Germany and divided Korea, Ho Chi Minh and his comrades might have accepted that this was the reality: especially as it became ever more clear that the United States intended to uphold the status quo with all their power. When Ngo Dinh Diem was proclaimed President of the 'Republic of Vietnam' in October 1955 compromise seemed impossible as he began to suppress all opposition, whether political or religious. In the North, in the Democratic Republic, the army shed all guerrilla characteristics and became a professional force. The particular role of Ho Chi Minh seemed increasingly to be performed in the international arena. As a rift opened between a 'revisionist' Soviet Union and a 'doctrinaire' China, Ho endeavoured to keep open communications, visiting Moscow and Peking frequently. He also cultivated friendly neutrals, such as Indonesia: in March 1959 he issued a communiqué jointly with Sukarno invoking the 'spirit of Bandung'. Any foreign visitor of any distinction would be welcomed in the presidential palace in Hanoi where Ho was adept at revealing the human face of Communism.

National Liberation Front Formed in South (1960)

Yet all the time the Communists looked forward to 'the end of the beginning'. This was brought about when, somewhere in the 'liberated area' of the South, a rally was held in December 1960 to establish the National Liberation Front. In a sense, this was a recognition of the division of the country, as the Front was now the organisational base for activity against the Diem regime. However, the Front was increasingly built up and reinforced by the North via the route which became known as the Ho Chi Minh Trail. It is argued that the year 1960 also saw the recognition of Le Duan as second in the hierarchy to Ho, representing the new generation of leaders.

The focus was now on the South, where despite ever-increasing American aid the West was not 'winning the war'. Diem, once the main hope, was regarded as an obstacle to improvement. On 1 November 1963 he was ousted in an army coup almost certainly promoted by the Americans. Three weeks later, President Kennedy was also killed. In 1963 there were 16 000 American 'advisers' in South Vietnam; two years later their number was over ten times greater. Vietnam had become an American obsession. The air bombing of the North began on orders from

President Johnson in February 1965. Interviewed by a Left-wing British journalist and television producer, Felix Greene, Ho declared: 'You have seen the country. You see the sufferings which air raids have caused our people. Who would wish this frightful war to continue? They give us no choice but to fight. We shall not give up our independence.'

Concern for the worsening conflict was expressed when the Commonwealth heads of government met in 1965. The Afro - Asian leaders were especially critical of the American escalation. Harold Wilson, as Britain's Labour Prime Minister, was pulled two ways. The Left wing of his party demanded an end to American aggression; the Foreign Office under Michael Stewart defended American policy calling uncertainly for an international conference. This was the situation as the Commonwealth leaders sought to find a formula. The best they could suggest was a Commonwealth exploratory mission. Nigeria and Ghana were to be participants.

Nkrumah Tries to Mediate (1966)

Early in 1966 President Johnson ordered that the bombing of the North be resumed after a temporary pause. This was condemned by several outside powers, including France. General de Gaulle wrote to Ho Chi Minh on 8 February 1966, stressing that peace could only be restored by a return to non-intervention; the United States was not named, but clearly this was in de Gaulle's mind. This was the background to an attempt by President Nkrumah of Ghana to break through the impasse. He had been in correspondence with Ho, and now determined to make a personal visit to Hanoi to search for peace.

Before departing, he sought an assurance from Lyndon B. Johnson that he would respond, asking that the talks should not be sabotaged by American air raids. Johnson's reply lacked enthusiasm, but contained a passage which afterwards struck Nkrumah's colleagues as ominous: 'If you go to Hanoi, Mr President, you will be in no danger of military action in Vietnam.'[24] Nkrumah flew to Rangoon, taking his Foreign Minister and a large party with him. There they boarded a Chinese plane and flew to Peking for preliminary discussions. When they arrived, the Chinese had to inform him that in his absence he had been deposed by a military coup in Ghana. He did not get to Hanoi. Although almost by chance, the Vietnam war had claimed another Head of State (its first victim being Ngo Dinh Diem). It was to terminate the careers of two more; Lyndon Johnson and Richard Nixon.

Ho received a visit from his friend and adversary Jean Sainteny in July 1966. They reminisced about old times, particularly their weeks together at Biarritz. Ho was not under any illusion: the Americans were erecting massive bases at Da-Nang and Cam Ranh Bay. He still hoped that France under de Gaulle would provide 'an opening to the west', whereby they could negotiate for *'engagement de dégagement'*. He did not know that ten years would have to run before on 2 July 1976 the National Assembly of the united Socialist Republic of Vietnam endorsed the unification of the nation, proclaiming Saigon to be Ho Chi Minh city.

As American pressure increased, so the response of the Democratic Republic and the National Liberation Front, the Viet Cong, also reached a new level. In the propaganda war, Ho and his men were sowing seeds of doubt within the United States. A notable convert to their point of view was Harrison Salisbury of the *New York Times* who argued that American withdrawal from the South would not produce a takeover by the North. He quoted Le Duan as promising that the Lao Dang stood for 'socialism in the north, democracy in the south'. The South could operate a mixed economy: the two parts of Vietnam would work it out 'as between brothers'.[25]

Tet Offensive Cracks American Resolve (1968)

This was the soft sell; the hard sell came with the Tet offensive, January – February 1968, when Viet Cong forces penetrated almost all American bases and even moved into Saigon. The operation was hideously expensive in lives, and yielded no immediate results; yet as at Dien Bien Phu they crashed through the enemy's psychological threshold. General Westmoreland might successfully call for reinforcements, until there were 510 000 American combat troops in Vietnam, with 50 000 South Koreans and smaller contingents from the Philippines, Australia and New Zealand: they could not secure victory. The climax was in sight: the seeds of doubt had been sown on almost every campus across America, in the churches, in the press, in Congress.

Ho Chi Minh was nearing the end of his long life. He died, as he had lived, without fuss. Some time before, he observed, 'My death? It won't interest anyone. It is what I have done today that counts.'[26] He died on 3 September 1969, after a heart attack. His funeral was attended by Kosygin and many leading statesmen, from China, Algeria and other ex-colonial countries. Sainteny represented France. Deputies of the Assembly of South Vietnam proposed sending a deputation to Hanoi, and Nguyen Xuan Oanh, acting Premier of South Vietnam during 1964 – 5, praised him in the Assembly as a Vietnamese hero: one who might be called an Asian Tito.

Ho's Prophecy: 'Total Victory'

Ho's will was read to the 250 000 people who came to the funeral. He deplored the split in the international Communist movement: 'I firmly believe that the brother countries and parties will unite again.' He accepted that victory was still distant, but 'total victory' was an 'absolute certainty'. He was writing 'in anticipation of the day when I go to join the revered Karl Marx and other revolutionary elders': 'Our country will have the singular honour of being a small nation whose heroic struggle has defeated two big imperialists, the French and the Americans.'[27]

It was no vain boast.

8

Kwame Nkrumah: The Pursuit of Black Unity

Kwame Nkrumah belongs to the age group of Nu and Aung San. Like them he came from a rural family, right outside the westernised professional class. Like Aung San (and also Sukarno and Ho Chi Minh) there was a family tradition of descent from ancestors of good pedigree, former chiefs. Unlike those others he grew up in a colony where higher education was still in its infancy. Overcoming great obstacles he obtained academic training in the United States. Unlike Aung San and Sukarno he was a model student, excelling despite his marginal position. Yet, like them, he saw university education as the portal to political struggle. When he returned to the Gold Coast he had been absent for 12 years: he had departed far too young to have made any mark. The African colony to which he returned was regarded by the British government as 'advanced' – in African terms – which meant that it had made a start on the road to self-government; however, the Colonial Office reckoned that the goal was still distant. Within four years of his return, Nkrumah had emerged as the acknowledged national leader whose stature required a rapid acceleration in the political process. The independence of Ghana in 1957 had a 'knock-on' effect on the other British African colonies similar to the knock-on effect of India's achievement in 1947 whereby Burma and Ceylon also emerged from their imperial past.

Like Martin Luther King, Nkrumah could say 'I have a dream': a dream of an Africa united and free. His African vision was consistent with other wider associations, notably those of the Commonwealth and the UN. One might suppose that this statesmanship would have gained him international acclaim. Instead he was denigrated, almost from the moment he emerged as a leader. In particular, the British press made him a bogeyman. Nehru was also hounded by part of the press led by the *Daily Express*, almost to the day of his death. Nehru was able to shrug off this carping criticism. For Nkrumah it was more than a nuisance because influential elements in Ghana were acutely sensitive to British comment. He responded defensively, becoming eventually what his enemies had called him all along: a dictator. Just as his rise was spectacular, so was his downfall. Yet was his fall due to hubris, the fatal *idée fixe* about power, which has overtaken so many world leaders, including Sukarno? The reader must judge from this account, written by someone who approached his subject with no preconceived ideas either way.

Village Childhood

Kwame Nkrumah was born in September 1909: like Nu he was Saturday's son. His mother, his father's senior wife, was living in a village, Nkroful, near the little town of Half Assini almost on the border of the French Ivory coast: it was there that his father, a goldsmith, practised his trade. The claim to be descended from Chief Aduku Addaie came through his mother's line.

Nkrumah's mother was converted to Christianity by a German Roman Catholic priest and the boy followed her into the Church. He attended a local school and then became a pupil-teacher at Half Assini. There he came to the attention of the Principal of the government teachers' training college. About this time the Prince of Wales' College at Achimota was opened and Nkrumah found himself there. He was fortunate; the Governor, Sir Gordon Guggisberg, was interested in higher education as an element in changing the structure of government and society. The Gold Coast had fallen back from the situation 50 years earlier when English-educated Africans had played a leading part in administration, Christian leadership, the judiciary and the learned professions. During Joseph Chamberlain's tenure of the Colonial Office all that had changed; Africans had been replaced by British. There remained an African elite, very conscious of their historic role in West Africa, usually termed 'the intelligentsia', and still dominant in the legal profession and private medicine. However, as in India, the British preferred the traditional leaders of society and emphasised the importance of the chiefs. In the coastal belt these were really only minor functionaries but in the middle belt, Ashanti, they were powerful.

Receives Best Education in Colony

This was the background to Guggisberg's efforts towards modernisation. He managed to attract to the new Achimota college a remarkable Principal, Alek Fraser, who had a long record of educating the leaders of society in Ceylon.[1] Achimota was organised on the lines of a British public school with the boarders grouped in 'houses' which were supposed to inculcate the team spirit: however, it was more than a boarding school. In the absence of a university college it was the nearest the Gold Coast had to an institution of higher education. Nkrumah (who had been given the Christian name of Francis) responded readily to this challenge. Fraser gave 'inspiration and encouragement' by his talks in chapel, but it was really the Vice-Principal, Dr Kwegyir Aggrey, who stirred up the young student and aroused his first thoughts about nationalism; though Aggrey firmly believed in partnership between White and Black. Looking back, Nkrumah pronounced that the 'Achimota days . . . were among my happiest'.[2]

He returned to teaching in Catholic schools, being chosen as the first African to teach at a seminary for future priests near Elmina. For a time he believed he had a vocation to be a priest himself but he reverted to a previous plan to save sufficient money to go to university.

Enters American College (1935)

His ambition was stimulated by Nnamdi Azikwe, a Nigerian, who had spent many years (1925 – 34) in the United States doing graduate work at Lincoln University and the University of Pennsylvania. When he returned to Africa to work in journalism it was to the Gold Coast he came in 1934. His encouragement stimulated the young Nkrumah. He had inadequate funds to go abroad but a relative advanced him some money and off he went in 1935.

Like Azikwe, Nkrumah enrolled at Lincoln University, Pennsylvania, founded in 1854 as a college for Blacks, which introduced a theological faculty in 1869 affiliated to the Presbyterian church. The library contained a collection of African materials. Nkrumah was to study at this somewhat remote, paternalistic institution until 1942, acquiring the degrees of Bachelor of Arts and of Theology. He worked his way through college in characteristic American fashion, taking menial jobs in the vacation, eventually settling on work as a steward at sea, like Ho Chi Minh. However his teachers recognised his exceptional qualities and he was given junior teaching posts which enabled him to register at the University of Pennsylvania, where he obtained his Master's degree and began to work towards a PhD, specialising in philosophy.

Increasingly he was attracted to Black America, first as a preacher in Black churches and then in civil rights organisations such as the NAACP and the Urban League. He met C.L.R. James with his individual brand of

Marxism and pan-Africanism (James had broken with the Comintern), and he studied the writings of Marcus Garvey which 'did more than any other to fire my enthusiasm'. An American academic writer has quoted a classmate of Nkrumah at Lincoln as asserting he acquired an anti-American complex during these years.[3] This really does not fit the evidence. In his *Autobiography* he reports a personal experience of racial harassment with restraint (p. 42). It is difficult to imagine a more ardent disciple of the American work ethic, combining spartan living with high academic endeavour: he was the epitome of the Get Up And Go philosophy. When Lincoln University awarded him an Honorary Doctorate (1951) his delight was obvious. If he later showed hostility to policies of the United States this was quite separate from his personal feelings about the American people.

Arrives in England (1945)

In May 1945 with the termination of the war in Europe and the easing of Atlantic travel he crossed over to Britain. He records: 'I quickly felt at home in England. . . . Nobody bothered about what you were doing and there was nothing to stop you getting on your feet and denouncing the whole of the British Empire' (pp. 48–9). His first intention was to continue his philosophy studies in London University, combined with reading for the Bar: but this was soon abandoned because of his ever-growing fascination with pan-African politics. His first acquaintance was George Padmore, the veteran opponent of colonialism from Trinidad. Nkrumah was hastily coopted into the preparations for a Pan-African Congress to be held in October 1945 in Manchester. This was the Fifth (or Sixth, according to one's definition) such Congress: most had taken place in Europe, but that preceding the Manchester meeting was held in New York in 1927.[4] The doyen of the movement was the sociologist W.E.B. Du Bois (1868–1963) who argued that the mainline American negro policy of accommodation to White America was harmful: he urged people to see 'Beauty in Black'.

The Africans had little reason to look to British political parties. When the Labour Party issued a statement of post-war aims in 1943 (*The Colonies: the Labour Party's post-war policy for the African and Pacific colonies*), it affirmed: 'For a considerable time to come these peoples will not be ready for self-government, and European peoples and States must be responsible for the administration of their territories.' Nkrumah was an omnivorous reader and certainly took in the meaning of this paternalistic pronouncement.

Helps Promote Pan-African Congress

In Manchester, Jomo Kenyatta attended to the preliminary work. The Manchester Congress was significant in representing the emergence of the Africans as a key element. Du Bois still presided, but the United States sent few other delegates. The Caribbean was well represented by (among others) C.L.R. James, George Padmore, Peter Milliard (a doctor from British Guiana practising in Manchester) and T.R. 'Otto' Makonnen, roped in like Nkrumah as organiser. Most of the Africans, apart from Kenyatta, were new names; political unknowns outside their own territories. There were several from the Gold Coast besides Nkrumah, notably Joe Appiah, a barrister and one of the Ashanti aristocracy, and Dr Kurankyi Taylor, another lawyer, a Fanti from the coast: a neighbouring tribe to Nkrumah's Nzima people. Other important Africans present were Wallace Johnson, the trades unionist from Sierra Leone, Peter Abrahams, South African writer, and – one of the few Francophone delegates – the poet Raphael Armattoe from Togo.

The communiqué issued afterwards, like the Bandung communiqué ten years later, was a general statement concerning the Rights of Man. However, the final resolutions addressed to the Colonial Powers and the colonised peoples provided an agenda for action: 'We demand for Black Africa autonomy and independence'; 'We affirm the right of all colonial peoples to control their own destiny. All colonies must be free from imperialist control, whether political or economic. . . . Today there is only one road to effective action – the organisation of the masses.'[5]

In the Gold Coast the last sentiment was potentially practical politics, for mass politicisation had begun among two important sections of the people of the coast, the cocoa farmers and the ex-servicemen: indeed, the cocoa farmers had first flexed their muscles in 1937 when they refused to sell to the European firms who bought 98 per cent of their crop (fixing the market) and also imposed a boycott on European imports. The war years had seen a boom in cocoa prices: in 1938 cocoa earned £5½ million for 300 000 long tons; by 1948, because of disease, production had fallen to 200 000 tons but earnings had increased to £41 million. Nevertheless, the farmers had to sell at a controlled price and vast sums were retained by Britain, exporting cocoa for dollars. This was to become a major grievance. The second group were returning soldiers, restless after service overseas. By 1945, 63 038 of the Gold Coast population were in the armed forces and 30 500 had served in the Burma campaign where two Divisions (the 81st and 82nd) came from West Africa. Most of the infantry soldiers were recruited from the more backward tribes of the north, but many NCOs and the few junior African officers were from the literate south. Perhaps more important, the motor transport required by a modern army was supplied with drivers by conscripting bus, lorry and taxi drivers from Accra and the other big towns. The others had gone willingly, but the drivers had a feeling of resentment from the start; army pay was less than their civilian earnings.

Gold Coast Unrest: Minor Political Concessions (1946)

This potentially explosive situation was not defused by the introduction of a new constitution in 1946. The governor, Sir Alan Burns, was a member of the Caribbean White upper class. For the first time there was an elected majority in the legislative council (18 out of 32 total). However, the elected members were chosen by an electoral college dominated by the chiefs and the clear intention was to provide political training for the chiefs and the so-called intelligentsia while the Governor retained all power. Burns believed he had answered political demand: 'The people are really . . . satisfied with the new constitution they have gained', he told the Commonwealth Parliamentary Association, adding, 'It is no good trying to hurry the Africans.' He forecast that the constitution would have a life of at least ten years: perhaps lasting till about 1970. Within two years it was condemned by the Commission of Enquiry into Disturbances appointed by the Labour Government as 'outmoded at birth'.

These events in his native land must have appeared insignificant to Nkrumah, engaged in building up a structure of organisations to develop an awareness of African identity and solidarity. He was Secretary of the West African National Secretariat, editor of a paper, *The New African*, and founder of the Coloured Workers' Association. Unlike most of those reading for the Bar or enrolled in university he felt a responsibility for less privileged Africans washed up on British shores, mainly seamen, who had no recognised place in Britain. He worked almost unbelievably long hours and subsisted on occasional cups of tea (rather as Krishna Menon had done during his long, lonely London years).

Nkrumah Asked to Organise Political Party (1947)

News about this dynamic activist was sent back to the Gold Coast, and he seemed just the man they needed to organise a political organisation to associate a mass following with the upper-middle-class political elite, who were already restless within the confines of the Burns constitution.

Nkrumah was told by his friend Ako Adjei (whom he had got to know in America) that a new organisation, the United Gold Coast Convention (UGCC), required an organising secretary. Some time after, he heard from Dr J.B. Danquah, a lawyer and a mainline member of the intelligentsia, urging him to take on the job. Nkrumah was undecided; was he really intended to promote the political interests of the intelligentsia? He consulted the West African National Secretariat: they urged him to go back. He made plans to return.

His Return: Was He a Communist?

When in November 1947 he arrived in Liverpool to embark for home he found that the passport officials were reluctant to let him go. The Special Branch had been watching him, and had accumulated an extensive dossier on his activities. The main question was: did he belong to the Communist Party? Later writers have answered this question with a resounding *Yes*. In his *Autobiography* Nkrumah adroitly sidesteps the question, acknowledging that he admired some of the British Communist Party leaders and rather unconvincingly declaring that he had a blank Party card among his possessions. Let us assume he was a Communist: what does that mean? In 1945 it was clear that 'there was little difference between Labour colonial policy and that of the Tories': the words are those of Nkrumah, but this opinion was shared even by moderate British Socialists, including the Fabian Colonial Bureau and Dr Rita Hinden, its Secretary. Creech Jones, the Colonial Secretary, had been a champion of colonial causes before he took office: now he was falling in with the policies of powerful officials like Sir Andrew Cohen.[6] Nkrumah could still admire certain Labour stalwarts, especially Fenner Brockway, but in general the party was a great disappointment. What more natural than that he should gravitate towards the Communist Party? This certainly did not mean that he had become a tool of Moscow, but that he made a shrewd assessment of which ideology was most likely to speed up progress in Africa.

The UGCC was founded at Saltpond on the coast on 29 December 1947 to work for 'government . . . of the people and their Chiefs'. J.B. Danquah, half-brother of a paramount chief, was the moving spirit, along with Akufo Addo, a close relation of Danquah, William Afori Atta, another relative of Danquah, Obetsibi Lamptey, from Accra, Ako Adjei, and now Nkrumah. All except the latter were lawyers, mostly flourishing lawyers. This became the Working Committee of the UGCC, but Nkrumah rapidly discovered that there was little else: there were only two branches, both inactive. Nkrumah decided to get out on the road. He was given an ancient, unreliable car and in this he made long journeys and addressed crowded meetings. His first appearance in Accra was on 20 February 1948; Danquah was in the chair; he assured the packed meeting that 'Kwame Nkrumah would never fail them.' Among the issues raised were ex-servicemen's grievances.

Riot by Returned Soldiers: Nkrumah Arrested

Two days later there was an ex-service demonstration. About 2000 formed a procession to take their demands to the Governor. They were halted by the police, stones were thrown, and the European Superintendent opened fire on the crowd, killing two and wounding five others. This started a riot; the big stores were looted, and the gates of the prison were battered down and some prisoners released. By then Nkrumah and Danquah had returned to Saltpond. When they heard the news they issued statements: Nkrumah demanded the recall of the Governor and called for a Constituent Assembly.

For some days the government did nothing, shaken by these unprecedented disturbances. Then, on 12 March, the 'Big Six' of the UGCC were arrested and taken to the remote northern territory where they were separated and held incommunicado.

In parliament, those on the Left pressed for an inquiry into the causes of the riots. When Willie Gallacher, the solitary Communist MP, questioned the Colonial Under-Secretary, Rees-Williams, on 1 March about the riots, Rees-Williams retorted, 'I guarantee that when the facts come to light' then Gallacher 'will not like them'. The old diehard, Lord Winterton, asked whether they were 'due to Communist dupes of the Third International, including the Communist Party in this country?' Rees-Williams replied darkly, 'There was certainly Communist incitement.'[7] By 8 March there were 27 dead and 227 wounded in the rioting; later it was disclosed that 2000 persons had been detained 'behind barbed wire'. When Reginald Sorensen inquired what steps were being taken to deal with grievances, Rees-Williams replied blandly that the attitude of the chiefs and native authorities was 'most helpful'.

Watson Commission Urges Reform (1948)

It was then announced that a Commission of Inquiry would be constituted, with Andrew Aiken Watson, KC, Recorder of Bury St Edmunds, as chairman. When the Watson Commission arrived, the Big

Six were released and called to give evidence. The remaining five had retained Dingle Foot, a leading barrister and Liberal MP, to advise them. Danquah's evidence was somewhat defensive, even apologetic: Nkrumah felt that their intention was to distance themselves as far as possible from his pronouncements and actions. All the allegations about his member- ship of the Communist Party were paraded and much was made of his role in London in leading a little group known as 'The Circle'. Its motto was 'Service, Sacrifice, Suffering' – not, one might have supposed, very different from the teaching of Christ – but its final goal was announced as 'a political party embracing the whole of West Africa, whose policy then shall be to maintain the Union of African Socialist Republics'. This was proof, according to the Commission, that: 'Mr Nkrumah has not really departed one jot from his avowed aim for a Union of West African Soviet Socialist Republics. . . . [He] has never abandoned his aims for a Union of West African Soviet Socialist Republics and has not abandoned his foreign affiliations connected with these aims.'

Commission Pillories Nkrumah

By inserting the word *Soviet* into the actual language of The Circle's credo the Commission managed to invest this document with sinister implications: it was worthy of Joe McCarthy, though his technique had not yet been launched. If the Watson Commission intended to drive a wedge between the radical secretary of the UGCC and the upper-class leaders they succeeded. The break came rapidly, though the complaints of the intelligentsia were forced. They objected because Nkrumah had set up a 'Ghana National College' for the education of students expelled because of their support during the banishment of the Big Six; they objected to his launching of the *Accra Evening News*, an anti-colonial voice which achieved immediate popularity; most of all they objected to his Committee on Youth Organisation, set up as a branch of the UGCC. This soon became the main vehicle for nationalist demand.

The Report of the Commission (which was not published until the autumn, when the Government had worked out its response) was strangely two-faced. The colonial government was upbraided for being out of touch; failing to grasp that the colony had been exposed to liberal ideas from the outside world: 'The star of rule through the Chiefs was on the wane', it declared. While urging rapid constitutional reform they concluded: 'We have no reason to suppose that power in the hands of a small literate minority will not be used to exploit the illiterate majority.' Nevertheless they recommended that a committee should be formed from Gold Coast leaders to chart a programme of reform. The Governor (1947–9), Sir Gerald Creasey, who was a Whitehall official, lacked a sure touch; despite the Watson Commission's comments on chiefly authority he selected a group strongly representative of the chiefs and their allies. The Chairman was Judge Henley Coussey. Of the 40 members, nine were chiefs; the remainder belonged to the old intelligentsia. Six from the UGCC were included: Danquah, Akufo Addo and Obetsibi Lamptey; and three from outside the Big Six: B.D. Addai, Combina Kessie from Ashanti and 'Pa' Grant, the father figure of the UGCC. Nkrumah was excluded: and as the other UGCC leaders remained preoccupied with their task, he strengthened his political standing with the public.

The UGCC working committee attempted to impose discipline. A meeting was held in August 1948, when Akufo Addo asked Nkrumah the question: 'Why do you persist in using the word Comrade as a term of address?' Pa Grant demanded his removal from office; other committee members thought he might be neutralised by making him treasurer. They knew that Nkrumah enjoyed a popularity which none of them could emulate. Through the Youth Organisation he was building up an alternative body of supporters, notably K.A. Gbedemah, educated at Achimota. He was almost as active and enterprising as Nkrumah. Other supporters were Kojo Botsio, Krobo Edusei, Dzenkle Dzewu: the young men.

Nkrumah Founds His Own Party: CPP (1949)

At length, at a meeting on 12 June 1949 at a sports ground in Accra, speaking to a crowd estimated at 60 000, Nkrumah announced the formation of the Convention People's Party (CPP), to create 'the new Ghana that is to be'. This move was timed to pre-empt the UGCC from dismissing him. The crowd sang 'Lead Kindly Light', which became the anthem of the CPP. It was Gandhi's favourite hymn: not exactly a call to revolution ('One step enough for me').

This was the scene when a new Governor arrived in August. Sir Charles Arden-Clarke, who had spent most of his career in northern Nigeria, Lugard's country, was a reliable paternalist. Next came publication of the Coussey report in October. The final recommendation (the committee had divided almost equally) was for an assembly of which two-thirds would be directly elected with one-third elected by the territorial councils of chiefs. The Colonial Office diluted these proposals, announcing a legislature of 100 members: 37 from the chiefs, 33 (rural) chosen by electoral colleges, five (urban) directly elected, two chosen by the Europeans, and three officials. The vote was restricted to house-holders in the towns and taxpayers in the rural areas. Creech Jones congratulated the committee on producing a constitution which would have the effect of cutting the CPP down to size. The Colonial Office Report, 1949–50, declared, 'The people of the Gold Coast . . . refused to be coerced into irresponsible action by a handful of extremists of the Convention People's Party'.

Crackdown on CPP: Jail for Leaders

When Nkrumah announced a programme of Positive Action, this was, in effect, a Gandhian campaign of civil disobedience. In addition he convened a People's Representative Assembly which was not confined to the CPP but included others. Positive Action was begun in January 1950. The government began by arresting the less important members of the CPP as a warning and only on 22 January was Nkrumah pulled in. He was arraigned on three different charges and sentenced to three periods of one year's imprisonment with hard labour to run consecutively.

There was no question of giving special treatment to a political prisoner, as in the case of Nehru. Nkrumah was thrown into a cell along with ten others. For eleven men there was one latrine bucket. They slept on the concrete floor. No reading or writing materials were allowed. Nkrumah managed to keep up a correspondence by writing on lavatory paper which he wheedled out of his cellmates.

Nkrumah Contests Election from Jail

The long sentence was punctuated by the announcement of a general election under the Coussey constitution to be held on 5 and 6 February 1951. Because, technically, his jail sentence was for one year, Nkrumah could register as a voter and then stand for election. He persuaded the CPP to nominate him as one of the two candidates for the Accra double-member constituency. Gbedemah unselfishly withdrew and stood for another seat. Nkrumah was able to write the party manifesto on his borrowed toilet paper, and smuggle other messages out of prison. The UGCC concentrated their resources against Nkrumah and his running mate, T. Hutton-Mills. The tribalism of the town's Ga majority was given heavy emphasis. They should reject this stranger, this Nzima. Despite all the propaganda, the electorate – often described as petit bourgeois – came down decisively for Nkrumah and the CPP. In Accra, Nkrumah headed the poll with 20 780 votes while Hutton-Mills was given 19 812.

Their UGCC opponents, both Ga and former friends, Obetsibi Lamptey (1630 votes) and Ako Adjei (1451 votes) were humiliated.

Dramatic CPP Victory (1951)

Throughout the colony in urban constituencies the CPP received 58 855 votes, while all others received only 5574. In the rural electoral colleges the CPP had 1938 votes and all others 780 votes. Because of the indirect system the UGCC was able to return three candidates: Sir Tsibu Darku and K.A. Busia, Chiefly dignitaries, and Tachie Meson, a business tycoon from Sekondi on the coast. Of these, Busia was to make his mark later: an Oxford graduate, the first African to be taken into the Colonial Service (in 1942), he was exactly the type the British would have preferred.[8] However, the unpalatable fact was that the CPP had won a resounding triumph.

After an awkward pause, while the Governor and the Colonial Secretary digested the unwelcome news, the release of Nkrumah and the other six CPP leaders still imprisoned was announced. Nkrumah emerged, drawn, and obviously still dazed, to a tumultuous welcome from virtually the whole of Accra.

Governor Accepts Nkrumah as Leader in Council

Making the best of the situation, Arden-Clarke invited Nkrumah to meet him and submit his list of names for the majority of the Executive Council who would now become Ministers. The dangerous Communist agitator had been transformed overnight into the Governor's principal councillor. It was a situation often to be repeated in the following years in British colonies. Out of the seven Africans who now took over as Ministers, all except one were CPP members: the odd man out was J.A. Braimah of the northern territory which had played no part in the election.[9]

What were the attitudes of the two leading figures? The Governor's position is shrewdly summed up by one observer: 'A deal with Nkrumah and the CPP would give the British a breathing space, perhaps a long one.' This was now the prayer of all British colonial administrators: 'Peace in our time'. The old vision of a British Empire lasting for centuries, like Rome, had faded. And so 'The government in Britain, and indeed the outside world as a whole, watched with amazement the steadily growing friendship between these two very different men, as they steered the Gold Coast towards independence.'[10]

In this as in subsequent encounters with Englishmen, Nkrumah was very sensitive to atmosphere. He could work with men whose background and beliefs were entirely opposed to his own, provided he was assured of their goodwill. Any suspicion that he was being deceived or double-crossed would induce extreme hostility. For the moment, all seemed well. He was aware that his powers were limited: 'The civil service, the police, the judiciary, defence and external affairs were all in the hands of the Governor and . . . all decisions thereon had to come from Whitehall' (p. 147). He settled for a gradualist policy. Late in October 1951 Labour gave way to a Churchill-led Conservative government. There was no reversal of policy: Nkrumah had been right in assessing their relative positions on Africa, only now the Tories were out to show that they had shed pre-war Conservatism. In March 1952, Nkrumah's ambiguous status as 'Leader of Government Business' was upgraded to that of Prime Minister. He pressed for further constitutional advance, and his proposals were published by the British Government as a White Paper in June 1953. Discussion in Cabinet was aided by the absence of Churchill – and also Eden – because of illness. The Colonial Secretary, Oliver Lyttleton, announced in October that all the proposals were accepted save only for the suggestion that the Gold Coast should at once be transferred from the Colonial Office to the Commonwealth Relations Office. On 28 April 1954, the Colonial Office Minister told parliament they had reached 'the last stage before the Gold Coast assumes full responsibility for its own affairs'.

He Secures Promise of Self-Government (1954)

Did Nkrumah's policy of accommodation mean following the middle way? Sometimes this seemed indicated, as when he told the legislature they must beware 'When we are freeing ourselves from one form of imperialism [against those who would] . . . bind us to another one which would swiftly undo all the work that has been done in recent years to foster . . . a free and independent nation'; 'As we would not have British masters, so we would not have Russian masters.'[11] Yet the CPP was becoming a political monolith, a 'Tammany-type machine' as an American observer wrote: no longer the party of the masses. This tendency was reinforced by Nkrumah's almost obsessive working habits. Because he sat at his desk from early morning until night he was not getting around to see what was happening among the ordinary people: and many of his henchmen were using their positions of power for personal or family advantage. All this surfaced when a second general election was called to provide a bridge to lead into that 'last stage' before independence.

The 1954 election was held under the same franchise as before (giving the vote to about half the adult population) but this time the whole country was divided into 104 single-member constituencies. There was keen competition to obtain the CPP ticket, and many would-be candidates not selected stood as 'rebels': altogether there were 323 candidates for the 104 seats. There was a rival party in the field, the Ghana Congress Party (GCP), founded in 1952 by Dr Busia; it included several of the erstwhile UGCC leaders, but despite some impressive names it operated from a narrow base. The GCP formed an electoral pact with the other opposition groups, among which the Northern People's Party (NPP) was the most formidable. Nkrumah dealt with the rebels by expelling 81 CPP members; many of them drifted over to the NPP. After the election, the CPP held 72 seats and the opposition 32. The NPP gained 16 seats, but only Busia was successful from the Congress, beating his CPP rival by nine votes; Danquah was defeated by over 1100 votes. Nkrumah refused to recognise the NPP in the new parliament as the official opposition.

Opposition Develops in Ashanti

During the 'last stage' an unexpected groundswell of opposition developed. Cocoa production had largely shifted from the coastal area, where disease had destroyed many cocoa trees, into Ashanti. The cocoa farmers in this middle belt felt the same grievances against the CPP government that earlier the southerners felt towards the British: they were carrying others on their backs. The initiative was taken by Bafuor Osei Akoto, a prosperous, go-ahead cocoa farmer of Kumasi. He organised a demonstration on 19 September 1954, out of which was born the National Liberation Movement (NLM), a name which in the past the CPP had employed. The new movement was endorsed by the Kumasi chiefs, and several rebels from the CPP joined. A dramatic fillip was given to the cause when three major CPP Ashanti leaders announced their adherence in January 1955: these were Joe Appiah, R.R. Amponsah and Victor Owusu, while from the coast Kurankyi Taylor (expelled from CPP in 1952) also declared for the NLM. Appiah and Taylor had taken part in the historic 1945 Manchester Congress. Appiah had been in England from 1944–54 and married the daughter of Stafford Cripps. His prestige stood high, and it made a sensation when he denounced the CPP for corruption and waste.

The big chance came in July 1955 when a by-election in the heart of Ashanti was caused by the death of its CPP MP. The NLM candidate won with almost 70 per cent of the vote. It seemed that their claims must be taken seriously. They demanded that the Gold Coast become a federation with four states: the north, Ashanti, the south, and Togoland (the former German colony, now divided between Britain and France). The CPP dismissed the NLM claims as irrelevant to the main issue: early independence for Ghana.

The response of Conservatives who followed colonial affairs in Britain was less than friendly to the NLM; one article asserted: 'It is not by breakaway and territorial fragmentation that opponents of a government in power should seek to get their way but by fighting the government as a nation-wide party and finally throwing it out.'[12] A Select Committee of the Gold Coast parliament – which the opposition refused to join – rejected federalism in July 1955. Nkrumah now asked for a constitutional adviser to be sent from England. In place of a constitutional expert, the Colonial Office despatched Sir Frederick Bourne, formerly an Indian Governor, and then Governor of East Pakistan. Was this a sinister move? Apparently not, as Bourne also advised against federalism.

London Imposes Conditions on Independence

The Colonial Secretary, now Lennox-Boyd, invited Nkrumah to visit London but he would not leave at this critical time. Lennox-Boyd then laid down that independence would only be granted if wanted by 'a substantial majority of the people'; if Bourne's proposals were accepted by NLM as well as CPP then they could go ahead: 'If he failed then there appeared to be no alternative but to call a general election' (p. 245). Nkrumah summoned a constitutional conference with Bourne in attendance; several organisations joined in but not the NLM and its allies. The atmosphere of uncertainty was reflected in an increased level of violence, including attacks aimed at Nkrumah (Law and Order was still the Governor's responsibility). Holding another general election might entail a general breakdown: Nkrumah again urged that the time was ripe for independence *now*. In parliament, Lennox-Boyd restated his position on 11 May 1956: 'If a general election is held Her Majesty's Government will be ready to accept a motion calling for independence within the Commonwealth passed by a reasonable majority in a newly elected legislature and then to declare a firm date for this purpose.'

CPP Win Another Election: Independence Conceded

So there was no escape. The second election in two years was fixed for July. The NLM endeavoured to expand its activities beyond Ashanti – largely at the urging of Kurankyi Taylor – and thereby became overextended. Despite all their expectations (and ample campaign funds) they did not do much better than the GCP in 1954. The CPP won 71 out of the total of 104 seats. The NPP won 15 in the north (one less than in 1954) and the NLM took 13 of the Ashanti seats. The difference in the popular vote was less dramatic: for the CPP, 398 141 (plus five uncontested seats, where presumably they could have had a landslide); for the combined opposition, 299 116 votes.

On 3 August Nkrumah introduced a motion in the legislature calling for independence; it was passed by 70 to 0 as the opposition boycotted the occasion. The Colonial Secretary announced that parliament would put this into effect. However, Nkrumah's own proposals for an independence constitution were vetoed in favour of a Colonial Office draft which imposed limitations on Ministerial authority in the new Ghana. A Public Service Commission controlled all appointments; there were 13 entrenched clauses which could only be altered by the vote of the five regional councils: a not altogether unbiassed observer called this 'Government by Civil Servants behind a Parliamentary façade'.[13] Lennox-Boyd visited Accra in January 1957 to inform Nkrumah that he had to accept these provisions, or forgo independence. He chose the lesser evil, and on 6 March 1957 Ghana became independent as a Dominion.[14] The name was symbolic, commemorating a West African kingdom originating about 800 AD whose boundaries were unknown. Ghana symbolised West Africa before it was carved up by the Europeans; it symbolised the African federation Nkrumah longed to assemble. As constitutional head of the new state, Arden-Clarke briefly became Governor-General until Lord Listowel (former Secretary of State for India and Burma) arrived.

Nkrumah had his first opportunity to meet his fellow Prime Ministers at a Commonwealth Conference, June–July 1957. Before their first meeting, Nkrumah called upon Harold Macmillan, who had become Prime Minister five months earlier. In his diary, Macmillan recorded that he 'certainly has considerable charm'. Nkrumah's first encounter with Nehru was less happy.

Nkrumah Meets Nehru (1957)

As Indian High Commissioner, Mrs Pandit had her brother staying with her. She invited Nkrumah to breakfast, and he first met Mrs Pandit's grand-daughter:

As he smiled at the baby she leaped out of her nanny's arms into his. It was a sweet sight. While this was going on at the front door Bhai was coming down the stairs obviously lost in thought. He came towards Nkrumah and without a preliminary greeting said "What the Hell do you mean putting your head on a stamp?" Fortunately he recovered himself immediately and in a moment both men were laughing.

However, reportedly, Nehru was not amused: 'From then on he considered Nkrumah an opportunist of the Sukarno stamp.'[15]

In 1958 Nkrumah was able to make a start on implementing his dream of African Union. He had convened a pan-African conference in Kumasi in 1953 but that had necessarily been limited to consultation. Now in April 1958 there was a conference of independent states. Black Africa could provide only three participants: Ghana, Liberia and Ethiopia, the oldest of them all. The other five were Egypt, Tunisia, Libya, Sudan and Morocco. In addition, Algeria (whose independence was not recognised until 1962) sent a delegation. Frantz Fanon, who was there, related: 'Dr Nkrumah made a point of receiving our delegates among the first. For more than one hour the Algerian problem in its relation to the liberation of the African continent was studied. Once again, the Ghanaian Chief of State pledged the support . . . of the people of Ghana.' Nkrumah promised to recognise the Provisional Government of Algeria: 'in the immediate future. . . . Africa must be free, said Dr Nkrumah in his inaugural speech. We have nothing to lose but our chains and we have an immense continent to win.'[16] It was rhetoric: but effective rhetoric.

In December 1958 Nkrumah convened another All-African Peoples Conference with representatives of 28 territories still under colonial rule to meet at Accra. He deliberately shared the limelight with Tom Mboya of Kenya who showed himself a brilliant chairman. Mboya declared that they were 'facing a rough patch in the independence struggle'; symbolised by the continuing detention of their leader, Jomo Kenyatta.

Help for Guinea Against French Pressure (1958)

Of more immediate consequence, Nkrumah stepped in to assist a West African neighbour in difficulty. De Gaulle had become President, determined to transform the French African empire into a francophone community of autonomous states. He invited them to decide by referendum whether to opt for autonomy, with full French support, or for independence outside the community. Only Guinea, led by the activist Sékou Touré, decided for independence in October 1958. France gave a demonstration of what this would entail: all French personnel were withdrawn, investment was suspended, and even government and economic facilities already installed were taken away. Nkrumah's response was immediate: on 23 November a Ghana–Guinea union was proclaimed, and the new partner was given a credit of £10 million. This allowed Guinea to survive, and by its example encourage its less confident neighbours, Senegal and French Sudan, to ask for independence, amalgamating as a new state, Mali.

Nkrumah also made an African tour, in which he built up his relationship with President Nasser, and went on to visit Nehru in India. Visits were very much in the air. In January 1960 Macmillan set out on a tour of Africa, first stopping in Ghana: 'Nkrumah was an engaging character with much charm of manner and courtesy', he writes. Ghana's intention of shortly becoming a republic was discussed and no objection was raised, though the British Prime Minister insisted this 'must follow an orderly course'. Macmillan recorded meeting Nkrumah's wife (he had married an Egyptian Coptic Christian) and noted 'the pride and pleasure which he took in his newly born son. Whatever may have been his public faults . . . he had many private virtues.'[17]

Referendum Endorses Republic (1960)

In order to obtain a republic, Nkrumah announced a popular referendum, though others taking this step had not considered a referendum necessary. Reportedly, he wrote to all Heads of Commonwealth governments inviting them to send observers to check the conduct of the elections. Most ignored his letter but Nehru 'denounced the idea as derogatory to the sovereignty of the new state and reproached Dr Nkrumah for ever issuing the invitation'. Not surprisingly he was 'upset'. The referendum was accompanied by an election for President: Danquah chose to oppose Nkrumah. The result showed a majority of 900 000 for the constitution (1 008 740 for, 131 425 against) and a slightly larger majority for Nkrumah as President (Nkrumah: 1 016 076; Danquah: 124 623). The most careful assessment decides that the vote was fair in the towns and in the south but was rigged in Ashanti and neighbouring areas. The conclusion is that Nkrumah would have otherwise won by the two-thirds majority which was the general election pattern.[18]

Now began the long-drawn-out tragedy of the Congo which, according to General H.T. Alexander, 'produced a fundamental change in Ghana's position *vis-à-vis* the West', while Basil Davidson observes 'experience in the Congo . . . seems to have formed for Nkrumah the final demonstration that policies of "tact", of "continuity", of conformity with Western wishes had nothing more to offer'. Writing from two very different political positions they draw the same conclusion: the Congo experience had a traumatic effect upon Nkrumah's view of Ghana's relations with Britain, the United States and the Commonwealth. Henceforward his concept of non-alignment was much more critical of Western motives in Africa and the Third World.

It was with great reluctance that the Belgians recognised Patrice Lumumba as a national leader. However, in elections to a National Assembly held on the eve of independence, Lumumba's party (*Mouvement National Congolais:* MNC) won 41 of the 137 seats. The next grouping in this hastily cooked-up Assembly gained only 13 seats. Manoeuvres to block him failed to stop the Assembly endorsing his claim to form a government, and he went ahead on 23 June 1960. Independence was granted one week later. In July the *Force Publique* which Belgium had created broke out in mutiny. Pleading danger to the many thousand Belgian nationals who remained in the Congo, paratroopers were flown in. One of their tasks, it emerged, was to support a breakaway movement in the mineral-rich province of Katanga producing the main Belgian investment. Lumumba appealed to the UN and then, failing a response, to the states of Africa.

Help for Lumumba in Congo

Nkrumah at once despatched a mission to Leopoldville. His choice of emissary was odd: Andrew Djin was a party hack who, when manager of the Cocoa Purchasing Company, had been censured by a Commission of Enquiry for 'irregularities', and was not a 'fit and proper person' to run the firm; though the Commission hinted that Nkrumah was 'indebted to Mr Djin'. Immediately after the Djin mission, Nkrumah sent his Chief of Defence Staff, the British Major-General Alexander to Leopoldville. In his view there was imminent danger of the Congolese mutineers and the Belgian soldiers being embroiled in conflict. On his own initiative Alexander went to the mutineers' barracks and persuaded them to lay down their arms. When he heard, Djin was furious at this move. Nkrumah decided to order the immediate airlift of two of the army's three battalions to Leopoldville to give muscle to the UN who, meanwhile, had established a mission in the Congo. These were the first forces to come in. They were supported by a contingent of Ghana police and various other services, such as doctors. They introduced some order into near-chaos.

Nkrumah gave total commitment to Lumumba from the start: other non-aligned were more cautious. Nehru hesitated. Perhaps because he considered Nkrumah an opportunist he instructed Krishna Menon at the

UN in New York to hold aloof and 'if pressed . . . vote against direct military assistance'. This was ironic as later India was to provide a complete brigade for the Congo.

Meanwhile, Lumumba had paid a brief visit to the UN. On his way back he halted in Accra. On 8 August he and Nkrumah put their signatures to a document intended to seal their partnership: they would form a Federal Union and 'any state or territory in Africa is free to join this Union'. This agreement was kept secret. It was as momentous – and as unfulfilled – as Churchill's offer in 1940 to form a Franco–British Union. From this moment, everything went wrong for Lumumba. On 5 September President Kasavubu dismissed his Prime Minister, although he secured a vote of confidence from both Houses of Parliament. Lumumba attempted to appeal to the public over the radio but he was turned away by Ghanaian troops acting under UN orders (heading the UN mission was Ralph Bunche). The Ghana representative, Djin, was totally ineffective in this emergency: when he visited UN headquarters he was informed that 'the Congolese no longer had any confidence in us'. He ascribed this loss of confidence to 'General Alexander's intrigue and subversive action'.

A few days later Lumumba was arrested, and then released. He had turned against the Ghana army and the same day (12 September) he gave an ultimatum to the Ghanaians 'to cease all activities in the Congo within one hour'. Nkrumah continued to despatch long letters of brotherly advice to the Prime Minister of the Congo but the situation had passed beyond both of them. Power was seized by the Congo army now controlled by Colonel Mobutu. In November the General Assembly of the UN recognised the government of Kasavubu on a vote which split the African states: Ghana, Guinea, Mali, Morocco and Egypt supported Gizenga as Lumumba's heir; the remainder, solidly francophone, voted for Kasavubu.

Meanwhile, the Ghanaian presence 'on the spot' ceased to be very relevant. Djin went back to Ghana and his role was assumed by Nathaniel Welbeck, an old associate of the President, who was a rabble-rousing speaker but no diplomat. The UN officials became increasingly irritated by his bumbling interventions. Having been declared persona non grata his residence was attacked by Congolese soldiers; Tunisian troops defending Welbeck suffered casualties. He was ignominiously bundled home by Alexander, and the Ghana mission closed.

All this time, Lumumba had been under house arrest in Leopoldville. On 27 November he slipped away, heading for Stanleyville and Gizenga. He was intercepted on 2 December. This roused Nkrumah to a fresh effort on his behalf. He asked Macmillan to intervene: 'It was quite wrong for other people to incarcerate a "legal Prime Minister".' In his whimsical way the British Prime Minister observed, 'This argument naturally had some appeal to me on general grounds': but he did not respond. To Nkrumah it seemed that the British – and also the United States and France – were behaving in a devious and cynical fashion, pretending to uphold the UN but in reality sanctioning the separatist regime of Tshombe in Katanga.[19]

Shocked by US–UK Response to Lumumba's Murder

Several Afro–Asian states withdrew their contingents in protest against the ineffectiveness of the UN: neither Ghana nor India withdrew. In January Lumumba passed into the custody of Tshombe; Nkrumah was at his wits' end. He told Macmillan that if any harm befell him 'it would have a most serious effect upon the relations of Ghana with the Commonwealth . . . the failure to help Lumumba would never be forgotten by the people of Africa.' Nevertheless, Lumumba was murdered: probably on the day he arrived in Katanga (17 January) though the details never became known. On 14 February 1961, the day after news of Lumumba's death was released, Nkrumah made a long broadcast over Ghanaian radio. He indicted the UN which had failed to preserve law and order; he castigated the failure to remove the Belgians and their mercenaries; he asked why 'modern and expensive armaments' were turned on unarmed peasants and he declared, 'The rulers of the United States, of the United Kingdom, of France . . . must answer these questions.'[20]

Unstated was the belief that the American Central Intelligence Agency had a hand in the downfall and death of Lumumba who had appealed to the USSR, and thereby upset the United States and also Britain (Macmillan wrote 'our long-term interests would best be served by . . . a Congo Government . . . largely depending on American rather than Russian aid and support'). Non-alignment could be tolerated, providing the Afro–Asians were non-aligned away from the USSR. One immediate consequence of the Congo experience was the division of the independent African states into two opposed groups. First, the francophone group (excluding Guinea and Mali) became known as the Brazzaville States. In January 1961, Ghana, Guinea, Mali, Egypt, Morocco and the Algerians launched the Casablanca group. In May 1961 African moderates joined the Brazzaville faction as the Monrovia States. There was also the Pan-African Movement for East and Central Africa (PAFMECA) in which Julius Nyerere took the lead. Nkrumah saw this as a contradiction, and was critical, thus annoying Nyerere who should have been a natural ally.

Nkrumah's disillusionment with Britain was displayed in his decision to terminate Alexander's services (despite cordial personal relations) and those of other officers from the UK. He accepted a Soviet offer to train army cadets, thus upsetting the Sandhurst-trained Ghanaians. However, there was no complete break with Britain. Macmillan's diary was still favourable: Nkrumah was 'moderate and reasonable'. Over the question of the expulsion of a racist South Africa from the Commonwealth he was cautious. When the Commonwealth Prime Ministers met to consider the issue in March 1961, others forced the pace: Nkrumah said publicly he had 'no wish for a showdown'. Macmillan eventually realised that only Australia and New Zealand would resist the pressure and advised South Africa not to press for readmission as a republic.

Asserts Non-Alignment not Pro-Soviet (1961)

That Nkrumah still desired friendship with Britain was demonstrated by his ardent wish for a visit by Queen Elizabeth. Busybodies in England tried to block the visit. Was it safe for Her Majesty to go to a land which was virtually Communist controlled? Nkrumah reassured Macmillan in a long letter (26 September 1961). He flatly denied:

> The suggestion, or rather the insinuation (for it is never overtly expressed) that Ghana under my leadership is veering more and more towards the Eastern bloc, and that there has been some implicit or secret understanding with the USSR . . . which compromises Ghana's fundamental position of neutrality. . . . Let me assure you that this is entirely without foundation. My visit to the USSR and to other Eastern countries has undoubtedly been very fruitful. . . . We are hoping to receive from the Russians increased technical assistance . . . just as we are also expecting increased technical assistance from Britain, the United States and Canada [this] must not be taken as an indication that we are leaning on some countries more than others.

Macmillan expressed relief that no 'shift of policy was taking place'.[21] The Queen's visit went ahead and 'the genial and warm-hearted people [of Ghana] gave her an unprecedented reception. . . . never had . . . the Queen looked happier or more charming.' So Macmillan was happy too.

A few months later *The Times* Africa Correspondent (W.P. Kirkman) wrote two long centre-page articles (25 and 26 June 1962) on the new African leaders which do more than most to illuminate Nkrumah's position.

The old-fashioned distinction between 'Extremists' and 'Moderates' beloved of the British . . . has to be scrapped. . . . These are labels that can properly be attached only to people with differing objectives. An Extremist in African terms would be a racialist who wanted to create a state hostile to all things European (Western or Eastern). A Moderate would be a man who saw the good in colonial administration. . . . The political leaders who count in Africa all have three aims in common. They want to create a viable state; they want to endow that state with a specifically African character; and they want . . . a respected place in world politics. . . . A reporter's task in Africa becomes extremely delicate. It is easy enough if one has made up one's mind to follow a particular line on any politician to select passages from his speeches which seem to prove one's point. But if all his current speeches are put together the line disintegrates. . . . The odd thing is not that one man can make seemingly incompatible statements without a stammer but that he probably means both or all statements with equal sincerity. . . . The smooth falsehoods of European politics are unknown. . . . The African politician's vulnerability to local and immediate circumstances can cause changes of position with bewildering rapidity in response to a variety of situations.

Kirkman saw Nkrumah as 'the Rousseau of the African revolution . . . Senghor is its Montesquieu and Dr Azikwe its Voltaire.' The politicians coming along in the states decolonised in 1960 'have benefited from the spadework done for them. . . . They have inherited . . . both the "African personality" that President Nkrumah sought with such labour, and the sophistication of the "Black Europeans".'

This analysis does much to elucidate what is often dismissed as Nkrumah's plunge into Communist (or was it Fascist?) dictatorship. Certainly he was becoming ever more a man on his own. Perhaps the incapacity of his lieutenants in the Congo made him feel he could rely only on himself. An indication of his worsening view of party faithfuls and their organisations had been revealed in his 'Dawn Broadcast to the Nation' delivered on 8 April 1961. He castigated those who had become wealthy by exploiting their political standing for private gain. Soon many of the old guard felt his hand upon them. Gbedemah and Botsio were asked to resign. Their places were taken by 'new men' who owed their rise entirely to Nkrumah, Tawia Adamafio, formerly Busia's lieutenant, and Coffie Crabbe among them. Nkrumah's style of politics had become 'the manipulation of factions', as Davidson observes.

Former Colleagues Tried for Bomb Plot

On 1 August 1962 on his return from a visit to Upper Volta, Nkrumah's party halted at a place called Kulungu. A bomb was thrown, a boy talking to the President was killed, and he was injured. Suspicion lighted on Adamafio and Nkrumah's friend of long ago, Ako Adjei, together with Coffie Crabbe. They were arrested along with others, supposedly their associates. The case did not come to trial until 1963. First, the lesser fry were tried and five out of seven found guilty of treason. Then in August 1963 the trial was begun of Adamafio, Adjei, Crabbe and two others. As in the first trial a Special Court presided over by Chief Justice Sir Arku Korsah heard their case. On 9 December judgment was delivered by the Chief Justice who took five hours to review the case. The three main defendants were acquitted although the other two were found guilty. Two days later Sir Arku Korsah was removed from the office of Chief Justice despite remaining a member of the Court of Appeal. The verdicts were set aside on 25 December by means of a law passed on 23 December empowering the President to quash any decision of the Special Court.

One Party State (1964)

The people of Ghana appear to have taken this development calmly, but for White liberal friends of Ghana this seemed like the parting of the ways. On 2 January 1964 a police constable shot at the President from close range. He missed, killing a security guard. The Commissioner of Police was dismissed along with eight other senior officers. Things were getting out of hand. Nkrumah announced another referendum to enable him to dismiss the judges and also to establish a one-party state. The referendum gave him a huge majority: 2 773 920 votes for and 2452 against the President. The result was patently a fraud, in Davidson's words.

The one-party state was authoritarian but not unrestrained. When Ako Adjei, Adamafio and Crabbe were given a second trial they were condemned to death: but the sentence was commuted by Nkrumah to life imprisonment. When Lieutenant-General J.A. Ankrah, commanding the Ghana army, was retired he was due for retirement anyway (he had come up through the ranks and served in Burma). The Winneba Ideological Institute and the party newspaper *The Spark* were viewed as instruments of international Communism, but were not particularly effective. More serious is the allegation that in these latter years Ghana was allowed to accumulate extravagant debts: an amount of £500 million is often quoted, though the true figure seems to have been about £120 million. The sudden fall in cocoa prices in 1964 was partly responsible, but on the positive side great new projects – Tema deep water harbour, and above all the Volta River Hydro-Electric scheme – had come into operation.

Evidence of Nkrumah's perilous position is given in an account by Mrs Pandit of an official visit to Ghana at this time:

> When I arrived in Accra he received me in his office and invited me to dinner. . . . He insisted on sending his own car to fetch me. An armed guard sat with the chauffeur, who took a circuitous route and we changed cars midway to the President's palace. I was most bewildered by these strange goings-on and even more so when Nkrumah told me that he stayed in a different place every night [as Sukarno had done in his last years]. He was then a nervous man and showed me the steel vest he wore under his shirt. The evening passed in a tense atmosphere.

Nkrumah and African Unity

In foreign policy, Nkrumah took a leading part in the new Organisation of African Unity (founded in 1963, this had ended the Casablanca/Monrovia division). Rhodesia had long presented an affront to Ghana and other Black African states, yet Nkrumah still valued the Commonwealth connection sufficiently to support Britain's compromise proposals. When Ian Smith proclaimed UDI in November 1965 this was too much. As before, in the Congo, Nkrumah burned to take action. A specially convened meeting of the Organisation of African Unity (OAU) called on those African states who belonged to the Commonwealth to sever their links with Britain. Nyerere was the first to break off relations; Nkrumah followed on 16 December, though the break was made without any display of hostility against Britain.

His Mission to Vietnam

The spectacle of a White-dominated state defying Afro-Asian opinion may have given the impulse to the decision to fly to Vietnam. Nkrumah must have realised the risk he was taking. Africa had its first military coup in 1958, in Sudan; the danger of military intervention was graphically illustrated in 1964 with army mutinies in Kenya, Tanganyika and Uganda; as recently as January 1966 the Nigerian coup had cost the lives of the Prime Minister and the Premiers of the Northern and Western regions. Knowing the risk he was taking, he still set out for Peking: why? The only credible explanation is that Nkrumah, with Rhodesia fresh in his mind, felt he could not tolerate superpower indifference to the Third World any longer.[22]

The aeroplane stopped at Cairo for a discussion with Nasser, and then at Delhi to consult Mrs Gandhi. So far, all appeared normal. Then on arrival at Peking he was told that a military coup had occurred in Ghana. The head of the Ghanaian army, Major-General Barwah, refused to surrender to the conspirators; he was shot out of hand. The Guard Regiment formed by Nkrumah for his protection fought the mutineers and only gave up when they threatened to kill Nkrumah's wife and three infants. The nominal head of the 'National Liberation Council', as it was styled, was the retired General Ankrah; the Deputy Chairman was J.W.K. Harlley, demoted after the abortive assassination attempt of January 1964. Nkrumah attributed the coup to the Black American ambassador Franklin Williams, alleging that he had offered $13 millions for carrying it out.[23] Certainly, the United States administration had vastly over-reacted to Nkrumah's book *Neo-Colonialism: The last stage of imperialism* (1965), though the views he advanced were becoming the commonplace of Third World writing.

Deposition and Exile (1966)

Most of the large entourage the President had brought with him quietly left him. With a select few, he flew to Guinea: the nearest point to Ghana where he would be accepted. President Sékou-Touré gave him a warm welcome. Nkrumah was given the honorary title of co-president. He settled at Conakry, the capital, expecting that his stay would be brief. He was to remain there for a further six years. He assembled a large secretariat, some 80 in number. His hopes seemed justified when on 17 April 1967 three lieutenants led a Reconnaissance Squadron of the army to seize the radio station and the former president's house. They proclaimed their achievement on Nkrumah's behalf: and then succumbed to a counter-attack. Two of them were executed, the third received 30 years in jail.

In 1969 the National Liberation Council handed over power to Dr Busia, the moderate politician amenable to Western counsels. During the three years he was in charge over £300 million in foreign debts were accumulated. Then on 13 January 1972 the army dismissed Busia; a group of officers led by Colonel Acheampong assumed control.

Death and Posthumous Rehabilitation

There was no hope for Nkrumah; he had contracted cancer and on 27 April 1972 he died in a Bucharest hospital, aged 63. The military leader, Colonel Acheampong, wanted him to have a state funeral. After much ceremony in Accra he was buried in his birth-place, Nkroful. Acheampong delivered a graveside eulogy: 'He waged a relentless war against colonialism and racism. . . . We mourn the loss of a great leader whose place in history is well assured.' The Colonel added 'Like all of us, Dr Nkrumah had his shortcomings.'

The verdict of two respected British historians is equally appreciative:

Nkrumah was perhaps the most typical African leader of his time – the lonely student abroad, the strident young politician in constant trouble with the colonial authorities, the prime minister who brilliantly guided his country through the troubled waters of independence, the dictator whose continent-wide ambitions proved too great a burden for his people to bear. The twenty years or so of African history from the end of the Second World War until 1965 could be called, without too much exaggeration, the age of Nkrumah.[24]

This verdict is underlined by the Secretary-General of the Commonwealth:

Who among those we now acknowledge as the great men of all time has not been flawed? Yet, on the whole, what history remembers are not the transient flaws, grave as they sometimes were, but their grand achievements that transcend time. . . . He contributed in important ways to a saner global society by his efforts to keep Africa a nuclear-free zone. He protested vigorously against atomic bomb testing in the Sahara and in June 1962 convened a 'World Without the Bomb' conference in Accra. . . . Its significance . . . lay in Nkrumah's assertion of Africa's right to contribute to the evolution of human destiny. . . . Now that he is no longer in the World of Men, Kwame Nkrumah lives still as a symbol.[25]

9

White Over Black: Kenyatta's Kenya

Kenyatta is the only one of the leaders we are considering who was almost certainly born before imperial rule was established in his land. His date of birth is uncertain – 1893 or maybe earlier. It was not until 1895 that Britain assumed responsibility for Kenya from the Imperial British East African Company (which had been established in 1888 with vague rights in the land). The new British Protectorate was partly a response to missionary pressure: Uganda was the scene of intense rivalry between Roman Catholics and Anglicans. Hence, at this early period the British were more interested in the country beyond the Great Lakes than in the less populated hills and forests in between. As early as 1891 a survey was made of a line for a proposed railway. Work began in 1896. African labour was not available, so the British imported labourers from India; they made good progress, and by 1899 had reached the hundredth mile. The line then began an ascent and entered the fertile upland country where the Kikuyu tribes dwelt. By 1901 the Uganda Railway, as it was called, was virtually complete. About midway a railway camp began to grow into a town: from nothing, Nairobi came into existence.

British Discover 'White Highlands'

Having built the railway – paid for by the British government out of an interest-free loan of £5 million – the colonial authority looked around for ways to increase its meagre revenues: use by a handful of missionaries was not the answer. The best solution seemed to be to encourage immigration by White British settlers. Foremost among these pioneers was Lord Delamere (1870–1931) who in 1903 was allotted 100 000 acres in Njoro, in the heart of the Kikuyu country. He later disposed of his holdings for £200 000 (and then acquired additional estates). As an alternative to ranching in Canada, Kenya seemed attractive to misfits among the British aristocracy. A steady trickle of upper-class settlers began to arrive; somewhat incongruous was an influx of Afrikaner farmers and hunters, displaced by the upheavals of the Boer War. After the Great War a stream of new immigrants, mainly ex-army officers, arrived. Each of these groups was accustomed to think in terms of command. The Africans were seen only as labourers by them. And so, under Delamere's leadership, Kenya was becoming White Man's Country: just as in South Africa or Rhodesia, except that it was more upper class in tone.[1]

Beside the 9000 Whites (1920), amid the estimated African population of perhaps 3 000 000 there were 30 000 Indians in Kenya. Indian merchants had traded on the coast for centuries; we have seen that Indian workers built the railway, and Indians largely ran the railway system when it became operational. In addition, there were a growing number of Indians in the lower grades of the administration and more and more Indian traders. Nairobi was largely built and supplied by Indians. After 1918 they were conscious that back in their mother country Gandhi was leading a campaign for self-government. They began to make political demands: which the Whites totally rejected. For the time being, Africans could do little else but watch this struggle. As yet they had no leaders capable of challenging White dominance. In the earliest phase of British rule the tribes had fiercely resisted the invaders, but this was the era when the White man had the final argument:

> Whatever happens we have got
> The Maxim Gun, and they have not.

Gradually the traditional leaders, the chiefs, were coopted into the basic structure of British administration. Education, the pathway to political emancipation in most British imperial possessions, had made little headway amongst Kenyan Africans by the 1920s. A knowledge of English was acquired in schools started by the missionaries, but these 'mission boys' (as the Whites dubbed them) could expect no more than lowly clerical jobs. This extraordinary situation, in which a tiny minority of expatriate Britishers had their own way in everything they wanted, was perpetuated into the 1950s.

The Africans as Helots

Hence the task confronting Kenyatta and other African politicians was of a different order from that faced by leaders in colonies without a White settler elite. The task was not to convince rulers in distant London that it was time to go, but to dislodge an alien *Herrenvolk* from their backs: the

White Tribe who were determined to hang on to power and privilege as in South Africa and Rhodesia. The only long-term advantage the Kenyan Africans had was that of numbers: whereas in South Africa there was one White to every five Blacks, and even in Rhodesia the proportion was one White to 25 Blacks, in Kenya there was one White to 400 Blacks. Unless the Whites could force the constitutional pace while the Africans were still unprepared, in the long run they must yield in an age in which democracy — the rule of the many — was the acclaimed belief of the Western world. Failing in their bid to emulate Southern Rhodesia, their subsequent strategy was to resist others' political claims. It was Kenyatta whose presence and personality hastened the end of White hegemony.

For almost 70 years he was ignored, humiliated, vilified, persecuted and hated by the White overlords. In the last 15 years of his long life he was accepted — even acclaimed — as their leader by the remaining Kenyan White population. For 30 years before then (1963) he was regarded by his own people as their champion. The attempt to destroy his position in Kenya by branding him as the mastermind behind the desperate Kikuyu attempt to regain the lands seized by the Whites, denounced as Mau Mau, backfired. Mau Mau led the British — the people of Britain — to question what they were doing in Kenya when the massacre at Hola Camp revealed that the masters had been reduced to repeating the horrors of Nazi brutality to obtain the acquiescence of their colonial subjects. After Hola the only question was how to regain some kind of moral credibility. And so Kenyatta, reviled and rejected, was at last recognised as the champion of Kenya's future development.

For the first 30 years of his life he was nobody, a non-person in White eyes; until he became a nuisance, a power for evil, and then at last the national leader. He who was to become Jomo Kenyatta was born as Kamau, son of Ngengi, near Gatundu on the Ngenda ridge, south-west of Mount Kenya, a peak over 17 000 feet high and almost in the centre of the territories soon to be a British colony.

Kikuyu Lands Seized

His people, the Kikuyu, had settled after inward migration like almost all Africans. In the nineteenth century the dominant tribe was the Masai, a Nilotic people originally from the north. They established their position by martial prowess but, clinging to traditional custom as herders of cattle, they were past their prime. The Kikuyu had taken to agriculture and thrived in the fertile, well-watered highlands. However, at the end of the nineteenth century they — and also the Masai — suffered a serious decline in population. This coincided with the first incursions of European explorers and they may have introduced the smallpox which decimated the local people. The rinderpest which killed so many of their cattle cannot be attributed to this cause.

Many of the Kikuyu survivors withdrew into their ancestral domain, abandoning the peripheral lands they had opened up. These they had acquired not by theft or sequestration from the original inhabitants but by some kind of trade-off, and they had legitimised their claim to these holdings by ritual observances. However, when the White pioneers arrived they regarded this as an empty country: just as the American pioneers had perceived the western prairies. The colonial authority subscribed to this view, designating this as Crown land, available for sale or lease. This view was corroborated by their dealings with the Masai, who as nomadic pastoralists viewed their grazing lands as a common tribal right. When the British made deals with a Masai tribe they believed they had done the right thing. But Kikuyu land occupation was not based on common ownership; it was not based on possession by an individual either, to retain or to dispose of; and so the British genuinely misunderstood the facts – at least in the early years.

Kenyatta Gets Basic Mission Training

Kenyatta (we had better call him that from the beginning) lost his father when only a boy. According to tribal custom his father's younger brother took his mother as his wife. He regarded his stepsons without affection. First his mother left her second husband, then Kenyatta departed to join his grandfather, a magician, a seer. His own life did not change: he tended the goats, the family's main wealth. One day, a Scottish missionary visited their village and addressed them. The listening boy decided he wanted to learn their 'magic' and made his way to their mission station at Thogoto. The role of the missionaries was to endow the government with moral authority: and this role was accepted by many of them to the end of British rule. But not by all: and external missionary influences, notably that of J.H. Oldham of the International Missionary Council, and C.F. Andrews, friend of Gandhi, exerted powerful pressures in the 1920s and 1930s.

Coming out of nowhere, Kenyatta took several years to emerge from total obscurity into a modest place in African politics. The dominant figure at Thogoto was the medical doctor, John Arthur. A few months after Kenyatta arrived in November 1909 he developed a serious chest infection. Dr Arthur adopted the drastic treatment of applying scalding poultices to his chest. He was pronounced cured. He resumed his elementary education and did not especially impress the missionaries. Instead of being earmarked for a clerical job he was apprenticed as a carpenter. He learned his trade from John Cook, in charge of industrial training. He was a big, bluff man, popular with the African youngsters, who left soon afterwards.

In February 1913 Kenyatta was circumcised; the initiation test by which a Kikuyu attained manhood.[2] In a manner typical of his whole life he did not undergo the gruesome tribal ceremony. Neither did he have an operation in hospital under an anaesthetic, which the missionaries urged. He underwent the ordeal in public, backed by his own tribal sponsor (who was, however, a Christian minister). The operation was performed by a Kikuyu hospital assistant with a sterile surgical knife. He also underwent the Christian initiation – baptism – in August 1914. He wished to take the names of the apostles John and Peter but this was considered presumptuous by the missionaries who limited him to one new name. To their annoyance he said he would be Johnstone (stone, rock, *petrus*, Peter). He declined further industrial training as a mason (even less highly regarded than being a carpenter) and set out for Nairobi, seeking employment with Cook.

The outbreak of war brought Kenya onto the world scene, for neighbouring Tanganyika was German East Africa. The colony had to await the arrival of Indian troops. A seaborne assault on the headquarters of German East Africa was mounted. Despite overwhelming numerical superiority, the expedition was bungled and repulsed. They settled down to a long-drawn-out overland penetration.

Wider Horizons, 1914–18

War brought a vastly increased demand for manpower, and Kenyatta had no difficulty getting work in Nairobi. According to George Delf he was engaged as a clerk in the Public Works Department on Cook's recommendation. What is established is that by 1916 he was working for Cook, now manager of an estate growing sisal near Thika. It was a sign of trust that he became wages clerk and collected the money from the bank 25 miles away each week.

The military forces had to be supplied by columns of porters, mainly drawn from the Kikuyu. At first they went willingly, but as tales were recounted of their suffering by death and disease they held back. Soon they were being rounded up at the point of a bayonet. Many ran away into Masai country, for the proud Masai refused to be carriers of burdens.

Kenyatta also departed to their country. Although rejecting conscription, the Masai were supplying the army with meat, and Kenyatta found a job as a clerk with an army contractor. When the war ended he returned to Nairobi and became manager of a European-owned store. He went to evening classes to improve his English, and adopted an individual style of European dress, wearing a broad-brimmed hat reminiscent of his ranching days. He now called himself K.N. Johnstone.

During the war years the White settlers had consolidated their community's position. They began to get their hands on the machinery of government, and played a big part in a post-war scheme of settlement by ex-servicemen from the United Kingdom. The war had literally devastated the Kikuyu. The official figure for losses among the porters was 27 000; but these were men accounted for, and amid enforced recruitment thousands simply disappeared: the total casualty list was probably 45 000. Added to this, the worldwide influenza epidemic took a severe toll: Dr Arthur reckoned the fall in the Kikuyu population at 130 000 out of a total of less than one million.

There was a severe post-war shortage of labour for hire, compounded by the arrival of new settlers. In 1919 the Whites were able to persuade Sir Edward Northey, the first Governor, to introduce compulsory labour, enforced by the lash. The same scandal had aroused British humanitarians to indignation against King Leopold's brutal regime in the Congo. Lionel Curtis warned J.H. Oldham (11 November 1920): 'Northey's regulations in East Africa are in danger of provoking in religious circles an agitation which, unless wisely handled at the outset will recall the agitation of fifteen years ago over Chinese labour on the Rand.'[3] However, in the 1920s the Nonconformist voice was no longer a power in England. There was no outcry. The Kikuyu had to improvise their own protest movement. What was particularly resented was the *kipande* or pass which Africans, and no others, were required to carry in a metal box around their necks. The *kipande* was filled in by the employer, and a man could not leave his employment and seek a job elsewhere without getting the pass endorsed first.

First Kikuyu Protest Leader: Thuku

The Kikuyu found their leader in Harry Thuku, born 1895, from a family of well-off farmers. He came to Nairobi in 1911 and was engaged as a clerk and then a telephone operator. He became friendly with Indians, particularly M.A. Desai, editor of the *East African Chronicle*, which publicised Kikuyu grievances. A Kikuyu Association had been formed in

1919, largely composed of chiefs in defence of their land, increasingly threatened by expropriation. In 1921, with Desai's assistance, Thuku founded the Young Kikuyu Association, the name echoing Gandhi's Young India.

The East African Indians were politically active on their own account. In January 1920, the first-ever election was held for the legislative council. All the Whites were enfranchised. The Indians demanded that they be included on a common roll, though they were prepared to accept property and educational qualifications which would leave the Whites as the major part of the electorate. Regarding the Africans as steeped in barbarism and incapable of political action, the Whites concentrated their ire upon the Indians, denouncing them as carriers of disease and moral degeneracy and characterising them as exploiters of the African population: though their only fault was to set up as traders in the rural areas as well as the town. Thuku infuriated the Whites by declaring that the Indians were the Africans' best friends. Onto this troubled scene appeared C.F. Andrews, who had stood beside Gandhi in his struggle in South Africa. He was in Kenya at the invitation of the Indian leaders. He advised them to identify, politically, with the Africans: advice not welcome to some who considered they were a more civilised race.

When he arrived at Nairobi station, there along with M.A. Desai and other Indians was Harry Thuku waiting to greet him. They all conferred at the home of a prominent merchant. Then Andrews left to continue his journey (on 26 October 1921). Thuku called out, 'Ask the King of England to stop the settlers using the *kiboko* [rhinoceros hide lash] on their labourers.' This warning about the settlers' ways was immediately brought home to Andrews when he was brutally assaulted by Whites at Nakuru station. He managed to resist being dragged from the train, but the assault was repeated at the next station. He had to go into hospital.

Thuku Banished without Trial

Thuku embarked upon a speaking tour. He questioned the absolute authority of the chiefs, and by implication that of the British government. On returning to Nairobi he was taken into custody, without being charged. Next morning, a crowd collected, demanding his release. When they became threatening the police fired a volley, killing 21, including women and boys. Without any trial, Thuku and three associates were transported to Mombasa, and thence exiled in the most remote, most unpleasant corner of Kenya. He was not permitted to return from exile for over eight years: at the end of 1930.

Kenyatta becomes an Urban African: Marriage

What was Kenyatta doing meanwhile? He has no place in Thuku's recollections of those days. In January 1920 he took a mission-educated Kikuyu, Grace Wahu, as his wife, and on 20 November 1920 his first son was born. In the eyes of the Church of Scotland members they were not properly married; something he wanted to rectify, but only in November 1922 did they obtain a civil marriage. By then he was installed in a good job. His benefactor, Cook, was now Superintendent of the Nairobi Water Supply, and Kenyatta became his stores clerk and meter reader at the exceptional salary of 250 shillings a month (Thuku had earned 140 shillings in government service). Subsequently he became an Interpreter at the High Court. In addition, his own family home at Dagoretti, about 20 miles from town, became a general store: Kinyata Stores.

At first 'Kenyatta' was a nickname, derived from the fancy Kikuyu belt which he and his wife both wore. Soon he was generally known as Johnstone Kenyatta. As a public servant he was barred from politics, though according to Delf he joined the Young Kikuyu Association in 1922. In any case, with Thuku banished, they had reached a dead end. As the most searching account of these years rightly observes:

> African politicians spent most of the 1920s and 1930s simply drawing attention to their existence. While the British genuinely acknowledged the importance of African interests there was little recognition of the people's ability to express these for themselves. . . . As the settlers strove to achieve self-government it was not a debate that Africans could attend, much less one in which they could participate.[4]

Did the British 'genuinely' acknowledge African interests? The White Paper of 1923 paid lip service to them: and not much more. The White Paper – the outcome of a tussle which no-one won – was largely precipitated by the confusion created by Churchill as Colonial Secretary. At the annual dinner of the East African Association in London in January 1922 he gave an undertaking on the future of the White Highlands and closed with the words, 'We do not contemplate any settlement or system which will prevent British East Africa or Kenya . . . looking forward in full fruition of time to complete responsible self-government.' The settlers hailed this as recognition of their claims, inflated by the success of the Southern Rhodesian settlers, numbering 33 000 among a population of 770 000, in securing full internal self-government in 1923 with an elected Ministry of their own choice.

Whites Reject Share in Government by Others

However, Churchill had already sent a directive to Governor Northey headed 'Equal Rights for Civilised Men', which conceded a common electoral roll for all: Europeans, Indians, Arabs, and eventually Africans. Northey dithered so long over announcing this reform that he was recalled in June 1922 and replaced by Sir Robert Coryndon, South African born, and one-time secretary to Cecil Rhodes. Coryndon attempted to parley with Delamere and other settler bosses. It was disastrous: on 3 February 1923 he cabled London, warning, 'Complete machinery has been prepared and stiffened recently to paralyse the functions of government.' On 13 February he wired: 'Colony is absolutely solid that . . . ultimate responsibility of government must remain in European hands and must not be diluted by being shared with Eastern race, alien in spirit and recognised as lacking in genius of government of backward subject races.'

In London, the Cabinet considered this craven response. The Duke of Devonshire, the new Colonial Secretary, quoted Coryndon as asserting that the introduction of military forces to subdue the European population of 9000 'is in my opinion out of the question' (CP 99(23) dated 14 February 1923). An invitation was issued to Delamere and his associates to come to London to consult; a similar invitation went to the Indians. A Kikuyu request to send a delegation also was refused.

Britain Asserts 'Trusteeship' Policy (1923)

How to resolve the impasse? Lugard came up with the peculiar proposal of a White Dominion taking in the Highlands while the rest of Kenya remained a Crown Colony. An alternative solution was propounded by J.H. Oldham in a conversation with Randall Davidson, Archbishop of Canterbury, on 19 March. Oldham advised 'No political power should be given to the Indians. . . . On the other hand the Europeans must not have political power either.' Kenya must 'take a step back in responsible government'. After many months of fruitless discussion, something like this formula was accepted at a Cabinet meeting on 20 July 1923: the famous Devonshire Declaration, issued as *Indians in Kenya* (Cmd 1922 of 1923). HMG, 'exercising a trust on behalf of the African population . . . cannot but regard the grant of responsible self-government as out of the question within any period of time which need now be taken into consideration'.

C.F. Andrews told Davidson (3 August 1923) that: 'nothing solid [was] gained at all. . . . The same old bad legislative council remains which has done all these evil deeds in the past. It is now stereotyped, and stronger than ever. . . . It has become as clear as possible that the Empire is a White Empire. . . . The exploitation of the natives will go on as greedily as ever.' Less emotionally, Curtis said much the same to Oldham (30 January 1924): 'We are always enunciating unimpeachable principles without being prepared to face the practicable consequences.' Kenya for the Africans was 'the only sound principle'; but in practice was 'never faced'.

The 1920s saw a number of outside official inquiries. The big question was 'Closer Union', promoted by that enthusiastic Milnerite federalist, L.S. Amery. He induced another Milnerite, Sir Edward Grigg, to become Governor on the death of Coryndon, with the expectation he would be made Governor-General of a federation of Kenya, Uganda and Tanganyika. With that in mind, a new and grander Government House was constructed in Nairobi, designed by the architect of imperialism, Herbert Baker.

What did this portend? Amery told parliament on 19 July 1927: 'East Africa . . . can never remain a purely black man's country, and it is never going to become White Man's country, even in the sense that South Africa has become a White Man's country.' The goal of trusteeship was reaffirmed by Amery: but if there was an East African Commission, would there be an African member, asked one MP? This, the Colonial Secretary replied severely, 'could hardly lead to good results'. Reassured, the Kenyan Whites considered the advantages of federation. Grigg, like every other governor, soon fell under their sway. As Ormsby-Gore, Colonial Under-Secretary, told Irwin: 'Ned Grigg has been thoroughly infected with Kenyitis' (24 October 1927). He anticipated the Whites getting responsible government 'by gradual changes rather than by sudden change as happened in the case of Southern Rhodesia'.

Grigg tried to sell his ideas to the Viceroy (22 September 1927): 'There is a chance here of developing a political system which thoroughly reflects the interests of all races.' And how? A common roll was 'impossible . . . madness'. Representation must be based not on numbers but on each community's

character, its education, its enterprise, its civilisation and the contribution it makes in all ways to the development of the country. . . . The Indian question is a small thing in East Africa compared with the vast problem of the future of White settlement in the midst of this huge mass of primitive African barbarism. . . . The White race knows in its heart that what it concedes to the Indian it must in the long run concede to the African.

What was Black Kenya doing while these debates went on among the White men? There was the Kikuyu Association. The leaders were chiefs, P.J. Karanja, Josiah Njonjo, Waruhiu Kungu and Koinange Mbu. All were moderates, good churchmen, supporters of government. In 1932 they changed the name to the Kikuyu Loyal Patriots; this was to avoid being confused with the Kikuyu Central Association (KCA) which started in 1924 in succession to the defunct Young Kikuyu Association founded by the exiled Thuku. The government discouraged the KCA, arguing that with the establishment of Local Native Councils in 1925, operating in the tribal reserves, there was adequate machinery for political representation. But the chairman of these Councils was always the District Commissioner and they were dominated by chiefs.

Kenyatta Enters Kikuyu Politics (1928)

The first move by the KCA was to present a petition to Ormsby-Gore in 1924; the eight who handed it in did not include Kenyatta. When next they organised to present evidence to the Hilton Young Commission on Closer Union, in 1928, they were led by their President, Joseph Kang'etha, and among the other six representatives was Kenyatta. Kang'etha was the founder of the KCA, and in 1925 he was elected to Fort Hall Local Native Council. Impressed by the admission ceremony, invoking an oath of loyalty to the Crown, he instituted an oath of loyalty for KCA members: to the Kikuyu people. This involved holding a Bible in one hand and a handful of earth in the other. Kang'etha asked Kenyatta to act as secretary, and also to be their spokesman in London. From May 1928, Kenyatta was editor of a periodical in Kikuyu called *Muigwithania* (perhaps 'The Unifier').

Grigg proposed setting up Land Boards by local legislation. Chief Koinange spoke to a committee of the legislature for his association while Kang'etha and Kenyatta represented the KCA view. Grigg commented: 'It was manifest that the two natives who appeared as representatives of the Kikuyu Central Association were incapable of understanding the provisions of the Bill . . . unintelligent opposition.' In December 1928 a KCA gathering administered an oath to Kenyatta that if he went to England he would not betray them and would return for further service. For their part, they pledged to support his wife and two children. Ultimately, it was his younger brother, known as James Johnstone, belonging to the police, who became Grace's chief helper: Kenyatta contributed nothing.

Kikuyu Emissary to London (1929)

He departed on 17 February 1929, despite a warning from the colonial authorities that the Secretary of State would refuse to see him in England. Isher Dass, a radical Indian, was on the same ship. On arrival in London, Kenyatta was at a loss how to obtain entry into the corridors of power. He turned for advice to C.F. Andrews and W. McGregor Ross, a Quaker who had been Kenya's Director of Public Works and also a lone voice condemning settler dominance, the *kipande*, and other instruments of repression. Their combined efforts did not achieve much more than an interview with Grigg, which led nowhere. He turned to the Left: to Fenner Brockway and Kingsley Martin and the Communist League Against Imperialism. Still failing to make progress, he paid a visit to the Soviet Union. Returning, he found himself in trouble: two English girl-friends were complaining about him. Ross advised him, 'Get back to Kenya, sharp.' Kenyatta ignored this advice. In January 1930 Drummond Shiels, a progressive, now Labour Colonial Under-Secretary, agreed to see him, along with Ross. Again, Kenyatta was treated to paternal advice, and Shiels added 'a small homily on the impetuosity of youth'. This, to a man nearly 40 years old! Grigg's view, communicated to Shiels (12 March 1930), was even more scathing: 'The importance attached to Kenyatta in England is really, therefore, ridiculous. He has done so little even for his Association during his absence that he has ceased to have any serious following here [in Kenya] as far as I can judge.'[5]

Kenyatta did enjoy a minor success: a letter to the *Manchester Guardian* (18 March 1930) and another in identical terms to *The Times* (26 March). He denied that the KCA was a subversive organisation. He listed their main grievances and concluded: 'The repression of native views on subjects of such vital importance to my people . . . can only be described as a short-sighted tightening up of the safety-valve of free speech, which must inevitably result in a dangerous explosion.' While he was kicking his heels in London, the future of Kenya was being decided by the White men, as before.

The Hilton Young inquiry had backfired. Only the chairman recommended closer union; the other three members, who included Oldham, turned it down. They deplored the settlers' resistance to London's policy: they enjoyed power without 'real responsibility'. Political demands by Africans could not be 'permanently resisted': then, 'numbers would come into play'. They wanted a franchise based on a 'civilisation test': the 'ideal to be aimed at is a common roll on an equal franchise with no distinction between races'. This was unwelcome to the Labour Colonial Secretary, Sidney Webb, Lord Passfield: 'The Colonial Office, heartily led by Webb, are determined to stop it', Wedgwood Benn told Irwin (10 April 1930). The question was referred to the Lord Chancellor, Sankey, who observed sarcastically, 'The argument adduced by Lord Passfield in favour of communal instead of common electorate omits to point out that [this] means the opinion of the dominant White settlers.' Webb replied (Cabinet Minute 21 (1930), dated 9 April), 'His advisers took a serious view of the situation which would arise were the common roll to be adopted . . . there would follow . . . a situation comparable in its gravity to that of 1923.' Uncertain, the Labour Cabinet reaffirmed the so-called 'Dual Policy': 'in no way inconsistent with trusteeship'.

Lord Delamere delivered his political swan song a few weeks later:

> As to the political future of the natives, there was ample scope for such development within the boundaries of the Reserves without bringing the natives within the fold of the White Man's politics. If that last safeguard is undermined, there will go with it in its fall the right of British people to claim that with their race, and their race alone . . . must lie the responsibility for . . . the development of the Empire in Africa. (*East African Standard*, 12 July 1930)

After his death, the new settler leader, Lord Francis Scott, adopted a less strident tone. Politics was less important than economics, for Kenya was suffering acutely from the world depression.

Interlude in Kenya (1930)

During these years Kenyatta went his own way in London. The Rosses continued to care for him; still urging him to return home, they arranged for the Anti-Slavery Society to pay for his passage. In September 1930 he did return to Kenya. Dr Arthur tried hard to bring him back into the Presbyterian fold, but he resisted pressure, particularly with regard to condemning female circumcision. 'He is a man of guile', recorded Arthur. He was also suspect to many of the Kikuyu as a Europeanised African. In January 1931, Thuku returned from exile. He completely outshone Kenyatta, who seized the chance to return to London offered by the formation of a parliamentary select committee to whom evidence on Kikuyu grievances might be presented. With a school teacher, F.G. Mockerie, as companion, and to some extent minder, on 2 May they left on the *Mazzini* for Genoa.

A few weeks later with the advent of the National Government the Kenya Whites found an even better friend in Cunliffe-Lister, the new Colonial Secretary. The select committee recommended that another Commission investigate the question of landholding in the Highlands. This seemed promising, but the Report of the Carter Commission, published in 1933, was heavily weighted towards the settler interest. It gave legal authority to the exclusive White Highlands and extended their area. Their recommendation was endorsed by the British Government in 1934. In a parliamentary debate Ormsby-Gore announced that the White area delimited by Carter would be doubled to 12 000 square miles. Approvingly, Grigg, back in Parliament, quoted Joseph Chamberlain's dictum, 'We are trustees for civilisation', adding 'Concentration on a political aim, or on education looking to a political aim is a very dangerous thing.'[6]

Wanderings: Trip to Soviet Union (1936)

Kenyatta was now at a loose end. The humanitarian, Charles Roden Buxton, arranged for him to go to Woodbrooke College, Selly Oak, where he improved his English. Then he fell in with George Padmore, still in his Comintern phase. After some time in Germany they arrived in Moscow where he was indoctrinated at the University of the Toilers of the East, where Ho Chi Minh studied. At this juncture, Padmore fell out with the Comintern, and this reflected on Kenyatta. As mysteriously as they had arrived, they now left. Kenyatta turned to the Rosses again and inquired about getting back to Kenya. He was told that the KCA had supplied funds, which Mockerie had pocketed, and then departed. Kenyatta took up journalism, contributing to *Labour Monthly* edited by Palme Dutt, but this was a stopgap. He earned modest amounts by working in the Phonetics Department in University College and as an informant in Kikuyu at the School of Oriental and African Studies. Then in 1936 he registered at the London School of Economics for a Diploma in Anthropology under Bronislaw Malinowski: this was a breakthrough, for Malinowski was the doyen of his discipline (they shared a mutual dislike and distrust of Indians). He was taken on as an extra in the film 'Sanders of the River', starring Paul Robeson, who was later pilloried as an Uncle Tom for his role as a faithful chief. The star befriended the extra: for he too was reacting against Western capitalism and made the pilgrimage to Moscow.

Writes *Facing Mount Kenya*

Kenyatta's purpose in studying anthropology was not just to acquire academic recognition but to refute the stereotype of 'African barbarism'. This eventually emerged in a book, *Facing Mount Kenya*. It is not clear whether it was all his own work or how much was compiled by Dinah Stock, an Irish extra-mural lecturer connected with the League Against Imperialism. He lived with her in platonic friendship. He had developed a knack for successful cadging, sometimes ignobly as when he ran up a bill for £200 with his impecunious landlady, Mrs Hocken.

Book Published, 1938: Adopts Name 'Jomo'

On Malinowski's recommendation, *Facing Mount Kenya* was accepted by Frederick Warburg. Wanting to have his own photograph as a frontispiece, Kenyatta turned to an acquaintance, Peter Mbiya, son of Chief Koinange, spending a year at Cambridge after higher education in America. The young aristocrat lent Kenyatta a tribal cloak. Also, he acquired a spear and grew a beard and thus assumed a traditional African appearance. Then there was the question of the name on the title page: 'Johnstone' was not in the least African. Kenyatta considered the matter with young Koinange and came up with Jomo: not a real name, but having a Kikuyu-sounding flavour. There was a farsighted introduction by Malinowski: 'The educated, intellectual minority of Africans, usually dismissed as "agitators" are rapidly becoming a force. They are catalysing an African public opinion even among the raw tribesmen.' He went on: 'By ignoring them, and treating them with contempt we drive them into the open arms of world-wide Bolshevism.'

In Kenyatta's own preface he declared: 'I owe thanks also to my enemies for the stimulating discouragement which has kept up my spirits to persist in the task.' That this was a dig at the likes of Ross and Andrews was made clear: 'The African is not blind. He can recognise these pretenders to philanthropy and in various parts of the continent he is waking up.' The missionaries are blamed for believing that the African was 'a clean slate on which anything could be written'. It was not a comfortable book, and it aroused the wrath of Dr Arthur in his retirement: 'A veneer of an ideal African home life. It is untrue.'

Facing Mount Kenya sold 517 copies (not unsatisfactory for those times), but the remaining stock was destroyed in the blitz. It was reprinted in 1953 when Kenyatta had achieved notoriety: Lord Hailey, compiler of the *African Survey*, described it as 'still the best book on the Kikuyu'.

Warburg gave an advance of £30 on publication which enabled him to return to Kenya that year to meet the negro American educationist Ralph Bunche (later widely known as the UN representative in the Congo).[7] Kenyatta renewed his contacts with the KCA; however, he was soon back in London. Probably he surmised that if he stayed he would inevitably get into hot water.

Peter Koinange returned for good in 1938. Son of a leading chief of proven loyalty, well educated in America and Britain, he might have seemed exactly the right person to pioneer African entry into the elite administration (the Kenya equivalent of Busia in Ghana). Instead, he was offered an inferior post in education at a salary less than a European without his qualifications. Hurt, he moved into the independent schools movement. His loyalist father's faith in the British was strained too far. On 7 May 1939 he told the Governor, Air Chief Marshal Brooke-Popham (perhaps the most feeble of the feeble inter-war governors), 'There are fifty well-educated Africans who are fully qualified to represent the Kikuyu Africans in Kenya Legislative Council.' A copy of this letter was sent to Arthur Creech Jones, then a vigilant critic of British policies in the colonies. A debate was initiated in the House of Commons on 7 June 1939, but of course had no effect. In 1940, Creech Jones founded the Fabian Colonial Bureau with the indefatigable South African, Rita Hinden, as secretary.

Marriage in Wartime Britain (1942)

The clouds of conflict were gathering. Kenyatta, with his well-developed sense of survival, left London with Dinah Stock to stay with another extra-mural lecturer at Storrington in Sussex. He settled in, cultivating a vegetable patch, and obtaining work as an agricultural labourer (thus avoiding any possibility of conscription). As the war dragged on, Kenyatta found occasional employment as a lecturer to the troops, so bored they would listen to anyone. He spoke on the iniquities of British imperialism in Africa; doubtless making his tiny contribution to the death-knell of pre-war Conservatism. He drank quite heavily (a drinking companion at the pub was the composer Arnold Bax). He befriended Edna Grace Clarke, staying with his hosts, and when her parents were killed in an air raid he provided comfort. They went through a form of marriage on 11 May 1942 and on 11 August 1943 Edna gave birth to a son, named Peter Magana.

Back in Kenya the war stirred up momentous changes. The government at once interned the leaders of the KCA and other quasi-political movements. Kenyatta's abrupt departure had been timely. With an enemy threat from Italian-occupied Ethiopia, a great military effort was launched: 75 000 soldiers were recruited in Kenya alone (the East African total was 280 000). Many of them fought in the Ethiopian campaign, in the Middle East, and later in Burma with the 11th East African Division. External threat gave the White leaders the opportunity to extend their grip on government. In particular, Major Cavendish-Bentinck was in a key position as Minister for Agriculture, Animal Husbandry and Natural Resources. The area of the White Highlands was extended: another $6\frac{1}{2}$ million acres were alienated. When in 1943 a Land Consolidation Bill was pushed through the White-controlled legislature the Governor, Sir Henry Moore, told Whitehall (12 June 1944): 'It did not seem to me either necessary or politically desirable to challenge the unofficial majority there.'

The change to Sir Philip Mitchell in 1944 was supposed to bring in an official less susceptible to settler pressure (he had been Governor of Uganda and Tanganyika), but although he introduced the rhetoric of multi-racialism there was no real change. The settlers adhered to the attitudes of 40 years earlier. Humphrey Slade, Chairman of the Electors' Union, assured Smuts (19 February 1946) that the Africans were 'just emerging from barbarism': they had no claim to greater representation in the legislature. This followed the appointment of *one* nominated African to the legislature in 1944: Eliud Mathu, an Oxford-educated Kikuyu.

Prominent in Pan-African Congress

Meanwhile, Kenyatta was getting back into the wider world of pan-African politics. He moved for a while to Manchester where he helped the West Indian Otto Makonnen to run his cafés with their Caribbean menus (local folklore alleges that Kenyatta owned two cafés or clubs in Manchester). The two linked up with Padmore and planned to hold the Pan-African Congress there. Also invited were Kwame Nkrumah and Peter Abrahams, a Black South African writer who made Kenyatta the ill-starred hero of his novel, *A Wreath for Udomo*. Abrahams portrayed Udomo as pulled between the call of Africa and his love affairs with English women. Someone who knew Kenyatta well during these English years says he lived in a state of constant tension. When the time came, he left his English wife without signs of emotional stress, even though she was again pregnant.

Triumphant Return to Kenya (1946)

Arriving at Mombasa on 24 September 1946 he was hailed as a folk hero. He took steps to re-establish his leadership. He cultivated Chief Koinange through his son Peter. The chief gave one of his daughters to Kenyatta in marriage, a sign of his higher status.[8] Peter offered him the post of Vice-Principal of the independent teachers' training college he had established at Githungiri: subsequently he took over as Principal when Peter went abroad. He also approached the Governor, asking to be nominated to the Legislative Council. Mitchell advised him to acquire experience on a local Native Council first. Then, in March 1947 he was appointed to the African Land Settlement Board.

Much more important, he became President of the Kenya African Union in June 1947: this was the successor to the KCA, disbanded in the war. At much the same time, Mitchell told the Colonial Secretary in a Despatch (no. 44 of 17 April 1946) that the African political associations merely produced 'high-sounding phrases which have largely taken the place of hard thinking'.

Before he left England, Kenyatta had attended a conference where he heckled Creech Jones, newly appointed to the Colonial Office. The former champion of the undermost peoples was being seduced by his officials. Their plan was to introduce 500 new White settlers into Kenya at a cost of £1 600 000, of which £900 000 would be advanced by the United Kingdom. The Fabian Colonial Bureau protested; but when Creech Jones addressed them on 9 January 1946 he defended the scheme. White settlement was essential; they must accept the Carter Report: 'it would be folly to discuss the liquidation of European settlement', which would lead to 'healthy development in the days to come'. He ended by claiming, lamely, 'On the whole the Labour Government is doing very well.'

Governor Mitchell was thinking on similar lines. There must be racial cooperation, aiming at 'a civilised state [with] the values and standards of Britain, in which everyone, whatever his origins, has an interest and a part', he told Nairobi Rotary (24 October 1947). In case this upset them, a year later he affirmed, 'Kenya is marching inevitably towards the creation of a new Dominion of the Commonwealth in which the British will, for a very long time ahead, be the controlling and directing force.' This theme was reiterated: 'The choice has been made, and this Kenya and all its people are for ever British' (*The Times*, 4 December 1948).

The move by Pandit Nehru to appoint Indian Commissioners in

territories where there was a substantial Indian population came as an irritant. Reluctantly, the Colonial Office agreed. For East Africa, the candidate was Apa B. Pant, son of an Indian prince who had run his state on Gandhian principles. The governors of Uganda and Tanganyika at once agreed, but Mitchell objected: 'He is said to be Left in sympathies, known to have been involved in sabotage in India . . . it is not beyond the realms of possibility that he is being sent here for that purpose.' Blandly, the Colonial Office replied, 'It seems agreed that he is quite a pleasant person . . . and is intellectually sound. He was at Balliol' (18 June 1948). Grudgingly, Mitchell acquiesced, but Pant was under observation from the minute he arrived. Doubtless suspicion deepened when Peter Koinange, on a visit to Delhi, declared, 'The people of East Africa were looking to India for guidance in their efforts to put an end to their exploitation by the Whites' (*The Hindu*, 6 August 1949).

Unrest among Returned Soldiers

Kenyatta was also closely watched by the Special Branch from the moment he returned. The problems of his country were now more complicated. Little had been done for demobilised African soldiers, and there was no land for them. Many drifted along to Nairobi, existing in shanty settlements on the outskirts. Others joined the thousands of the land-hungry who, excluded from the White Highlands, made illegal holdings and were labelled Squatters. One important element was the 'Forty Group', young men circumcised in 1940. They mostly saw military service outside Kenya and were pugnacious, often rowdy. Claiming to be Kenyatta's followers, they were frequently an embarrassment. He endeavoured to preach the Protestant ethic of honesty, integrity, hard work: 'If we want freedom we must eschew idleness, for freedom will not come falling from heaven.' He tried to reach out to the Luo, Kamba, and other less sophisticated tribes, though his main support was among the Kikuyu people. The emphasis was always upon one Kenya; he did not exclude the Europeans, though he demanded equality for all.

Kenyatta Concentrates on Educational Uplift

For five years he preached a programme of reform, concentrating on education, centred at Githungiri. Near there at Gatundu he built himself a stone house, declaring, 'On this hill I am free. I hate to go into Nairobi. I want to run away from there.'

The Outbreak of 'Mau Mau'

While he was speaking of freedom, others were starting to act to eject the British. It was all on a minor scale, though in 1947 a European police inspector was killed in a skirmish and other violent actions followed. In 1948, the term Mau Mau was first mentioned. It is not clear whether this was just a mishearing of the Kikuyu word *muma* for an oath, or if there was another explanation.[9] Certainly there was an underground movement, entry into which was by oath and ceremonial initiation. There were higher degrees, the second being that of warrior, and initiation was increasingly harsh, bizarre to Western minds (though the admission ceremonies in some American fraternity houses seem equally bizarre). There were maiming attacks on cattle owned by Whites and a gap began to open between 'loyalist' Kikuyu and the guerrillas.

All this created a dilemma for Kenyatta. He must retain majority support among the Kikuyu, whose degree of involvement in the underground struggle was unknown. He wanted to keep his links with the British Left, who were apt to be upset by 'terrorism'. In his speeches he distanced himself from Mau Mau.

The British rulers replied with the usual mixture of carrot and stick. In 1948, Mitchell announced that *four* nominated Africans would be included in the new legislature. They were chosen by the Governor from a panel submitted by the Native Councils; Kenyatta was not one of them. Mathu, the model of a colonial moderate, had induced the old legislature to accept an end to the *kipande*. In the new Council the Whites rejected this. Sir Bernard Glancey, a former Indian Governor, was brought out to review the question. After months of inquiry he recommended that any African who could fill out a form in English be exempted from finger-printing. The non-Europeans rejected this palliative, but the Glancey Report was approved by a Council majority composed of the official bloc and the Whites. There seemed little mileage in moderation.

Mau Mau Outlawed (1950)

In 1950 Mau Mau was outlawed as a prohibited organisation. There followed a general strike in Nairobi called by the East Africa Trades Union Congress whose leader was the veteran Makhan Singh. There were violent clashes with the police before the strike was broken and its leader deported. Kenyatta's main activity in 1950 was to organise the Kenya Land Petition, along with Fenner Brockway, acting for what was now the Congress of Peoples Against Imperialism: 16 700 square miles of agricultural land had been alienated for White occupation. Brockway recorded his impression of Kenyatta in 1950: 'He seemed unchanged, aquiline features, tall, a cloak over his shoulders, an ivory-topped stick in his hand, sometimes smiling radiantly, sometimes severe, a fascinating showman.'

Kenyatta Publicly Condemns Mau Mau

By the time Brockway presented his petition to parliament with its 158 642 names (many recorded in blood), the government had changed and Kenyatta had been jailed. His public stance on Mau Mau was clear enough. On 26 July 1952 he told a crowd of 50 000 at Nyeri: 'The Kenya African Union claims this land as its own gift from God. . . . The Kenya African Union speaks in daylight. He who calls us the Mau Mau is not truthful. We do not want to know this Mau Mau.' This seemed clear enough, yet on 16 August he was visited by a group of eight young men, including Waruhui Itote, who became 'General China'. He had served in Burma, and Kenyatta contrasted the fighting he had done for the British with the coming fight for the people of Kenya. On 24 August he again addressed a mass meeting in company with Harry Thuku, Eliud Mathu, and the imposing loyalist chief, Waruhiu. Kenyatta was the star speaker. He called on the crowd to raise their hands to curse Mau Mau, adding, 'Mau Mau has spoiled the country. Let Mau Mau perish forever.' He went on to demand racial equality. As *The Times* writer observed, there was 'ample warning' that revolt was brewing but Mitchell and the Colonial service chose to ignore it.

Kenyatta Arrested: Convicted for Mau Mau (1953)

In September a new Governor arrived: Sir Evelyn Baring. He was driven to Government House circuitously to avoid hostile White demonstrators. On 7 October Chief Waruhui was assassinated. Two days later, Baring asked London for emergency powers. On the night of 20/21 October, Kenyatta was arrested and spirited off to a remote district. Simultaneously the Emergency was proclaimed. There followed a series of killings of Europeans. The trial of Kenyatta followed, opening on 24 November 1952 and continuing until 8 April 1953. By staging the trial in a remote spot, Kapenguria, far from Nairobi, the government hoped to avoid publicity; instead, Kapenguria became a focus of world attention. Indian lawyers rallied to his defence; first, A.R. Kapil and Pio Pinto (a Goan, later detained under the Emergency). More distinguished figures arrived, including Chaman Lall, friend of Nehru and eminent parliamentarian. The defence was led by D.N. Pritt. He was successful in demonstrating that this was really a political trial. He discredited much of the prosecution evidence, which relied heavily upon one witness, Rawson Macharia, who was rewarded with a government scholarship at Exeter University. When the weary business was over, Kenyatta concluded: 'I have done my best, and if all the other people had done as I have done Mau Mau would not be as it is now. You, the British made it what it is, not Kenyatta.'

When this travesty of British justice was finished, the magistrate (specially brought in, and flown out of Kenya immediately afterwards) sentenced Kenyatta and his companions to seven years' hard labour, followed by indefinite restriction. Pritt appealed against the verdict, and then against the way the Court was constituted (the magistrate, specially appointed, had been appointed to the wrong district). It was of no avail; the appeal courts, up to the Privy Council, confirmed the verdict, though blatantly unconstitutional and illegal.[10]

Banished: Severe Captivity

Kenyatta, with the others, was sent to Lokitaung, near Lake Rudolf on the Sudan border: for several months they were loaded with chains. Pritt was fortunate to get out of Kenya without being lynched. A particular venom was directed against Nehru for his stand. Thus Michael Blundell, who later took up the politics of multi-racialism: 'There are few Europeans in Kenya who do not insist that New Delhi through its official and non-official representatives in East Africa has encouraged and aided the rebellion of the Mau Mau.' They felt a 'burning hostility' to Nehru, he exclaimed (*New York Times*, 19 July 1953). Now it was hoped that Kenyatta would be forgotten. His house at Gatundu was razed to the ground; its stones were carted away and the site used for other purposes. No communication was permitted with him. There was complete silence. But far from Kenyatta being forgotten, his presence brooded over the whole political scene.

The Uprising Suppressed

Two brigades of British troops arrived in Kenya, while battalions of the King's African Rifles were brought in from Uganda and Tanganyika. A network of local security was set up, with Home Guards to defend the Kikuyu villages. Outlying Kikuyu homesteads were pulled down and their inhabitants moved into new villages behind barbed wire, as in Malaya, and later in South Vietnam. Colonel Arthur Young, head of the City of London police force, had reorganised the police in Malaya: now he was brought in to do the same job in Kenya. All this had its effect. Even when Mau Mau attacks inflicted severe casualties, as in the Lari massacre, their own losses were heavier. Slowly the jungle fighters were driven away from areas of settlement and survived only in the Aberdare mountains. By 1955, the back of the revolt was broken.

Renewed European confidence was reflected in the immigration figures; in 1955, 4000 came in to settle, including 1134 dependents. Between 1948 and 1955 the total White population had increased from 29 660 to 52 400. It was to peak at 55 759 (1962). Few of these new arrivals settled on the land; most were in urban occupations, such as lawyers, accountants, estate agents, the retail trades and construction firms. Most were British, though about a thousand Italians were admitted and smaller numbers of other Europeans. Almost all adopted the settler mentality.

The Emergency contributed to positive thinking, both in the political and economic spheres. In February 1954, the first Tory Colonial Secretary, Oliver Lyttleton, visited Kenya and persuaded the Whites to accept a minimal participation by non-Whites in government. The Council of Ministers was reconstituted with six official members and six non-officials, of whom three were Europeans (including the reactionary Cavendish-Bentinck), two Asians, and one African: it was not much. Some Europeans realised that times were changing. Led by Blundell they sought to maximise the 'politics of multi-racialism'. The rest dug themselves in.

Young Africans Rise Up

New African leaders were emerging, notably Tom Mboya and Oginga Odinga. As members of the Luo tribe they could not be accused of Mau Mau sympathies. Mboya was born in 1930 and grew up in Kikuyu country. Educated at Catholic schools and then given technical training at Jeannes School, he was employed by Nairobi City Council as a Sanitary Inspector: about the highest level of African recruitment. He records that a White woman entered his laboratory, looked round, and asked, 'Is there anybody here?': Mboya replied, 'Is there something wrong with your eyes?' Infuriated, she organised a petition to get him sacked, but fortunately his superiors backed him up.[11] He became a trades union leader and in 1954 went to India to study union organisation. He was a negotiator. Oginga Odinga was more radical, more demanding.

Government Repression Continues: Mass Internment

Although Mau Mau was on the decline, the government response was increasingly repressive. On 24 April 1954 in *Operation Anvil* the security forces made a sweep through Nairobi, arresting every African on the street and detaining 35 000 Kikuyu. There was no suggestion that they were jungle fighters: just Kikuyu. Numbers built up until there were 88 000 in the detention camps. In December 1954, Colonel Young resigned prematurely. There was a new Colonial Secretary, Lennox-Boyd, and his answers to parliamentary questions were not reassuring: Young felt that the police did not 'command the trust and confidence of the public'. The powers of the Home Guard were 'liable to abuse owing to lack of discipline'. It was plain that Young had disagreed sharply with Baring.

However, a more imaginative development was the plan by R.J.M. Swynnerton, *To Intensify the Development of African Agriculture* (1955). This involved consolidating holdings, issuing freehold titles to farmers who had previously been Crown tenants, and at last permitting Africans to grow coffee. As a result, the value of crops on smallholdings was doubled.

Although the level of rebellion was much reduced, the ferment among Africans only increased. Horrific stories were coming out of the camps about beatings and bullying; mainly by the guards recruited from distant tribes, but often supervised by the White officers. Baring seemed to be quite removed from all this. He was a diplomat, not an administrator, and as Lyttleton had told Young, 'He is too intelligent for his job.' When Harold Macmillan succeeded Eden as Premier he called for 'something like a profit and loss account for each of our Colonial possessions'. By far the largest drain was in East Africa, running a deficit, on average, 1954−6, of £49 million a year.[12] Kenya was virtually bankrupt. Lennox-Boyd still imagined independence was far off: 1975 was his target date as late as 1959. But events proved too much.

The Lyttleton constitution broke down in 1956. Lennox-Boyd negotiated an improved offer; but the Africans newly elected in 1957, including Mboya and Odinga, were unsatisfied. They wanted an African majority in the legislature, the release of Kenyatta, and early independence. On 6 December 1958, Mboya met Lennox-Boyd in London to present him with the evidence that Kenyatta had been framed in 1952. Rawson Macharia admitted that his statement at the trial was perjury. Lennox-Boyd declined to reconsider the matter. Kenyatta's guilt was a matter of belief not evidence.

1959: Kenyatta's Freedom Still Restricted

In 1959, Kenyatta's sentence of seven years' hard labour was completed. He was not set free, but was moved a few miles (still in the Lake Rudolf border country) and installed in a small government bungalow. He was allowed to have his family with him, and had a radio set. Otherwise, he was still incommunicado. He received an allowance of £9 per month. Rumour said he was a broken man, and was drinking the whole time (though how he managed on £9 a month was not explained).

The Horror of Hola Camp

The Conservative benches, with their active 'settler' members, were shaken by news which now emerged from Kenya. Most of the detainees had been released by 1959 after an elaborate process of psychological 'rehabilitation', but the hard core were confined in the remote Hola Camp. There, on 3 March, the guards inflicted terrible punishment on 85 recalcitrant prisoners. Eleven were killed, two with fractured skull and jaw, the rest with fractures on legs and arms. At first an attempt was made to pretend they had died through drinking contaminated water, but the truth came out. After an official inquiry, the Kenya Attorney-General admitted there had been use of 'illegal force'. But nobody was punished; two prison officers were retired.[13] Hola was renamed Galole: but there could be no wiping out of the impact of the tragedy.

London: A New Constitutional Initiative (1960)

After the general election of October 1959, Macmillan replaced Lennox-Boyd by Iain Macleod, who had been convinced by Hola that it was time for rapid change. A conference was convened in January 1960 at Lancaster House. The African delegation insisted that Peter Koinange (who had taken refuge in Ghana as a Mau Mau suspect) must attend. The Colonial Office refused. Five days of bargaining ensued, before a typically British fudge was agreed: a blank pass would be issued which would enable Koinange to attend. All this upset the White delegations. In the end a fancy constitution was agreed. Of the 65 seats in the new legislature, 33 would be elected from common roll constituencies (though the franchise was still restricted). Twenty seats were reserved: ten for the Whites, eight for Asians, and two for the Arabs. In these reserved seats candidates were required to obtain the support of 25 per cent of their own community in the constituency before facing election by a multi-racial electorate.

On 1 January 1960 the Emergency was formally ended. Almost, it seemed, as a counterblast to the new spirit of cooperation, the Kenya government issued a report compiled by one F.D. Corfield which purported to be the history of Mau Mau. The allegations made against Kenyatta at his trial were repeated unaltered, even though the falsity of much of the evidence had been proved.[14]

Kenya: No Way Back for Kenyatta

At the end of 1959 a new Governor took over from Baring: Sir Patrick Renison. On 31 March he announced that 'the release of Jomo Kenyatta would be a danger to security'; he followed this up by a sensational broadcast in which he spoke of 'the African leader of darkness and death'. 'His return would tend to glorify Mau Mau . . . when the emphasis should be on how much Mau Mau and Jomo Kenyatta retarded that advance' towards self-government. The reply by the African political leaders was to nominate Kenyatta as the President of the newly-formed Kenya African National Union (KANU). The government vetoed his nomination. Even Blundell, the supposed White liberal, opposed his release.

Meanwhile the Tory Right was fulminating against Macleod. At their 1960 annual conference, Patrick Wall announced to loud applause: 'We should make it crystal clear that until black Africans have shown they fully appreciate their responsibilities there can be no further constitutional advance in Kenya.'

1961 Kenya Election: KANU Demand Kenyatta's Release

As preparations for the Kenyan general election went ahead, the slogan *Uhuru*, 'freedom', was heard throughout the land. Every election meeting, whether in the 'open' or reserved seats, was accompanied by chanting from the crowds of *Uhuru Na Kenyatta*, and all the candidates were challenged to declare where they stood on his liberation. One European contest was particularly significant: that in the Rift Valley seat. In the all-White primary, Cavendish-Bentinck received 1545 votes while 542 went to Blundell: just enough, by 34 votes, to qualify. He was abused as a traitor for his supposedly anti-White activities at Lancaster House. When the actual election took place, with African participation, Blundell gained 20 009 votes and Cavendish-Bentinck 2051. KANU also experienced internal pressures as Odinga challenged Mboya for the leadership, alleging that he was lukewarm about Kenyatta's release.

On the eve of the poll, in January 1961, Mboya paid a quick visit to

New Delhi to implore Nehru to help in securing Kenyatta's release. Would he raise the matter at the forthcoming Prime Ministers' meeting in March? He was told that this was a 'delicate matter'; Nehru would discuss the release informally, but it could not be included on the agenda (*The Hindu*, 5 and 6 January 1961).

KANU Victory Thwarted by Whites

Mboya stood for a Nairobi constituency where most of the Africans were not of his own tribe. He triumphantly expressed the new politics of Kenyan nationalism by gaining 90 per cent of all the votes. When all was over, in February, KANU had won 19 seats with 67 per cent of the poll. The recently-formed alternative, the Kenya African Democratic Union (KADU) won 11 seats on 16 per cent of the votes. KANU told the Governor they would only form a Ministry if Kenyatta were released; the Governor turned them down. Eventually, KADU agreed to form a government without making this stipulation. Blundell and his New Kenya group supported them (although he had enlisted under the KANU banner during the election). Still lacking a majority, this coalition was reinforced by specially nominated members brought in by the Governor.

Kenyatta Free at Last

It seems clear that Renison's hard line in February 1961 had the backing of the British government: mainly because Macmillan would not risk a Tory revolt over Kenyatta's release.[15] However, Kenyatta was moved out of barren Lodwar to a more attractive location and allowed to receive visitors. On 1 August Macleod announced that restrictions on him were lifted. The Kenya government had rebuilt his house on his old plot of land, and there he returned in mid-August. On 22 August Renison held a meeting with the 'leader of darkness and death'. It was brief and tense. Macleod left the Colonial Office that autumn to become Leader of the House of Commons. He was replaced by the dilatory, smooth-talking Reggie Maudling.

Early in November Kenyatta visited London again. Macmillan reflected gloomily, 'If we have to give independence to Kenya it may well prove another Congo. If we hold on, it will mean a long and cruel campaign' (19 December 1961). Yet another constitutional conference was convened, February–March 1962. It resulted in an arrangement described later by *The Times'* Africa correspondent as 'elaborate nonsense'; a compromise seeking to reconcile the KADU wish for . devolution to regions (like Busia's plan in Ghana) and KANU's demand for a unitary state.[16] Kenyatta announced, 'I hope the British public will be aware of the subtle, professional public relations move', underlying the concessions made by Maudling to KADU (*The Times*, 2 March 1962).

A New-Style Governor

In January 1963 Renison was replaced by Malcolm MacDonald, renowned for the relaxed, open-shirt style which had been so successful in southern Asia. Soon after his arrival, Duncan Sandys (under whom the Commonwealth and Colonial Offices now combined) came to Kenya to assist in sorting out the legacy of the Maudling muddle.

Kenyatta Joins Constitution-Making

MacDonald went to work with both KANU and KADU leaders. He observed that Kenyatta was assiduous in his attendance at their meetings: not taking the lead, but 'when he did speak it was with clarity and authority': the Governor concluded: 'He was the wisest and perhaps strongest as well as the most popular potential Prime Minister of the independent nation-to-be.'[17] With Sandys' help, in mid-April they put the final touches to 'what was probably the most complicated colonial constitution ever produced'.

Kenyatta Leads Country into Independence

This was put to the test in another election held in May. KANU won a substantial majority in the Lower House and took a narrow lead in the Senate. On 1 June Kenyatta became the first Prime Minister, with full internal self-government. MacDonald comments: 'On that very day Kenyatta's character seemed to grow. . . . He became energetic, indeed dynamic; he became decisive; he became masterful. . . . When disagreements arose he insisted that . . . his Ministerial colleagues should accept his final considered view; and they conformed to his wish.'

On 31 December 1963, Kenya achieved independence, and one year later became a Republic, with Kenyatta as President. Thereafter (in November 1964), KADU merged into KANU, some of its leaders becoming Ministers.

His Acceptance of the Whites

During the 15 years during which he led his independent country, Kenyatta guided his people through a number of crises. His first priority was to reassure the Whites. This was aided by the British government coming up with generous compensation for White farmers who sold out. By soft-pedalling the importance of Mau Mau, replacing the slogan *Uhuru* by *Harambee* ('all pull together') he gave symbolic assurances: and when Kenya, especially Nairobi, entered into a building boom, British construction firms profited. Foreign visitors, especially to the wild life reserves, gave a boost to the flourishing tourist industry. To the Kenyan Whites Kenyatta became 'The Squire'. He was less magnanimous to the Indians who had done so much more for him: those who would not adopt citizenship found themselves squeezed out, even though more Asians than Whites became citizens.[18] African capitalism began to flourish and an elite with a vested interest in the regime gathered around the President.

Although Kenyatta lived a relatively simple life, preferring his old home at Gatundu and using the former Government House merely as a presidential office, he did acquire a very substantial agricultural estate, and a private fortune (subsequently bequeathed to his family). So did most senior African politicians and civil servants. The White Minister for Agriculture, Bruce MacKenzie, was retained until 1970 to give confidence to the remaining White farmers. When in May 1965 the government published its policy paper, *African Socialism and its Application to Planning in Kenya*, this rejected expropriation or full nationalisation as measures of land reform. This caused something of a split within KANU, with Odinga leading the radicals and Mboya the moderates. Odinga was ousted from his position as Vice-President and took his followers off to form the Kenya People's Union (KPU). One, Bildad Kaggia (detained with Kenyatta), stood as KPU candidate in 1966 and defeated his KANU opponent.

The worst blow came when Mboya was assassinated in July 1969. The motive of the killer, a Kikuyu, was obscure; however, the Luo crowd at his requiem mass demonstrated against Kenyatta as the leading Kikuyu. There was a revival of oath-taking as virtually all Kikuyu vowed 'to keep the flag in the House of Mumbi'; meaning to preserve Kikuyu pre-eminence.

Survives *Coup d'Etat* (1971)

A general election was held in January 1970, and although KANU was the only party there was a selection process reminiscent of the 1960 primaries in which almost half the sitting MPs were rejected, including five Cabinet Ministers. In 1971 there was an attempted *coup d'état*: by now a common occurrence in Africa. There had been army mutinies in

1964 in all three East African states, but these were quickly suppressed with British assistance. Now, there were a motley group of conspirators whose figurehead was Major-General Ndolo, the Kamba Chief of Staff. He was replaced by another Kamba, Major-General Mulinga. The whole affair fizzled out.

Dies the Grand Old Man (1978)

By now, Kenyatta was taking things more easily: *Mzee*, the Old Man or Grand Old Man, was a living legend. The management of everyday affairs devolved upon the Vice-President, Daniel Arap Moi, a member of the Kalenjin coastal tribe and originally of KADU. When eventually Kenyatta died on 22 August 1978, unexpectedly, at Mombasa he succeeded to the presidency without challenge, rather to the surprise of many. Kenyatta's state funeral was attended by the Prince of Wales on behalf of the Queen, by Morarji Desai (then Prime Minister) and Apa B. Pant from India, and by the principal leaders of African countries. He was interred in a mausoleum next to the parliament building. It was an astonishing metamorphosis for the primitive child of the tribe, the evil genius of Mau Mau to end up, in the words of Duncan Sandys, as 'the father figure of all Africa and respected by all'.[19]

Afterthoughts

It seems unnecessary to produce a lengthy conclusion. The reader should have been convinced that these eight men did indeed become the instruments of their countries' re-emergence into the international community. They overturned the old order and re-established respect and dignity for their peoples. In some cases, these emancipated peoples have continued to retain as much freedom as any of us can expect in these dangerous decades at the end of the twentieth century. For some, independence has in the end meant only deprivation of civil and political rights: in the worst cases, repression more harsh than under Western colonialism.

Do these eight leaders demonstrate any kind of pattern? One feature they all possessed was the capacity to speak to their audience, the ordinary people of their land. Some were accomplished orators; others, such as Ho Chi Minh and Nehru, communicated in an almost conversational way. All managed to get across to the peasant and the man in the street that the struggle for independence was *their* struggle. All had that quality – so overworked in our political vocabulary – of charisma, magic, creating an awareness in the ordinary man and woman that they were in the presence of someone very special.

Out of the eight, Nehru began life with the advantage of privilege; although Jinnah also had a father who was a successful entrepreneur. All the rest came from families outside the westernised, urban elite in which political awareness had developed. The fathers of Sukarno and Ho were school teachers, with limited access to the knowledge which would benefit their sons. The others were right outside the extensive network of colonial communication, though only Kenyatta began life with *nothing* in his favour.

Most of these leaders were started on their way upwards by the ladder of Western higher education, though none but Nehru received a formal university education in the metropole. For Ho Chi Minh, Communist ideological training provided a substitute for academic training: also in a European setting, in Paris and Moscow. Once again, only Kenyatta had to struggle on his own with almost no formal education until, late in life, he attached himself to the University of London.

Another feature common to almost all these leaders was the ability to express themselves with polish and with force in the language of the colonial power. Jinnah produced no book or booklet of a political or ideological nature. He wrote effective speeches, and drafted forceful political memoranda; but authorship seems never to have appealed to him. Aung San also left no writings for publication. The remainder were authors of standing. Three – Nehru, Nu, and Nkrumah – wrote autobiographies which are remarkable expressions of their respective personalities.

Do their personalities show any common features? All, at different times in their lives, withdrew from the bustle of street politics, the manoeuvring and manipulating of the committee room and the conference hall. Nehru saw jail as a refuge; later, after independence, he yearned for the solitude of the hills. Aung San had the ability to draw apart, even when in company; he may have found illness a means of psychological liberation from the demands made upon him. Jinnah spent years in London, away from all the pressures of politics. In part this was not of his choice: he was in political limbo. But he chose to linger when others were urging him to return. Nu tried in vain to free himself from politics and find satisfaction in authorship; in the end he found freedom in detention, and when let out took refuge in a monastery in India for a while, seeking spiritual release. Kenyatta spent long, lonely years in London when he could have made his way back to Kenya. Although others had to endure imprisonment, none like him had to pass ten long years in solitary confinement: an experience which would have destroyed most men, but left him prepared to confront his destiny.

The only leader to flinch from solitude was Sukarno; the only one who was temperamentally an extrovert. But he too had to endure being apart, in those years when the Dutch sent him into exile and at the end of his life when the generals banished him.

Withdrawal from the world is a recognised part of the experience of the great spiritual leaders of Asia and Africa: the Buddha, Jesus Christ, Muhammad. It is part of the mythology of leaders of history. In the West the politician who goes away or disappears is then forgotten. Not so in Asia and Africa.

It is also an element in Afro-Asian ideas about the great man that he renounces physical love for the sake of his people. Among these leaders, two – Kenyatta and Sukarno – clearly found women seductive, and could not have enough of them. Aung San, in his short life, found support and strength in the loyalty of his wife. For all the rest, marriage seems to have meant relatively little, and to have been renounced almost with relief. The place of Lady Mountbatten in Nehru's hours of trial has not been explored in this book. It is intriguing, but forms no part of the Nehru myth: that he sacrificed the treasure of marriage for his country. For

Nkrumah, Nu and Ho, the women in their life seem to have been unimportant.

Are we getting any closer to a group portrait of Afro-Asian leadership? One feature of high position is that the way to the top entails passing by friends, sometimes treading upon rivals. How ruthless were these eight leaders? The mildest, certainly, was U Nu. Yet when he faced total breakdown in his country soon after independence he cast off his nervous Cabinet colleagues and went on, virtually alone. Again, in 1958, he severed the political loyalties formed long before when they had all perceived the fight against imperialism as a shared struggle. This did not count: he attacked those who opposed *his* strategy.

Nehru would pay almost any price for unity – too high a price sometimes – but he could be ruthless, as when he turned his back on Subhas Bose and at the end, when Krishna Menon let him down. As to the rest, Aung San was coldly calculating where political advantage and loyalty conflicted. Nkrumah dismissed his closest comrades if they stood in the way. Ho, despite the 'Uncle Ho' image, was prepared to fight remorselessly in any power struggle. Sukarno had no compunction in pushing aside worthy comrades like Sjahrir. It was only rough justice when he was pushed aside. Who said a good Prime Minister is a good butcher? If that is true in England, where the realities are so elaborately concealed beneath the pretences, how much more true it is in the new states of Asia and Africa where butchery is all too often undisguised.

However different their personal qualities and styles, these men had an iron will and determination at the core of their characters. Doubtless this is true of all leaders capable of withstanding the stress of high political life. This willpower enabled them to decide when the critical moment had arrived to challenge the colonial overlord: whether that moment came soon, or after long delay and disappointment. They rose to the occasion; they triumphed. For some there was a fall to come at length. The way in which they overcame disaster, or wilted, is another measure of their comparative stature.

Let us leave these men to history, where they are sure of a place.

Notes and References

1 The Edifice of Empire

1. In *The Encyclopedia Americana* (1963 edn), vol. X, p. 300, 'Empire' rather surprisingly has this definition: 'A form of political organisation which is much older than the modern national state, and may well outlive it'.
2. James Bryce, *The Ancient Roman Empire and the British Empire in India* (London, 1914), pp. 32, 77. The *Encyclopedia Americana* article (above) observes that it is in 'the British Empire that modern imperialism has found its most notable creation – the greatest since the days of the Roman Empire. . . . British imperial policy has traditionally been guided by the concept that *imperium* (rule) must be supplemented by *libertas* (Liberty).' The author of these complimentary sentiments is a Princeton professor.
3. Rajendra Prasad, *Autobiography* (Bombay, 1957), p. 131.
4. Henri Brunschwig, *French Colonialism, 1871–1914; Myths and realities* (London, 1966), p. 82. See also pp. 57 and 129–30 for quotations following. The English edition is a revised version of the original in French, 1960.
5. D.K. Fieldhouse, *The Colonial Empires* (London, 1966), p. 306.
6. Dennis J. Duncanson, *Government and Revolution in Vietnam* (London, 1968), p. 98.
7. Fieldhouse, *Colonial Empires*, p. 308.
8. Paul Leroy-Beaulieu, *De la colonisation chez les peuples modernes* (5th edn, Paris, 1902: 1st edn 1874), vol. I, pp. 491–2.
9. Duncanson, *Government and Revolution*, p. 87
10. J.S. Furnivall, *Colonial Policy and Practice: A comparative study of Burma and Netherlands India* (Cambridge, 1948), p. 227.
11. J.H. Boeke, *The Structure of the Netherlands Indian Economy* (New York, 1942).
12. Robert Delavignette, *Freedom and Authority in French West Africa* (London, 1950), p. 149.
13. Elliott Roosevelt, *As He Saw It* (New York, 1945), p. 115. Quoted in Bernard B. Fall, *The Two Viet-Nams* (New York, 1963), p. 51.
14. *The Times*, 27 October 1942.
15. This and subsequent quotations from British Cabinet Ministers is taken from J.E. Williams, 'The Joint Declaration on the colonies: an issue in Anglo–American relations, 1942–1944', *British Journal of International Studies* (1976), no. 2, pp. 267–92.

2 The Nation Builders

1. Washington was as much the centre of a personality cult as any present-day Afro-Asian leader. When the Senate discussed the title of their new Head of State they favoured 'His Highness, the President of the United States, Protector of their Liberties'.
2. H.A.L. Fisher, *History of Europe*, 3 vols (London 1935: one volume edn, 1936), p. 951.
3. Ibid., p. 917.
4. Ibid., p. 959.
5. Thomas Carlyle, *On Heroes, Hero-Worship and the Heroic in History*, London 1841: Lecture I, 'The Hero as Divinity'. Compare the verdict of one of Washington's

biographers: Paul Van Dyke, *George Washington, the Son of his Country, 1732–1775* (New York, 1931), pp. 4–5: 'If young Washington had been among the hundreds scalped at Braddock's defeat [in 1755] it would have had on the political development of the world a deeper and more durable effect than if the young Napoleon had been killed at the bridge of Lodi.'

6.   V.I. Lenin, *The Teachings of Karl Marx* (1914: English edn, London, 1931), 'Materialist Conception of History'.

3   The Winding Path of M.A. Jinnah

1.   Stanley Wolpert, *Jinnah of Pakistan* (New York, 1984), p. 26. This work will be the source for several quotations in the pages following.

2.   Azim Husain, *Fazl-i-Husain: A political biography* (Bombay, 1946), p. 99.

3.   Ibid., pp. 309–10.

4.   An interesting analysis of the source of Jinnah's arguments is R.J. Moore, 'Jinnah and the Pakistan Demand', *Modern Asian Studies*, vol. 17 (1983), no. 4, pp. 529–61.

5.   N. Mansergh (ed.), *The Transfer of Power, 1942–7* (henceforth cited as *TOPI*), vol. I, 'The Cripps Mission' (London, 1970), p. 327.

6.   Z.H. Zaidi, *M.A. Jinnah–Ispahani Correspondence, 1936–1948* (Karachi, 1976), p. 449.

7.   Norval Mitchell, *Sir George Cunningham* (Edinburgh, 1968), p. 105.

8.   Penderel Moon (ed), *Wavell, the Viceroy's Journal* (London, 1973), p. 229.

9.   B.B. Misra, *The Indian Political Parties* (Delhi, 1976), p. 564. Quoting from the Alexander papers.

10.   *TOPI*, vol. VII, p. 540.

11.   Zaidi, *Correspondence*, p. 490.

12.   *TOPI*, vol. X, p. 12.

13.   Ibid., p. 102.

14.   Ibid., pp. 299–301.

15.   *TOPI*, vol. XI, pp. 898–900, and Alan Campbell-Johnson, *Mission With Mountbatten* (London, 1951: paperback edn 1985), p. 131.

16.   *Constituent Assembly of Pakistan, Debates*, vol. I, no. 2, pp. 18–20. Reproduced in Tinker, 'Tradition and Experiment in Forms of Government', C.H. Philips (ed.), *Politics and Society in India* (London 1963), p. 161; also by Wolpert, *Jinnah of Pakistan*, p. 339.

17.   Mitchell, *Sir George Cunningham*, pp. 141, 144.

4   Jawaharlal Nehru: The Fading Dream

1.   J. Nehru, *An Autobiography* (London, 1936), p. 561.

2.   Vijaya Lakshmi Pandit, *The Scope of Happiness: A personal memoir* (London, 1979), p. 56.

3.   J. Nehru (ed.), *A Bunch of Old Letters: written mostly to Jawaharlal Nehru and some written by him* (Bombay, 1958), p. 12. This invaluable collection will be frequently quoted.

4.   B.N. Pandey, *Nehru* (London, 1976), p. 92.

5.   S. Gopal, *The Viceroyalty of Lord Irwin, 1926–1931* (Oxford, 1957), pp. 94–100.

6.   Pandit, *Scope of Happiness*, p. 107.

7.   Nehru, *A Bunch of Old Letters*, pp. 307–12, 313–14, 319–54.

8.   Taya Zinkin, *Reporting India* (London, 1962), p. 217.

9.   S. Gopal, *Jawaharlal Nehru: A biography* (London 1975), vol. I, p. 255.
10. *Autobiography, Postcript, Five Years Later*, p. 609.
11. *TOPI*, vol. I, p. 219.
12. Ibid., p. 693.
13. R.J. Moore, *Churchill, Cripps and India, 1939–1945* (Oxford, 1979), p. 119.
14. B.B. Misra, *The Indian Political Parties* (Delhi, 1976), p. 385.
15. Ibid., p. 390.
16. *TOPI*, vol. IV, p. 769.
17. *TOPI*, vol. VI, p. 439.
18. Ibid., pp. 851–9.
19. Philip Ziegler, *Mountbatten: The official biography* (London, 1985), p. 328.
20. Gopal, *Jawaharlal Nehru*, vol. I, p. 327, quoting Patel; Abul Kalam Azad, *India Wins Freedom* (Bombay, 1959), p. 317; Michael Brecher, *Nehru: A political biography* (Oxford, 1959), p. 317.
21. Pandit, *Scope of Happiness*, p. 212.
22. *TOPI*, vol. IX, pp. 122–3, 131.
23. *Constituent Assembly Debates*, vol. 10, no. 3, p. 49. Quoted in Tinker, *Experiment With Freedom, India and Pakistan, 1947* (London, 1967), p. 121.
24. *TOPI*, vol. X, pp. 756–7.
25. The position of Abul Kalam Azad, the leading Muslim nationalist, is debatable. He asserts in *India Wins Freedom* that he resisted partition, yet persons present at the AICC vote claim that Azad observed: 'The door is open. We should walk through it.'
26. Alan Campbell-Johnson, *Mission With Mountbatten* (London, 1985), p. 189.
27. S. Gopal, 'Nehru and Science: Aspirations and achievements', *Inter-disciplinary Science Reviews*, vol. 10 (1985), no. 2.
28. U Nu, *Saturday's Son* (New Haven, Connecticut, 1975), p. 234.
29. Pandit, *Scope of Happiness*, p. 315.
30. *The Times*, 4 June 1964.

5 Country Boys Force the Pace: Aung San and Thakin Nu

1.   Hugh Tinker (ed.), *Burma; The struggle for independence, 1944–48* (hereafter *Struggle*), (HMSO, 1984) vol. II, pp. 117, 180.
2.   Thakin Nu, *Burma Under the Japanese: Pictures and portraits* (London, 1954), p. 77.
3.   *Struggle*, vol. I, pp. 109, 110.
4.   Maung Maung (ed.), *Aung San of Burma* (The Hague, 1962). The letter is reproduced in facsimile between pp. 64–65.
5.   *Struggle*, vol. I, pp. 265–6.
6.   Ibid., pp. 262–4.
7.   Ibid., p. 549.
8.   Ibid., pp. 856–7.
9.   U Nu, *Saturday's Son* (New Haven, Connecticut, 1975), pp. 115–16.
10. *Struggle*, vol. I, p. 770.
11. *Struggle*, vol. II, p. 204.
12. Ibid., p. 299, footnote.
13. *TOPI*, vol. IX, pp. 488, 503.
14. *Struggle*, vol. II, pp. 364–72.

15. Ibid., p. 194.
16. Ibid., pp. 769–71.
17. Nu, *Saturday's Son*, pp. 340–1.
18. Ibid., p. 141.
19. 'The Outline of Ti Pitaka', Pitaka Translation Society, 1st Instalment, 1981, 2nd Instalment (Three Parts), 1982, 3rd Instalment (Three Parts), 1982. Issued in mimeographed typescript, Rangoon.

6 Sukarno and the Vocabulary of Revolution

1. Thomas Stamford Raffles, *The History of Java* (London, 1817), vol. I. A translation of the Bharata Yudha is included: the quotation is on p. 433.
2. S. Takdir Alisjahbana, *Indonesia: Social and Cultural Revolution* (Kuala Lumpur, 1966), pp. 138–9.
3. Bernhard Dahm, *Sukarno and the Struggle for Indonesian Independence* (English language edn, Ithaca NY, 1966), p. 93.
4. Raffles, *History of Java*, vol. II, p. 70, gives the prophecy of Jayabhaya in a footnote: the prophecy ends, 'By the year 2100 there will be an end of Java entirely.' The Javan year 2100 is 2173 AD.
5. Alisjahbana, *Indonesia*, pp. 139–41.
6. Dahm, *Sukarno*, pp. 166–70.
7. Alisjahbana, *Indonesia*, p. 170.
8. This version is quoted by Dahm, *Sukarno*, p. 215, note 17, after going through a process of multiple translation: English–Dutch–German–English. The original version was published in *Asia* (New York, November 1940), pp. 595–9, under the title, 'The Parting of the Ways'. Nehru's words, though not dissimilar, reflect his peculiar love–hate relationship with England:

> Fascism and Nazism were anathema to us, and the horrors of Central Europe produced a powerful reaction on India. . . . Yet we saw and felt . . . the day-to-day humiliation and exploitation of our own people. We were not wise or clever enough to understand that, though Fascism and Nazism were definitely bad, imperialism was not so bad after all. . . . This declaration of the British government [in August 1940] means the final breaking of such slender bonds as held our minds together, it means the ending of all hope that we shall ever march together. I am sorry; for in spite of my hostility to British imperialism . . . I have loved much that was England and I should have liked to keep the silken bonds of the spirit between India and England.

It does seem clear that here as elsewhere Sukarno took a quotation and deliberately adapted it to his own way of thinking.

9. Mountbatten, *Report to the Combined Chiefs of Staff by the Supreme Allied Commander, South-East Asia, Post Surrender Tasks* (1969), para. 42.
10. Mountbatten, *Post Surrender Tasks*, paras. 67–71 and note 35.
11. In his reminiscences, Khrushchev says he considered 'a fancy stadium seemed like a waste of money'. '"Why do you want a stadium?" I asked Sukarno. "As a place to hold public rallies"' he said.' Sukarno also insisted that the two leaders should pose for photographers as though they were actually working on the site: 'Sukarno had a theatrical streak in him, and, frankly it lowered him somewhat in my eyes. . . .

You'd never find Nehru building a stadium at great expense just so he could have a bigger audience.' *Khrushchev Remembers: The last testament*, Strobe Talbott (ed.) (London, 1974), p. 314. Khrushchev also ridiculed Sukarno's womanising: 'He loved women. He couldn't have enough of them. His reputation was scandalous. He simply couldn't control his passions' (*Khrushchev Remembers*, p. 321).

12. On 13 December 1964 Radio Jakarta stated Sukarno was 'walking with a limp from a swollen leg and looked tired from overwork'.
13. *The Times*, 5 October 1965.
14. The 'Cornell Paper' was issued by the Modern Indonesia Project of the Southeast Asia Program. It consists of 162 typed papers with a covering letter dated 10 January 1966.

7 The Long March of Ho Chi Minh

1. Nguyen The Anh, 'How did Ho Chi Minh become a proletarian?', *Asian Affairs* (June 1985): this demonstrates how little we actually know of his early life.
2. Jean Lacouture, *Ho Chi Minh* (Paris, 1967), p. 30. This work, *Le Procès de la Colonisation Française*, appeared as a booklet in 1925 though parts of it previously appeared in *l'Humanité*. Another edition was published in Hanoi in 1962.
3. The photograph appears in M.N. Roy's *Memoirs* (Bombay, 1964). Nguyen Ai Quoc is seated next to Katayama Sen, founder of the shortlived Socialist People's Party. He left Japan in 1914 and never returned, as did Kondo Elizo and Manabe, lesser figures in Japanese radical politics. It is not clear why Fall, *The Two Viet-Nams* (New York 1963), p. 82 states that when Roy knew Nguyen at the University of the Toilers of the East in 1924 he struck Roy as 'an unimpressive personality' because the text of the memoirs ends in 1921.
4. This unsavoury episode is depicted by Hoang Van Chi, *From Colonialism to Communism* (London, 1964), p. 18, who alleges that the betrayal was furthered by the son of Phan's best friend, Nguyen Thuong Hien, among others. It also appears in John T. McAlister, *Viet Nam: The origins of a revolution* (New York, 1969), p. 83. The version given here differs slightly, based on Ralph Smith's reading of contemporary newspapers.
5. It seems worth relating this not altogether significant story in detail because it is one of the few episodes in his pre-war life for which there is full documentation: see J. Davidson, *Indo-China: Signposts in the storm* (Malaysia, 1979), pp. 22–4. Some authorities, e.g. Fall, *The Two Viet-Nams*, p. 96, and *The Times* obituary, 4 September 1969, state that Cripps defended Nguyen Ai Quoc. The latter is the only source for information about Li Sam.
6. Hoang Van Chi, *From Colonialism to Communism*, p. 59, declares that it was in 1941 that Ho changed his name. Davidson, *Indo-China*, pp. 24–5, is more vague but says much the same. McAlister, *Viet Nam*, p. 148, says he already had the name Ho Chi Minh in 1941. Ralph Smith, *Viet-Nam and the West* (London, 1968), pp. 110–11, believes he made the change in 1943. Dennis Duncanson, *Government and Revolution in Vietnam* (London, 1968), p. 153, ascribes the change to 1943.
7. Lacouture, *Ho Chi Minh*, pp. 64–5. One is tempted to wonder if Ho, that widely-read man, knew Shelley:

> See the mountains clasp high heaven
> And the waves clasp one another,

No sister-flower would be forgiven
If it disdained its brother;
And the sunlight clasps the earth

However, 'Love's Philosophy' ends, 'What are all these kissings worth/if thou kiss not me?' which was not then an option for Ho.

8. Fall, *The Two Viet-Nams*, p. 99. Lacouture, *Ho Chi Minh*, suggests he was arrested some time after July 1942 (p. 64) and released in the spring of 1943 (p. 70). Duncanson, *Government and Revolution*, p. 153, gives August 1942 for his arrest and says he was released 'a year later'. Smith, *Viet-Nam and the West*, p. 110, states Ho 'spent all of 1942 and the first month of 1943 in a Chinese prison'. Hoang Van Chi and Davidson pass over the question. McAlister, *Viet Nam*, p. 147, states he was released on 16 September 1943. He also quotes a thesis by King Chen (p. 148, note 2) where Chang's denial that Ho was jailed appears.

9. Reproduced in M. Charlton and A. Moncrieff, *Many Reasons Why: The American involvement in Vietnam* (London, 1978), p. 9. This is a BBC documentary history broadcast September–November 1977. There will be more quotations from the many people Charlton interviewed in a classic BBC marathon.

10. Lacouture, *Ho Chi Minh*, p. 88.

11. *Documents Relating to British Involvement in the Indo-China Conflict 1945–1965*, Cmd 2834, 1965 (hereafter cited as *Documents*).

12. There is a good account of the meetings by Davidson, *Indo-China*, pp. 44–6. He also reproduces the convention in full.

13. As revealed by Bidault after the death of Ho Chi Minh: see *Le Monde*, 10 September 1969.

14. French hardliners in Saigon or Paris also sabotaged Blum's own attempt to reach a compromise with Ho. According to Bernard Fall's commentary on Truong Chinh, *The August Revolution* (Hanoi, 1962) (American ed, 1963), an appeal telegraphed by Blum in an attempt to head off the conflict was held up for four days in Saigon and only transmitted to Saigon after fighting had begun: see p. 155, note 40.

15. Vo Nguyen Giap, *People's War, People's Army*, (Hanoi, 1961; American ed, 1962) esp. p. 127.

16. Truong Chinh, *August Revolution*: note by Fall, p. 155, note 40.

17. *Documents*, pp. 64–5. Frantz Fanon observed, 'We are reminded that Ho Chi Minh, during the most tragic hours of the war in Indochina never ceased to mark the difference between colonialism and the French people': *Towards the African Revolution* (London, 1980), p. 99 (trans: *Pour la Révolution Africaine* (Paris, 1964).

18. For Bidault's prediction, see Davidson, *Indo-China*, p. 74. For Navarre's assessment and that of Giap see Fall, *The Two Viet-Nams*, pp. 122–5.

19. *Documents*: the commitment to elections is on pp. 84–5. The whole conference spans pp. 68–87. The final declaration was issued unsigned.

20. S. Gopal, *Jawaharlal Nehru: A biography*, vol. II, (London, 1979), p. 227. U Nu, *Saturday's Son* (New Haven, Connecticut, 1975), pp. 243–4.

21. A bitter attack upon the excesses committed at this time is made by Hoang Van Chi, *From Colonialism to Communism*. Doubt is cast on its reliability by Ralph Smith. Hoang worked for Ho for almost ten years, then in 1955 escaped to Saigon: the book may be seen as Saigon propaganda. For Giap's admission of 'errors' in full, see above pp. 209–10, the 'Lime Pot' poem, p. 232.

22. Lacouture, *Ho Chi Minh*, pp. 173–4.

23. *Documents*, p. 125, for the British statement of 9 April 1956. The full correspondence on elections begins p. 96.

24. Perhaps it was over-subtle to read into this statement the implication that he was in danger of military action in Ghana.

25. *The Times*, 16 January 1967.

26. *Le Monde*, 5 September 1969: an appreciation by Jean Lacouture. In the same issue Jacques Decorry wrote that Ho had inspired no personality cult; he was respected, but not canonised.

27. *The Times*, 10 September 1969.

8 Kwame Nkrumah: The Pursuit of Black Unity

1. When Fraser had arrived in Ceylon he announced that his task would be to train the leaders of a self-governing country: which he did! W.E.F. Ward, *Fraser of Trinity and Achimota* (Oxford, 1965).

2. Nkrumah, *Ghana: The autobiography of Kwame Nkrumah* (Edinburgh, 1957), esp. pp. 14–20. This lively autobiography is the main source for Nkrumah's life before making his mark in politics. All quotations with page references and no other attribution come from the *Autobiography*.

3. W. Scott Thompson, *Ghana's Foreign Policy, 1957–1966*, (Princeton, New Jersey, 1969), p. 24, quoting Professor K.A.B. Jones-Quartey, a fellow Ghanaian.

4. Colin Legum, *Pan-Africanism* (London, 1962), argues that the origins of the movement stem from the London Congress of 1900. Others begin with the Paris Congress of 1919, the first under the leadership of Du Bois. Nkrumah accepted this view. In its communiqué this was referred to as 'the Fifth Congress'.

5. Legum, *Pan-Africanism*, pp. 133–7 for resolutions, which are not quite consistent with Legum's own account of their purport (p. 32) which affirms that the Congress declared that, 'Africans as a last resort may have to appeal to force in their efforts to achieve them, even if force destroys them and the world.'

6. *Autobiography*, p. 58. See the present writer's *Separate and Unequal: India and the Indians in the British Empire, 1920–1950* (London, 1976), pp. 277–8, for the uneasy performance of Creech Jones before the Fabian Colonial Bureau when he admitted feeling that he was 'on trial'.

7. In an attempt to embarrass Labour, the Conservative MP, J. Langford-Holt, asked what 'subversive and inflammable material' had been found among Nkrumah's possessions? Had it included *Revolution in the Colonies* by Arthur Creech Jones? The answer was 'Yes'.

8. Dennis Austin, *Politics in Ghana* (London, 1964), p. 147, points out that Busia was actually rejected in two constituencies and owed his preferment to the decision of Dr Asafu Adjaye not to claim the seat he had won.

9. To demonstrate the quality of the new team, Sorensen asked to be told their qualifications. In a written answer, the Colonial Secretary revealed that all had respectable academic or professional qualifications, except J.A. Braimah, a secondary-school leaver.

10. Basil Davidson, *Black Star* (London, 1973), p. 81, Roland Oliver and Anthony Atmore, *Africa Since 1800* (Cambridge, paperback, 1977), p. 230.

11. See *West Africa*, 6 March 1954, and D.G. Anglin in *Canadian Journal of Economics and Political Science* (May 1958).

12. *Commonwealth and Colonial Affairs*, December 1954: quoted by David Goldsworthy,

Colonial Issues in British Politics, 1945−1961 (London, 1971), p. 305.

13.   Geoffrey Bing, *Reap the Whirlwind* (London, 1968), pp. 189−93. Provides a detailed account of the negotiations.

14.   Nkrumah's *Autobiography* appeared on Independence Day, having been completed the October before.

15.   Vijaya Lakshmi Pandit, *The Scope of Happiness* (London, 1979), p. 307. She dates this meeting to 1959 but specifically states it was the 'first meeting' between them. The Sukarno comparison is quoted by Scott Thompson, *Ghana's Foreign Policy*, p. 51. It is here stated that Nkrumah told Nehru that the Ghana parliament was erecting a statue of its leader and received the retort that in India this could only happen when a leader had died. It seems unlikely that two such snubs could have been administered.

16.   Frantz Fanon, *Towards the African Revolution* (London, 1980) trans: *Pour la Révolution Africaine* (Paris, 1964), pp. 151−2, 157. Fanon became Algeria's envoy in Accra in 1960.

17.   Harold Macmillan, *Pointing the Way, 1958−1961* (London, 1972), pp. 121−3. This volume in his long autobiography, *Winds of Change*, contains most material concerning Nkrumah. There will be further quotations, not given page references (there are also references in the preceding volume). It was in a speech at Accra on 9 January that Macmillan first declared, 'The wind of change is blowing right through Africa.' Nkrumah commented, 'No ordinary wind, but a raging hurricane.'

18.   Commonwealth observers: Bing, *Reap the Whirlwind*, pp. 295−6 (Bing was then Attorney-General); Referendum, Austin, *Politics in Ghana*, pp. 387−95. H.L. Bretton, *The Rise and Fall of Kwame Nkrumah* (London, 1967), describes the referendum as 'farcical' (p. 49), a 'coup against the people of Ghana' (p. 148), but he also says that in the 1956 election 'Violations against the election code had been so widespread as to raise doubts about the validity' of the result (p. 14). Austin had every opportunity to follow the course of that election and found no cause to question its validity.

19.   This is also the view reached quite independently by Conor Cruise O'Brien, *To Katanga and Back* (London, 1962), see esp. pp. 4, 261, 268.

20.   Kwame Nkrumah, *Challenge of the Congo* (London, 1967), p. 130. Note the view of Scott Thompson, *Ghana's Foreign Policy*, p. 157: 'Lumumba's death . . . was a watershed in Ghana's foreign policy and in Nkrumah's thinking.'

21.   For a full account of this episode, see Macmillan, *Pointing the Way*, pp. 460−72. Khrushchev's view of Nkrumah's place in East−West relations is pertinent:

> A most interesting, intelligent and highly educated man, but he didn't have a sufficiently clear perception on political and social issues. For one thing he had been brought up on English culture. . . . Even after his country gained its independence all the officers in the Ghanaian army were still Englishmen. What kind of independence is that? . . . I'd say that given more favourable conditions he might have publicly declared a Socialist course for Ghana. But he never made such a declaration. Leaders like Kwame Nkrumah and Modibo Keita [President of Mali, deposed 1968] will rise again and choose the correct path to the future, the path of scientific socialism.

(Khrushchev Remembers: The last phase, pp. 334−7).

22.   Bretton, *Rise and Fall*, p. 216, quotes the *Sunday Telegraph*, 30 January 1966, as

suggesting he embarked on the journey to avoid presenting the 1966 budget: a singularly unconvincing explanation.

23. Nkrumah published his own version of the coup in *Dark Days in Ghana* (1968), see esp. p. 49.
24. Oliver and Atmore, *Africa Since 1800*, p. 289.
25. Shridath S. Ramphal, *Nkrumah and the Eighties* (London, 1981), pp. 3, 7, 16.

9   White Over Black: Kenyatta's Kenya

1. The term 'White Man's Country' was invoked as a kind of 'open sesame' for the European penetration of the more temperate areas of Africa. It was first used in relation to Kenya by (Sir) Charles Eliot, Commissioner for East Africa, in 1902.
2. In his admirable biography, *Kenyatta* (London, 1972), Jeremy Murray-Brown points out that the Kikuyu normally underwent circumcision at the age of 16 or 17 and surmises that he might have been born about 1897. However, announcing his death, Kenya State Radio said he was born 'about 1889'. Kenyatta always gave his date of birth as 1893 (e.g. at his trial). The delay in his undergoing the ritual can be explained by the lack of a father and his precipitate departure from his home. It is always dangerous for any Westerner to make guesses about the age of an African or Asian based upon a conception of ageing derived from an entirely different set of social pressures.
3. For this chapter, materials collected for two of Hugh Tinker's previous works, *Separate and Unequal* (London, 1976) and *The Ordeal of Love: C.F. Andrews and India* (Delhi, 1979) are relevant. Most of these materials were never introduced into those works. The main sources pertaining to this study are International Missionary Council (the Oldham papers), Lambeth Palace Archive (Randall Davidson papers), India Office Records (Private Office Papers of the Secretaries of State – Kenya, and private correspondence of Lord Irwin), Public Record Office (Colonial Office, Kenya series), Rhodes House, Oxford (Anti-Slavery Society and Creech Jones papers), Colonial Office Library, now FCO Library (pamphlets, sessional papers), Chatham House (press cuttings on East Africa), Cambridge University Library (Smuts papers on microfilm). As elsewhere, source references will be kept to the minimum.
4. Carl G. Rosberg and John Nottingham, *The Myth of 'Mau Mau': Nationalism in Kenya* (New York, 1966), p. 88.
5. Murray-Brown, *Kenyatta*, pp. 122, 125.
6. *House of Commons Debates*, vol. 314 (9 July 1936). Lord Hailey in his monumental *African Survey* (London, 1938, rev. edn, 1957), p. 750, estimates that by 1933, 10 345 square miles had been alienated to the Whites: 11.8 per cent was under cultivation, 40.7 per cent was used for stock, 20 per cent was occupied by African squatters and 27.5 per cent was unused. In 1938, 5 053 448 acres were under White occupation but a mere 546 602 acres (11 per cent) were being farmed by the Whites.
7. Kenyatta's biographers do not mention this visit. The evidence comes from a group photograph in Harry Thuku's *Autobiography* (Nairobi, 1970), Plate XVIII, where Thuku and Kenyatta are seated on either side of Bunche.
8. Kenyatta later acquired a fourth wife: a sign of high status according to traditional African ideas, but not according to Western Christian standards: and he was still,

nominally, a Christian. When asked whether he believed in polygamy he replied, 'I do not call it that'. Three of his wives outlived him.

9. For a detailed discussion, see Donald L. Barnett and Karari Njama, *Mau Mau From Within*, (Nairobi, 1966; paperback edn 1970), esp. pp. 53–5. An alternative meaning is given as *Uma Uma* (Out, Out). In his introduction to Robert Buijtenhuijs, *Mau Mau After Twenty Years: The myth and the survivors* (The Hague, 1973), Ali Mazrui suggests the cry was really *Mao Mao* (after all, they had a 'General China' as a leader). This seems far-fetched.

10. For a detailed account, see Montagu Slater, *The Trial of Jomo Kenyatta* (London, 1955). W.P. Kirkman observes (*Unscrambling an Empire* (London, 1966), p. 55): 'His trial in an English setting would almost certainly not have produced a conviction.' The magistrate, Judge Thacker, received a secret payment of £20 000 for the trial on the personal instruction of the Governor. See Charles Douglas-Home, *Evelyn Baring: The last pro-consul* (London, 1978), p. 247.

11. Tom Mboya, *Freedom and After* (London, 1963), p. 29.

12. D.J. Morgan, *The Official History of Colonial Development*, vol. 5, *Guidance Towards Self-Government in British Colonies, 1941–1971* (London, 1980), pp. 96, 99. This does not distinguish between the relative deficits of the three territories: that of Kenya was responsible for at least £35 million per annum.

13. *Documents Relating to the Death of Eleven Mau Mau Detainees*, Cmd 778 (1959). Macmillan seems to have been under the impression that those responsible would be punished. Writing to Lennox-Boyd (23 June 1959), he said: 'When the present disciplinary trials are over [there were no trials] Governor can reply and set out the organisational changes he proposes. . . . The most notorious figures can pass on or be transferred to other jobs or colonies', *Riding the Storm, 1956–1959* (London, 1971) p. 735. Apart from the two guilty prison officers, the chain of command was not touched.

14. *Historical Survey of the Origins and Growth of Mau Mau*, Cmd 1030 (1960).

15. This is convincingly argued by David Goldsworthy, *Colonial Issues in British Politics, 1945–1961* (London, 1971), p. 370, where he states that the question of Kenyatta's release was considered in Cabinet in February 1961.

16. *Report of the Kenya Constitutional Conference*, Cmd 1700 (April 1962). The comment on Maudling's compromise is by W.P. Kirkman, *Unscrambling an Empire* (London, 1966), p. 69. Chapters 4 and 5 of this book provide an excellent account of Kenya, 1960–3.

17. Malcolm MacDonald, *Titans and Others* (London, 1972), pp. 245–53. MacDonald places much stress on Kenyatta's temperate habits at this time though in his last two years of banishment he had drunk 'in gross excess' (p. 260).

18. By July 1969, 41 per cent of Asians and 10 per cent of Europeans left in the country had become citizens. By then, the White population had fallen from 55 759 to 40 593: still much higher than the post-war total.

19. *The Times*, 23 August 1978. A massive three-column, page-long obituary was printed (from which certain details have been abstracted here).

Guide to Further Reading

EMPIRES

In the Palmy Days

Henri Brunschwig, *French Colonialism 1871–1914: Myths and realities* (Pall Mall, London, 1966).

Henri Deschamps, *Les Méthodes et Doctrines Coloniales de la France du XVI siècle à nos jours* (Collection Armand Colin, Paris, 1953).

D.K. Fieldhouse, *The Colonial Empires; A comparative survey from the 18th Century* (Weidenfeld & Nicolson, London, 1966).

Jean Ganiage, *L'expansion coloniale de la France sous la troisième république* (Payot, Paris, 1968).

Prosser Gifford and William Roger Louis (eds), *France and Britain in Africa; Imperial rivalry and colonial rule* (Yale University Press, New Haven, Connecticut, 1971).

A.D.A. Kat Angelino, *Colonial Policy* (Nijhoff, The Hague, 1931), vol. I *General Principles*; vol. II, *The Dutch East Indies*.

V.G. Kiernan, *The Lords of Human Kind* (Weidenfeld & Nicolson, London, 1969).

V.I. Lenin, *Imperialism; The highest stage of capitalism*, 1917, (Progress, Moscow, 1966) (13th rev. edn).

James Morris, *Pax Britannica* (Faber, London, 1968); *Farewell the Trumpets* (Faber, London, 1978).

K.M. Pannikkar, *Asia and Western Dominance* (Allen & Unwin, London, 1953).

Herbert J. Priestley, *France Overseas: A study of modern imperialism* (Appleton Century, New York, 1938).

Stephen H. Roberts, *The History of French Colonial Policy, 1870–1925* (Nelson, Edinburgh, 1929; re-issued Frank Cass, 1963).

Ronald Robinson and John Gallagher, *Africa and the Victorians* (Macmillan, London, 1963).

In Decline

Stewart C. Easton, *The Rise and Fall of Western Colonization: A historical survey from the early nineteenth century to the present* (Praeger, New York, 1964).

Rupert Emerson, *From Empire to Nation: The rise to self-assertion of Asian and African peoples* (Harvard University Press, Cambridge, Mass., 1960).

J.S. Furnivall, *Colonial Policy and Practice: A comparative study of Burma and Netherlands India* (Cambridge University Press, 1948).

John Gallagher, *The Decline, Revival and Fall of the British Empire* (Cambridge University Press, 1982).

David Goldsworthy, *Colonial Issues in British Politics 1945–1961: From 'Colonial Development' to 'Wind of Change'* (Clarendon Press, Oxford, 1971).

R.F. Holland, *European Decolonisation, 1918–1981: An introductory survey* (Macmillan, London, 1985).

W.P. Kirkman, *Unscrambling an Empire: A critique of British colonial policy 1956–1966* (Chatto & Windus, London, 1966).

P.N.S. Mansergh, *The Commonwealth Experience* (Weidenfeld & Nicolson, London, 1969).

R.J. Moore, *Escape from Empire: The Attlee Government and the Indian Problem* (Clarendon Press, Oxford, 1983).

D.J. Morgan, *The Official History of Colonial Development*, vol. 5, *Guidance Towards Self-Government in British Colonies, 1941–1971* (Macmillan, London, 1980).

JINNAH AND THE EMERGENCE OF PAKISTAN

The Rise of Muslim Political Feeling

Azim Husain, *Fazl-i-Husain: A Political biography* (Longmans, Bombay, 1946). An account of provincial politics by the son of the Punjabi leader. Reveals the shifting ground on which Jinnah had to operate.

Wilfred Cantwell Smith, *Modern Islam in India* (Gollancz, London, 1946). Banned in India, this is a forceful book: unfortunately his conclusions turned out all wrong.

Choudhry Khaliquzzaman, *Pathway to Pakistan* (Longmans, Lahore, 1961). Egocentric, sometimes unreliable; but a good example of a Muslim leader who, initially close to the Congress and Nehru, ended up emigrating to Pakistan.

Peter Hardy, *The Muslims of British India* (Cambridge University Press, 1973). A scholarly historical survey from earlier times.

Jinnah

Hector Bolitho, *Jinnah: Creator of Pakistan* (Murray, London, 1954). Written by a professional biographer, not an Asian specialist. Nonetheless he did a good job and preserved information which might have disappeared.

Z.H. Zaidi (ed.), *M.A. Jinnah–Ispahani Correspondence, 1936–1948* (Forward Publications Trust, Karachi, 1976). Probably the most illuminating of these studies because it demonstrates how little Jinnah revealed himself, even to one he trusted completely.

Stanley Wolpert, *Jinnah of Pakistan* (Oxford University Press, New York, 1984). The 'definitive study', based on exhaustive research. 'Life and Times' treatment bringing in the British, Congress, everybody. But he does not penetrate into the inner man.

Ayesha Jalal, *Jinnah: The sole spokesman* (Cambridge University Press, 1985). A brilliant analysis, showing how weak Jinnah's political position was. Unfortunately she pushes the argument to extremes, ending up claiming that Pakistan was forced on a reluctant Jinnah by Nehru and the Congress!

Nicholas Mansergh (ed. in chief), *The Transfer of Power, 1942–7* (HMSO, London). For Jinnah, vols VI (1976), VII (1977), VIII (1979), IX (1980), X (1981), XI (1982), XII (1983) are all relevant. This series provides the principal source of most of Jalal and much of Wolpert. Overwhelming to the average reader, who should sample volumes VII and X which give a blow-by-blow picture of the most important negotiations.

The Pakistan Movement

It is somewhat artificial to make this a separate entry, but the four books listed below focus more widely than just on Jinnah.

Richard Symons, *The Making of Pakistan* (Faber, London, 1950). A pioneer interpretation by one who was present during the birth-pangs of the new nation.

Khalid Bin Sayeed, *Pakistan: The formative phase* (Pakistan Publishing House, Karachi, 1960). Perhaps the most thorough and penetrating study.

Chaudhri Muhammad Ali, *The Emergence of Pakistan* (Columbia University Press, New York, 1967). By the most senior Muslim civil servant, whose advice was of key importance to the Muslim politicians (though not to Jinnah).

A.B. Rajput, *The Muslim League, Yesterday and Today*, Muhammad Ashraf, Lahore, 1948). Not in the same class as those above: but useful.

(In addition, the books in the next section listed as 'The Political Scene' are relevant.)

NEHRU AND INDIA

Biographical

Jawaharlal Nehru, *An autobiography* (Bodley Head, London, 1936). Still the most illuminating portrait; revealing in its mixture of frankness, detachment, and emotionalism. A great book.

Jawaharlal Nehru, *The Discovery of India* (Signet Press, Calcutta, 1946; paperback edn, 1981). A curious mixture of history, politics, and autobiography. Written when Nehru was unsure about the future.

Jawaharlal Nehru (ed.), *A Bunch of Old Letters; Written mostly to Jawaharlal Nehru and some written by him* (Asia Publishing House, Bombay, 1958). The 366 letters included date from 1917 to 1948. Though a few are included for effect (G.B. Shaw, Harold Laski), the great majority clearly reflect Nehru's personal feelings: many from Gandhi, many from Edward Thompson, the writer, four from Cripps (the last in 1942) and none from Attlee.

Michael Brecher, *Nehru: A political biography* (Oxford University Press, London, 1959). The first serious study, written while Nehru was still at the peak of his achievement. The author acquired a close familiarity with his subject.

B.N. Pandey, *Nehru* (Macmillan, London, 1976). Given access to the extensive collection of material in the possession of Mrs Pandit he produced a fine work. An understandable element of hero-worship.

Sarvepalli Gopal, *Jawaharlal Nehru: A biography* (Jonathan Cape, London), vol. I, *1889–1947* (1975), vol. II, *1947–1956* (1979), vol. III, *1956–1964* (1984). The authorised work, backed up by a research team, and based on full access to Nehru's own collected papers. Gopal was criticised for weighting his study so heavily to the years of the premiership. However, the second volume is the most successful, when Nehru was in his prime; the last, covering the sad decline, is candid although (necessarily) not altogether objective. Nehru's humanity and personal dignity come through well.

Vijaya Lakshmi Pandit, *The Scope of Happiness: A personal memoir* (Weidenfeld & Nicolson, London, 1979). The autobiography of a lady distinguished in her own right, but containing intimate glimpses of her brother from youth to age.

B.R. Nanda, *The Nehrus: Motilal and Jawaharlal* (Allen & Unwin, London, 1962). By the curator of the Nehru Memorial Museum and Library. Readable, informative, valuable, occasionally subjective.

Nicholas Mansergh, *The Transfer of Power, 1942–7*, is just as relevant to Nehru as to Jinnah. Additionally, vol. I (1970) is important for Nehru.

The Political Scene

B.B. Misra, *The Indian Political Parties: An historical analysis of political behaviour up to 1947* (Oxford University Press, Delhi, 1976). The major part of this long book is devoted to the period 1920–47. The author is second to none in the comprehensive thoroughness of his research, but his treatment will be considered old-fashioned by many. Although he came to manhood during those years he achieves a detachment not found in any other contemporary Indian writer.

R. Sunthralingam, *Indian Nationalism: An historical analysis* (Vikas, Delhi, 1983). Also thorough, detached and more concise.

V.P. Menon, *The Transfer of Power in India* (Longmans, London/Calcutta, 1957). This study by the former constitutional adviser has fixed an interpretation on the British–Congress–League dialogue (often a diatribe) which no subsequent work can affect, it seems. Fortunately, it is for the most part accurate.

Alan Campbell-Johnson, *Mission With Mountbatten* (Robert Hale, London, 1951; paperback, 1985). Under a deceptively chatty style the author provides shrewdly percipient portraits of Mountbatten, Gandhi, Nehru and Jinnah. Remaining as constitutional Governor-General until June 1948, Mountbatten's press officer stayed with him.

Hugh Tinker, *Experiment With Freedom: India and Pakistan, 1947* (Oxford University Press, London, 1967).

Nehru's India

So many books on the later Nehru years: how to select a handful?

W.H. Morris-Jones, *Parliament in India* (Longmans, London, 1957). The institution in its palmy days.

Selig S. Harrison, *India: The most dangerous decades* (Princeton University Press, New Jersey, 1960). A non-sensational view of the pressures of language and regionalism which many have warned herald the break-up of Nehru's India.

A.H. Hanson, *The Process of Planning: A study of India's Five Year Plans, 1950–1964* (Oxford University Press, London, 1966). A detailed survey of the centralised mechanism over which Nehru presided personally.

Francine R. Frankel, *India's Political Economy, 1947–1977* (Princeton University Press, New Jersey, 1978). On its appearance I described this as 'massive, tightly argued, carefully researched . . . a comprehensive analysis'.

BURMA: AUNG SAN AND NU

Before the Japanese Invasion

Little is to be found about the Thakins; the following are relevant:

John F. Cady, *A History of Modern Burma* (Cornell University Press, Ithaca, New York, 1958). About half of this substantial book is devoted to the period 1920–40.

Maung Maung, *Burma's Constitution* (Nijhoff, The Hague, 1959). Also contains chapters on the inter-war years.

Marjorie Proctor, *The World My Country: The story of Daw Nyein Tha of Burma* (Grosvenor Books, London, 1976). A slight book from an MRA perspective. Impinges on the early life of the wife of Aung San.

Wartime

Ba Maw, *Breakthrough in Burma: Memoirs of a revolution, 1939–1946* (Yale University Press, New Haven, Connecticut, 1968). A bombastic work by the Japanese-appointed Head of State; often unreliable. Full of flavour.

Thakin Nu, *Burma Under the Japanese: Pictures and portraits* (Macmillan, London, 1954). Written soon after the events described; typical of Nu's relaxed approach to all critical situations.

Maung Maung (ed.), *Aung San of Burma* (Nijhoff, The Hague, 1962). An anthology of *pièces d'occasion*; the nearest approximation to a biography or memoir.

Louis Allen, *Burma; The longest war* (Dent, London, 1985). The main theme is the military conflict but there are useful passages on the BNA and 'the Resistance'.

Hugh Tinker (ed.), *Burma: The Struggle for Independence*, vol. I, *From Military Occupation to Civil Government, January 1944 to August 1946* (HMSO, London, 1983).
Not recommended for the casual reader: those prepared to dig should find some nuggets.

Admiral Mountbatten, *Report to the Combined Chiefs of Staff by the Supreme Allied Commander South-East Asia, 1943–45* (HMSO, London, 1951). Contains a section on his dealings with Aung San and his comrades.

The Struggle for Independence

Maung Maung Pye, *Burma in the Crucible* (Khittaya, Rangoon, n.d. (1951?). Among the first accounts; by a newspaper editor.

Hugh Tinker, *The Union of Burma: A study of the first years of independence* (Oxford University Press, London, 1957; (4th edn, 1967). While the main narrative is concerned with the decade 1948–57, there is an account of events leading up to independence, recorded a few years afterwards.

Hugh Tinker, (ed.), *Burma: The Struggle for Independence*, vol. II, *From General Strike to Independence, August 1946 to January 1948* (HMSO, 1984). Again, an exhaustive study (it exhausted its editor anyway).

F.S.V. Donnison, *Burma* (Ernest Benn, London, 1980). A general survey, deriving its interest from the author being Chief Secretary, February–November 1946.

U Nu, *U Nu-Saturday's Son* (Yale University Press, New Haven, Connecticut, 1975). His life story written in his serene later years. Should be read, even if none of those listed above are read.

SUKARNO AND INDONESIA

Before the Dutch Withdrawal

Bernhard Dahm, *Sukarno and the Struggle for Indonesian Independence* (English-language edition revised from original German version (1966) Cornell University Press, Ithaca, New York, 1969). The most thorough and illuminating work on the period to August 1945, giving many insights into Sukarno's early life.

The Revolutionary Period

George M. Kahin, *Nationalism and Revolution in Indonesia* (Cornell University Press, Ithaca, New York, 1952). The pioneer study; the author arrived in Indonesia soon after the

Second World War and observed much for himself: though somewhat through the spectacles of an American patriot of 1776, outraged by the enormities of George III.

Soetan Sjahrir, *Out of Exile* (John Day, New York, 1949). Letters written while Sjahrir was exiled by the Dutch colonial authorities.

Benedict R.O. Anderson, *Java in a Time of Revolution: Occupation and resistance, 1944–1946* (Cornell University Press, Ithaca, New York, 1972). A detailed study of nationalist struggle under the Japanese and thereafter leading to the Dutch 'police action'. Treatment is revisionist: cf. Reid (below), 'Anderson's book has emphatically lost the optimism of Kahin's' yet clearly from the same stable. Contains useful 'Who's Who' of Indonesian personalities.

Anthony Reid, *The Indonesian National Revolution, 1945–1950* (Longmans, Victoria, Australia, 1974). An impressive work because so much is concentrated into a relatively brief compass.

Arnold Brackman, *Indonesian Communism: A history* (Praeger, New York, 1963). The author reported from South-East Asia, 1945–55, and interviewed many participants. The work also covers the period to 1961, and appears increasingly Cold War in tone.

S. Takdir Alisjahbana, *Indonesia: Social and cultural revolution* (Oxford University Press, Kuala Lumpur, 1966). Not a straightforward history, but unique insights into Sukarno from personal observation from 1927 onward. Also important for later Sukarno years, as the author became increasingly disillusioned.

Lord Mountbatten, *Report to the Combined Chiefs of Staff by the Supreme Allied Commander, South-East Asia, Post Surrender Tasks* (HMSO, London, 1969). Publication was long delayed in deference to Dutch (and French) susceptibilities: the report was compiled in the first six months of 1947. Although of limited importance on Sukarno and revolt against Dutch, establishes what the British thought they were doing there. Also gives earliest evidence on certain key dates, e.g. date of transfer of Indonesia/French Indo–China to SEAC given as 15 August 1945; others cite 13 and 14 August.

Louis Allen *The End of the War in Asia* (Hart-Davis, London, 1976). Importance lies in use of Japanese sources, many being participants in events, 1942–6.

Sukarno's Indonesia

Bernard Dahm, *History of Indonesia in the Twentieth Century* (Pall Mall, London, 1971). Again, a translation from German. Masterly survey of period 1900–70. Though not in the same detail, it is in the same class as his previous work.

Herbert Feith, *The Decline of Constitutional Democracy in Indonesia* (Cornell University Press, Ithaca, New York, 1962). A very detailed study of the years December 1949–March 1957. Though disillusionment was inevitable, the author clings to the Kahin ideal. Essential reading for the dedicated student.

Donald Hindley, *The Communist Party of Indonesia, 1951–1963* (California University Press, Berkeley, 1966). Another highly concentrated work casting light on relations between Sukarno and PKI.

J.D. Legge, *Sukarno: A political biography* (Allan Lane, London, 1972). A competent pulling together of most of the works cited above.

Arnold Brackman, *Indonesia: The Gestapu Affair* (American–Asian Educational Exchange, New York, 1969), gives a Right-wing interpretation of the fall of Sukarno.

Brian May, *The Indonesian Tragedy*, Routledge, London, 1978. More concerned with Suharto than Sukarno and discusses the 'development myth'.

HO CHI MINH AND VIETNAM

Early Days

Jean Lacouture, *Ho Chi Minh* (Editions de Seuil, Paris, 1967). Perhaps overstates the 'Uncle Ho' aspect, but provides detailed biography.

Hoang Van Chi, *From Colonialism to Communism: A case history of North Vietnam* (Pall Mall, London, 1964). As a disillusioned fellow traveller Hoang paints a grim picture of the years after 1954 but his brief account of Ho's early life gives assurance of authenticity.

J. Davidson, *Indo-China: Signposts in the storm* (Longman, Malaysia, 1979). His background chapters include material on Nguyen/Ho not found elsewhere. As a work which covers the conflict to its end this probably provides the best overall survey although the mandarin manner of the professional diplomat is not absent.

Bernard B. Fall, *The Two Viet-Nams: A political and military analysis* (Praeger, New York, 1963). Includes a chapter (6) 'The Rise of Ho Chi Minh'. The most moving and persuasive account of the conflict, covering the French period and the initial years of American involvement.

War After War

Ellen J. Hammer, *The Struggle for Indochina, 1940–1955: Viet Nam and the French experience* (Stanford University Press, California, 1954; 2nd edn, 1966). Reflects a time before American innocence turned to guilt.

Dennis J. Duncanson, *Government and Revolution in Vietnam*, (Oxford University Press, London, 1968). By a British scholar-official disillusioned by all the failures of Vietnam.

John T. McAlister, *Viet Nam: The origins of revolution* (Knopf, New York, 1969). A thoughtful analysis of both sides in the Franco–Vietnamese war.

Vo Nguyen Giap, *People's War, People's Army* (Hanoi, 1961; issued in facsimile, Praeger, New York, 1962, with a profile of Giap by Fall).

Truong Chinh, *The August Revolution* and *The Resistance Will Win* (Hanoi, 1962, 1960; issued in facsimile Praeger, New York, 1963, as *Primer for Revolt* with an introduction by Fall).

Ralph Smith, *Viet-Nam and the West* (Heinemann, London, 1968). An interpretation of Vietnamese nationalism.

Michael Charlton and Anthony Moncrieff, *Many Reasons Why: The American involvement in Vietnam* (Scolar Press, London, 1978). Because communicated through interviews, somewhat scrappy; but gives a sense of immediacy.

Documents relating to British involvement in the Indo-China Conflict, 1945–1965, Cmd. 28340 (HMSO, London, 1965). Discreet, but includes basic documents.

New York Times, *The Pentagon Papers* (New York, 1971). Not really useful for this study, but to be read as a contrast to the bland British selection of documents.

R.B. Smith (Ralph Smith), *An International History of the Vietnam War*: vol. I, *Revolution Versus Containment, 1955–61* (Macmillan, London, 1983); vol. II, *The Struggle for South-East Asia, 1961–65* (Macmillan, London, 1985). This massive work (to be completed: vol. III, *Limited War, 1965–70*, and vol. IV, *The Denouement, 1970–76*) treats all the actors as small figures in a gigantic scene, but *inter alia* includes important material on Ho Chi Minh.

NKRUMAH AND GHANA

Before Independence

David E. Apter, *The Gold Coast in Transition* (Princeton University Press, New Jersey, 1955). Pioneer study.

F.M. Bourret, *Ghana: the road to independence, 1919–1957*, Oxford University Press, London, 1960.

J.D. Fage, *Ghana: A historical interpretation*, 1959 (University of Wisconsin Press, 1966). A brief, cogent introduction.

Kwame Nkrumah, *Ghana: The autobiography of Kwame Nkrumah* (Nelson, Edinburgh, 1957). A straightforward, frank, personal narrative, very different from Nehru's introspective autobiography. Either this is what it seems – a glimpse into an appealing personality – or else it is deliberately designed to disguise the author's motivation. The second hypothesis is not accepted here.

Basil Davidson, *Black Star: A view of the life and times of Kwame Nkrumah* (Allan Lane, London, 1973). An overview tracing the story from the return in 1947 to Nkrumah's death. Sympathetic, but not uncritical.

Dennis Austin, *Politics in Ghana, 1946–1960* (Oxford University Press, London, 1964). A balanced and detailed study which actually covers the years till 1963. Perhaps overemphasises the importance of elections in the academic fashion of that time, but provides the indispensable information on the period.

The International Scene

Kwame Nkrumah, *Africa Must Unite* (Heinemann, London, 1963). Visionary.

W. Scott Thompson, *Ghana's Foreign Policy, 1957–1966: Diplomacy, ideology, and the new state* (Princeton University Press, New Jersey, 1969). The equivalent of Austin in external affairs; a detailed, well researched, though basically unsympathetic account.

Colin Legum, *Pan-Africanism* (Pall Mall, London, 1962). This book ranges far beyond Nkrumah's impact on pan-Africanism. It includes numerous quotations from his speeches/writings.

David Kimche, *The Afro-Asian Movement: Ideology and foreign policy of the Third World* (Israel Universities Press, Jerusalem, 1973). Like Legum he paints a wide canvas, but in so doing gives insights on Nkrumah.

Kwame Nkrumah, *Challenge of the Congo* (Nelson, London, 1967). A detailed, highly charged view of the Congo up to 1965.

H.T. Alexander, *African Tightrope: My two years as Nkrumah's Chief of Staff* (Pall Mall, London, 1965). The personal experience of a conventional soldier in unexpected circumstances.

The Last Years

Geoffrey Bing, *Reap the Whirlwind: An account of Kwame Nkrumah's Ghana from 1950 to 1966* (Macgibbon & Kee, London, 1968). Verbose, including many irrelevancies, but invaluable as a first-hand view of Nkrumah's task and its frustrations.

Henry L. Bretton, *The Rise and Fall of Kwame Nkrumah: A study of personal rule in Africa* (Pall Mall, London, 1967). An account by an American professor who was there: vitiated by his antipathy to his subject.

Kwame Nkrumah, *Dark Days in Ghana* (published in Conakry?, 1968). A sombre account by the deposed president, justifying his actions. Contains a variety of first-hand information.

Shridath S. Ramphal, *Nkrumah and the Eighties; Kwame Nkrumah Memorial Lectures 1980* (Third World Foundation Monograph 9, London, 1981). Not a book, the text of lectures, providing a significant assessment of the role of a Commonwealth statesman.

KENYATTA AND KENYA

Elspeth Huxley, *White Man's Country: Lord Delamere and the Making of Kenya*, 2 vols (Macmillan, London, 1930). Scarcely mentions the Africans.

Jomo Kenyatta, *Facing Mount Kenya* (Secker & Warburg, London, 1938, reprinted 1953). Contains elements of autobiography. Described in *The Times* obituary as, 'Probably the most impressive book that any British African leader [sic] has written in sociology or politics'.

Roland Oliver, *The Missionary Factor in East Africa* (Longmans, London, 1952).

L.S.B. Leakey, *Mau Mau and the Kikuyu* (Methuen, London, 1952). In the copy I read someone had inscribed 'Racist Imperialist'. Unjust, but understandable.

Documents Relating to the Death of Eleven Mau Mau Detainees, Cmd 778 (1959). Now that most university libraries and some big city libraries have British Sessional Papers on microfiche, readers should be able to locate this highly disturbing account of one of the worst episodes in any British colony.

George Delf, *Jomo Kenyatta: Towards truth about the Light of Kenya* (Gollancz, London, 1961). The author was denied access to Kenyatta, still exiled, but he produced a preliminary biography of value.

George Bennett and Carl G. Rosberg, *The Kenyatta Election: Kenya, 1960–1961* (Oxford University Press, London, 1961). Election studies were then in vogue, but this one does illuminate the moment of change in Kenya.

George Bennett, *Kenya: a political history, the colonial period* (Oxford University Press, London, 1963). Concise, thoroughly researched.

Josiah M. Kariuki, *'Mau Mau' Detainee: The account by a Kenya African of his experiences in detention camps, 1953–1960* (Oxford University Press, Nairobi, 1963). Restrained and powerful indictment of the camps.

Tom Mboya, *Freedom and After* (André Deutsch, London, 1963). The autobiography of an African leader, without rancour, despite White humiliation.

Carl G. Rosberg and John Nottingham, *The Myth of 'Mau Mau': Nationalism in Kenya* (Praeger, New York, 1966). Sets out to write an African social and political history within the colonial framework. Impressively documented.

Jomo Kenyatta, *Suffering Without Bitterness: The founding of the Kenya nation* (East Africa, Nairobi, 1968). Based on Kenyatta's own writings.

Harry Thuku, *An Autobiography* (Oxford University Press, Nairobi, 1970). Unpretentious memories of the pioneer nationalist who stood up as a 'loyalist' during Mau Mau.

Jeremy Murray-Brown, *Kenyatta* (Allen & Unwin, London, 1972). A remarkable example of biography almost as a detective inquiry. Extensively utilised in this study.

Robert Buijtenhuijs *Mau Mau After Twenty Years: The myth and the survivors* (Mouton, The Hague, 1973). A detached reassessment, showing how Kenyatta skilfully merged the contributions of the jungle fighters, the new politicians like Mboya, and the 'loyalists' into a new Kenya blend.

Valerie Cuthbert, *Jomo Kenyatta: The burning spear* (Longmans, London, 1982). A capable biography in the light of the years after independence.

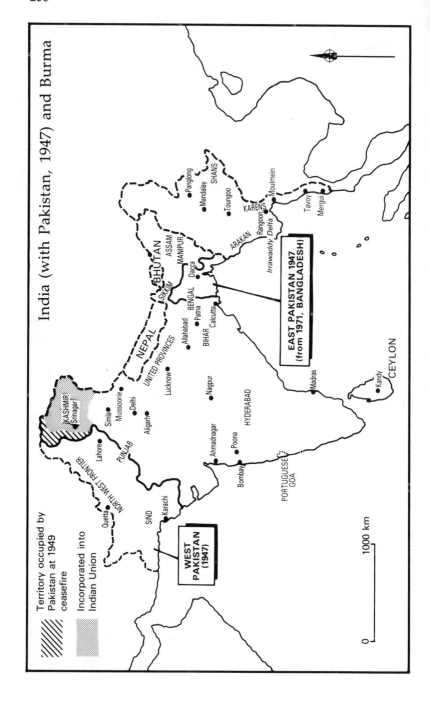

India (with Pakistan, 1947) and Burma

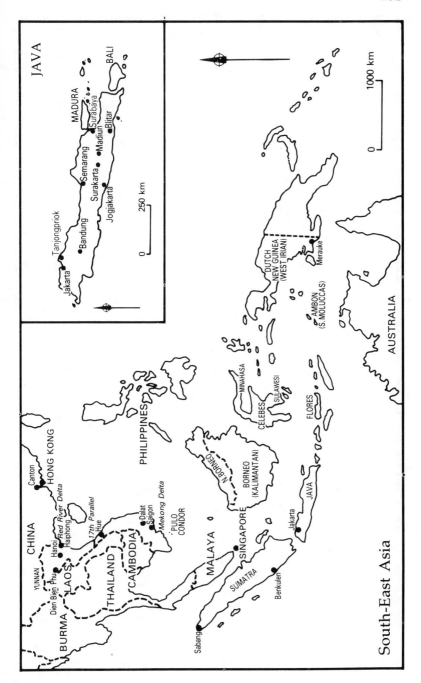

South-East Asia

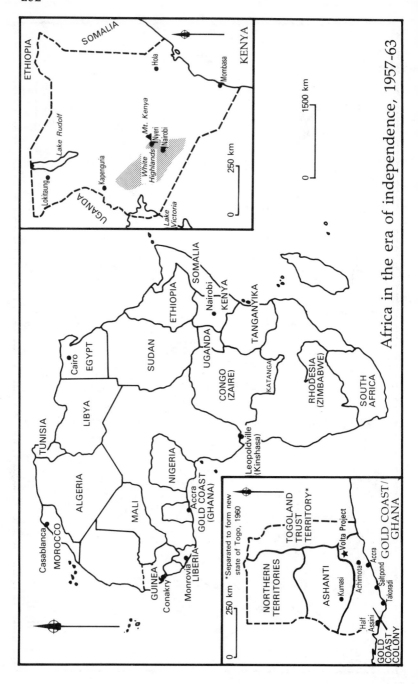

Africa in the era of independence, 1957-63

Index

Africans and Asians commonly known by the last name (e.g. Jinnah, Kenyatta, Nehru, Nkrumah) are listed under the last name. Others known by their full names (e.g. Aung San, Ho Chi Minh) are listed under the first name, ignoring any honorific prefix: thus Abdul Rahman, Tungku.

Abdul Rahman, Tungku, 25
Abrahams, Peter, 185, 224
Abul Kalam Azad, Maulana, 43, 45, 52, 56, 57, 62, 82, 83, 87, 243 ch.4, n25
Accra, 186, 188, 190, 191–2, 200, 205;
Accra Evening News, 189
Acheampong, Colonel, 206–7
Acheson, Dean, 146
Achimota college, 182–3, 190
Acland, Sir Richard, 9
Aden, xi, 4
Afghanistan, 17, 45, 72, 93
Afori Atta, William, 187
Africa, 4, 8–9, 181, 185, 203, 205
Afrikaners, 208–9
Aga Khan, 41, 47, 48, 84
Aggrey, Dr Kwegyir, 183
Ahmadnagar, 84
Ako Adjei, 187, 192, 204
Akufo Addo, 187, 190
Alexander, A.V., 55–6, 61
Alexander, General H.T., 198, 199, 200, 202
Algeria, 10, 11, 171, 179, 197, 201
Aligarh, 41, 53, 132
Allahabad, 70–1, 73, 81, 82
Ambedkar, Dr B.R., 51, 54
Ambon (Amboina), 136, 149–50
Amery, L.S., 217
American Colonies, 2, 27–8
Amir Sjarifuddin, 142–3, 146
Amritsar, 6, 72
Anawratha, King, 125
Andrews, C.F., x, 211, 214, 216–17, 219, 222
Ankrah, Lieut.General J.A., 204, 206
Annam, 11, 12, 160, 166
Anti-Fascist Organisation, 104; later Anti-Fascist People's Freedom League (AFPFL), 105, 107–15, 117–19, 121, 123
Anti-Slavery Society, 220
Appiah, Joe, 185, 194
Arakan, 103, 123

Arap Moi, Daniel, 237
Arden-Clarke, Sir Charles, 190, 192, 196
Arku Korsah, Sir, 204
Arthur, Dr John, 211, 213, 220, 222
Ashanti, 182, 185, 194–5, 196, 198
Asoka, Emperor, 1
Assam, 50
Atlantic Charter, 19, 133
Atomic Bomb, 106, 137, 166, 207
Attlee, Clement, 58, 61, 89, 97, 109–10, 116, 118–19, 121
Aung San, Bogyoke, 26, 34, 37–8, 79, early days, 97–100, ally of Japan, 100–4; opposes British plans, 104–13, enters government, 113–16; negotiates independence agreement, 116–17; shapes political future, 117–20; assassinated, 120; legacy, 125, 126, 158, 165, 181, 239
Aurangzeb Khan, 53
Austin, Dennis, xv, 247 ch.8, n8, 248 n18
Australia, xiv, 3, 4, 139, 145, 147, 179
Austria, 1, 29, 31–5
Auchinleck, Sir Claude, 108
Ayub Khan, Field Marshal, 123
Azikwe, Nnamdi, 183, 263

Baldev Singh, 60, 62
Bali, 127
Ba Maw, Dr, 79, 98–9, 101–4
Banaras, 52
Bandung, 128, 141, 149; Conference, 151, 177, 185
Banerjee, S.N., 43
Bangladesh, 22
Bangkok, 101, 167
Bao Dai, Emperor, 25, 166–7, 170, 174
Ba Pe, 102, 112, 115, 118
Barbados, 2, 8, 27
Bardoli, 80
Baring, Sir Evelyn, 228, 231, 233, 250 n10
Barwah, Major-General, 206

Ba Sein, 113, 115, 116
Batavia, 2, 14, 136; *see also* Jakarta
Bax, Arnold, 223
Beel, Dr Louis, 144, 147, 148
Belgium, 145, 199
Ben Bella, Ahmad, xiii
Bengal, 44, 48, 49, 50−1, 53, 64−5, 89, 90
Benkulen, 133
Benn, Wedgwood, 220
Berkeley, Bishop George, 2
Besant, Annie, 71, 77
Bevin, Ernest, 143
Bhabba, Homi, 94
Bhatnagar, S.S., 94
Biarritz, 170, 179
Bidault, Georges, 170, 173
Bihar, 84, 86
Blitar, 136, 157
Blum, Léon, 160, 163, 171
Blundell, Michael, 229, 230, 233, 234
Bogor, 155, 157
Bolivar, Simon, 26−7
Bombay, 42−5, 51, 66, 85
Borodin, Mikhail, 161−2
Bose, *see* Sarat Chandra Bose *and* Subhas
    Chandra Bose
Bourne, Sir Frederick, 195
Brahmans, 69−70, 127
Braimah, J.A., 192
Bright, John, 4
Britain, British Empire, x, xii, 1−9, 13, 19−20,
    25−6, 93, 163, 176, 184, 223, 241 ch.1,
    n2; *see also* Commonwealth
Brockway, Fenner, 187, 219, 227−8
Bryce, James, 5
Bucharest, 206
Buddhism, 17, 36, 67, 98, 123, 125; Buddhist
    scriptures, 124−5
Budi Utomo, 15
Bunche, Dr Ralph, 200, 223
Burma, xi, xiii, xiv, 3, 7, 10, 13, 15, 18, 21, 28,
    79, 83, 93, 97−104; the postwar
    independence struggle, 104−21;
    problems in the new state, 121−5, 126,
    134, 148, 181, 185, 204
Burma Independence Army (BIA), 101−2
Burma National Army (BNA), 102−3, 105−7,
    109, 118, 122, 135
Burmah Oil Company, 99−100
Burmese Way to Socialism, 123
Burns, Sir Alan, 186
Busia, Dr K.A., 192, 194, 203, 206, 223, 234
Butler, Sir Harcourt, 70, 72
Buxton, Charles Roden, 221
Byzantium, 1

Cabinet Mission Plan (1946), 56−7, 60, 61,
    64, 86−7, 88−9, 90
Cairo, 206
Calcutta, 59, 66, 74, 100
Cambodia, 12, 13, 170
Cambridge, 70−1, 97
Campbell-Johnson, Alan, 92
Canada, 3, 4, 27, 202
Caribbean, 1, 8, 14
Carlyle, Thomas, 36−7, 38
Carter, Sir Morris, 221, 225
Casablanca group of states, 201, 205
Castro, Fidel, xii
Cavendish-Bentinck, F.W., 224, 230, 233
Cavour, Count Camillo, 28−9, 31, 32−4
Central Intelligence Agency (CIA), 155−6,
    201
Ceylon, xi−xii, 4, 8, 9, 21, 93, 167
Chaman Lall, 229
Chang Fa-kwei, Marshal, 164−5
Chiang Kai-shek, Marshal, 81, 162, 165
Chiefs, 165, 181−2, 186, 187, 189, 190, 209,
    214, 223, 228
China, 10, 17, 18, 28, 74, 80, 82, 85, 93, 94−5,
    100, 153, 159, 161−2, 164−5, 168−9,
    172
Chins (tribe), 117, 122
Chit Hlaing, 98
Chit, Thakin, 114
Chou En-lai, 17, 151
Churchill, Randolph, 4
Churchill, Winston S., 9, 19, 37, 48, 51−2,
    193, 200, 215−16
Civil disobedience, 7, 45, 72−3, 75, 81, 83−4,
    191
Cobden, Richard, 4, 32
Cochin-China, 11, 12, 162−3, 169−70, 171
Cocoa, 185, 194, 199
Cohen, Sir Andrew, 187
Colijn, Hendrikus, 131
Colombo, xi−xii
Colonial Office (Whitehall), 181, 182, 190−1,
    193, 197, 225, 226, 232
Coloured Workers' Association, 186
Commonwealth, 64, 93, 119−20, 178, 181,
    198, 199, 205, 225
Communists, Communist Party, 15, 37, 109,
    129, 152, 154, 156, 160, 163, 170,
    187−8
Communist International (Comintern), 18,
    160−1, 164
Conakry, 206
Confrontation (Konfrontasi), 153
Congo, 198−202, 203, 205, 234; French
    Congo, 10

Congress, *see* Indian National Congress
Congress of Oppressed Nationalities, 74, 162
Congress of Peoples Against Imperialism, 238
Congress Socialist Party, 77
Conservative Government and Party, 187, 193, 195, 232, 233
Constituent Assembly, of India, 38, 58, 60–1, 86; of Pakistan, 66, 88–9, 92; of Burma, 115; of Ghana, 188
Convention People's Party (CPP), 190–6
Cook, John, 212, 215
Corfield, F.D., 233
Coryndon, Sir Robert, 216
Coussey, Justice Henley, 190, 191
Crabbe, Coffie, 203–4
Creasey, Sir Gerald, 190
Cranbourne, Lord, 20
Creech Jones, Arthur, 187, 191, 223, 225, 247 ch.8, n6, n7
Crewe, Lord, 5
Cripps, Sir Stafford, 51, 55–6, 82–3, 85, 88, 91, 94, 97, 116, 163, 194
Cromwell, Oliver, 68
Cunliffe-Lister, Sir Philip, 221
Cunningham, Sir George, 53, 54, 68
Curtis, Lionel, 6, 213, 217

Dacca, 41, 68
Dakar, 12
Dalat, 137, 170
Dange, S.A., 18
Danquah, J.B., 187, 188–9, 190, 194, 198
Davidson, Basil, xv, 198, 203, 204
Davidson, Archbishop Randall, 216–17
de Gaulle, *see* Gaulle, Charles de
de Graaff, A.C.D. *see* Graaff, A.C.D. de
de Jonge, B.C. *see* Jonge, B.C. de
Delcassé, Theophile, 11
Delf, George, 212, 215
Delhi, 51, 56, 66, 68, 108, 116, 226, 229, 234
Desai, Morarji, 213–14, 237
Devonshire, Duke of, 216
Dewantoro, 134
Dewey, Lieut.Colonel Peter, 168
Dhani, Air Vice Marshal Omar, 154
Dien Bien Phu, 173, 179
Disraeli, Benjamin, 3
Djin, Andrew, 199–200
Dominions, Dominion Status, 3, 5, 6, 9, 20, 64, 65, 75, 90, 105, 119, 196; *see also* Commonwealth
Dorman-Smith, Sir Reginald, 105, 106–11, 112–13
Du Bois, W.E.B., 184–5

Dulles, John F., 173
Durban, xi
Dutch Empire, 1, 2, 4, 14–16, 18, 19, 25, 126–7
Dyarchy, 6, 7, 8

East Pakistan, 67, 68, 195
Eden, Sir Anthony, 193, 231
Egypt, 147, 198, 200–1
Elizabeth II, Queen, 202, 237
Elphinstone, Mountstuart, 4
Ethiopia, 147, 151, 197, 224
Eurasians, 16, 152
'Extremists' in colonial politics, 43, 86, 203

Fabian Colonial Bureau, 187, 223, 225
Fall, Bernard, 165
Fanon, Frantz, xiii, 197, 246 n17
Fazl Huq, 48–9, 50, 53, 66
Fazl-i-Husain, 43, 47, 48, 66
Ferry, Jules, 10
First World War, *see* World War I
Flores (Lesser Sunda Islands), 132
Fontainebleau conference (1946), 170–1
Foot, Dingle, 189
Force 136 (SOE), 103–4
France, French Empire, 1, 4, 10–14, 19, 22, 25, 159, 180, 197–8, 201
Frontier Areas (Burma), 115, 117
Furnivall, J.S., 14

Gallacher, William, 188
Gambetta, Léon, 10
Gandhi (Gandhy), Feroz, 81
Gandhi, Indira, 206
Gandhi, *Mahatma*, 6–7, 18, 23, 28, 42, 44–7, 49, 52, 58, 62, 65, 66, 71–8, 82–4, 89, 90–2, 98, 108, 130–1, 166, 190–1, 209, 211, 214
Garibaldi, Giuseppe, 28, 31–4, 128
Garvey, Marcus, 184
Gatundu, 226, 229, 236
Gaulle, Charles de, 168, 178, 179, 197
Gbedemah, K.A., 190–1, 203
Geneva, 93, 173, 176
Genoa, 31
Gerbrandy, Pieter, 141
Germany, German Empire, 4, 26, 32, 49, 77, 81, 83, 195
Ghana, xiv-xv, 22, 178, symbolism, 196, 232; *see also* Gold Coast
Ghana Congress Party (GCP), 194, 196
Ghulam Hidayatullah, 66
Giap, *see* Vo Nguyen Giap
Gibraltar, xi

Githungiri, 225, 226
Gizenga, Antoine, 200
Gladstone, William Ewart, 5, 35
Glancey, Sir Bernard, 227
Goa, 94
Gokhale, G.K., 43
Gold Coast, 151, 181, 185–96; *see also* United
　　Gold Coast Convention (UGCC)
Graaff, A.C.D. de, 129–131
Gracey, Major General Douglas, 167–8
Great War, *see* World War I
Grigg, Sir Edward, 9, 217–19, 221
Graham, Dr Frank, 146
Guggisberg, Sir Gordon, 182
Guided Democracy, 152
Guinea, 197–8, 200–1, 206
Gujarat, Gujaratis, 42, 44

Hague, The, 14, 16, 141, 143, 148
Hailey, Lord, 222, 249 ch.9 n6
Haiphong, 169, 171
Half Assini, 182
Halifax, Lord, 20–1; *see also* Irwin, Lord
Hanoi, 163, 166, 167, 169, 178
Harlley, J.W.K., 206
Harrow, 70–1, 97
Hartini (wife of Sukarno), 154–5, 157
Hatta, Mohammad, 130, 132, 133–4, 137,
　　142, 146–7, 148, 150, 151, 162
Hawthorne, Major General D.C., 141
Helfrich, Admiral, 141, 143
Helliwell, Colonel Paul, 165
Hilton Young, Sir Edward, 218–19
Hinden, Dr Rita, 187, 223
Hindus, 36, 41, 44, 46, 49, 51, 59, 67, 85, 87
Hitler, Adolf, 133, 153
Ho Chi Minh (Nguyen Ai Quoc), xiv, 18, 25,
　　34, 37–8; conspiratorial life as Nguyen
　　Ai Quoc, 158–64; as Ho, assumes
　　leadership in revolution, 165–76; elder
　　statesman, 176–80; 181, 183, 221, 238,
　　240
Ho Chi Minh City (Saigon), 179
Ho Chi Minh Trail, 177
Hola Camp, 232
Hong Kong, 18, 163
Hoover, President Herbert, 20
Hull, Cordell, 20
Humanité, French newspaper, 160
Hutton Mills, Tommy, 191
Hyderabad, 35, 51

Independence for India League, 74
India, xiii, xiv, 3–8, 13, 15, 17, 18, 19, 21, 22,
　　126, 145, 148, 181, 230

Indian Army, 5, 7–8, 13, 35, 67, 106, 108,
　　113, 141–2, 167–8, 212
Indian Civil Service, xi, 8, 71, 108
Indian legislature, 38, 43, 46, 53–4, 61–2, 73
Indian National Army (INA), 85–6, 103
Indian National Congress, 5, 8, 40, 42–3, 49,
　　51–2, 65, 71, 90–1, 113
Indians in Kenya, 214, 216, 225–6, 227, 230,
　　236
Indo-China, 11, 19, 21, 106, 161, 171; *see also*
　　Vietnam
Indo-China Communist Party, 162, 164
Indonesia, xiv, 14–16, 21, 106, 127–57, 161
Indonesian military/paramilitary forces, 135,
　　138, 141–3, 145, 147, 150
Inggit Garnasih (wife of Sukarno), 129, 134
Inns of Court (London legal centre), 42, 71
Interim Government of India, 52, 57–60, 62,
　　87, 89, 90
Iqbal, Muhammad, 49
Iraq, 5
Ireland, 4, 28
Irian, *see* New Guinea
Irwin, Lord, 47, 75, 76, 217; *see also* Halifax,
　　Lord
Isher, Dass, 219
Iskander Mirza, Colonel, 56, 67
Islam, *see* Muslims
Ismailis, 41
Ispahani, M.A.H., 59, 69
Ismay, Lord, 64
Italy, 28–35

Jakarta, 136, 140–1, 143, 146, 155
Jamaica, 2, 9
James, C.L.R., 183–5
Japan, 13, 16–17, 19, 21, 50–1, 80, 83, 98,
　　100–6, 107, 108, 126, 130, 133–5, 165,
　　167
Java, 2, 28, 108, 127, 129, 133–4, 136
Jayakar, M.R., 76
Jayaprakash Narayan (JP), 77, 80, 81, 84,
　　86–7, 88, 91
Jinnah, Dina (daughter), 47, 69
Jinnah, Fatima (sister), 47, 69
Jinnah, Mohammad Ali, xii, 5, 6, 24–5, 26,
　　29, 34, 38–9; nationalist politician,
　　42–7; turns to separatism, 48–53;
　　campaign for Pakistan, 53–65; head of
　　state, 66–8
Jinnah, Ratanbai (wife), 47, 69
Jogjakarta, 35, 127, 143, 145, 148
Johnson, Louis, 82–3
Johnson, President Lyndon, 178
Jones, Arthur Creech, *see* Creech Jones
Jonge, B.C.de, 16, 131

Kachins (tribes), 117, 122
Kamba (tribe), 226, 237
Kandy, 107, 167
Kang'etha, Joseph, 218
Kapenguria, 228–9
Kapil, A.R., 228
Karachi, 42, 49, 66, 67, 68
Karens (ethnic group), 101–2, 103, 117, 121, 122, 124, 136
Kasavubu, President Joseph, 200
Kashmir, 67, 70, 71
Katanga, 199, 201
Kawabe, General Masakazu, 102
Kennedy, President John F., 177
Kenya, xv, 8, 9, 22, 38, 39, 197, 205, 208–21, 225–37
Kenya African Democratic Union (KADU), 234–5, 237
Kenya African National Union (KANU), 233–6
Kenya People's Union (KPU), 236
Kenya African Union, 223, 228
Kenyatta, Edna (wife), 223–4
Kenyatta, Grace (wife) 215, 218
Kenyatta, Johnstone/Jomo, 26, 38–9; in obscurity, 208–18; envoy in Europe, 218–24; becomes Kenya's leader, 225–8; jailed, becomes martyr, 228–34; emerges to claim independence, 234–7
Kenyatta, Peter Magana (son), 223
Khaliquzzaman, Choudhry, 51, 79
Khan Sahib, Dr, 53, 66
Khilafat (Caliphate) movement, 45
Khojas (trading community), 42
Khrushchev, Nikita, 244–5, ch.6 n11, 248 n21
Kikuyu (tribe), 208, 210–18, 220, 222, 226–7, 229, 236
Kikuyu Association, 213–14, 218
Kikuyu Central Association, 218–19, 223
Kipling, Rudyard, 3, 40
Kirkman, W.P., 202–3, 350 n10
Knight, Sir Henry, 111, 112
Koinange Mbu, Chief, 218, 223, 225
Koinange, Peter Mbiya, 222–3, 225, 226, 232
Koiso, General Kuniaki, 136
Kojo Botsio, 190, 203
Komite Nasional Indonesia Pusat (KNIP), 138–9, 145
Korea, 93, 153, 179
Kosygin, Aleksey, 179
Kripalani, J.B., 91
Krishna Menon, V.K., 64, 77, 88, 90, 94–5, 186, 199, 240
Kumasi, 197
Kuo Min-tang (KMT), 74, 100, 161, 162, 168
Kyan Nyein, 111, 114–15, 116–17, 120, 122, 123

Labour Government, 1929–31, 75, 193, 219–20; 1945–51, 52, 107, 225
Labour Party, 184
Lahore, 72, 75
Lahore Resolution (the 'Pakistan' resolution), 50, 64
Laniel, Joseph, 172–3
Laos, 170, 173
Lattre de Tassigny, General de, 172
League Against Imperialism (*becomes* Congress of Peoples Against Imperialism), 74, 76, 130, 163, 219, 222
League of Nations, 6
Leclerc, General Jacques, 167–8, 169–70
Le Duan, 176, 177, 179
Lenin, Vladimir Ilich, 18, 24, 37, 160–1, 166
Lennox-Boyd, Alan, 195, 196, 231–2, 250 n13
Leopoldville, 199, 200
Let Ya, Bo, 101, 120
Liaqat Ali, Nawabzada, 60, 61–2, 64, 66, 67–8, 88, 90
Liberia, xiv, 151, 197
Libya, 197
Lincoln University (Pennsylvania), 183–4
Linlithgow, Lord, 81
Listowel, Lord, 121, 196
Linggajati agreement, 144–5
Liverpool, 187
Löfgren, S., 172
Lokitaung, 229
London School of Economics, 221
London University, 184, 221, 238
Loseby, F.H., 163
Lothian, Lord, 77, 97
Lucknow, 44, 51, 74
Lugard, Lord, 190, 216
Lu Han, General, 168
Lumumba, Patrice, 199–201
Luo (tribe), 226, 230, 236
Luzon, 166
Lyttleton, Oliver, 193, 230–1

MacArthur, General Douglas, 106, 139–40
McCarthy, Joe, 189
Macaulay, Thomas, 4
MacDonald, Malcolm, 235
MacDonald, Ramsay, 47
Macharia, Rawson, 229, 231
Mackenzie, Bruce, 236
Macleod, Iain, 232, 234
McMahon Line, 93
Macmillan, Harold, 196, 198, 201, 202, 231, 234, 248 n17 250 n13
Madagascar, 10
Madiun, 147

Madras, 74
Maeda Minoru, Vice-Admiral, 135, 136, 138
Magwe, 117
Mahalanobis, Professor P.C., 94
Mahmudabad, Raja of, 69
Majlis Sjuro Muslimin Indonesia, *see* Masjumi
Makarios, Archbishop, xiii
Makhan Singh, 227
Makonnen, T.R., 185, 224
Malaya, 3, 13, 19, 21, 85, 106, 113, 133, 137,
   139, 230; *becomes* Malaysia, 149, 153
Mali, 198, 200, 201, 248 n21
Malinowski, Bronislaw, 221–2
Mallaby, Brigadier A.W., 141
Malta, xi, 9
Manchester, 184–5, 224; *Manchester
   Guardian*, 219
Manchuria, 103
Mandalay, 79, 103, 122, 123, 165
Mandela, Nelson, xii
Manipur, 103
Mao Tse-tung, xii, 172, 176
Martin, Kingsley, 219
Marx, Karl, Marxism, 15, 21, 37, 77, 100, 109,
   128, 131, 180, 184; *see a¹so* Communism
Marxist League (Burma), 121
Marhaen, 131
Masai (tribe), 210–11, 213
Masani, Minoo, 77
Masjumi, 135, 145, 150
Mathu, Eliud, 224, 227
Maudling, Reginald, 234–5
'Mau Mau' 227–31, 232, 233, 236
Mauritius, 2
Mazzini, Giuseppe, 28, 29, 30–1, 33, 34, 128
Mboya, Tom, 197, 230, 231, 233–4, 236
Meerut, 88
Mehta, Ferozeshah, 43
Mendès-France, Pierre, 174
Menon, V.P., 90
Mergui, 119
Metternich, Prince, 29
Miéville, Sir Eric, 65
Milan, 31
Military coups, 123, 150, 154–6, 177,
   205–6, 236–7
Milliard, Peter, 185
Missionaries, 10, 36, 101, 132, 182, 208–9,
   211–12
Mitchell, Sir Philip, 224–8
Mobutu, Colonel Joseph, 200
'Moderates' in colonial politics, 43, 203
Mohammad Ali, 43, 44, 45, 46
Mombasa, xi, 215, 225, 237
Monrovia group of states, 201, 205

Mons (ethnic group), 123
Montagu, Edwin, 6, 44
Montesquieu, Charles, 263
Montgomery, Field Marshal Lord, 115
Moore, Sir Henry, 224
Morarji Desai, *see* Desai, Morarji
Morley, John, 5, 47; Morley–Minto Reforms,
   43
Morocco, 13, 171, 197, 200, 201
Moscow, 24, 161, 163, 177, 187, 221, 238
Moulmein, 102, 104
Mountbatten, Admiral (1946: Lord), 61,
   62–5, 68, 85–6, 89–92, 94, 103–7,
   111, 139–43, 167, 168
Mountbatten, Edwina, 85, 239
Moutet, Marius, 169
Mugabe, Robert, xiii
Muhammad Ali, Chaudhri, 60
Muhammad Saadullah, 50
Munro, Sir Thomas, 4
Murphey, Peter, 104
Muslim League (All-India Muslim League),
   41, 43, 45–6, 52–4, 60–5, 78, 85, 89
Muslims, 8, 36, 43, 47, 48–9, 59, 67, 85, 87,
   132–3
Musso, 129, 146
Mussoorie, 72
Mya, Thakin, 102, 115, 120
Myaungmya, 117

Naidu, Sarojini, 44
Nairobi, 208, 212–15, 225, 226, 230–1, 234
Nam Bo, *see* Cochin China
Naoroji, Dadabhai, 43
Naples, 32
Napoleon, 1, 29, 242 ch.2 n5
Nasser, Gamal Abdel, xiii, 206
Nasution, General Haris, 148, 150, 155–6
Nationalism, 30, 46, 50, 74, 106, 108, 126,
   129, 160, 177, 180, 234, 241 ch.1 n1
National Liberation Movement (Gold Coast),
   194–6
Natmauk, 99
Navarre, General Henri, 173
Nazimuddin, Khwaja, 53, 66
Nazis, 81, 85, 133
Nehru, Indira (daughter), 71, 77, 81; *see also*
   Gandhi, Indira
Nehru, Jawaharlal, xii, 5, 26, 29, 37–9; begins
   duel with Jinnah, 48–9, 55–6, 58–9;
   aligns with Mountbatten against Jinnah,
   62–3, 65; years of preparation, 70–5;
   front-rank leader, 75–81; wartime, 81–
   4; approach to independence, 85–8;
   leads interim government, 88–92; rises

to opportunities after independence, 92−4; final decline, 94−6; relation to other national leaders, 97, 98, 113, 116, 126−7, 130−2, 133, 147, 149, 151, 158, 162, 174, 181, 191, 196−7, 198, 199, 225, 229, 234, 238−9, 244 ch.6 n8, 245 ch.6 n11

Nehru, Kamala (wife), 71, 72, 77

Nehru, Motilal (father), 46−7, 70, 71, 74−5

Nehru, Vijaya (sister), 71, 72; *see also* Pandit, Vijaya Lakshmi

Netherlands, *see* Dutch Empire

New Guinea, 132, 137, 148, 149, 151−3

Ne Win, General, 101, 102, 122

New York, 31, 184; *New York Times*, 179

New Zealand, 3, 147, 179

Nghe-An province, 159, 163, 176

Ngo Dinh Diem, President, 175, 177−8

Nguyen Ai Quoc, *see* Ho Chi Minh

Nguyen Duy Trinh, 176

Nguyen Hai Thanh, 165

Nguyen Tuong Tam, 169

Nguyen Xuan Oanh, 179

Nigeria, 196, 205

Nixon, President Richard, 178

Nkrumah, Kwame, 22, 24, 26, 29, 37−9; youth, and years abroad, 182−7; enters Gold Coast politics, 187−90; forms own party, wins general election, 190−2; approach to independence, 192−6; as international statesman, 196−203; autocratic style leads to downfall, 203−6; reputation restored, 206−7, 239−40, 248 n2

Non-violence, *see* Civil disobedience

Northey, Sir Edward, 213, 216

Northern Ireland, 51

Northern People's Party (Ghana), 194

North West Frontier Province, 53, 54, 57, 66, 68

Nu, Thakin (U Nu), 27, 38−9, 93, 94−5, reluctant politician, 98−100, 103−4; withdrawal, 109; political comeback, 115−20; becomes prime minister, 120−1; post-independence trials, 121−4; takes refuge in religion, 124−5; 126−7; portrait of Ho Chi Minh, 174−5; 181, 182, 239−40

Nyerere, Julius, 201

Obetsibi Lamptey, 187, 190, 192

Office of Strategic Services (OSS), 158, 165, 168

Oginga Odinga, 230, 231, 233, 236

Oldham, J.H., 211, 213, 216, 219

Organisation of African Unity (OAU), 205

Ormsby-Gore, W.G.A., 217, 218, 221

Ottama, U, 98

Pacific, 18, 21

Padmore, George, 184−5, 221, 224

Paine, Thomas, 27

Pakistan, xiii, xiv, 21, 24, 38, 50−1, 52, 55−7, 60, 62−8, 90, 91, 94, 123, 148

Palme Dutt, 221

Pan-Africanism, 184, 197

Pandit, Mrs Vijaya Lakshmi, 72, 76, 78, 88, 95, 196−7, 205

Panglong agreement, 117−18

Pant, Apa B., 226, 237

Pant, Govind Bhalabh, 78

Parliament, 47, 61, 217

Parsis, 45, 67

Partai Kommunis Indonesia (PKI), 129, 136, 144, 150, 152

Partai Nasional Indonesia (PNI), 129−30, 150

Partai Nasional Indonesia Bahru (New PNI), 131

Patel, Sardar Vallabhai, 59, 62, 67, 79, 81, 84, 87, 89−91

Patel, Vithalbhai, 47

Patna, 77, 124

Patti, Major Archimedes, 158, 165, 166

Pearl Harbor, 81

Peking, 24, 177−9, 205

Pembela Tanah Air (Peta), 135, 136, 138, 141, 143

Pemuda (Young Indonesia), 135, 136, 141, 142, 156

Pennsylvania, University of, 183

Perks, Captain J.P.H., 141

People's Volunteer Organisation (PVO), 109−10, 118, 120−1, 138

Pethick-Lawrence, Lord, 54−5, 58, 85, 97, 109−10, 116

Petit, Sir Dinshaw, 45; Ratanabai, *see* Jinnah, Ratanbai

Pham Van Dong, 161, 173, 176

Phan Boi Chau, 162

Philippines, 19, 20, 25, 103, 134, 137, 179

Plural Society, 16, 98, 214, 230, 236

Poland, 80

Poona, 84

Portugal, 1, 94

Press (Newspapers), 5, 181; *see also Accra Evening News, Humanité, Manchester Guardian, New York Times, Times*

Prince of Wales, 237

Princes (in India), 7, 35, 90

Prison, 73, 76−7, 81, 84, 126, 130, 132, 164−5, 191, 229, 231−2, 239

Prisoners of War (POWs), 140–2, 167
Pritt, D.N., 163, 229
Punjab, 7, 44, 48, 49, 50–1, 53–4, 57, 61, 64, 72, 86, 89, 90, 94

Quetta, 68
Quezon, President Manuel, 25

Rafi Ahmad Kidwai, 78
Raffles, Sir Stamford, 128
Rajagopalachari, C., 51, 78, 79, 81, 83
Rajendra Prasad, 62, 78, 80
Rance, Sir Hubert, 111–15, 119
Rangoon, 99, 100, 103, 106, 107–9, 110, 115, 124, 172, 178; Rangoon police, 112; Rangoon University, 99
Ratna Sari Dewi (wife of Sukarno) 154–5
Red Flags (Burmese Communists), 109, 117
Rees-Williams, D.R., 188
Renison, Sir Patrick, 233–5
Renville agreement, 146
Revolt in colonies, 2, 7, 13, 15, 18, 98–9, 162–3, 171–3, 227–31
Rhodesia, xiii, 8, 205–6, 209–10, 215, 217
Robeson, Paul, 221
Robespierre, Maximilien, 95
Rome, 1, 2, 30, 31, 34, 36, 192
Roosevelt, Elliott, 19
Roosevelt, President Franklin D., 18–20, 62, 82, 145, 165
Ross, W. McGregor, 219, 221, 222
Round Table Conference (London), 47, 77
Rousseau, Jean Jacques, 203
Rowlatt Acts, 6, 7, 45
Roy, M.N. (alias of N.N. Bhattacharaya), 18, 77, 161, 163, 245 ch7 n3
Russia, 1, 17, 18, 33; *see also* Soviet Union

Saigon, 167–8, 179
Sainteny, Jean, 159, 166, 168–9, 171, 178–9
Salisbury, Harrison, 179
Saltpond, 187, 188
Sandhurst, 202
Sandys, Duncan, 235, 237
Sankey, Lord, 220
Sapru, Sir Tej Bahadur, 47, 76
Sarat Chandra Bose, 65
Sarekat Islam, 15, 128
Saw, U, 110, 112, 113, 116, 120
Saya San, 98
Sayyid Ahmad Khan, Sir, 41–2
School of Oriental and African Studies (London), xi, 221
Scott, Lord Francis, 220
Second World War, *see* World War II

Sékou Touré, President, 197, 206
Senanayake, D.S., 25
Senegal, 11, 17, 171, 198
Senghor, President Léopold, 203
Shanghai, 162, 163
Shans (ethnic group), 117
Shaukat Ali, 44, 49
Shiels, Dr Drummond, 219
Shinwell, Emmanuel, 9
Shwe Dagon Pagoda, 108
Sicily, 28, 30, 31–2
Sikandar Hyat Khan, Sir, 48–9, 50–1, 66
Sikhs, 51, 54–5, 62, 67, 68, 94, 167
Simla, 52, 56, 81, 84, 86, 90, 94
Simon Commission (Indian Statutory Commission), 46, 47
Sind, 49, 54, 62–3
Singapore, 106, 133, 137, 163
Sitaramayya, Pattabhi, 80
Sjahrir, Sutan, 127, 131, 132, 133–7, 139, 142–5, 147, 148–9, 240
Slade, Humphrey, 224
Slim, General Sir William, 105
Smith, Ian, 205
Smith, Ralph, xiv, 245 ch.7 n4, 246 n21
Smuts, Field-Marshal J.C., 20, 51, 224
Soe, Thakin, 100, 101, 103, 105, 109, 111, 113, 122
Sorensen, Reginald, 188, 247 ch.8 n9
South Africa, 3, 5, 6, 8, 20, 185, 202, 209–10, 214
South East Asia, 4, 17
South East Asia Command (SEAC), 139–40
South Vietnam, 174–6, 177, 179
Soviet Union, 23, 74, 79, 80, 82, 146, 153, 174, 176–7, 201, 202, 219
Spain, 1, 27, 29, 79
Spoor, General S.H., 143
Sri Lanka, *see* Ceylon
Srinagar, 68
Stalin, Joseph, 124, 159, 163
Stanley, Oliver, 9, 20
Stewart, Michael, 178
Stock, Dinah, 222–3
Subbarayan, P., 83
Subhas Chandra Bose, 74–5, 77, 78, 79–80, 85, 103
Sudan, 197, 205; French Sudan, 198
Sudirman, Colonel, 141, 143
Suez, xi, xii
Suharto, General, 155–7
Suhrawardy, H.S., 51, 53, 59, 64
Sukarno, xiv, 25, 29, 37–9; political apprenticeship and banishment, 127–33; Japanese sponsorship, 134–7;

uneasy independence leadership, 138–48; constitutional presidency, 148–51, monumentalism, 151–4; downfall, 154–7; his place in history, 197, 238–40, 224–5 ch.6 n11, n12
Sukarno (son, Guntur), 134
Sulawesi (south Celebes), 148–9
Sumatra, 133, 134, 136, 137, 139, 145
Sun Yat Sen, 161
Surabaya, 127, 128, 141–2
Sureté, 162–3
Suzuki, Colonel Keiji (Bo Mogyo), 100–2, 135
Switzerland, 30, 32, 33, 74
Sylhet, 51
Syria, 13

Tagore, Rabindranath, x, 77, 134
Takdir Alisjahbana, 129, 131–2, 133, 134
Tan Malaka, 18, 136, 144, 147, 148, 161
Tanganyika, 205, 212, 217, 226, 229
Tantabin, 110
Tavoy, 102, 117
Tawang, 94
Tawia Adamafio, 203–4
Taylor, Kuranki, 185, 194, 196–7
Tehran, 20
Terauchi, Hisaichi, Field Marshal, 137
Tet offensive (1968), 179
Thailand, 13, 101, 103, 124, 162
Thakins (Dobama Asi-Ayone), 99, 113, 114
Than Tun, Thakin, 100, 101–3, 105, 106–8, 109, 114, 120–22
Thant, U, 100, 152
Thein Pe (*Tet Pongyi*), 100, 103, 111, 114
Theosophy, 70, 71, 77, 128
Thierry d'Argenlieu, Admiral, 168–9, 171
Thirty Comrades, 101, 164
Thomson, David, xv
Thuku, Harry, 213–15, 220
Tilak, B.G., 43
Times, The, 119, 151, 156, 202, 219, 228, 234, 250 n19
Tin Tut, U, 108, 113–15, 120
Tito (Josip Broz), 179
Tjokroaminoto, Omar Said, 128
Togoland, 195
Tojo Hideki, General, 134, 136
Tokyo, 102, 103, 104
Tonking, 10, 12, 162, 168, 172
Toungoo district, 100, 103, 122
Tours (Loire), 160
Trevelyan, Sir Charles, 4
Trotsky, Leon, 23
Truman, President Harry S., 144

Truong Chinh, 163–4, 175, 176
Tshombe, Moise, 201
Tunisia, 10, 197, 200
Tun Ok, Thakin, 101, 102, 107, 109
Turkey, 44–5

Uganda, 205, 208, 217, 226, 229
Unionist Party (Punjab), 46, 52, 53
United Gold Coast Convention (UGCC), 187–90, 191–2, 194
United Nations, 114, 145, 150, 151–3, 199–201
United Provinces, 44, 70, 76, 78, 84
United States of America, 3, 4, 18–21, 82, 102, 145, 147–8, 159, 167, 172–3, 174, 177, 178–9, 180, 181, 199, 201, 206
University of Toilers of the East, 161, 221
Untouchables, 51, 60, 67, 77, 124
Upper Volta, 204

Van Mook, Dr H.J., 130, 134, 141, 143, 145–7
Van Der Post, Laurens, 140
Verdun, 17
Victor Emmanuele, King, 32, 33
Vienna, 36
Viet Minh (Viet-Nam Doc-Lap Dong-Minh), 164, 166, 169, 171–2, 176
Vietnam, xiv, 11, 12, 17, 21, 38, 39, 93, 137, 153, 159–79, 205
Vinoba Bhave, 81
Volksraad (Dutch East Indies), 15–16, 133
Volta river hydroelectric scheme, 205
Voltaire (Jean François Arouet), 203
Vo Nguyen Giap, 163–4, 165, 172–3, 175, 176

Wakema, 98–9
Wall, Patrick, 233
Waruhui Kungu, 218, 228
Waruhui Itote ('General China'), 228
Washington (American capital), 20
Washington, President George, xii, 24, 26–7, 241 ch.2 n1, n5
Watson Commission (Commission of Enquiry into Disturbances in the Gold Coast), 186, 188–90
Wavell, Field Marshal Lord, 52, 55–61, 63, 68, 84–9, 108, 113, 116
Webb, Sidney (Lord Passfield), 220
Welbeck, Nathaniel, 200
West African National Secretariat (London), 186–7
Westerling, Captain R.P.P. ('Turk'), 149

Western education, 25, 41, 98, 181, 182–3, 238

Westmoreland, General William, 179

Whampoa Military Academy, 161

White Flags (Burmese Communists), 109, 118, 121

Whitehall, xiv, xv, 111

White Highlands (Kenya), 208, 215–16, 221, 224, 226

White settlers, 2, 8, 208–9, 213, 225, 230, 232, 236

Wikana, 136, 138

Wilhelmina, Queen, 15, 144

Wilkie, Wendell, 19

Williams, Franklin, 206

Willingdon, Lord, 76

Wilson, Harold, 178

Winneba Ideological Institute, 204

Winterton, Lord, 188

Wisara, U, 98

World War I, 5–6, 17, 71, 126, 159, 209, 212–13

World War II, 8, 13, 49, 51, 52, 80, 223–4

Wyatt, Woodrow, 56, 60–1

Yamamoto Moichiro, Colonel, 135

Young, Colonel Arthur, 230, 231

Young, Sir Edward Hilton, *see* Hilton Young

Young Italy, 28, 30

Young Kikuyu Association, 214, 215, 218

Yugoslavia, 119

Yunnan, 164, 166, 169, 172

Zaire, *see* Congo

Ziarat, 68

Zinkin, Taya, 80

Zinoviev, Grigory, 161